Economic Modelling at the Bank of England

INTERNATIONAL STUDIES IN ECONOMIC MODELLING

Series Editor

Homa Motamen

Executive Director
Canadian Imperial Bank of Commerce
Securities Europe Ltd
London

Economic Modelling in the OECD Countries
H. Motamen

Modelling the Labour Market
M. Beenstock

Input-Output Analysis
M. Ciaschini

Models of Disequilibrium and Shortage in Centrally Planned Economies
C. Davis and W. Charemza

In preparation

Economic Models of Trade Unions
P. Garonna

Recent Modelling Approaches in Applied Energy Economics
O. Bjerkholt

New Directions in International Commodity Modelling
W. C. Labys
O. Guvenen
J. B. Lesourd

Economic Modelling at the Bank of England

Edited by

S. G. B. Henry

Director of Research,
Economics Division,
Bank of England.

and

K. D. Patterson

Reader in Applied Econometrics,
University of Reading.
Economic Adviser,
Bank of England.

CHAPMAN AND HALL
LONDON • NEW YORK • TOKYO • MELBOURNE • MADRAS

UK	Chapman and Hall, 11 New Fetter Lane, London EC4P 4EE
USA	Chapman and Hall, 29 West 35th Street, New York NY10001
JAPAN	Chapman and Hall Japan, Thomson Publishing Japan, Hirakawacho Nemoto Building, 7F, 1-7-11 Hirakawa-cho, Chiyoda-ku, Tokyo 102
AUSTRALIA	Chapman and Hall Australia, Thomas Nelson Australia, 480 La Trobe Street, PO Box 4725, Melbourne 3000
INDIA	Chapman and Hall India, R. Seshadri, 32 Second Main Road, CIT East, Madras 600 035

First edition 1990

Typeset in 10/12 Sabon by
KEYTEC, Bridport, Dorset
Printed in Great Britain by
St Edmundsbury Press Ltd, Bury St Edmunds, Suffolk

ISBN 0 412 357100 (HB)

British Library Cataloguing in Publication Data
Henry, S. G. B.
Economic modelling at the Bank of England. –
(International studies in economic modelling).
1. Great Britain. Economic conditions. Econometric models
I. Title II. Patterson, K. D. (Kerry David) 1947–
III. Series
330.9410011
ISBN 0-412-35710-0

Library of Congress Cataloging-in-Publication Data
Economic and financial modelling for policy analysis/edited by
S. G. B. Henry and K. D. Patterson. – 1st ed.
p. cm. – (International studies in economic modelling)
Includes bibliographical references.
ISBN 0-412-35710-0
1. Finance–Great Britain–Econometric models. I. Henry, S. G.
B. II. Patterson, K. D. III. Series.
HG186.G7E36 1990
332.1'01'5195–dc20 90-1606
CIP

Contents

Contributors vii
Foreword ix
Editors' introduction xi

1 **A three sector model of earnings behaviour** 1
D. J. Mackie
with appendix by N. Hatch

2 **Stockbuilding and liquidity** 49
T. S. Callen, S. G. Hall and S. G. B. Henry

3 **Interest elasticity of consumers' expenditure** 73
M. J. Dicks

4 **Measuring the risk of financial institutions' portfolios: some suggestions for alternative techniques using stock prices** 107
S. G. Hall and D. K. Miles

5 **The long run determination of UK monetary aggregates** 127
S. G. Hall, S. G. B. Henry and J. B. Wilcox

6 **A capital asset pricing model with time-varying betas: some results from the London stock exchange** 167
S. G. Hall, D. K. Miles and M. P. Taylor

7 **An empirical model of companies' debt and dividend decisions: evidence from company accounts data** 187
G. Chowdhury and D. K. Miles

8 **Modelling the flow of funds with an application to the demand for liquid assets by the UK personal sector** 223
D. G. Barr and K. Cuthbertson

9 **Optimal control of stochastic non-linear models** 247
S. G. Hall and M. J. Stephenson

Index 257

Contributors

D. G. Barr	Bank of England
T. S. Callen	Bank of England
G. Chowdhury	Department of Economics, North Eastern University, Boston, IL, USA
K. Cuthbertson	Department of Economics, University of Newcastle, and Bank of England
M. J. Dicks	Bank of England
J. S. Flemming	Bank of England
S. G. Hall	Bank of England
N. Hatch	Bank of England
S. G. B. Henry	Bank of England
D. J. Mackie	Morgan Guaranty Trust Company, London
D. K. Miles	Department of Economics, Birkbeck College London
K. D. Patterson	Department of Economics, University of Reading, and Bank of England
M. J. Stephenson	Bank of England
M. P. Taylor	Department of Economics, City University, and Bank of England
J. B. Wilcox	Bank of England

Foreword

J. S. FLEMMING

The Bank of England's role as a leading central bank involves both formal and informal aspects. At a formal level it is an adviser to HM Government, whilst at an informal level it is consulted by domestic and overseas institutions for advice on many areas of economic interest. Such advice must be grounded in an understanding of the workings of the domestic and international economy—a task which becomes ever more difficult with the pace of change both in the economy and in the techniques which are used by professional economists to analyse such changes.

The Bank's economists are encouraged to publish their research whenever circumstances permit, whether in refereed journals or in other ways. In particular, we make it a rule that the research underlying the Bank's macroeconometric model, to which outside researchers have access through the ESRC (Economic and Social Research Council) macromodelling bureau, should be adequately explained and documented in published form. This volume expands the commitment to make research which is undertaken within the Economics Division of the Bank of England widely available. Included here are chapters which illustrate the breadth of interests which the Bank seeks to cover. Some of the research is, as would be expected, directly related to the specification of the Bank's model, but other aspects are also well represented.

I believe that this sample of our work will withstand the scrutiny of our peers in the economics profession, as well as informing readers of what we do and thus illuminating their understanding of the workings of both the Bank and the economy.

Introduction

S. G. B. HENRY AND K. D. PATTERSON

The papers collected together in this volume are a representative sample of quantitative research undertaken recently in the Economics Division of the Bank of England. It is quite usual for economic advisory teams in the UK, the USA and Europe to have a continuous programme of applied econometric research. In the Bank's case this programme spans many aspects of economics, involving both macroeconomic and microeconomic elements. The macroeconomic research is largely directed at the maintenance and development of a quarterly model, which is at the centre of the production of forecasts and advice on macroeconomic policy issues. This is a considerable activity given the pace with which economic ideas, econometric practice and, indeed, the economy itself change. The Economics Division of the Bank also undertakes research of a microeconomic nature including, for example, studies of the efficiency of financial markets, and of the interrelationship between companies' decisions on debt and equity issues and corporate dividend payments. Throughout the programme of research there is an interest in identifying, and where possible quantifying, the links between the real and financial sectors of the economy.

In this book we have selected research papers written by our colleagues within the Economics Division which illustrate these facets of empirical research. We consciously decided not to include material on the more short-term activities relating to reporting and briefing, although these often use quantitative material and techniques, and play an important role in the provision of informed advice to policy-makers. The reason for this decision was that it was felt that a more consistent and self-contained collection could be made by concentrating upon applied econometric research. Within these limits, the chapters illustrate the diverse applications of modern applied econometrics carried out in the Economics Division. The topics selected are generally of considerable policy relevance, and they also illustrate, we hope, an important set of techniques which can be deployed to analyse economic problems.

In the first chapter Hatch and Mackie present the results for a model of earnings as currently used in the Bank model. In this approach earnings are disaggregated into three sectors: manufacturing; a sector composed of the non-manufacturing private and public sectors; and non-manufacturing public corporations. There are several reasons for disaggregating earnings in this way, with perhaps the most important being the possibility that the determinants of earnings differ quite markedly between sectors. If this is the case, using an aggregate equation would tend to blur these sectoral differences and exclude potentially important behaviour. The results reported in this chapter show that there are significant intersectoral effects in the disaggregated earnings equations. That is, each of the preferred equations includes earnings from at least one other sector as an explanatory variable of earnings in that sector. This is important evidence that, along with familiar determinants of wage inflation like labour productivity, inflationary expectations and unemployment, comparisons of wage settlements between sectors have an independent role in wage bargaining.

Apart from this feature of the model there are two further notable aspects of Mackie's approach. First the overall model is subjected to elaborate testing with, in particular, the necessary and sufficient conditions for subsystem homogeneity imposed in the model, and then it is tested for data consistency. Second, an illustration is provided of the practical issues which can arise in the operation and maintenance of an empirical model. After the original model was estimated by Mackie it was discovered that the data for the retentions ratio variable could be improved if allowance was made for the changes in the tax system in the early 1970s. This argument was advanced by the Macroeconomic Bureau at Warwick University (Fisher *et al.*, 1989). Accordingly, in an appendix to this chapter, Hatch investigates the results of re-estimating the original Mackie model using new data, including the revised definitions for the retentions ratio. His results show that these changes produce differences from the original estimates, although their broad features remain very similar upon re-estimation.

In Chapter 2, Callen, Hall and Henry exploit co-integration methods to model the difficult area of stockbuilding. One of the central concerns of this chapter is the relationship between stocks and liquidity, which both share the common characteristic, as far as the firm is concerned, of being easier and less costly to change than employment and the capital stock. The model which best fits the data—here the aggregate of stocks of finished goods and work in progress for the manufacturing sector—can be motivated by portfolio allocation considerations. That is, the firm's decision to hold stocks and liquid assets depends upon relative rates of return for these variables along with the more usual output variable (although, if sales data were separately available, that would, in principle, be preferable). The modelling methodology first requires estimation of an equation determining the equilibrium or target stock level. The theoretical basis of this equation is the maximization of a static nominal profit function, and is described in section 2.2. Some motivation for the dynamics of the empirical equation is provided by an extension of the static model to a dynamic cost-minimization problem given costs of adjusting stock levels.

An important contribution of this chapter is the extension of the usual scale variables used in modelling stock levels to include a measure of the variance of output (as a proxy for the variance of sales). Although it has been recognized that uncertainty is likely to play an inherent part in determining stock levels, there has not been much success in previous work in incorporating this into an empirical model. The procedure reported in this chapter, which is based on the GARCH-M procedure due to Engle *et al.* (1987), results in a two-equation system—one equation for stock levels and one for output—and provides estimating equations which include the variance of output. The empirical success of the model is assessed in section 2.4, where logarithmic and levels versions of the equations are reported. In particular, there is evidence that stock levels are positively related to the variance of output, and that a range of cost and financial variables are influential in determining stock levels.

In the third chapter Dicks reports new evidence for the UK on the interest elasticity of consumers' expenditure. This is an issue of profound policy significance. In this chapter, Dicks shows that, although the issue is by no means settled, the weight of evidence does suggest a modest positive interest elasticity of private saving. Moreover, interest rate effects appear to have increased (in both size and significance) during the 1980s, a period in which competition in the UK financial markets increased as a result of the Government's policy of deregulation. There appear to be two reasons why the effectiveness of changes in interest rates on consumption expenditure could have increased. Firstly, the policy of liberalizing financial markets has led to a weakening of the liquidity constraints which previously restricted households' choice. This will have had the effect of permitting consumers to move closer to their desired (life-cycle) levels of expenditure, as they may now find it easier to borrow through periods when income is temporarily low, so maintaining a smoother consumption profile over time. Secondly, there is the effect produced by a larger proportion of households who are now affected by changes in interest rates. Dicks' findings suggest that the latter effect may dominate, at least in the short run, implying that the leverage of monetary policy may have been strengthened as a result of deregulation of the financial markets.

After briefly summarizing previous research, Dicks presents detailed econometric evidence in the form of new models of consumers' expenditure for both non-durables and durables based on UK data. These equations are now incorporated into the Bank's short-term model of the UK economy. A distinct part of the chapter is devoted to the analysis of the links between consumption and developments in the housing market. In summary, these results show that, although changes in mortgage lending are found to have a strong effect on durables spending, no role can be found for housing variables in the non-durables equation.

In Chapter 4, Hall and Miles are concerned with the analysis of a question which has important practical implications: how can regulatory authorities assess the capital adequacy of the financial institutions that they supervise? The central problem is how to assess whether an institution has issued sufficient equity capital to reduce the probability of bankruptcy to an acceptably low level. This in turn depends on the volatility of the value of an institution's assets and liabilities.

A standard approach to this problem is to try to estimate directly the probability of default. If the variability of returns on each different class of assets and liabilities and the correlation between these returns are known, then the probability of default of the financial institution holding these assets is simply a matter of numerical calculation. A difficulty arises, however, since it is very hard to make accurate estimates of the riskiness of returns on individual assets (both because of lack of data and because even when data are available the variability of returns may well change over time). In this chapter an alternative technique is explored which aims to overcome both these problems by basing calculations of the risk associated with an institution's balance sheet on its stock market valuation. Of course, such an approach assumes that the stock market has sufficient information on the values of underlying assets and liabilities to evaluate companies correctly. The approach allows an implicit valuation of balance sheet items for which secondary markets do not exist.

Hall and Miles aim to gauge the riskiness of the institution from a measure of deviations of stock market valuations around the market's expectation. If it is assumed that these deviations are normally distributed, it is possible to calculate the probability that the value of the institution's equity falls to zero (i.e. that the institution goes into default within a certain period). The basic analysis is directed at developing a model of expected market valuations. To do this Hall and Miles apply the capital asset pricing model (CAPM) in which the expected capital gain on a share equals the safe rate of interest plus a risk premium given by the correlation of the share price with a diversified portfolio (the institution's beta) multiplied by an indicator of the market's attitude to risk. The main difficulty that arises with this application is that the betas themselves are expectations based on past movements in asset prices and can be expected to change over time. Therefore, Hall and Miles report implementation of two methods of estimation which make different assumptions about how the market computes the expected variances and covariances of stock prices from past data, and hence calculate the betas of individual institutions. The empirical results show the stock market valuations of the big four banks measured relative to the variability of their market valuations, and these indicate that default probabilities were at relatively high levels in the late 1970s and again in the middle 1980s. In all cases, however, the estimated probability of bankruptcy one period ahead remained very low.

In Chapter 5 Hall, Henry and Wilcox are concerned with the determinants of a number of monetary aggregates—in particular M0, M1, M3 and M4. The two-stage methodology of first identifying a long-run equation for each variable of interest and then combining this in a dynamic equation is exploited. The authors initially consider M0, the narrowest of the monetary aggregates, and find that a co-integration analysis using M0, real expenditure and price variables by themselves does not lead to a co-integrating vector. The key to extending this set of variables is in recognizing that the widespread introduction of cash dispensers and credit cards has altered the demand for M0, given levels of real expenditure and prices. Once this is taken into account through the introduction into the co-integration analysis of what are broadly called 'innovation' variables, it is possible to find a co-integrating vector. The second stage of the modelling methodology is then implemented to provide what is a relatively simple dynamic specification for (the logarithm of) M0. Further applications of this methodology are reported for M1, M3 and M4—although, because of the particular considerations necessary for each monetary aggregate, this procedure is far from mechanical. Hall *et al.* report that income, prices and interest rates do not by themselves provide a co-integrating vector for M1, and innovation is again at the centre of explaining why this is so. The wide-scale introduction of interest-bearing cheque accounts in the 1980s markedly changed the nature of M1, and including a variable which captures this change, in addition to the usual variables, does provide a co-integrating vector. Attention is then turned to the broader monetary aggregates M3 and M4. Here, Hall *et al.* find important roles for measures of wealth and inflation but, perhaps surprisingly, do not identify significant interest rate effects.

In Chapter 6 Hall, Miles and Taylor report estimation of the CAPM using data from the London Stock Exchange. According to the CAPM the required excess return on a risky asset is proportional to its non-diversifiable risk, with the covariance of the asset return with the return on the market portfolio acting as a sufficient statistic for this risk. However, empirical tests of the CAPM have not generally been favourable, with variables other than the required covariance turning out to be significant. Several explanations of the failure of the simple CAPM have been put forward, but Hall *et al.* pursue a different line of enquiry. In particular, they suggest that the relevant covariance is not that based on the unconditional covariances but the covariance conditioned on information up to the time that the expectation is formed, i.e. the conditional covariance. Further, if returns above the market return are generated by a (conditional) heteroscedastic process then there will be variation over time in the asset betas (the ratio of the covariance of the asset return with the market return to the variance of the market return). The modelling framework for this analysis is the GARCH formulation due to Bollerslev (1986), and the data are monthly data on the share prices of firms quoted on the London Stock Exchange. Portfolios were formed for four sectors—mechanical engineering, financial, electrical and chemical—and the return on the market portfolio was based on the *Financial Times* (FT) 500 share index. Overall, the results suggest a rejection of both the traditional CAPM and the extension to a consumption-based CAPM due to Breeden (1979). The authors conclude that risk characteristics have changed over time, with time variation in both conditional variances and covariances, and it is necessary to extend the CAPM to take this into account.

In Chapter 7 Chowdhury and Miles provide an assessment of the financial behaviour of the company sector using microdata. This is an example of empirical work which is undertaken at the Bank but is not specifically directed at developing the Bank's macroeconomic model. Instead, the work is a free-standing piece of research, offering insights into the behaviour of the company sector, which is of considerable use in background assessment of (and briefing upon) developments in the company sector. Chowdhury and Miles seek to explain the factors underlying the long-term financial decisions of some 650 quoted UK-based companies. Information about these companies was taken from their published accounts and used to model their dividend payments and long-term debt flows. In addition, the company accounts data were used to describe other financial characteristics of the firms, such as tax exhaustion, gearing and new equity issues, in ways which bring out the diversity of the company sector, something which is not feasible with aggregate data.

The econometric estimation of a model of firms' dividend and debt decisions was designed to assess the relative effects of items of company expenditure and receipts, the cost of funds (as reflected by relative interest rates), the tax position of the firm, considerations of capital gearing and liquidity, statutory controls and risk as reflected by the volatility of recent income. The econometric results show that current and past profits, tax payments and investment expenditure were prime determinants of debt and dividend decisions. A company's gearing and liquidity position were also found to be significant, with both dividend payments and debt issues lower when gearing was higher or when liquidity was lower. Lagged stocks of debt, financial assets and the square of the change in the rate of return on capital were all found to be significant factors explaining debt issues and dividend payments. Dividend payments appeared to be much more sensitive to tax rates and interest rates than were debt issues, with tax effects particularly powerful. The model suggests that, as a result of the recent changes in company tax capital, gearing will in future be lower and dividend payments higher (for a given level of income). It is clear that dividend controls had a major negative impact on payments of dividends during periods when they were in force. However, it was found that this was fully offset by a surge in distributions in the years following abolition of restraint. The operation of the 'corset' had no discernible effect on debt issues. Vindication for the choice of a disaggregated data base is provided by the diversity in behaviour across companies evident in the empirical results which are described in some detail.

Perhaps one of the areas most ripe for new ideas in model building, particularly as embodied in large-scale macroeconometrics, has been the determination of the flow of funds. Recall that each sector's saving, i.e. broadly the difference between income and expenditure plus net transfers for each sector, is allocated amongst a range of financial instruments. It is the allocation of such savings into these financial instruments that we are referring to by the term flow of funds. Although most macroeconomic models of which we are aware embody little by way of contemporaneous feedback between the real and financial sectors, and in particular the flow of funds, this is not to say that there may not be, at least potentially, longer-run influences of such flows onto the real side of the economy. For example, in the Bank model (Patterson *et al.*, 1987; Harnett and Patterson, 1988; Chapter 3 of this volume) there are, with a lag, important effects from financial flows onto consumption expenditures.

In Chapter 8 Barr and Cuthbertson report some of the results from an initiative set up within the Economics Division of the Bank, and known internally as the flow of funds project, for a thorough examination of the links between real and financial variables. In the first phase of the project the focus is on the allocation of the flow of funds, with other work directed at the possibility of higher-level integrated decisions and the endogenization of rates of return. In the work reported here Barr and Cuthbertson assume a two-stage budgeting process for each sector (Deaton and Muellbauer, 1980), the first stage of which determines the total flow of funds, which is then to be allocated amongst a range of financial instruments in the second stage. The theoretical allocation model is the almost ideal demand system (AIDS) approach due to Deaton and Muellbauer. This is modified to take into account the particular characteristics of a model which allocates financial, rather than consumption, flows. Barr and Cuthbertson combine the AIDS approach, which provides equilibrium or target shares for each of four liquid assets for the personal sector (notes and coins, sight deposits, time deposits and building society deposits), with the Granger–Engle co-integration approach to dynamic modelling. Thus error feedback equations (EFEs) are used which provide estimates of both the dynamics of short-run behaviour and equilibrium shares for the flow of funds into these assets for the personal sector. This approach is then extended to personal sector liabilities (e.g. bank lending) and capital uncertain assets (e.g. equities and gilts). Overall, the approach seems very fruitful in what has, historically, been a difficult area for empirical work (Keating, 1985; Courakis, 1988).

In Chapter 9 Hall and Stephenson are concerned with the optimal control of stochastic non-linear models. They note that, whilst there is now a large literature on the application of optimal control techniques to macroeconomic models, there has not been much progress in establishing a practical algorithm for the direct calculation of optimal control solutions for non-linear stochastic models. The algorithms which exist generally work by linearizing a deterministic form of the non-linear model. In contrast, Hall and Stephenson approach the problem directly. Their first step is to reformulate the objective function to isolate the stochastic elements of an optimal control solution. They then suggest using stochastic simulation techniques to estimate the variances of the endogenous variables in non-linear model. This leads to the development of an algorithm to solve the full stochastic optimal control problem. The standard objective function in optimal control problems is then extended to include terms in the variances of the target variables. This is because a realistic element of policy design is the need to minimize variation around desired levels of target variables, rather than just focusing on the levels of these variables. The techniques are then illustrated with an application using the Bank of England's quarterly model. The objective function in this example penalizes deviations of the current account of the balance of payments from zero, using government current expenditure on goods and services as the control variable.

In preparing this volume the editors have benefited from the help and encouragement of a number of colleagues in the Economics Division. We would particularly like to thank John Flemming and Christopher Taylor for advice and encouragement on this work. Lisa Millham provided valuable help in the preparation of charts, Fran Robinson made a number of useful editorial suggestions and Tracey Jacobs typed successive versions of the chapters accurately and (more surprisingly) cheerfully. Lastly our thanks go to the authors themselves for their efforts in preparing this book.

REFERENCES

Bollerslev, T. (1986) Generalized autoregressive conditional heteroskedasticity. *Journal of Econometrics,* **31**, 307–28.

Breeden, D. T. (1979) 'An intertemporal asset pricing model with stochastic consumption and investment opportunities. *Journal of Financial Economics,* 7, 265–96.

Courakis, A. S. (1988) Modelling portfolio selection. *Economic Journal,* **98**, 619–42.

Deaton, A. and Muellbauer, J. (1980) *Economics and Consumer Behaviour,* Cambridge University Press, Cambridge.

Engle, R. F., Lilien, D. M. and Robbins, R. P. (1987) 'Estimating time varying risk premium in the term structure: the ARCH-M model. *Econometrica,* **55**, 391–407.

Fisher, P. G., Tanna, S. K., Turner, D. S., Wallis, K. F. and Whitley, J. D. (1989) Comparative properties of models of the UK economy. *National Institute Economic Review,* No. 129, 69–87.

Harnett, I. and Patterson, K. D. (1988) An analysis of changes in the structural and simulation properties of the Bank of England quarterly model of the UK economy. *Economic Modelling*, 5, 20–56.

Keating, G. (1985) The financial sector of the London Business School model, in *Advances in Monetary Economics* (ed. D. Currie), Croom Helm, London.

Patterson, K. D., Harnett, I., Robinson, G. and Ryding, J. (1987) The Bank of England model of the UK economy. *Economic Modelling*, 4, 397–530.

1

A three-sector model of earnings behaviour

D. J. MACKIE

1.1 INTRODUCTION

In this chapter we discuss some research undertaken in order to improve the properties of the earnings equations in the Bank of England's quarterly macroeconomic model of the UK economy.

The labour market in the Bank model is currently disaggregated into three main sectors: the manufacturing sector (which includes those public corporations defined as manufacturers in the 1980 Standard Industrial Classification (SIC)), the non-trading public sector and a sector which incorporates the non-manufacturing private sector and non-manufacturing public corporations. (The last sector is referred to in this chapter as the non-manufacturing sector, for ease of exposition.[1]) Although there is a model variable for earnings in public corporations, which plays an important part in ensuring that public sector income is accurately modelled in forecasts and simulations, the level of this variable depends solely on earnings in the non-manufacturing sector (which includes the majority of public corporations).

Most of the quarterly macroeconomic models of the UK economy have a degree of disaggregation in the labour market similar to that in the Bank model, while the annual models tend to work with highly aggregate labour markets.[2] (For a survey of the labour markets in the main UK models see Wallis *et al.* (1986).) One possible interpretation of this is that in the short run interactions between sectors are very important in the wage determination process while in the long run wages are determined entirely by

[1] It is referred to as the 'other' sector in the Bank of England model manual.
[2] An exception to this is the National Institute's quarterly model which has a single aggregate earnings equation. Nevertheless, the National Institute does recognize the importance of intersectoral effects when modelling earnings (e.g. Foster *et al.*, 1986).

fundamental forces of supply and demand. There can be no doubt, however, that a certain degree of disaggregation provides advantages not only in giving a model a richer dynamic structure but also if the determinants of wages differ markedly across sectors.

An important result presented in this chapter is that intersectoral effects are important in the wage determination process. Each of the preferred equations has earnings in at least one of the other sectors as an explanatory variable. Other important determinants of nominal earnings in these equations are labour productivity, consumer prices, inflationary expectations, personal sector taxes and employers' labour taxes, although the last variable only has an effect in the short run. Another important result is that participants in the labour market who are not currently employed (defined here as the short-term unemployed) do not exert much influence on nominal earnings.

In this chapter we analyse the disaggregated earnings equations as a subsystem of the Bank model and look at the properties of this subsystem. In particular, we consider the issue of homogeneity between nominal earnings and prices and derive the necessary and sufficient conditions for the subsystem to exhibit homogeneity of degree one. These restrictions are imposed and tested. In addition to considering the properties of the earnings subsystem, we examine the simulation properties of the equations when they form part of the larger Bank model.

The analytical and econometric approach taken is discussed in section 1.2, the estimation results are presented in section 1.3, the dynamic properties of the equations are discussed and some simulation results when the equations are incorporated into the Bank model are reported in section 1.4, and in section 1.5 some conclusions are presented and areas for future work are suggested.

1.2 THE ANALYTICAL AND ECONOMETRIC APPROACH

1.2.1 The bargaining model

A common approach to deriving a wage equation suitable for estimation is to consider a union bargaining model in which employers and employees bargain about the level of nominal wages and employers set the level of employment unilaterally. The estimated equations reported here lie broadly within this framework. The economic theory underlying this approach is discussed extensively elsewhere (e.g. Nickell, 1982; Nickell and Andrews, 1983; Nickell, 1984) and thus is not repeated in detail here.

The approach in these models is to specify a utility function for the firm and the union and the level of utility which would apply to each participant if no agreement was reached. The resulting wage agreement is usually assumed to be the Nash solution to the bargaining game, although this simply refers to the nature of the equilibrium rather than to the problem of how the equilibrium is actually achieved in a dynamic sense. Nickell (1984) points out that these models suggest equations for the level of nominal wages, and the equations presented here are of this form but with earnings rather than wages as the dependent variable. A number of different empirical models suitable for estimation could be derived from this approach depending not only on the specification of the two objective functions and the situation where no agreement is reached, but also on the proxies which are used for the various unobservable variables.

These models tend to consider a single unionized firm or sector; by contrast, in this chapter we analyse three sectors, all of which are unionized to some extent. The results derived from a model with a single unionized sector can be extended to the case of several unionized sectors as long as there is no collusion between different sectors, i.e. each sector regards earnings in the other sectors as predetermined when it enters its own bargaining procedure. However, earnings in the other sectors will form an important part of the bargaining process (for a similar assumption see Smith and Holly (1985)).

According to the equations presented in the next section the most important determinants of nominal earnings are trend labour productivity, the short-term unemployment rate, consumer prices, inflationary expectations, incomes policies, personal sector income taxes (including National Insurance contributions) and employers' labour taxes. In addition, because of the disaggregated nature of the labour market, each of the earnings equations includes earnings from at least one of the other two sectors as an explanatory variable.

1.2.2 Labour productivity

A long moving average of actual labour productivity (output per head) is the important variable in these equations for explaining the long-run trend increase in real earnings. The use of an eight-quarter moving average is an attempt to remove cyclical influences and proxy trend productivity. However, a drawback of this measure is that any change in productivity will influence earnings whether it represents a change in trend productivity or not. Nevertheless, this approach seems preferable to the rather atheoretical practice of incorporating a time trend. There are alternative measures of productivity which could have been used, e.g. the capital-to-labour ratio. Earlier work in this area did investigate the use of a measure of trend productivity derived from the manufacturing production function in the Bank model. However, it did not prove to be as successful as a moving average of output per head. Hall and Henry (1987) consider several different measures of trend productivity in an aggregate earnings equation, and they argue that their results provide some grounds for preferring a moving average of output per head as the relevant trend variable.

There are several ways in which the inclusion of trend productivity in a wage equation can be justified. In the union bargaining model described by Nickell and Andrews (1983), for example, trend productivity can be used as a proxy for the real wage growth in the economy as a whole which workers might expect if they failed to obtain employment in the unionized firm or sector, and also as a proxy for the 'base' level of real wages. Regarding the latter, Nickell and Andrews assume that employees' utility is a function of post-tax real wages relative to a base level of wages which takes account of the growth in real wages over time. In addition, the level of productivity enters as part of the firms' production function. Another approach to the inclusion of trend productivity is contained in the recent paper by Rowlatt (1986) where it forms one of the variables which defines the nominal wage increase considered acceptable by employers and employees and the long-run warranted real wage. The latter variable refers to the real wage considered by employees to be fair in the long run. It is a function of productivity, the terms of trade and the retentions ratio.

1.2.3 Unemployment

The appearance of unemployment in wage equations has a long history. In the context of a bargaining model the inclusion of unemployment can be justified because a union's utility is likely to be influenced by the conditions in the labour market outside the unionized sector which will affect any workers who fail to find employment in that sector. As the prospects for alternative employment decline, employees become less likely to increase the risk of losing their current job by pushing for a large real wage increase. Important relevant variables include both employment in the other sectors and unemployment. However, there may be seniority effects (e.g. Oswald and Turnbull, 1985; Oswald, 1986) where labour market conditions outside the unionized sector have very little effect on the bargaining position adopted by the union. The use of short-term unemployment (defined as those unemployed for less than 26 weeks) rather than total unemployment is an attempt to have a measure of conditions in the labour market which excludes persons who have ceased to be very active in terms of looking for a job. This does not, of course, imply that all the long-term unemployed are 'voluntarily unemployed'. One possibility is that such persons would accept a job at the going real wage but perceive that the probability of obtaining a job is relatively low. This could be a consequence of demand-side factors, e.g. firms reducing their demand for the long-term unemployed because of the erosion of their human capital, or of supply-side factors, e.g. the unemployed becoming discouraged from applying for jobs because of the large number of refusals that they have received. If the long-term unemployed are largely inactive in the labour market, the union's utility may only be influenced by the number of short-term unemployed, i.e. those individuals who form the effective competition for other jobs. A number of other researchers have found that the short-term unemployed affect wage behaviour more than the long-term unemployed (e.g. Layard and Nickell, 1986; Hall and Henry, 1987; Nickell, 1987).

The measure of conditions in the labour market used in the equations is the reciprocal of the short-term unemployment rate which gives a non-linear response of earnings to changes in the short-term unemployment rate and a non-constant elasticity.[3] It could be argued that including unemployment in this manner is an alternative to including a structural mismatch variable (e.g. the absolute change in the proportion of manufacturing employees used by Layard and Nickell (1986)), since the latter variable will reduce the estimated effect of the recent rise in total unemployment on wages. Of particular interest, given recent UK experience, is the effect of unemployment on real wages. It could be argued that the UK's recent experience indicates that the unemployment elasticity of real wages is not very large. For example, from 1979 to 1985 real earnings in the manufacturing sector grew by around 2.7% per annum while total unemployment increased from 1.1 million to 3.1 million. This compares with real earnings growth of 2.5% per annum from 1963 to 1978 while total unemployment increased from 0.5 million to 1.2 million. These figures do not appear to be consistent with the traditional Phillips curve. However, if the relevant pressure of demand variable is short-term unemployment rather than total unemployment, then there would have been less downward pressure on real earnings over recent years since, although short-term unemployment rose sharply in 1980, it has been broadly flat since then. Even so, the evidence presented here is that the effect of short-term unemployment on real earnings is also very weak.

1.2.4 Prices and inflationary expectations

In many wage equations distributed lags on prices are used to capture the effects both of lagged adjustments to past price changes and of expectations of future inflation. The approach taken here is to include lags of consumer prices to capture the former effect and, in addition, to include an explicit inflationary expectations term to capture the latter effect. It ought to be noted that the use of consumer prices concentrates on real consumption earnings which are of relevance to employees rather than own-product real earnings of relevance to employers. The work here does not investigate

[3]Nickell (1987) presents a number of arguments in support of a non-linear relationship between wages and unemployment. Of course, the term used in the estimation work reported here is not the only manner in which non-linearities could have been introduced.

whether this distinction is important, and further work should consider the issue more fully. (See, for example, Carruth and Oswald (1987) for an analysis of the use of real consumption earnings or the real product wage as the dependent variable in a wage equation.)

A priori, it is likely that price expectations will be important in an earnings equation since wage bargains will be influenced not only by past movements in the cost of living but also by what is likely to happen in the future. There are a number of ways of incorporating expectations of inflation, but the method chosen here is to assume that expectations are rational. The equations are estimated by the McCallum errors-in-variables technique using instrumental variables (McCallum, 1976a, b).

1.2.5 Incomes policies

It is apparent from even the briefest encounter with the literature that there is little agreement regarding how to model incomes policies or even which periods should be considered pertinent. This is an important issue in the estimation of an earnings equation since, of the 21 years since 1966, 13 were affected by incomes policies of one sort or another. The most common technique is the use of (1, 0) dummies. However, a particular coefficient on such a variable would be open to different interpretations, e.g. it could indicate a severe policy which was very ineffective or a mild policy which was very effective. The use of a single dummy variable has the drawback of restricting the overall effect of all the policies to be identical. However, using an individual dummy for each policy has the effect of significantly reducing the degrees of freedom available. One way around the degrees-of-freedom problem is for the researcher to select those periods which, according to his priors, are the most important.

The approach adopted here eschews the traditional approach of using dummy variables and instead uses an index which attempts to measure the severity of each policy. This allows different policies to have different effects while economizing on the degrees of freedom used. This technique is discussed by Desai *et al.* (1984) and Whitley (1986), and a recent example of its use in an earnings equation is given by Rowlatt (1986). The construction of the index proceeds by comparing the stated norm associated with each policy with an estimate of how earnings would have behaved in the absence of the policy, i.e.

$$\text{severity index} = \Delta W_t^c - \text{NORM}_t \qquad (1.1)$$

where ΔW_t^c is the counterfactual growth in earnings in the absence of the policy and NORM_t is the rate of growth of earnings desired by the government which is implied by each incomes policy. The simplest approach to proxying ΔW_t^c is to use either ΔW_{t-1} or ΔP_{t-1}, and the estimation here uses ΔW_{t-1}. One drawback of this approach is that once an incomes policy has been in effect for a number of quarters ΔW_{t-1} may no longer be a good proxy for ΔW^{e}_{t}. An alternative approach which attempts to take account of differing severities of incomes policies is to estimate an equation of the form

$$W_t = \lambda \mathrm{IP}_t \mathrm{NORM}_t + (1 - \lambda \mathrm{IP}_t)\delta Z_t \tag{1.2}$$

where IP is a (1, 0) dummy and Z_t is a vector containing the other determinants of earnings. An example of this approach is given by Wren-Lewis (1985). However, given the number of non-linear constraints which would need to be imposed, this method would not be feasible for the equations in this chapter.

The incomes policy variables used in the estimation work differ across sectors because ΔW^{e}_{t} is proxied by lagged earnings growth for each sector. In addition, the public sector variable takes account of a period of additional pressure on public sector wages, the so-called $N - 1$ policy of the early 1970s (see Mackie (1987) for further details).

Apart from the need to take account of the periods during which incomes policies were in effect, additional problems are caused by earnings rising in anticipation of an incomes policy coming into effect and earnings exhibiting a certain amount of catching-up following the ending of a policy. The former problem is ignored here by assuming that the opportunities for bringing forward wage settlements were quite limited. Catch-up effects are more important, and are alluded to by those who argue that incomes policies only moderated real wage growth in the short run, if at all. While the dynamic structure of many wage equations will ensure that the level of the real wage will return asymptotically to what it would have been in the absence of an incomes policy, some researchers include explicit dummy variables to ensure a quicker catch-up of real wages. However, given that it is not at all obvious a priori how to model the dynamic effects of an incomes policy correctly, the inclusion of lagged values of the policy variables in the estimation work reported here represents an attempt to allow the data to determine the cumulative effects of a policy. It is possible that there is a simultaneity problem with the incomes policy variable if high earnings growth in any quarter led to a revision to the norm for that quarter. This issue has been investigated by Desai *et al.* (1984) and Whitley (1986), but is ignored in the estimation work reported here.

1.2.6 Taxes

Personal sector taxes will be an important explanatory variable if unions bargain, at least to some extent, in terms of post-tax wages. The variable used in the estimation work is the retentions ratio which measures the proportion of pre-tax earnings which are retained after tax. It incorporates the effects of basic rate personal taxes, employees' National Insurance contributions and personal tax allowances. It also takes account of the reduced rates of income tax which existed for some of the estimation period.

Employers' labour taxes will directly affect the level of real profits and will therefore be an important factor in the bargaining process from the employers' point of view.[4] The variable used in the estimation work takes account of employers' National Insurance contributions, National Insurance surcharge and employers' other contributions (e.g. to pension funds). In addition, the variable which enters the non-manufacturing earnings equation takes account of selective employment tax (the tax on employment in the services sector levied between 1966 and 1973).

1.2.7 Wages, earnings and hours

The theory discussed in this section refers to wage settlements, while the estimated equations reported in the next section refer to earnings. Other researchers have handled the distinction between wages and earnings in a variety of ways. Rowlatt (1986) notes that her investigations of the issue of the dependence of manufacturing earnings on hours proved unpromising, and the equations she presents have the first difference of earnings as the dependent variable without any explicit account being taken of the number of hours worked. In contrast, Holly and Smith (1987) explicitly adjust the Department of Employment manufacturing earnings data to obtain a series for wages. Thus for the manufacturing sector they have

$$W_{\mathrm{m}} = \frac{\mathrm{WAEM}}{1.3H - 0.3\mathrm{NH}}$$

where WAEM is average earnings in manufacturing, H is average hours worked in manufacturing and NH is normal working hours worked in manufacturing. This can be rearranged to give

$$\mathrm{WAEM} = 1.3(H - \mathrm{NH})W_{\mathrm{m}} + \mathrm{NH}W_{\mathrm{m}}$$

which implies that overtime working receives a premium of 30% over the normal hourly rate. There are problems in acquiring the data for this exercise for the other sectors. Outside the manufacturing sector, data are only available on an annual basis. Whether the number of hours worked is an important variable in explaining earnings is obviously an empirical matter and further work should be undertaken to investigate this issue.

1.2.8 Relativities and the equations as a system

The inclusion among the explanatory variables of earnings in other sectors can be justified in a bargaining framework because relativities could either

[4]Strictly speaking the variable used in the estimation work should be called employers' non-earnings labour costs. It is referred to as labour taxes for ease of exposition.

enter a union's utility function directly or because wages in the other sectors will affect the utility of those who fail to remain employed in any particular sector. It is because each of the earnings equations includes earnings in one or more of the other two sectors as explanatory variables that they form a simultaneous system. The three earnings equations can be written as a system as follows:

$$AY = BX + U \tag{1.3}$$

where A and B are matrices of polynomials in the lag operator L, Y is a vector containing the three earnings variables, X is a vector of predetermined explanatory variables and U is a vector of disturbances. If earnings in each sector were determined totally independently of earnings in the other sectors, then A would be a diagonal matrix. However, this is not found to be the case and interaction between different sectors is an important part of the inflationary process. Given the probable simultaneities the following procedure was adopted. The equations were initially estimated as individual structural equations using instrumental variable estimation to ensure consistent, albeit inefficient, estimates of the parameters. Once a parsimonious representation of the data was obtained, the equations were estimated by a systems method to increase the efficiency of the estimates. In the event, none of the preferred equations contain the contemporaneous value of earnings in either of the other two sectors as explanatory variables. It follows that the system is not simultaneous contemporaneously, although it is simultaneous in a short-run dynamic sense and in the steady state. Nevertheless, estimating the equations as a system will increase the efficiency of the estimates if the contemporaneous disturbances across the equations are correlated. Apart from the gain in efficiency there is a further advantage in estimating the equations as a system, which is that cross-equation parameter restrictions can be imposed.

It is usually considered appropriate that there should be no money illusion in the wage bargaining process, at least in the long run, and so an investigation of this restriction is of some importance. Using the characterization of the system in Equation (1.3) the reduced form can be expressed as

$$Y = A^{-1}BX + A^{-1}U \tag{1.4}$$

If the polynomials in the lag operator are all solved for $L = 1$, then the elements of the maxtrix $A^{-1}B$ are the static steady state coefficients for each of the predetermined variables. These are the variables of interest when examining the theoretical long-run properties of the equations, rather than the coefficients in the single-equation static steady state solutions.

It is the appropriate elements of the matrix $A^{-1}B$ corresponding to prices in the vector X which determine the homogeneity, or otherwise, of earnings with respect to prices in the long run. The cross-equation restrictions to be tested are that the three relevant coefficients, which are highly non-linear functions of the elements of the matrix A and of the elements of the column of the matrix B which refers to prices, are each equal to unity. A sufficient but not necessary condition for long-run homogeneity of nominal earnings with respect to prices is that each individual structural equation exhibits homogeneity of nominal earnings with respect to the nominal price terms which appear as explanatory variables (i.e. consumer prices and other earnings). The appropriate restrictions for this sufficient condition are easy to impose and test in each individual equation. The necessary and sufficient condition for homogeneity requires that the highly non-linear cross-equation restrictions are imposed on the system. These restrictions are derived and imposed in the next section when the three equations are estimated as a system.

1.3 THE ESTIMATION RESULTS

In this section we initially present the results of estimating the three individual structural equations by instrumental variables. The equations are then re-estimated as a system both to take account of the possibility that the contemporaneous residuals in each of the structural equations are correlated and to impose the cross-equation restrictions discussed in the previous section. The discussion in this section concentrates on the static steady state properties of the equations and focuses attention on the systems nature of the earnings equations. The short-run dynamic behaviour of the equations is illustrated in the next section which discusses the simulation properties in the context of the Bank model. The mnemonics used in the equations are those in the Bank of England model manual.

1.3.1 Manufacturing earnings

The individual structural equation estimated for manufacturing earnings was derived from an equation of the following general form:

$$\begin{aligned}\ln \mathrm{WAEM}_t = {} & \sum_{i=1}^{4} \alpha_i \ln \mathrm{WAEM}_{t-1} + \beta \mathrm{LPROM}_{t-1} \\ & + \sum_{i=0}^{3} \gamma_i \mathrm{RSTUR}_{t-i} + \sum_{i=0}^{4} \delta_i \ln \mathrm{PC}_{t-i} \\ & + \sum_{i=0}^{4} \varepsilon_i \ln \mathrm{WAPS}_{t-i} + \sum_{i=0}^{4} \phi_i \ln \mathrm{RET}_{t-i} \\ & + \sum_{i=0}^{4} \lambda_i \ln \mathrm{LABM}_{t-i} + \mu \mathrm{TDAYWK}\end{aligned}$$

$$+ \eta + \theta \text{DEPC}_t + \sum_{i=0}^{1} \Psi_i \text{IP1}_{t-i} \quad (1.5)$$

where WAEM is an index of average earnings per head in manufacturing, DEPC_t is the expectation of inflation over the year beginning in the current quarter, LPROM is trend productivity in manufacturing, PC is the price deflator for total consumption, RET is the employees' retentions ratio, WAPS is average earnings per head in the non-trading public sector, LABM is employers' labour taxes, RSTUR is the reciprocal of the short-term unemployment rate, IP1 is the incomes policy dummy for manufacturing, TDAYWK is a dummy for the 3 day week and ln indicates the natural logarithm of the variable. Further details of all the variables used are given in Mackie (1987).

Equation 1.5 was estimated with quarterly data from 1966 Q1 to 1983 Q4 using instrumental variables. The inflationary expectations term was replaced by actual inflation over the same period and instrumented appropriately. In addition, the contemporaneous terms for prices, other earnings and the reciprocal of the short-term unemployment rate were treated as endogenous variables (see Table 1.1 for further details).

After a reasonably parsimonious version of Equation 1.5 was obtained, non-manufacturing earnings (WOO) were included in the equation. The final equation is given as Equation (1) in Table 1.1. A number of test statistics are reported for each equation.[5] $Z_1(4)$ and $Z_2(4)$ are both test statistics for residual autocorrelation up to and including fourth order appropriate for the case of instrumental variable estimation. They differ according to how the test statistic is calculated. $Z_1(4)$ is a test of the likelihood ratio type calculated in the way suggested by Godfrey (1983), while $Z_2(4)$ is a modified Lagrange multiplier test calculated in the manner suggested by Breusch and Godfrey (1981). These two tests are not necessarily asymptotically equivalent (Breusch and Godfrey, 1981). Both test statistics are distributed χ^2 with four degrees of freedom. $Z_3(4)$ and $Z_3(8)$ are four- and eight-period-ahead forecasting tests, which are distributed $\chi^2(4)$ and $\chi^2(8)$ respectively, and $Z_3(\rho)$ is Sargan's test for the validity of the instruments, which is distributed $\chi^2(\rho)$.

For the forecasting tests reported here the data from 1984 Q1 to 1985 Q4 were put aside at the beginning of the estimation work and not utilized again until the forecasting test statistics were constructed on the basis of the final parsimonious equations. Specifically, the tests were not evaluated at each stage in the specification search and used as a selection criterion. As a result these tests genuinely confront the models with new data (Harvey, 1981, pp. 186–7). After the forecasting tests were performed in this manner the equations were re-estimated over the whole sample period.

[5] For a full discussion of how the test statistics are constructed see Mackie (1987).

Table 1.1 Manufacturing earnings (the dependent variable is $\ln WAEM_t$)

	Equation (1) (unconstrained equation)	*Equation (2) (price homogeneity imposed)*	*Equation (3) (price homogeneity and Δ_1 on ln LABM imposed)*
$\ln WAEM_{t-1}$	0.67329	0.69397	0.69804
	(13.16)	(14.45)	(14.64)
$LPROM_{t-1}$	0.08443	0.10217	0.10996
	(2.40)	(3.21)	(3.62)
$RSTUR_t$	0.00034	0.00033	0.00029
	(3.14)	(3.12)	(3.18)
$\ln PC_{t-1}$	0.29836	0.24709	0.24732
	(3.22)	(3.02)	(3.03)
$\ln PC_{t-2}$	−0.19154	−0.19075	−0.19080
	(2.60)	(—)	(—)
$\ln WAPS_{t-3}$	0.10258	0.10090	0.09512
	(4.50)	(4.44)	(4.43)
$\ln RET_{t-1}$	−0.21278	−0.17680	−0.15153
	(3.96)	(4.01)	(5.05)
$\ln LABM_t$	−0.85272	−0.80191	−0.84516
	(3.71)	(3.56)	(3.87)
$\ln LABM_{t-1}$	0.76419	0.86442	0.84516
	(3.24)	(3.93)	(—)
$\ln WOO_{t-1}$	0.13524	0.14878	0.15032
	(2.95)	(3.35)	(3.39)
Constant	−0.10652	−0.32004	−0.29621
	(0.39)	(1.60)	(1.50)
$DEPC_t$	0.37676	0.31189	0.29256
	(5.71)	(8.61)	(11.06)
$IP1_t$	−0.02942	−0.03728	−0.03816
	(1.06)	(1.39)	(1.43)
$IP1_{t-1}$	−0.17558	−0.16567	−0.15405
	(5.16)	(5.03)	(5.25)
TDAYWK	−0.05678	−0.05730	−0.05818
	(9.16)	(9.27)	(9.58)
SEE	0.00565	0.00565	0.00564
$Z_1(4)$	6.76	8.67	8.66
$Z_2(4)$	10.70	12.33	12.38
$Z_3(4)$	4.37	4.67	4.53
$Z_3(8)$	9.35	8.53	8.01
$Z_4(6)$	8.28	9.37	9.76
Wald statistics for linear restrictions		1.39 ($\chi^2(1)$)	2.00 ($\chi^2(2)$)

The estimation was performed on quarterly data from 1966 Q1 to 1983 Q4 using instrumental variables. The additional instruments were $\Delta_4 \ln PC_{t-1}$, $\Delta_4 \ln PC_{t-2}$, $\Delta_4 \ln PFO\$_t$, $\Delta_4 \ln WULC_t$, $\Delta_4 \ln WPC_t$, $\Delta_4 \ln EER_{t-1}$, $\Delta_4 ERUK_{t-1}$ and RUR_{t-1}. In addition, the general form included $\ln WOO_{t-1}$, $\ln WAPC_{t-1}$, $\ln WPC_t$ and $\ln EER_{t-1}$ in the instrument set. The *t* statistics are given in parentheses.

Equation (1) is well determined with a standard error of 0.56% and all the variables discussed in the Appendix, Section A1.2, appear in the equation correctly signed. Both WAPS and WOO enter the equation, although neither of them appear contemporaneously. This result contrasts with the recent work of Holly and Smith (1987) who fail to find any significant effect of non-manufacturing earnings in their manufacturing wages equation. The static steady state of the equation is given by

$$\begin{aligned}\ln \text{WAEM} = {} & 0.25842\text{LPROM} + 0.00104\text{RSTUR} \\ & + 0.32696 \ln \text{PC} + 0.31398 \ln \text{WAPS} \\ & + 0.41395 \ln \text{WOO} - 0.65128 \ln \text{RET} \\ & - 0.27097 \ln \text{LABM} - 0.32604 \end{aligned} \tag{1.6}$$

The equation is slightly over-homogeneous in the static steady state with respect to the nominal price and wage variables, with the sum of the coefficients on PC, WAPS and WOO coming to 1.05. A discussion of the appropriate orders of magnitude of the coefficients is better left until the equations are examined as a system to take account of the simultaneity in the static steady state between WAEM, WOO and WAPS. However, there are two important variables in Equation (1) which do not enter the static steady state and hence need to be discussed here.

The equation suggests that there is an important role for inflationary expectations in the wage bargaining process. In the static steady state this variable is zero. However, in an economy with a positive inflation rate it is likely to be an important transmission mechanism for inflationary shocks. It is difficult to determine the appropriate size of the coefficient on inflationary expectations a priori. Nevertheless, we can attempt to evaluate its importance by looking at its impact effect on the level of WAEM. The impact elasticity of manufacturing earnings with respect to inflationary expectations is given by 0.37676DEPC_t. Thus, if, for example, inflationary expectations are originally at 10% and individuals then expect inflation to rise to 11%, this will increase WAEM by 0.4% in the current period. The inflationary expectations term will have longer-run dynamic effects but these are somewhat harder to disentangle analytically.

The equation also suggests that incomes policies have a significant effect on earnings in the short run. As discussed above the inclusion of lagged values of the policy variable was an attempt to allow the data to determine the cumulative effect of a policy, and it is interesting to note that the first lag of the incomes policy term is more significant than the contemporaneous term. In the static steady state the incomes policy term would, of course, be zero.

On the issue of residual autocorrelation the results are somewhat inconclusive in that one of the test statistics is marginally significant at the 95%

level while the other is insignificant. Mackie (1987) presents some further evidence which suggests that we cannot reject the hypothesis of no residual autocorrelation. If there is any residual autocorrelation, it is not of a simple form because the coefficients on each of the four lags of the residuals in an auxiliary regression are not significantly different from zero.

The equation does fairly well on the forecasting test, particularly when it is considered that it is quite a demanding test when performed in the way outlined above. The forecast errors (actual minus predicted) from the eight-quarter test are shown in Table 1.2.[6] Although none of these errors is significantly different from zero, the equation does show a tendency to consistently underpredict, at least since mid-1984. One possible explanation for the forecasting errors in the context of this equation is that inflationary expectations have not, in fact, followed inflation down and hence nominal earnings have remained higher than the equation would predict.

It is interesting to note that these forecasting errors are, in fact, relatively small during a period when many would argue that real manufacturing earnings have grown unexpectedly quickly. According to the equation an important part of the explanation for the recent rapid growth in real earnings is the slow feedthrough of the effects of the rise in labour productivity in the early 1980s. While a certain amount of this increase in productivity was cyclical, and part was due to an exceptional amount of labour shedding, it has nevertheless meant that firms could afford high pay settlements.

It was mentioned earlier that a sufficient but not necessary condition for the system as a whole to exhibit homogeneity with respect to prices is for each individual equation to be homogeneous with respect to the nominal price and wage variables. Equation (2) in Table 1.1 gives the results of imposing single-equation homogeneity. The imposition of the constraint is not rejected at the 95% confidence level with a Wald statistic of 1.39 (distributed $\chi^2(1)$). However, the sizes of some of the coefficients have changed. The static steady state of Equation (2) is given as

$$\begin{aligned} \ln \mathrm{WAEM} = {} & 0.33386\mathrm{LPROM} + 0.00108\mathrm{RSTUR} \\ & + 0.18410 \ln \mathrm{PC} + 0.32971 \ln \mathrm{WAPS} \\ & + 0.48616 \ln \mathrm{WOO} - 0.57772 \ln \mathrm{RET} \\ & + 0.20426 \ln \mathrm{LABM} - 1.04578 \end{aligned} \tag{1.7}$$

Perhaps the most important change between Equation 1.6 and Equation 1.7 is that the long-run coefficient on employers' taxes has changed sign. In order to remove a perverse long-run effect from this variable a constraint was imposed so that ln LABM only enters as a first difference. This is given

[6] These forecast errors are the difference between two logarithms. Thus a forecast error of 0.01 can be interpreted as a 1% error on the level of the variable.

Table 1.2 Forecast errors in Equation (1)

	Q1	*Q2*	*Q3*	*Q4*
1984	−0.00457	−0.00793	0.00593	0.00535
1985	0.01269	0.00587	0.00988	0.01182

as Equation (3) in Table 1.1, and the Wald statistic for the two restrictions is 2.0 (distributed $\chi^2(2)$). In fact, this restriction on ln LABM is not rejected when imposed on Equation (1) with a Wald statistic of 0.34 (distributed $\chi^2(1)$). The static steady state solution of Equation (3) is given by

$$\begin{aligned}\ln \text{WAEM} = {} & 0.36415\text{LPROM} + 0.00096\text{RSTUR} \\ & + 0.18718 \ln \text{PC} + 0.31501 \ln \text{WAPS} \\ & + 0.49781 \ln \text{WOO} - 0.50182 \ln \text{RET} \\ & - 0.98096 \end{aligned} \tag{1.8}$$

There is evidence of some residual autocorrelation in Equations (2) and (3), although there is disagreement between the test statistics. In addition, Equation (3) forecasts the period 1984 Q1 to 1985 Q4 better than Equation (1) with smaller forecast errors through most of this period.

1.3.2 Non-manufacturing earnings

The individual structural equation estimated for non-manufacturing earnings was derived from an equation of the following form:

$$\begin{aligned}\ln \text{WOO}_t = {} & \sum_{i=1}^{4} \alpha_i \ln \text{WOO}_{t-i} + \beta \text{LPROO}_{t-1} \\ & + \sum_{i=0}^{3} \gamma_i \text{RSTUR}_{t-i} + \sum_{i=0}^{3} \delta_i \ln \text{PC}_{t-i} \\ & + \sum_{i=0}^{3} \varepsilon_i \ln \text{WAPS}_{t-i} + \sum_{i=0}^{3} \phi_i \ln \text{RET}_{t-i} \\ & + \sum_{i=0}^{3} \lambda_i \ln \text{LABN} + \mu \text{TDAYWK} + \eta \\ & + \theta \text{DEPC}_t + \sum_{i=0}^{1} \psi_i \text{IP2}_{t-i} \end{aligned} \tag{1.9}$$

where WOO is the average earnings per head in the non-manufacturing sector (including the majority of public corporations), LPROO is trend productivity for the whole economy, LABN is employers' labour taxes which includes the effects of selective employment tax and IP2 is the incomes policy dummy for non-manufacturing.

Equation 1.9 was estimated with quarterly data from 1966 Q2 to 1983 Q4 using instrumental variables, replacing inflationary expectations by

Table 1.3 Non-manufacturing earnings (the dependent variable is $\ln WOO_t$)

	Equation (4) (unconstrained equation)	*Equation (5) (Δ_l on ln LABN imposed)*	*Equation (6) (price homogeneity imposed)*	*Equation (7) (price homogeneity and Δ_l on* ln LABN *imposed)*
$\ln WOO_{t-1}$	0.38042	0.38274	0.38036	0.39265
	(3.11)	(3.14)	(3.15)	(3.22)
$\ln WOO_{t-2}$	0.20302	0.21073	0.20298	0.22190
	(1.63)	(1.70)	(1.65)	(1.80)
$\ln WOO_{t-3}$	−0.24130	−0.21260	−0.24132	−0.18839
	(1.97)	(1.81)	(1.99)	(1.66)
$LPROO_{t-1}$	0.19387	0.23307	0.19372	0.28215
	(1.39)	(1.77)	(1.42)	(2.47)
$\ln PC_{t-1}$	0.89975	0.95240	0.90001	0.95321
	(3.67)	(4.02)	(3.75)	(4.00)
$\ln PC_{t-2}$	−0.65844	−0.65792	−0.65824	−0.68699
	(3.05)	(3.06)	(—)	(—)
$\ln WAEM_{t-1}$	0.82467	0.79338	0.82463	0.77674
	(4.60)	(4.53)	(4.65)	(4.45)
$\ln WAEM_{t-2}$	0.40825	0.45799	−0.40842	−0.46911
	(2.25)	(2.67)	(2.29)	(2.73)
$\ln LABN_t$	−0.78838	−0.95369	−0.78956	−0.90454
	(1.66)	(2.19)	(1.80)	(2.09)
$\ln LABN_{t-1}$	1.01684	0.95369	1.01686	0.90454
	(2.30)	(—)	(2.32)	(—)
Constant	2.33871	2.49595	2.34096	2.28728
	(3.65)	(4.07)	(4.31)	(4.18)
$DEPC_t$	0.13410	0.13743	0.13442	0.09414
	(1.64)	(1.69)	(2.03)	(1.66)
$Z_1(4)$	5.75	6.36	5.68	6.52
$Z_2(4)$	7.56	8.22	7.44	8.74
$Z_3(4)$	9.38	12.15	8.87	12.01
$Z_3(8)$	12.79	15.71	12.31	15.71
$Z_4(6)$	6.00	6.60	6.00	6.88
SEE	0.01528	0.01524	0.01516	0.01533
Wald statistics for linear restrictions		0.75 $(\chi^2(1))$	0.00004 $(\chi^2(1))$	1.29 $(\chi^2(2))$

The estimation was performed on quarterly data from 1966 Q2 to 1983 Q4 using instrumental variables. The additional instruments were $\Delta_4 \ln PC_{t-1}$, $\Delta_4 \ln PC_{t-2}$, $\Delta_4 \ln PFO\$_t$, $\Delta_4 \ln WULC_t$, $\Delta_4 \ln WPC_t$, $\Delta_4 \ln EER_{t-1}$ and $\Delta_4 ERUK_{t-1}$. In addition, the general form included $\ln WAPC_{t-1}$, $\ln WPC_t$, $\ln EER_{t-1}$, $\ln PPOX_{t-1}$ and RUR_{t-1} in the instrument set. The t statistics are given in parentheses.

actual inflation and treating the contemporaneous terms for prices, other earnings and the reciprocal of the short-term unemployment rate as endogenous variables (see Table 1.3 for further details).

After a reasonably parsimonious version of Equation 1.9 was obtained, manufacturing earnings were included and the final equation is given as Equation (4) in Table 1.3. This equation is rather less well determined than the corresponding equation for manufacturing earnings, with a standard error of 1.5%, and a number of the variables which entered the general form were excluded during the specification search, in particular the reciprocal of the short-term unemployment rate, the employees' retentions ratio and the incomes policy dummy. In addition, only one of the other earnings terms appears as an explanatory variable. Although some of the important explanatory variables are missing from the equation, WOO will be influenced by these variables via the WAEM terms. This will become apparent when we consider the three equations as a system.

The static steady state solution of Equation (4) is given as

$$\ln \mathrm{WOO} = 0.29470\mathrm{LPROO} + 0.36681 \ln \mathrm{PC} + 0.63299 \ln \mathrm{WAEM} + 0.34728 \ln \mathrm{LABN} + 3.55503 \qquad (1.10)$$

Equation 1.10 is almost exactly homogeneous in the nominal price and wage variables with the sum of the coefficients on PC and WAEM equal to 0.9998. Another feature of this equation is that LABN has a positive coefficient, which in the single-equation context is an incorrect sign. The equation does not reject a first-difference restriction on the ln LABN terms with a Wald statistic of 0.75 (distributed $\chi^2(1)$). This is given as Equation (5) in Table 1.3. The nominal price homogeneity restriction is not rejected in either Equation (4) or Equation (5). Inflationary expectations play a role in the WOO equation but they are less well determined than in the WAEM equation.

There does not appear to be any residual autocorrelation in any of these equations. However, their forecasting performance is rather worse than for the WAEM equation. The forecast errors for Equation (4) from the eight-quarter test are given in Table 1.4. Although none of these forecast errors is significantly different from zero the equation does show a marked tendency to overpredict. This contrasts with the WAEM equation and is much harder to understand given recent UK experience. It may be due to the weight given to WAEM in the WOO equation which leads to a relatively large solution value of WOO over this period.

Table 1.4 Forecast errors in Equation (4)

	Q1	*Q2*	*Q3*	*Q4*
1984	−0.02571	−0.02653	−0.04109	−0.02562
1985	−0.03382	−0.04626	−0.01437	−0.03449

1.3.3 Non-trading public sector earnings

Attempts were made to derive an equation for earnings in the non-trading public sector (WAPS) in an analogous manner to the other two earnings equations. However, a specification search beginning from a general form similar to Equations 1.5 and 1.9 did not prove very successful. It is possible that earnings in the public sector depend much more on institutional arrangements than private sector earnings, at least in the short run. As a consequence of this it is likely to prove difficult to model public sector earnings in a manner comparable to private sector earnings.

In order to derive an equation for WAPS the starting point was the presumption that in the long run comparability is maintained between WAPS and WAEM. In the short run there can be substantial deviations from this relationship. Hence, public sector earnings could be modelled in the simplest possible manner as

$$\alpha_i(\mathrm{L}) \ln \mathrm{WAPS}_t = \beta_i(\mathrm{L}) \ln \mathrm{WAEM}_t \qquad (1.11)$$

where $\alpha_i(L)$ and $\beta_i(L)$ are polynomials in the lag operator. This is similar to the approach taken in the London Business School model (Budd *et al.*, 1984). The final parsimonious equation for WAPS, given as Equation (8) in Table 1.5, augments Equation 1.11 with a number of additional variables. CATCH75 is a dummy variable to take account of a period of exceptionally rapid catch-up of public sector earnings during 1975 and CLEGG is a dummy variable to take account of the effects of the Clegg Commission on pay comparability. Apart from all the incomes policies which affected both public and private sectors, the incomes policy variable used in this equation (IP3) additionally takes account of the $N - 1$ policy which the Conservative Government implemented towards the end of 1970 with regard to public sector wage settlements. It is to be expected that incomes policies would have an important effect on public sector earnings in so far as the government has a direct influence on wage settlements. It is interesting to note that it is the first lag of the incomes policy variable which is important rather than the contemporaneous term; this is also a feature of the manufacturing earnings equation. The reciprocal of the short-term unemployment rate was also included in the equation, with the contemporaneous term being regarded as endogenous (see Table 1.5 for further details). The static steady state solution of Equation (8) is given as

$$\ln \mathrm{WAPS} = 0.96470 \ln \mathrm{WAEM} + 0.00079\mathrm{RSTUR} \qquad (1.12)$$

The reciprocal of the short-term unemployment rate has a small direct influence in this equation and it is under-homogeneous in WAEM. The homogeneity restriction is not rejected by the data to give Equation (9) in Table 1.5.

Neither Equation (8) nor Equation (9) appears to suffer from residual autocorrelation and they both pass the forecasting test. The forecast errors

Table 1.5 Non-trading public sector earnings (dependent variable is $\ln WAPS_t$)

	Equation (8) *(unconstrained equation)*	*Equation (9)* *(price homogeneity imposed)*
$\ln WAPS_{t-1}$	0.33730	0.34973
	(3.03)	(2.87)
$\ln WAPS_{t-3}$	0.39078	0.41075
	(3.35)	(3.23)
$\ln WAPS_{t-4}$	−0.13348	−0.14942
	(1.24)	(1.27)
$\ln WAEM_{t-1}$	0.98941	1.04859
	(6.89)	(6.83)
$\ln WAEM_{t-3}$	−0.78462	−0.86699
	(2.84)	(2.92)
$\ln WAEM_{t-4}$	−0.58295	−0.58123
	(1.82)	(1.65)
$\ln WAEM_{t-5}$	1.16782	1.19936
	(4.89)	(4.59)
$\ln WAEM_{t-8}$	−0.39857	−0.41079
	(4.34)	(—)
$RSTUR_t$	0.00259	0.00428
	(1.47)	(2.96)
$RSTUR_{t-1}$	−0.00497	−0.00728
	(1.90)	(3.22)
$RSTUR_{t-2}$	0.00270	0.00384
	(2.14)	(3.56)
$IP3_{t-1}$	−0.19701	−0.20061
	(2.66)	(2.47)
Constant	0.81701	0.69727
	(4.24)	(3.66)
CATCH75	0.068191	0.06596
	(3.28)	(2.89)
CLEGG	0.04358	0.04136
	(3.59)	(3.12)
$Z_1(4)$	3.52	4.24
$Z_2(4)$	4.47	5.55
$Z_3(4)$	3.37	2.53
$Z_3(8)$	8.57	8.20
$Z_4(4)$	3.27	4.23
SEE	0.01813	0.01992
Wald statistics for linear restrictions		2.07 ($\chi^2(1)$)

The estimation was performed on quarterly data from 1966 Q2 to 1983 Q4 using the instrumental variables option on TSP. The additional instruments were RUR_{t-1}, $RSTUR_{t-3}$, $RSTUR_{t-4}$, $RSTUR_{t-5}$ and $RSTUR_{t-6}$. The t statistics are given in parentheses.

for Equation (8) from the eight-quarter test are given in Table 1.6. None of the forecast errors is significantly different from zero and, in fact, the forecasting performance of this equation is in some sense better than those

Table 1.6 Forecast errors in Equation (8)

	Q1	*Q2*	*Q3*	*Q4*
1984	−0.00043	0.00408	0.03049	0.02173
1985	−0.01718	−0.02033	−0.02621	0.00043

of the WAEM and WOO equations since the errors are both positive and negative rather than being persistently positive or negative.

1.3.4 The properties of the system

It has been stressed in this chapter that the earnings equations in the Bank model need to be examined as a system to take account of the interaction between sectors. Despite the fact that the three preferred final equations do not contain any contemporaneous other-earnings terms as explanatory variables, the system is simultaneous in a short-run dynamic sense and in the static steady state. We now consider the matrix of static steady state coefficients (the matrix $A^{-1}B$ in Equation 1.4 evaluated at $L = 1$). If we consider the three unconstrained equations ((1), (4) and (8) in Tables 1.1, 1.3 and 1.5 respectively), then the $A^{-1}B$ matrix evaluated at $L = 1$ is as follows:

$$\begin{bmatrix} \ln \text{WAEM} \\ \ln \text{WOO} \\ \ln \text{WAPS} \end{bmatrix} =$$

$$\begin{bmatrix} 0.594 & 0.280 & 1.101 & -1.497 & -0.623 & 0.330 & 0.00296 \\ 0.376 & 0.472 & 1.063 & -0.948 & -0.394 & 0.556 & 0.00187 \\ 0.573 & 0.270 & 1.062 & -1.444 & -0.601 & 0.319 & 0.00365 \end{bmatrix} \begin{bmatrix} \text{LPROM} \\ \text{LPROO} \\ \ln \text{PC} \\ \ln \text{RET} \\ \ln \text{LABM} \\ \ln \text{LABN} \\ \text{RSTUR} \end{bmatrix}$$

Because of the interaction between sectors, any variable which appears in a single equation will appear in all three equations in the steady state. Thus the trend growth in earnings in each of the sectors is determined by productivity growth in both manufacturing and the economy as a whole. Of particular importance with regard to the coefficients on LPROM and LPROO are the implications for the share of labour income in value added. If the growth of real earnings were to exceed the growth of productivity this would lead, *ceteris paribus*, to a decline in the share of profits in value added. However, firms might resist such a decline and respond by either increasing prices or reducing employment. Some commentators see such a mechanism as an important part of the explanation of stagflation in the 1970s (e.g. Bruno and Sachs, 1985). Over the period 1966–84, manufacturing productivity grew on average by 2.8% per annum while whole-economy productivity grew by 2% per annum. Over the same period real earnings in the manufacturing, non-manufacturing and public sectors grew by 2.4% per annum, 2.1% per annum and 1.9% per annum respectively. The coefficients in the above matrix imply that, *ceteris paribus*, if productivity grew at its historical average then real earnings in the manufacturing, non-manufacturing and public sectors would grow at 2.3% per annum, 2.0% per annum and 2.2% per annum respectively. These figures suggest that in this set of equations there does not appear to be any tension over the division of value added between labour income and profits. However, larger coefficients on LPROM and LPROO might imply a problem in this respect.

All the equations are slightly over-homogeneous in consumer prices in the static steady state. In the WAEM and WAPS equations the retentions ratio has a coefficient larger (in absolute terms) than −1. This implies that personal sector taxes have a very powerful effect on earnings, and it could be argued that these coefficients are implausibly large. Employers' taxes have an important effect on WAEM and WAPS, although the effect is incorrectly signed in the WOO equation. The reciprocal of the short-term unemployment rate has a very weak effect in all three equations. As mentioned earlier not only does the form of this variable imply a non-linear response of earnings to the short-term unemployment rate but, in addition, the elasticity of the response varies with the short-term unemployment rate. The elasticity of earnings with respect to the reciprocal of the short-term unemployment rate is given by

$$C_{ij}\text{RSTUR}$$

where C_{ij} is the appropriate element of the $A^{-1}B$ matrix. Table 1.7 gives the percentage decline in earnings induced by a rise of 100 000 in short-term unemployment at the levels of employment and unemployment prevailing in 1978 and 1985. It illustrates how the effect of short-term unemployment on earnings has fallen with the rise in short-term unemployment. (Over this period short-term unemployment rose from 0.85 million to 1.34 million.) Short-term unemployment has the largest influence on public sector earnings. This is perhaps surprising given that the public sector is probably insulated the most from market-related shocks.

Table 1.7

	1978	*1985*
WAEM	−1.12	−0.45
WOO	−0.71	−0.28
WAPS	−1.38	−0.55

The next system examined corresponds to the equations where price homogeneity is imposed and employers' labour taxes no longer appear in the static steady state solution (Equations (3), (7) and (9) in Tables 1.1, 1.3 and 1.5 respectively). The system appears as follows:

$$\begin{bmatrix} \ln \text{WAEM} \\ \ln \text{WOO} \\ \ln \text{WAPS} \end{bmatrix} = \begin{bmatrix} 0.871 & 0.585 & 1.000 & -1.200 & 0.00293 \\ 0.467 & 0.806 & 1.000 & -0.643 & 0.00157 \\ 0.871 & 0.585 & 1.000 & -1.200 & 0.00377 \end{bmatrix} \begin{bmatrix} \text{LPROM} \\ \text{LPROO} \\ \ln \text{PC} \\ \ln \text{RET} \\ \text{RSTUR} \end{bmatrix}$$

The coefficients on productivity have increased relative to the unconstrained case and it could be argued that they imply implausibly large effects which may lead to some tension in the division of value added between labour income and profits. However, the coefficients on the retentions ratio have declined. The coefficients on the reciprocal of the short-term unemployment rate have remained remarkably stable.

1.3.5 Estimating the earnings equations as a system

The individual structural equations were estimated by instrumental variables to ensure consistency. However, a gain in efficiency can be attained by estimating the equations in a manner that takes account of any cross-equation correlation in the residuals. Furthermore, estimating the three equations as a system allows the imposition of cross-equation restrictions which enables the price homogeneity restriction to be imposed in a more general manner by placing constraints on the appropriate elements of the $A^{-1}B$ matrix. These constraints are both necessary and sufficient for price homogeneity in the static steady state rather than simply sufficient. The estimation method used was the three-stage non-linear least-squares method, and the equations chosen to form the system were the three equations (1), (4) and (8) (Tables 1.1, 1.3 and 1.5 respectively).

Because of the nature of the estimation procedure only one diagnostic test statistic is reported. $Z_5(3)$ is a likelihood ratio type test for first-order residual autocorrelation calculated along the lines suggested by Breusch and Godfrey (1981). It takes account of correlation between the contemporaneous residual for each equation and the lagged residuals from the other two equations, as well as its own lagged residual. It is distributed $\chi^2(3)$.

The results of estimating the unconstrained system are given in Equations (10), (15) and (20) in Tables 1.8, 1.9 and 1.10 respectively. In the WAEM and WOO equations the majority of the parameter estimates are similar to those in the individual structural equations and, in general, the standard errors of the parameter estimates decline. In addition, the standard errors of these two equations have declined. In the WAPS equation some of the parameter estimates seem to have changed by a larger degree, although again there is a decline in the standard error of the equation. The static steady state of this system is as follows:

$$\begin{bmatrix} \ln \text{WAEM} \\ \ln \text{WOO} \\ \ln \text{WAPS} \end{bmatrix} = \begin{bmatrix} 0.633 & 0.227 & 1.076 & -1.416 & -0.403 & 0.221 & 0.0024 \\ 0.399 & 0.373 & 1.059 & -0.893 & -0.254 & 0.363 & 0.0015 \\ 0.600 & 0.215 & 1.020 & -1.341 & -0.382 & 0.209 & 0.0023 \end{bmatrix} \begin{bmatrix} \text{LPROM} \\ \text{LPROO} \\ \ln \text{PC} \\ \ln \text{RET} \\ \ln \text{LABM} \\ \ln \text{LABN} \\ \text{RSTUR} \end{bmatrix}$$

The main characteristics of the system are the same as when the equations were estimated individually: all three equations are over-homogeneous in prices, the coefficients on the retentions ratio are greater than unity (in absolute terms) in the WAEM and WOO equations, the effects of short-term unemployment are very weak and employers' labour taxes are again incorrectly signed in the WOO equation.

In order to derive the necessary and sufficient conditions to ensure homogeneity in the static steady state we write the expression $AY = BX + U$ from Equation 1.3 more generally as

$$\begin{bmatrix} \alpha(L) & \beta(L) & \gamma(L) \\ \delta(L) & \varepsilon(L) & 0 \\ \phi(L) & 0 & \lambda(L) \end{bmatrix} \begin{bmatrix} \ln \text{WAEM} \\ \ln \text{WOO} \\ \ln \text{WAPS} \end{bmatrix} = \begin{bmatrix} \mu(L) \\ \eta(L) \\ 0 \end{bmatrix} \begin{bmatrix} \text{LPROM} \\ \text{LPROO} \\ \ln \text{PC} \\ \ln \text{RET} \\ \ln \text{LABM} \\ \ln \text{LABN} \\ \text{RSTUR} \end{bmatrix}$$

(assuming for convenience that $U = 0$). $\alpha(L)$, $\beta(L)$, $\gamma(L)$, $\delta(L)$, $\varepsilon(L)$, $\phi(L)$, $\lambda(L)$, $\mu(L)$ and $\eta(L)$ are all polynomials in the lag operator. For clarity of exposition we consider only the third column of the matrix B which corresponds to $\ln$ PC in the vector X. By pre-multiplying the matrix B with the inverse of the matrix A, the three long-run coefficients can be written as

$$\frac{\varepsilon(L)\lambda(L)\mu(L) - \beta(L)\lambda(L)\eta(L)}{\lambda(L)\alpha(L)\varepsilon(L) - \gamma(L)\phi(L)\varepsilon(L) - \lambda(L)\delta(L)\beta(L)} = C_{13} \tag{1.13}$$

$$\frac{\alpha(L)\lambda(L)\eta(L) - \delta(L)\lambda(L)\mu(L) - \gamma(L)\phi(L)\eta(L)}{\lambda(L)\alpha(L)\varepsilon(L) - \gamma(L)\phi(L)\varepsilon(L) - \lambda(L)\delta(L)\beta(L)} = C_{23} \tag{1.14}$$

$$\frac{\beta(L)\phi(L)\eta(L) - \phi(L)\varepsilon(L)\mu(L)}{\lambda(L)\alpha(L)\varepsilon(L) - \gamma(L)\phi(L)\varepsilon(L) - \lambda(L)\delta(L)\beta(L)} = C_{33} \tag{1.15}$$

Table 1.8 System estimation: manufacturing earnings (dependent variable is ln WAEM)

	Equation (10) (unconstrained equation)	*Equation (11) (cross-equation homogeneity imposed on all three equations)*	*Equation (12) (cross-equation homogeneity imposed on ln WAEM and ln WOO)*	*Equation (13) (cross-equation homogeneity imposed on all three equations and Δ_1 imposed on ln LABM and ln LABN)*	*Equation (14) (cross-equation homogeneity imposed on ln WAEM and ln WOO and Δ_1 imposed on ln LABM and ln LABN)*
ln $WAEM_{t-1}$	0.67606 (15.67)	0.68926 (16.23)	0.68117 (16.00)	0.69114 (16.13)	0.67973 (15.97)
$LPROM_{t-1}$	0.08932 (3.05)	0.10070 (3.56)	0.09753 (3.48)	0.11229 (4.13)	0.10165 (3.82)
$RSTUR_t$	0.00035 (3.69)	0.00036 (3.80)	0.00035 (3.70)	0.00029 (3.59)	0.00033 (4.00)
ln PC_{t-1}	0.29436 (3.69)	0.24559 (3.36)	0.26810 (3.64)	0.24222 (3.29)	0.26930 (3.65)
ln PC_{t-2}	−0.19539 (2.89)	−0.18853 (2.86)	−0.19228 (2.93)	−0.18341 (2.76)	−0.19188 (2.93)
ln $WAPS_{t-3}$	0.10021 (5.12)	0.10374 (5.28)	0.10294 (5.36)	0.09754 (5.08)	0.10231 (5.35)
ln RET_{t-1}	−0.19983 (5.27)	−0.17961 (5.02)	−0.18909 (5.24)	−0.14832 (5.63)	−0.18026 (6.16)
ln $LABM_t$	−0.84974 (4.21)	−0.79900 (3.98)	−0.82142 (4.12)	−0.86241 (4.37)	−0.84313 (4.35)
ln $LABM_{t-1}$	0.79279 (3.85)	0.88585 (4.50)	0.85036 (4.36)	0.86241 (—)	0.84313 (—)
ln WOO_{t-1}	0.13925 (3.53)	0.14995 (—)	0.14579 (—)	0.15251 (—)	0.14646 (—)
Constant	−0.13630 (0.63)	−0.32856 (1.86)	−0.24342 (1.39)	0.29363 (1.66)	−0.23072 (1.33)
$DEPC_t$	0.35681 (9.06)	0.31651 (11.44)	0.33320 (11.37)	0.29588 (13.33)	0.32802 (12.46)

Table 1.8 Contd.

	Equation (10) (unconstrained equation)	*Equation (11) (cross-equation homogeneity imposed on all* three equations)	*Equation (12) (cross-equation homogeneity imposed* on *ln WAEM and* ln WOO*)*	*Equation (13) (cross-equation homogeneity imposed on all three equations and Δ_1 imposed on ln LABM* and *ln LABN*)	*Equation (14) (cross-equation homogeneity imposed on* ln WAEM *and ln* WOO and Δ_l imposed on ln LABM *and* ln LABN*)*
$IP1_t$	−0.02885	−0.03556	−0.03202	−0.03664	−0.03212
	(1.19)	(1.48)	(1.35)	(1.51)	(1.35)
$IP1_{t-1}$	−0.17013	−0.16783	−0.16908	−0.15432	−0.16573
	(6.06)	(5.92)	(6.01)	(5.86)	(6.23)
TDAYWK	−0.05650	−0.05698	−0.05663	−0.05836	0.05706
	(10.32)	(10.31)	(10.34)	(10.63)	(10.57)
SEE	0.00502	0.00509	0.00505	0.00514	0.00505
$Z_5(3)$	4.88			6.88	5.78
Wald test for restrictions		10.55 ($\chi^2(3)$)	0.91 ($\chi^2(2)$)	15.06 ($\chi^2(5)$)	4.00 ($\chi^2(4)$)

The estimation was performed on quarterly data from 1966 Q2 to 1983 Q4 using the non-linear three-stage least-squares method. The additional instruments were RUR_{t-1}, $RSTUR_{t-4}$, $RSTUR_{t-5}$, $RSTUR_{t-6}$, $\Delta_4 \ln PC_{t-1}$, $\Delta_4 \ln PC_{t-2}$, $\Delta_4 \ln PFO\$$, $\Delta_4 \ln WULC$, $\Delta_4 \ln WPC$, $\Delta_4 \ln EER_{t-1}$, $\Delta_4 ERUK_{t-1}$. The t statistics are given in parentheses.

Table 1.9 System estimation: non-manufacturing earnings (dependent variable is $\ln WOO_t$)

	Equation (15) (unconstrained equation)	*Equation (16) (cross-equation homogeneity imposed on all three equations)*	*Equation (17) (cross-equation homogeneity imposed on* ln WAEM *and* ln WOO*)*	*Equation (18) (cross-equation homogeneity imposed on all three equations and Δ_1 imposed on* ln LABM *and* ln LABN*)*	*Equation (19) (cross-equation homogeneity imposed on* ln WAEM *and ln WOO and Δ_1 imposed on* ln LABM *and* ln LABN*)*
$\ln WOO_{t-1}$	0.37154	0.37690	0.37446	0.38643	0.38512
	(3.36)	(—)	(—)	(—)	(—)
$\ln WOO_{t-2}$	0.19339	0.19428	0.19518	0.22311	0.22016
	(1.72)	(1.72)	(1.73)	(1.96)	(1.93)
$\ln WOO_{t-3}$	−0.25092	−0.25190	−0.25093	−0.18476	−0.18366
	(2.27)	(2.28)	(2.27)	(1.76)	(1.75)
$LPROO_{t-1}$	0.15780	0.15957	0.16214	0.28285	0.28211
	(1.27)	(1.29)	(1.31)	(2.68)	(2.68)
$\ln PC_{t-1}$	0.86829	0.84176	0.84631	0.90474	0.90588
	(3.93)	(3.89)	(3.91)	(4.15)	(4.15)
$\ln PC_{t-2}$	−0.60728	−0.61094	−0.61373	−0.63640	−0.63798
	(3.18)	(3.20)	(3.21)	(3.28)	(3.29)
$\ln WAEM_{t-1}$	0.80831	0.80677	0.80859	0.73325	0.73616
	(5.00)	(4.98)	(4.99)	(4.61)	(4.63)
$\ln WAEM_{t-2}$	−0.37576	− 0.35687	−0.35988	−0.42638	−0.42568
	(2.31)	(2.25)	(2.26)	(2.72)	(2.71)
$\ln LABN_t$	−0.82589	−0.74167	−0.75208	−0.90183	−0.90937
	(1.92)	(1.85)	(1.87)	(2.26)	(2.28)
$\ln LABN_{t-1}$	1.04967	1.04629	1.05228	0.90183	0.90937
	(2.62)	(2.61)	(2.62)	(—)	(—)
Constant	2.47773	2.33623	2.34537	2.29915	2.30322
	(4.37)	(4.71)	(4.72)	(4.56)	(4.57)
$DEPC_t$	0.19037	0.17705	0.17679	0.13521	0.13568
	(3.20)	(3.43)	(3.42)	(2.91)	(2.92)

Table 1.9 Contd.

	Equation (15) (unconstrained equation)	*Equation (16) (cross-equation homogeneity imposed on all three equations)*	*Equation (17) (cross-equation homogeneity imposed on* ln WAEM *and* ln WOO*)*	*Equation (18) (cross-equation homogeneity imposed on all three equations and Δ_1 imposed on* ln LABM *and* ln LABN*)*	*Equation (19) (cross-equation homogeneity imposed on* ln WAEM *and ln* WOO *and Δ_1 imposed on* ln LABM *and* ln LABN*)*
SEE	0.01387	0.01388	0.13888	0.01414	0.01414
$Z_5(3)$	4.88			6.88	5.78
Wald test for restrictions		10.55 ($\chi^2(3)$)	0.91 ($\chi^2(2)$)	15.06 ($\chi^2(5)$)	4.00 ($\chi^2(4)$)

See footnote to Table 1.8.

Table 1.10 System estimation: non-trading public sector earnings (dependent variable is ln $WAPS_t$)

	Equation (20) (unconstrained equation)	*Equation (21) (cross-equation homogeneity imposed on all* three equations)	*Equation (22) (cross-equation homogeneity imposed on ln WAEM and* ln WOO)	*Equation (23) (cross-equation homogeneity imposed on all three equations and* Δ_1 *imposed on ln LABM* and *ln LABN*)	*Equation (24) (cross-equation homogeneity imposed on* ln WAEM *and ln* WOO and Δ_1 imposed on ln LABM *and* ln LABN)
ln $WAPS_{t-1}$	0.37838	0.43848	0.38103	0.43786	0.38030
	(4.10)	(4.55)	(4.14)	(4.54)	(4.13)
ln $WAPS_{t-3}$	0.35267	0.35395	0.35380	0.35218	0.35306
	(3.68)	(3.45)	(3.70)	(3.43)	(3.70)
ln $WAPS_{t-4}$	−0.12690	−0.14630	−0.12567	−0.14543	−0.12201
	(1.40)	(1.51)	(1.39)	(1.50)	(1.36)
ln $WAEM_{t-1}$	0.89908	0.92627	0.89441	0.92301	0.89027
	(8.05)	(7.77)	(8.02)	(7.74)	(7.99)
ln $WAEM_{t-3}$	−0.64976	−0.70297	−0.63292	−0.71398	−0.63607
	(2.86)	(2.91)	(2.79)	(2.95)	(2.81)
ln $WAEM_{t-4}$	−0.65174	−0.68393	−0.66612	−0.67740	−0.66733
	(2.41)	(2.36)	(2.47)	(2.34)	(2.47)
ln $WAEM_{t-5}$	1.14804	1.17519	1.14430	1.18582	1.15078
	(5.70)	(5.47)	(5.70)	(5.51)	(5.74)
ln $WAEM_{t-8}$	−0.37048	−0.36068	−0.37054	−0.36205	−0.37148
	(4.93)	(—)	(4.94)	(—)	(4.95)
$RSTUR_t$	0.00081	0.00210	0.00073	0.00212	0.00069
	(0.88)	(2.43)	(0.80)	(2.45)	(0.75)
$RSTUR_{t-1}$	−0.00237	−0.00395	−0.00225	−0.00401	−0.002215
	(1.66)	(2.81)	(1.59)	(2.86)	(1.57)
$RSTUR_{t-2}$	0.00154	0.00245	0.00147	0.00249	0.00145
	(2.04)	(3.36)	(1.96)	(3.40)	(1.94)
$IP3_{t-1}$	−0.18034	−0.16567	−0.18452	−0.16229	−0.18400
	(2.96)		(3.04)	(2.50)	(3.04)

Table 1.10 Contd.

	Equation (20) (unconstrained equation)	*Equation (21) (cross-equation homogeneity imposed on all* three equations)	*Equation (22) (cross-equation homogeneity imposed on ln WAEM and* ln WOO)	*Equation (23) (cross-equation homogeneity imposed on all three equations and* Δ_1 *imposed on ln LABM* and *ln LABN*)	*Equation (24) (cross-equation homogeneity imposed on* ln WAEM *and ln* WOO and Δ_l imposed on ln LABM *and* ln LABN)
Constant	0.84472	0.64464	0.84049	0.64848	0.84155
	(5.24)	(4.12)	(5.22)	(4.14)	(5.23)
CATCH75	0.06480	0.05815	0.06376	0.060488	0.06532
	(3.68)	(3.10)	(3.64)	(3.22)	(3.72)
CLEGG	0.04072	0.03472	0.04050	0.03497	0.04091
	(3.97)	(3.22)	(3.96)	(3.24)	(4.01)
SEE	0.01539	0.03472	0.01540	0.01649	0.01540
$Z_5(3)$	4.88			6.88	5.78
Wald statistics for		10.55	0.91	15.06	4.00
restrictions		$(\chi^2(3))$	$(\chi^2(2))$	$(\chi^2(5))$	$(\chi^2(4))$

See footnote to Table 1.8.

where C_{ij} refers to the (i, j)th element in the matrix $A^{-1}B$. The constraints to be imposed are that $C_{13} = C_{23} = C_{33} = 1$. In order to impose these constraints it is necessary to note that C_{33} is a linear function of C_{13}, i.e.

$$C_{33} = -\frac{\phi(L)}{\lambda(L)} C_{13} \tag{1.16}$$

This implies that the three constraints given in expressions 1.13, 1.14 and 1.15 cannot be imposed as they stand. Rather, the constraint $\phi(L) = -\lambda(L)$ replaces expression 1.15, and expressions 1.13 and 1.14 are imposed after substituting $\phi(L) = -\lambda(L)$. The intuitive explanation for this is that the only nominal price variable entering the WAPS equation is WAEM, and if the WAEM equation is homogeneous of degree one with respect to prices then WAPS will be as well if the long-run coefficient on WAEM in the WAPS equation is unity. This will be so if $\phi(L) = -\lambda(L)$.

The results of imposing the three constraints are given in Equations (11), (16) and (21).[7] These restrictions are rejected by the data with a Wald statistic of 10.55 (distributed $\chi^2(3)$). The particular problem appears to be the restriction on the WAPS equation. Imposing this restriction on its own gives a Wald statistic of 8.30 (distributed $\chi^2(1)$). This is an interesting result given that the data accepted this restriction in the individually estimated structural equation (Equation (9) in Table 1.5). The explanation for this is that the increase in efficiency brought about by the systems estimation has increased the ability of the data to reject any particular restriction.

When price homogeneity is imposed on the three equations the long-run coefficients on employers' labour taxes become incorrectly signed. Imposing first differences gives Equations (13), (18) and (23) with a static steady state solution

$$\begin{bmatrix} \ln \text{WAEM} \\ \ln \text{WOO} \\ \ln \text{WAPS} \end{bmatrix} =$$

$$\begin{bmatrix} 0.864 & 0.577 & 1.000 & -1.141 & 0.00350 \\ 0.461 & 0.800 & 1.000 & -0.609 & 0.00187 \\ 0.864 & 0.577 & 1.000 & -1.141 & 0.00519 \end{bmatrix} \begin{bmatrix} \text{LPROM} \\ \text{LPROO} \\ \ln \text{PC} \\ \ln \text{RET} \\ \text{RSTUR} \end{bmatrix}$$

Although the price homogeneity and first-differencing of employers' labour taxes restrictions are jointly rejected by the data, with a Wald statistic of 15.06 (distributed $\chi^2(5)$), the steady state coefficients look quite reasonable with the exception of the productivity terms which, it could be argued,

[7]In order to impose the constraints, the expressions 1.13 and 1.14 (after substituting $\phi(L) = -\lambda(L)$) have to be solved as a set of simultaneous equations in two of the parameters selected as the parameters to be constrained.

imply implausibly large effects since the sum of the coefficients on LPROM and LPROO exceed unity in all three equations.

Imposing restrictions on the long-run consumer price coefficients in just the WAEM and WOO equations and allowing the long-run coefficient in the WAPS equation to be determined freely is not rejected by the data with a Wald statistic of 0.91 (distributed $\chi^2(2)$). These are given as Equations (12), (17) and (22).

The final equations chosen at this stage are Equations (14), (19) and (24) in Tables 1.8, 1.9 and 1.10 respectively. In addition to the imposition of price homogeneity for the long-run coefficients on prices in the WAEM and WOO equations, employers' labour taxes only enter as first differences. Thus there is only a short-term effect from a shock to employers' taxes. The Wald statistic for these four restrictions is 4.00 (distributed $\chi^2(4)$). The static steady state solution to Equations (14), (19) and (24) is

$$\begin{bmatrix} \ln \text{WAEM} \\ \ln \text{WOO} \\ \ln \text{WAPS} \end{bmatrix} = \begin{bmatrix} 0.700 & 0.492 & 1.000 & -1.241 & 0.0022 \\ 0.376 & 0.752 & 1.000 & -0.666 & 0.0012 \\ 0.659 & 0.463 & 0.942 & -1.169 & 0.0020 \end{bmatrix} \begin{bmatrix} \text{LPROM} \\ \text{LPROO} \\ \ln \text{PC} \\ \ln \text{RET} \\ \text{RSTUR} \end{bmatrix}$$

1.4 THE DYNAMIC PROPERTIES OF THE EARNINGS EQUATIONS

In order to examine the dynamic properties of the earnings equations a version of the system consisting of Equations (14), (19) and (24) was re-estimated over the whole data period available (i.e. 1966 Q2 to 1985 Q4) to give the equations presented in Table 1.11. The purpose of re-estimating the equations over an extended data set was to make use of the data reserved previously for the forecasting tests. The static steady state solution is

$$\begin{bmatrix} \ln \text{WAEM} \\ \ln \text{WOO} \\ \ln \text{WAPS} \end{bmatrix} = \begin{bmatrix} 0.764 & 0.385 & 1.000 & -1.071 & 0.00207 \\ 0.287 & 0.701 & 1.000 & -0.402 & 0.00078 \\ 0.723 & 0.364 & 0.946 & -1.013 & 0.00180 \end{bmatrix} \begin{bmatrix} \text{LPROM} \\ \text{LPROO} \\ \ln \text{PC} \\ \ln \text{RET} \\ \text{RSTUR} \end{bmatrix}$$

Table 1.11 Earnings equations used in simulations (estimated as a system with cross-equation homogeneity imposed on ln WAEM and ln WOO and Δ_1 imposed on ln LABM and ln LABN)

	Dependent variable		
Independent variable	ln $WAEM_t$	ln WOO_t	ln $WAPS_t$
ln $WAEM_{t-1}$	0.70303 (16.83)	0.64931 (4.08)	0.84812 (7.67)
ln $WAEM_{t-2}$		−0.51531 (3.28)	
ln $WAEM_{t-3}$			−0.57611 (2.56)
ln $WAEM_{t-4}$			−0.65085 (2.43)
ln $WAEM_{t-5}$			1.12210 (5.71)
ln $WAEM_{t-8}$			−0.36764 (5.06)
ln WOO_{t-1}	0.11248 (—)	0.52103 (—)	
ln WOO_{t-2}		0.26790 (2.34)	
ln WOO_{t-3}		−0.14580 (1.42)	
ln $WAPS_{t-1}$			0.40128 (4.45)
ln $WAPS_{t-3}$	0.09746 (5.00)		0.32025 (3.35)
ln $WAPS_{t-4}$			−0.11879 (1.36)
$LPROM_{t-1}$	0.12427 (5.52)		
$LPROO_{t-1}$		0.19850 (1.87)	
ln PC_{t-1}	0.28980 (3.98)	0.81003 (3.66)	
ln PC_{t-2}	−0.19746 (3.00)	−0.58716 (2.96)	
ln RET_{t-1}	−0.17415 (5.95)		
Δ_1 ln $LABM_t$	−0.73941 (3.88)		
Δ_1 ln $LABN_t$		−1.00289 (2.49)	
$RSTUR_t$	0.00035 (4.27)		0.00053 (0.56)
$RSTUR_{t-1}$			−0.00188 (1.28)
$RSTUR_{t-2}$			0.00129 (1.68)

Table 1.11 Contd.

Independent variable	*Dependent variable*		
	$\ln WAEM_t$	$\ln WOO_t$	$\ln WAPS_t$
$IP1_t$	−0.03189 (1.31)		
$IP1_{t-1}$	−0.16210 (5.97)		
$IP3_{t-1}$			−0.17604 (2.93)
TDAYWK	−0.05754		
CATCH75			0.06364 (3.63)
CLEGG			0.03949 (3.88)
Constant	−0.08783 (0.56)	1.69394 (3.60)	0.85411 (5.35)
$DEPC_t$	0.31342 (12.48)	0.15871 (3.34)	
SEE	0.00518	0.01470	0.01559

The estimation was performed on quarterly data from 1966 Q2 to 1985 Q4 using the non-linear three-stage least-squares method. For the additional instruments see the footnote to Table 1.8. The t statistics are given in parentheses.

The static steady state is broadly similar to the system estimated over the shorter data period. This system of equations is stable with all the eigenvalues lying within the unit circle. The mean lag of the system is just over five quarters.[8]

One way of examining the dynamic properties of the earnings equations is to incorporate them into the Bank model and to run some simulation experiments.[9] These simulation exercises take the form of examining how the model behaves in response to a shock to one or more of the exogenous variables, where the solution path of the model after the shock has been administered is compared with a base case. These simulations do not, of course, isolate the dynamic properties of the earnings subsystem independently of the dynamic properties of the rest of the model, neither do they have any particular policy prescriptions. Rather, they simply illustrate the marginal properties of the Bank model. Nevertheless, they are informative and assist in determining whether the equations should ultimately form part of the Bank model.

[8]The author is grateful to Stephen Hall for supplying a program to calculate the eigenvalues of the system.

[9]Mackie (1987) derives the analytic dynamic steady state for the system of equations.

The simulation results are now discussed. Two exogenous shocks were considered: an increase in world prices and an increase in government current expenditure. The simulations were run on a 10 year simulation base with the exchange rate constrained throughout.

1.4.1 An increase in world prices

In this simulation all world prices (including world unit labour costs) are raised 2% above the base throughout. A shock of this sort primarily feeds into UK domestic inflation via the unit value indices for imports which in turn feed into manufacturers' wholesale prices. The transmission into domestic prices occurs fairly slowly, with manufacturers' wholesale prices fully reflecting this increase in world prices after only about 4 years. There is a further lag of 1 year before consumer prices rise above the base to the full extent of the initial shock (i.e. 2%). Whole economy average earnings initially respond more slowly than consumer prices with a consequent small decline in real earnings. After about 3 years, however, average earnings overshoot prices slightly and there is a small increase in real earnings until the final year of the simulation when whole economy real earnings are almost unchanged relative to the base (Fig. 1.1). The different sectors respond at different rates to the price shock, with the fastest sector being non-manufacturing which responds slightly more quickly than the manufacturing sector over the first 5 years of the simulation (Fig. 1.2). The non-manufacturing earnings equation has the largest impact elasticity with

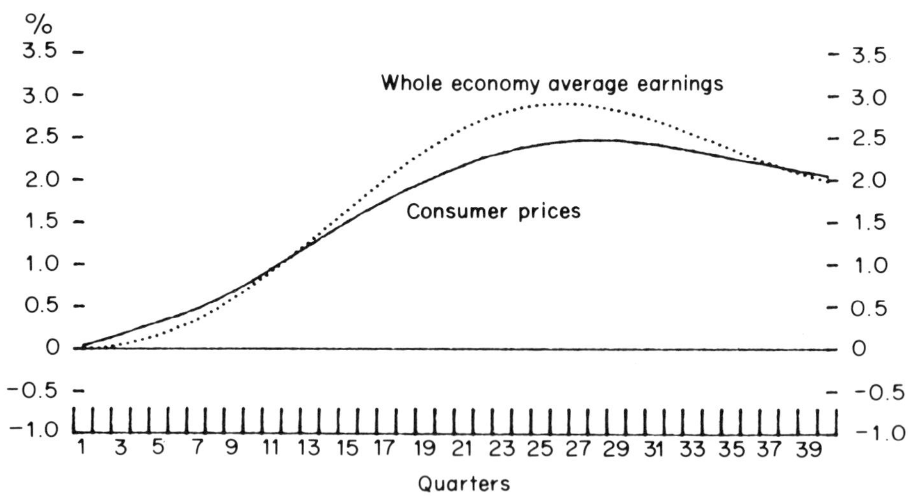

Fig. 1.1 Increase in world prices: prices and average earnings (percentage differences from base).

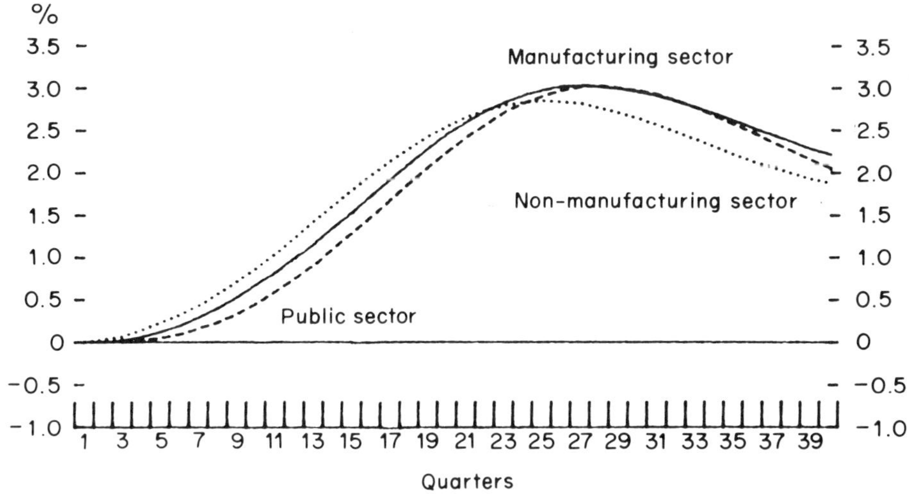

Fig. 1.2 Increase in world prices: relative response in earnings (percentage differences from base).

respect to consumer prices (0.81 compared with 0.29 for manufacturing). Earnings in the non-trading public sector are the slowest to respond since the price shock only feeds in indirectly via manufacturing earnings. Futhermore, although during the course of the simulation non-trading public sector earnings appear to catch up with manufacturing earnings, by the end of the simulation period they reach only 93% of the response of manufacturing earnings. This is very close to the long-run response of 0.95.

It is important to know the degree to which domestic prices in the model are homogeneous with respect to world prices in the long run. A plausible simulation property, with the exchange rate constrained, would be homogeneity of degree one so that an x% increase in all world prices would eventually lead to an increase of x% in UK domestic prices. This simulation suggests that the model does in fact have this property. This follows from the proposition that homogeneity of degree one in the individual price and earnings equations in the model is a sufficient but not necessary condition that the model as a whole will exhibit homogeneity of degree one if the exchange rate is constrained. Consumer prices increase relative to the base by more than 2% after about 6 years but turn down again after about 8 years and end the simulation period exactly 2% above the base.

Turning to the real side of the economy, we find that domestic output never deviates by more than 0.5% from the base (Fig. 1.3). Initially gross domestic product (GDP) is slightly above the base as the initial beneficial shock to competitiveness increases exports and reduces imports. However, as domestic prices respond, the expansionary effect from net trade declines

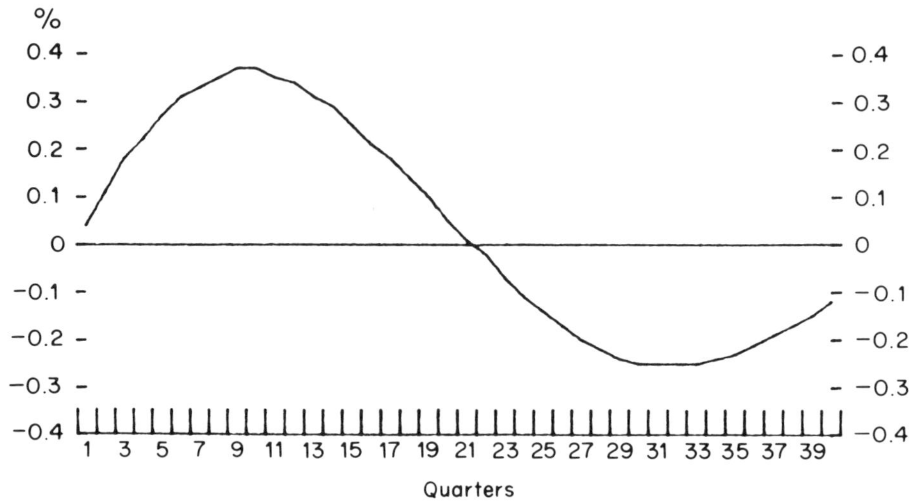

Fig. 1.3 Increase in world prices: GDP (percentage differences from base).

and GDP falls below the base after about 6 years. Investment responds initially to the increase in activity but eventually falls below the base. Consumers' expenditure remains broadly unchanged for about 7 years as an increase in expenditure on consumer durables from about the third year broadly offsets a decline in expenditure on non-durables. However, after about 8 years expenditure on consumer durables also falls below the base. Expenditure on non-durables is below the base throughout primarily because of inflationary losses on liquid assets and wealth. The increase in expenditure on consumer durables, relative to the base, is partly due to lower real interest rates which affect this category of consumption directly and lower nominal interest rates, brought about by a lower public sector borrowing requirement (PSBR), which affect consumption via mortgage lending.

Initially both total unemployment and short-term unemployment fall below the base as output expands (Fig. 1.4). After about 4 years the former declines by around 60 000 while the latter declines by around 30 000. After just over 5 years both rise above the base as the stimulus to domestic output is reversed.

1.4.2 An increase in government expenditure

In this simulation government current expenditure is increased by £400 million (1980 prices) per quarter throughout. The effects of this shock are illustrated in Figs 1.5 to 1.8. There is a very small inflationary effect in this simulation with consumer prices only around 0.75% above the base after

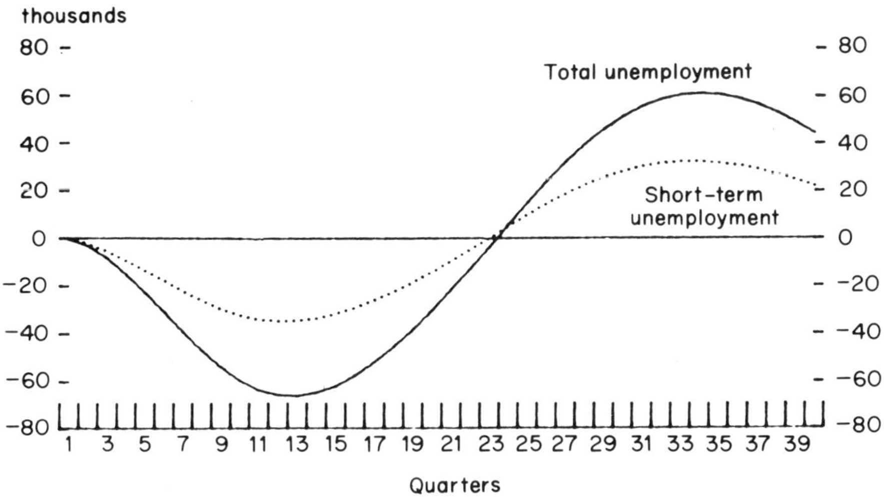

Fig. 1.4 Increase in world prices: unemployment (levels differences from base).

10 years (Fig. 1.5). However, about two-thirds of this increase in prices is due to an increase in local authority receipts of rates which in the model finance a part of the increase in government current expenditure.

This simulation again illustrates how weak the Phillips curve effect is in

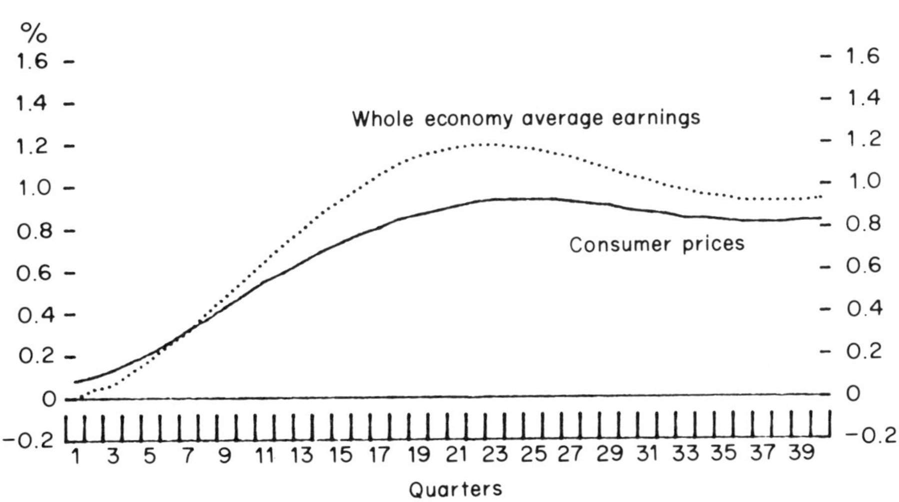

Fig. 1.5 Increase in government expenditure: prices and average earnings (percentage differences from base).

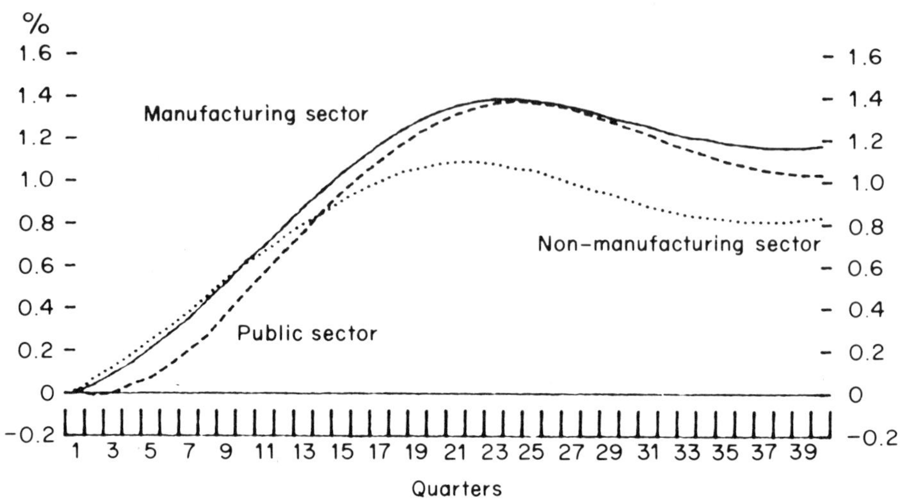

Fig. 1.6 Increase in government expenditure: relative response in earnings (percentage differences from base).

these equations. Early on in the simulation the level of short-term unemployment is almost 70 000 lower than in the base, which corresponds to a change in the short-term unemployment rate from around 4.57% to 4.32%. At this level of short-term unemployment rate, the changes induced by this simulation, *ceteris paribus*, would lead to an increase in the real wage of

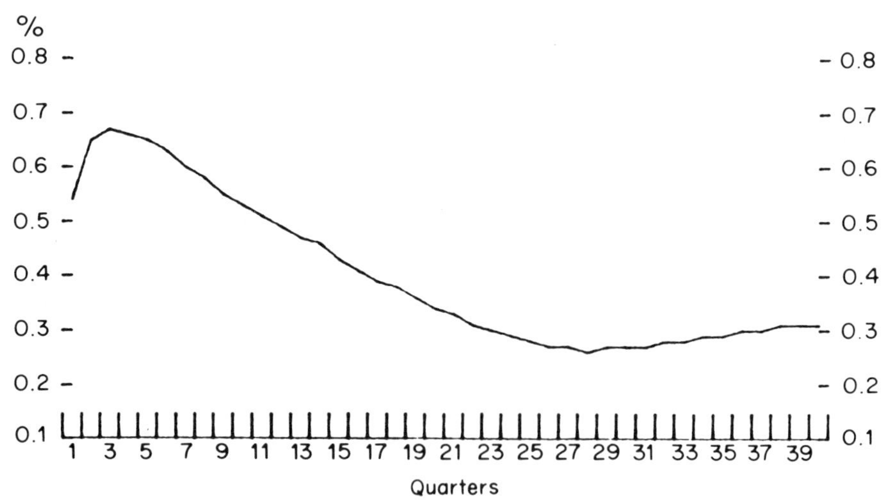

Fig. 1.7 Increase in government expenditure: GDP (percentage differences from base).

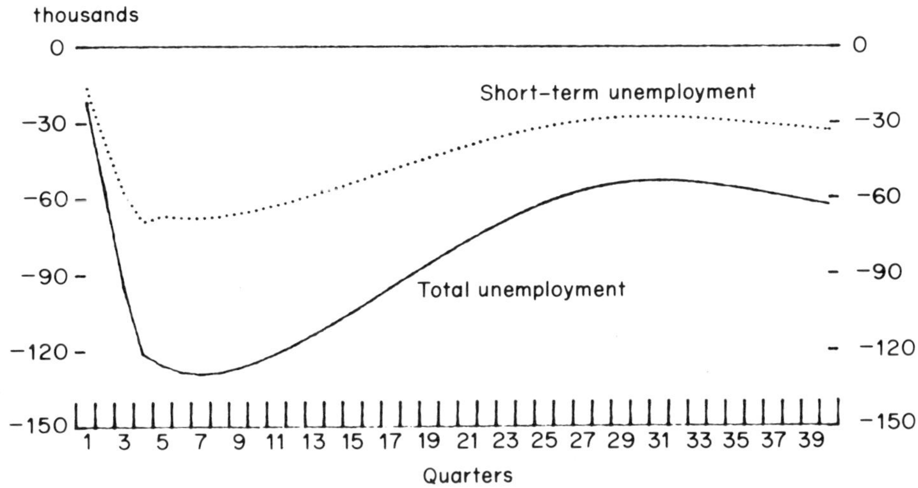

Fig. 1.8 Increase in government expenditure: unemployment (levels differences from base).

0.25% for the manufacturing and non-trading public sectors and about 0.1% for the non-manufacturing sector.

The level of GDP is higher than the base throughout the simulation period although there is considerable crowding out as the simulation proceeds (Fig. 1.7). The reason for this crowding out is an appreciation in the real exchange rate, which occurs as a result of the small rise in domestic prices with the exchange rate constrained, which depresses output in the manufacturing and non-manufacturing sectors. In addition, the increase in the PSBR puts upward pressure on nominal interest rates.

1.5 CONCLUSIONS AND SUGGESTIONS FOR FURTHER WORK

The aim of the research reported here was to improve the earnings equations in the Bank of England macroeconomic model of the UK economy. However, as with any research project, there remain many issues which require further investigation. In this section we draw some conclusions from the work already undertaken and discuss how future work might proceed.

The equations presented in this chapter appear to be an adequate representation of earnings in the three disaggregated sectors with plausible theoretical and empirical properties. Although the system of equations is not contemporaneously simultaneous, there are nevertheless important intersectoral effects and as a consequence the equations have a fairly rich dynamic structure. Other variables found to be important in determining nominal earnings are labour productivity, consumer prices, inflationary expectations, personal sector taxes and employers' labour taxes, although the last variable only has an effect in the short run. An important result of this research is that short-term unemployment does not have a very powerful effect on earnings.

The intersectoral effects in these equations may imply a certain amount of nominal inertia in the inflationary process. Since earnings in each sector depend on lagged earnings in the other sectors as well as lagged prices, a shock to prices may take longer to feed through fully to earnings than if earnings simply depended on past prices. This, along with the small effect from short-term unemployment and the large increases in labour productivity in the early 1980s, may provide part of the explanation of why the growth of nominal earnings has remained relatively high recently despite falls in inflation.

One question which is often asked of a disaggregated labour market is whether there is a leading sector. There are two ways in which this notion might be interpreted. The first is that within any annual wage round a particular sector might temporally lead the other two sectors. This would occur if an annual wage round existed as a well-defined phenomenon and different groups of employees settled at the same time each year. However, the model presented here does not really address this issue. The second possible interpretation of the notion of a leading sector is that a particular sector might respond more quickly to a shock than the other sectors. With this interpretation the leading sector may vary according to the nature of the shock. The simulations reported earlier indicate that the non-manufacturing sector is the leading sector in response to a shock to prices. This property can also be seen from the coefficients on consumer prices in the WAEM and WOO equations. The public sector will lead very slightly in response to an unemployment shock with a slightly larger impact elasticity than in the manufacturing sector. Finally, and perhaps surprisingly, the manufacturing sector will lead in response to an incomes policy shock because the incomes policy variable enters the manufacturing earnings equation contemporaneously (as well as lagged once) whilst only occurring with a lag in the public sector equation.

The simulations reported here illustrate the dominance of the cost-push approach to pricing behaviour in the Bank model. With the exchange rate constrained, the two main channels through which demand pressures can affect prices are via short-term unemployment influencing earnings and employed factor utilization rates affecting manufacturing profit margins, and it has been amply demonstrated that the former effect is very weak in the equations reported here.

As has been mentioned earlier, an important feature of these equations is the influence of productivity on real earnings. If the sum of the coefficients on the two productivity terms in the equations exceeds unity, then a balanced increase in productivity of 1% will lead to a rise of more than 1% in real earnings. It might be considered desirable to impose restrictions on the equations to ensure the shares in value added remain constant in the steady state. However, it is not really feasible to impose the necessary and sufficient conditions in the way that price homogeneity has been imposed because the two sets of restrictions would become extremely complicated. Further work should investigate the imposition of sufficient conditions to ensure constant shares in value added which could probably be imposed along with the price homogeneity restrictions.

The estimated equations suggest that there is an important role for inflationary expectations in the wage bargaining process. Apart from price expectations a disaggregated labour market could also incorporate sectoral wage expectations, i.e. earnings in any one sector will be influenced not only by expectations of price inflation but also by expectations of earnings in the other two sectors. This is something which could be investigated further.

One issue which has received a certain amount of attention recently in the literature is the appropriate role of corporate profits in determining wage behaviour. Carruth and Oswald (1987) find empirical evidence that profits (real profits per unit of capital stock) have a direct influence on real product wages. They argue that this result is consistent with microeconomic industrial relations data (e.g. Gregory *et al.*, 1985, 1987). The model presented by Rowlatt (1986) also includes a term in profits (real profits per unit of private sector output) which has a significant effect in her preferred equation. In contrast, Hall and Henry (1987) failed to find any empirical support for the inclusion of a real profits term in an aggregate earnings equation. The evidence on this issue is, at this stage, rather inconclusive and hence would warrant some further research which could be carried out within the context of the disaggregated model presented here.

DATA DEFINITIONS (Variables not previously defined)

EER	effective UK exchange rate index
ERUK	UK exchange rate against US$ (index)
PC	price deflator for total consumption
PFO$	world dollar price of oil
PPOX	producer price of manufacturing output (excluding food, drink and tobacco)
RSTUR	reciprocal of the short-term unemployment rate
RUR	reciprocal of the unemployment rate
WAPC	index of average wages in public corporations (Bank estimate)
WOO	average earnings in the 'other' sector

WPC major six consumer prices
WULC competitors' unit labour costs: manufacturing

APPENDIX: RE-ESTIMATING THE BANK WAGE EQUATIONS

N. Hatch

A1.1 Introduction

In this appendix we discuss the results of re-estimating the model described in the main chapter using Department of Employment data, and a revised definition of the retentions ratio.

A1.2 Data

For this extension to the model discussed in the main chapter, it was decided to construct a consistent set of data using Department of Employment indices, since the data used in the previous study were derived from several different sources. The whole economy average earnings (WSDE) and manufacturing average earnings (WAEM) indices were available directly from the *Gazette*. An index was then constructed for non-trading general government (WAPS). In order to construct the final residual index for non-manufacturing earnings (WOO) the indices had to be weighted by both employment and the relative level of earnings across sectors. The employment weights were taken directly from the model and the nominal earnings weighting factors were calculated from the *Blue Book* (Tables A1.1 and

Table A1.1 Revised earnings sector

Variable description	*Units*	*Model code*	*Source*
DE whole economy earnings[a]	1985 = 100	WSDE	DE *Gazette*
DE manufacturing earnings	1985 = 100	WAEM	DE *Gazette*
DE general government earnings[a]	1985 = 100	WAPS	DE *Gazette*
DE non-manufacturing[b]	1985 = 100	WOO	Constructed by residual from DE series
CSO whole economy earnings[a]	£ per quarter per man	WS	CSO

DE, Department of the Environment.
[a]Including an adjustment for HM Forces pay.
[b]Includes public corporations, private services, primary production, agriculture and construction.

Table A1.2 De-indexation factors

Variable	*Factor*[a]
WAPS	19.32
WAEM	21.81
WOO[b]	18.95
WSDE	19.74

[a]The factors are calculated using the *Blue Book* such that WSDE × 19.74 = WS in 1977 Q1.
[b]The following relationship is used to obtain earnings in the non-manufacturing private sector (WOO):

$$\begin{aligned}\text{WOO} \times 18.95 \times \text{LOTH} &= (\text{WSDE} \times 19.74 \times \text{LE}) \\ &\quad - (\text{WAPS} \times 19.32 \times \text{LEG}) \\ &\quad - (\text{WAEM} \times 21.81 \times \text{LEMF})\end{aligned}$$

A1.2). This resulted in there being two measures of whole economy average earnings on the Bank model, the first derived from the Central Statistics Office (CSO) measure of wages and salaries (WS) and the second from the Department of Employment's whole economy average earnings index (WSDE). The two measures were assumed to be equal in 1977 Q1. A simple equation is used to link the two series thereafter, with the residual from the linking equation representing the degree of mismatch between the two measures of earnings. A major advantage of using the Department of Employment based series is that not only are they internally consistent but they are also available on a monthly basis. Nevertheless, we still have the option of using the CSO data and in some circumstances this may be preferable. Existing earnings data were retained prior to 1977 because the Department of Employment data were not available on a consistent basis.

A1.3 Retentions ratio

The three-sector system of earnings equations on the Bank model includes a retentions ratio term in the manufacturing earnings (WAEM) equation. The version of the system discussed earlier has a short-run coefficient on the retentions ratio of −0.174 with a highly significant t value. When the long-run static solution was calculated for the earning system as a whole the retentions ratio has coefficients of −1.07, −0.40 and −1.01 for manufacturing, non-manufacturing and general government sectors respectively. The means of calculating the ratio is shown in Table A1.3 using the standard rate of taxation (TRY) as a basis for its construction. Unfortunately, however, the taxation variable used did not take account of 'full earned income relief' which was operational up to 1973 Q2. Therefore the correct measure of the tax rate to use is TRYE. Since, for the period prior to 1973, TRYE is less than TRY (because of the relief), the adjusted retentions ratio

Table A1.3

(a) Old retentions ratio

$$\text{RET} = \text{TXA} + \frac{(\text{TXB})(\text{TRY})/100}{\text{WS}}$$

where

$$\text{TXA} = 1 - \left(\frac{\text{TRY}}{100} + \frac{\text{YJCN}}{\text{YWS}}\right)$$

$$\text{TXB} = \frac{100\text{TARR}/\text{TRY} + \text{MSCR}}{4(\text{NTAS} + 1.45\text{NTAM})}$$

(b) New retentions ratio

$$\text{RET} = \text{TXA} + \frac{(\text{TXB})(\text{TRYE})/100}{19.739837\text{WSDE}}$$

where

$$\text{TXA} = 1 - \left(\frac{\text{TRYE}}{100} + \frac{\text{YJCN}}{\text{DEYW}}\right)$$

$$\text{TXB} = \frac{100\text{TARR}/\text{TRYE} + \text{MSCR}}{4(\text{NTAS} + 1.45\text{NTAM})}$$

$$\text{DEYW} = \frac{19.739837(\text{WSDE})(\text{LE})}{1000}$$

TRT standard rate of income tax
TRYE basic/standard tax rate on income subject to full earned income relief
YJCN National Insurance contributions paid by employees and self-employed
WS average earnings CSO
YWS income from wages and salaries
TARR reduction in income tax due to existence of reduced rates
MSCR aggregate married, single and child tax allowances
NTAS number claiming single allowance
NTAM number claiming married allowance
WSDE average earnings index
LE employees in employment

is higher than the one originally used. After 1973 Q2 the two measures of the tax rate are the same. Table A1.3 gives details of the new (corrected) measure of the retentions ratio.

A1.4 Re-estimation

The new earnings data and corrected retentions ratio were used in the re-estimation of the three equation earnings system. The same estimation period (1966 Q2–1985 Q4) and method (three-stage least-squares) were applied. No attempt was made during the re-estimation to remodel the dynamics of the system. The cross-equation homogeneity restrictions on the manufacturing and non-manufacturing equation were also imposed. The earnings data enter the re-estimated equations in index form rather than as nominal series. This should represent no problem in itself because the equations are in logarithmic format.

In general the results of the re-estimation were very similar to the original specification of the model. However, the coefficient on the retentions ratio was much smaller than in the original system. This was found to be due partly to data revisions and partly to the new earnings data, but primarily to the use of the corrected taxation variable. It was also found that relaxation of the homogeneity restrictions tended to reduce the coefficient still further. The impact effect in the final re-estimated model was 30% smaller than in the old model, and the long-run effect was between 40% and 45% smaller. The *t* value was reduced from 6.0 in the original specification to around 2.5 in the re-estimated system.

(a) Average earnings in manufacturing

$$
\begin{aligned}
\ln \text{WAEM} = {} & \underset{(16.3)}{0.7470814} \ln \text{WAEM}_{-1} + \underset{(3.9)}{0.0926633} \frac{1}{8} \sum_{i=2}^{9} \ln \left(\frac{\text{MPRO}}{\text{LEMF}} \right)_{-i} \\
& + \underset{(2.3)}{0.0002215035} \left(\frac{\text{LE} + \text{LSE} + \text{LU}}{\text{LUST}} \right) \\
& + \underset{(3.3)}{0.02734244} \ln \text{PC}_{-1} - \underset{(2.1)}{0.1620931} \ln \text{PC}_{-2} \\
& + \underset{(2.5)}{0.05039052} \ln \text{WAPS}_{-3} - \underset{(2.5)}{0.1209214} \ln \text{RET}_{-1} \\
& - \underset{(9.4)}{0.0602848}\, \text{D741} + \underset{(11.1)}{0.2781885}\, \text{DEPC} - \underset{(0.4)}{0.01258942}\, \text{IP1} \\
& - \underset{(4.6)}{0.1465952}\, \text{IP1}_{-1} - \underset{(3.8)}{0.8438736} \\
& \times \ln \left(\frac{\text{DEYW} + \text{YECO} + \text{YECN} + \text{YECS}}{\text{DEYW}} \right) \\
& + \underset{(-)}{0.8438736} \ln \left(\frac{\text{DEYW} + \text{YECO} + \text{YECN} + \text{YECS}}{\text{DEYW}} \right)_{-1} \\
& + \underset{(-)}{0.09489} \ln \text{WOO}_{-1} - \underset{(3.2)}{0.3457466}
\end{aligned}
$$

where DEYW = 19.739837WSDE(LOTH + LEG + LEMF)/1000, $\bar{R}^2 =$ 0.999, SE = 0.006, DW = 1.7 and the data are for 1966 Q2 to 1985 Q4.

(b) Average earnings: non-trading public sector

$$\begin{aligned}\ln \mathrm{WAPS} = {} & \underset{(2.9)}{0.2844632} \ln \mathrm{WAPS}_{-1} + \underset{(2.2)}{0.2493875} \ln \mathrm{WAPS}_{-3} \\ & + \underset{(1.0)}{0.1037444} \ln \mathrm{WAPS}_{-4} + \underset{(3.7)}{0.04348184}\,\mathrm{CLEGG} \\ & + \underset{(3.0)}{0.06029121}\,\mathrm{CT75} \\ & + \sum_{i=1}^{8} \alpha_i \ln \mathrm{WAEM}_{-i} + \sum_{i=0}^{2} \beta_i \left(\frac{\mathrm{LE} + \mathrm{LSE} + \mathrm{LU}}{\mathrm{LUST}}\right)_{-i} \\ & - \underset{(3.3)}{0.2405629}\,\mathrm{IP3} + \underset{(2.1)}{0.1039326}\end{aligned}$$

where

$$\alpha_1 = \underset{(7.2)}{1.03303},\ \alpha_2 = 0,\ \alpha_3 = \underset{(2.7)}{-0.7228093},\ \alpha_4 = \underset{(0.8)}{-0.2569231},$$

$$\alpha_5 = \underset{(2.8)}{0.6772469},\ \alpha_6 = 0,\ \alpha_7 = 0,\ \alpha_8 = \underset{(4.2)}{-0.3946951}$$

$$\beta_0 = \underset{(0.7)}{0.0008237988},\ \beta_1 = \underset{(1.2)}{-0.002140297},\ \beta_2 = \underset{(1.7)}{0.001551848}$$

$\bar{R}^2 = 0.999$, SE $= 0.019$, DW $= 1.7$ and the data are for 1966 Q2 to 1985 Q4.

(c) Average earnings: 'other' sector

$$\begin{aligned}\ln \mathrm{WOO} = {} & \underset{(—)}{0.46009} \ln \mathrm{WOO}_{-1} + \underset{(2.6)}{0.2847003} \ln \mathrm{WOO}_{-2} \\ & - \underset{(2.1)}{0.1997314} \ln \mathrm{WOO}_{-3} \\ & + \underset{(2.6)}{0.2651546} \frac{1}{8} \sum_{i=2}^{9} \ln \left(\frac{\mathrm{GDPO}}{\mathrm{LE} + \mathrm{LSE}}\right)_{-i} + \underset{(4.7)}{0.9650075} \ln \mathrm{PC}_{-1} \\ & - \underset{(3.9)}{0.7279398} \ln \mathrm{PC}_{-2} + \underset{(3.2)}{0.4988331} \ln \mathrm{WAEM}_{-1} \\ & - \underset{(1.9)}{0.2809209} \ln \mathrm{WAEM}_{-2} + \underset{(2.2)}{0.1010923}\,\mathrm{DEPC} \\ & - \underset{(2.1)}{0.8038095} \ln \left(\frac{\mathrm{DEYW} + \mathrm{YECO} + \mathrm{YECN} + \mathrm{TSET}}{\mathrm{DEYW}}\right) \\ & + \underset{(—)}{0.8038095} \ln \left(\frac{\mathrm{DEYW} + \mathrm{YECO} + \mathrm{YECN} + \mathrm{TSET}}{\mathrm{DEYW}}\right)_{-1} \\ & + \underset{(3.0)}{0.7923684}\end{aligned}$$

where $\bar{R}^2 = 0.999$, SE = 0.14, DW = 1.95 and the data are for 1966 Q2 to 1985 Q4.

Data definitions for variables not previously defined:

CLEGG	Dummy variable to take account of Clegg Commission on pay in the public sector
CT75	A dummy variable to take account of particularly rapid earnings growth in the public sector
D741	Dummy for the three day week
IP3	Incomes policy dummy for the non-trading public sector
GDPO	Output measure of GDP
LEG	Employees in the non-trading public sector
LEMF	Employees in manufacturing
LOTH	Employees in the non-manufacturing sector (LE-LEG-LEMF)
LSE	Self employed
LU	Unemployed
LUST	Short-term unemployment (up to 26 weeks)
MPRO	Manufacturing output
TSET	Selective employment tax
YECN	Employers' National Insurance contributions
YECO	Employers' other contributions
YECS	Accruals of National Insurance surcharge.

REFERENCES

Breusch, T. S. and Godfrey, L. (1981) A review of recent work on testing for auto-correlation in dynamic simultaneous models, in *Macroeconomic Analysis: Essays in Macroeconomics and Econometrics* (eds D. Currie, R. Nobay and D. Peel), Croom Helm, London.

Bruno, M. and Sachs, J. D. (1985) *Economics of Worldwide Stagflation*, Harvard University Press, Cambridge, MA.

Budd, A., Dicks, G., Holly, S., Keating, G. and Robinson, B. (1984) The London Business School econometric model of the UK. *Economic Modelling*, **1**(4), 355–420.

Carruth, A. A. and Oswald, A. J. (1987) Wage inflexibility in Britain *Oxford Bulletin of Economics and Statistics* (Special Issue), **49**, 59–78.

Desai, M., Keil, M. and Wadhwani, S. (1984) Incomes policy in a political environment: a structural model for the UK 1961–1980, in *Applied Decision Analysis and Economic Behaviour* (ed. A. J. Hughes Hallett), Nijhoff, Dordrecht.

Foster, N., Henry, S. G. B. and Trinder, C. (1986) Public and private sector pay: some further results, Discussion Paper No. 120, National Institute of Economic and Social Research.

Godfrey, L. G. (1983) On the uses of misspecification checks and tests of non-nested hypothesis in empirical econometrics. *Economic Journal* (Supplement), **94**, 69–81.

Gregory, M., Lobban, P. and Thomson, A. (1985) Wage settlements in manufacturing, 1979–84: evidence from the CBI pay databank. *British Journal of Industrial Relations*, **23**, 339–57.

Gregory, M., Lobban, P. and Thomson, A. (1987) Pay settlements in manufacturing industry, 1979–84: a micro-data study of the impact of product and labour market pressures. *Oxford Bulletin of Economics and Statistics* (Special Issue), **49**, 129–50.

Hall, S. G. and Henry, S. G. B. (1987) Wage models. *National Institute Economic Review*, February, No. 119, 70–5.

Harvey, A. C. (1981) *The Econometric Analysis of Time Series*, Philip Allan, Oxford.

Holly, S. and Smith, P. (1987) A two-sector analysis of the UK labour market. *Oxford Bulletin of Economics and Statistics* (Special Issue), **49**, 79–102.

Layard, R. and Nickell, S. (1986) Unemployment in Britain. *Economica* (Supplement), **53**, S121–69.

McCallum, B. T. (1976a) Rational expectations and the natural rate hypothesis: some consistent estimates. *Econometrica*, **44**, 43–52.

McCallum, B. T. (1976b) Rational expectations and the estimation of econometric models: an alternative procedure. *International Economic Review*, **17**, 484–90.

Mackie, D. J. (1987) A three sector model of earnings behaviour, Bank of England Discussion Paper, Technical Series No. 16.

Nickell, S. J. (1982) A bargaining model of the Phillips curve, Centre for Labour Economics Discussion Paper No. 130, London School of Economics.

Nickell, S. J. (1984) The modelling of wages and employment, in *Econometrics and Quantitative Economics* (eds D. F. Hendry and K. F. Wallis), Blackwell, Oxford.

Nickell, S. (1987) Why is wage inflation in Britain so high? *Oxford Bulletin of Economics and Statistics* (Special Issue), **49**, 103–28.

Nickell, S. J. and Andrews, M. (1983) Unions, real wages and employment in Britain 1951–79. *Oxford Economic Papers* (Supplement), **35**, 183–206.

Oswald, A. J. (1986) Wage determination and recession: a report on recent work. Centre for Labour Economics Discussion Paper No. 243, London School of Economics.

Oswald, A. J. and Turnbull, P. (1985) Pay and employment determination in Britain: what are labour contracts really like? *Oxford Review of Economic Policy*, **1**, 80–97.

Rowlatt, P. A. (1986) A model of wage bargaining, Government Economic Service Working Paper No. 91 (Treasury Working Paper No. 44).

Smith, P. and Holly, S. (1985) Wage and employment determination in the UK, Centre for Economic Forecasting Discussion Paper No. 137, London Business School.

Wallis, K. F. (ed.), (1986) *Models of the UK Economy*, Oxford University Press, Oxford.

Whitley, J. D. (1986) A model of incomes policy in the UK, 1963–79. *Manchester School of Economic and Social Studies*, **54**, 31–64.

Wren-Lewis, S. (1985) Private sector earnings and excess demand from 1966 to 1980. *Oxford Bulletin of Economics and Statistics*, **47**, 1–18.

2

Stockbuilding and liquidity

T. S. CALLEN, S. G. HALL

AND S. G. B. HENRY

2.1 INTRODUCTION AND MOTIVATION

There are two distinct themes in this chapter, both of which have been the subject of quite intensive study in the literature. The first theme, which occupies roughly the first half of the chapter, is concerned with the relationship between company liquidity and stockbuilding. This is one aspect of a wider question of the relationship of company liquidity to company expenditure as a whole. Co-integration methods are used to explore this question. The second theme taken up subsequently emphasizes explicit dynamic modelling of the stockbuilding decision, treating it as optimal and intertemporal. This introduces two additional elements into the empirical modelling conducted in the first part of the chapter. These elements are the problems of introducing a co-integrating vector into a forward-looking model and allowing for the conditional variance of sales as a determinant of stockbuilding. Before describing the theoretical underpinnings of the models to be estimated later, some additional motivation for these two themes is provided.

First, in considering the relationship between stocks and liquidity, it needs to be recognized that both stocks and liquidity probably play a buffer role for the company, while variables that are more costly to change (e.g. employment, investment) adjust more slowly to their long-run levels. The buffering role of stocks is well known: if there are quadratic adjustment costs in output, it is optimal for a firm to let stocks absorb a proportion of any change in demand and then stock levels gradually adjust to the new equilibrium. Liquid assets may also play a buffering role because holdings of liquid assets and/or bank borrowing are less costly to change than other items in the accounts. The implication behind such an interpretation is that disequilibrium in liquidity from its long-run target level probably affects other company sector variables. Recognition of this feature led to the company sector adjustment system developed in the Treasury, for example, where disequilibrium financial effects were included in real company sector equations. The benefits of using co-integration methods for such a model are then obvious: the residual generated in estimation of the co-integrating vector for liquidity can be interpreted as the deviation of liquidity from its long-run desired level. Ireland and Wren-Lewis (1988), for example, find that disequilibrium liquidity, when measured in this way, was significant when entered into a stocks equation (as well as other company sector equations), indicating that stocks and liquidity are in a sense jointly determined: one method of increasing liquidity in the short term is to decrease stockholding.

Co-integration techniques can be used to investigate both stocks and liquidity, and this question will be explored in section 2.3. To anticipate somewhat, the results suggest that there is an important relationship between companies' holdings of stocks (of finished goods), liquid assets and liquid liabilities (in the form of bank borrowing). However, the findings do not confirm that this relationship is consistent with disequilibrium effects. Instead it appears that portfolio-type considerations are important in the firms' decision to hold stocks and liquid assets and, as with any allocative decision, the respective holdings depend on relative rates of return as well as scale variables.

The empirical tests reported later experiment with two ways of including financial effects in stockbuilding equations. The first includes the actual level of real gross liquid assets and real bank borrowing in the stocks equation. The second approach uses the probable determinants of the allocation between liquidity and stocks in the stocks equation. The main result in the latter approach is that the borrowing and lending rate prove to be important (equal but with opposite signs), with the obvious interpretation that the difference in rates or the 'cost of liquidity' determines both holdings of gross liquid assets and the level of bank borrowing. As the interest rate spread declines, the cost of holding liquidity decreases and both the holding of liquid assets and the level of bank borrowing should increase. Thus, stockholding is in part dependent upon the relative cost of stockholding (which we describe later) and of holding liquidity. The interpretation of models which use liquidity levels directly is not so clear. Probably the most convincing interpretation is that liquidity is acting as a proxy variable. If stock and liquidity levels have a common subset of regressors which we cannot identify or cannot measure accurately, the actual level of liquidity may proxy the effect that these variables have on stocks. These regressors are most likely to be the costs and benefits of holding stocks and liquidity. While we use a cost-of-stockholding term (derived by Kelly and Owen (1985)), which includes both costs and benefits of stockholding, and a cost-of-liquidity term, it is possible that these terms do not accurately reflect true costs and benefits. An alternative interpretation is that the use of liquidity variables in expenditure equations is capturing 'rationing' effects. This appears to be the interpretation behind the widespread use of *net* liquidity effects, i.e. they indicate a borrowing constraint upon the firm, so that when the constraint is relaxed borrowing increases and companies' expenditure, including that on stocks, expands.

The second theme of this chapter investigates equations which result from explicit optimization with forward-looking behaviour for the stockbuilding decision. This takes as its point of departure a number of recent papers on company sector behaviour which have focused on intertemporal optimization under rational expectations. The seminal work of Sargent (1978) on the demand for labour has been followed by a number of studies which seek to treat the firms' expectations of future variables in an explicit way. This work includes that of Nickell (1984) and Henry and Wren-Lewis (1984) on the labour market and Hall *et al.* (1986) on the determination of stock levels. One common finding amongst these, and many other papers, is that there is a root which is close to unity in the dynamic process under consideration. This means that the long-run solution for the model is poorly determined, and this finding is a cause for some concern. This is related to the concept of co-integration already discussed and, in this context, this finding of a near-unit root takes on an even more serious aspect as a symptom of non-cointegration is the lack of a well-defined long-run solution.

Following the investigation of the co-integration properties of a range of stockbuilding models, we extend the models in two ways. Firstly, a co-integrating vector, once found, is introduced into an explicit forward-looking model. Second, theory suggests that the conditional variance of output is a major determinant of the stock level; the more uncertain the level of output the more stocks are held, and so there is a need to identify a co-integrating vector which includes this uncertainty term. Therefore in the second half of this chapter co-integrating vectors are estimated which include terms in the conditional variance of output using a generalization of the ARCH in mean (GARCH-M) process proposed by Engle *et al.* (1987). The co-integrating vector is then entered into the forward-looking model by developing a new parameterization of the model which isolates the levels solution in a single term while incorporating the restrictions of the rational expectations hypothesis (REH) in a set of forward first-difference terms. This new parameterization can easily be interpreted as a generalization of the standard error-correction model (ECM) to include a polynomial lead operator in the first-difference terms as well as the standard polynomial lag operator. We shall term this model a generalized error-correction model (GECM).

The chapter has the following plan. In section 2.2 we outline a simple model of stock behaviour and some estimation problems based on GARCH-M.

Section 2.3 is then devoted to co-integration and ECMs of the relationship between stockbuilding, liquidity and other financial variables. In section 2.4 the estimation results for the GARCH-M are presented, and in section 2.5 some conclusions are given.

2.2 STOCKBUILDING BEHAVIOUR AND EXPECTATIONS

2.2.1 Determining equilibrium stock levels

We see the firm as solving a highly complex non-linear intertemporal cost-minimization problem which involves direct production costs, costs associated with potential stock-outs, costs of stock holding and complex dynamic costs of adjustment. The full solution to such a problem is difficult and would yield a Euler equation for stocks which would be highly non-linear and particularly sensitive to the precise assumptions regarding the functional form of the chosen model. To avoid these complexities the optimization problem is separated into two parts: first we consider a static problem which gives rise to what might be regarded as the long-run solution for the firm; next dynamic elements are entered by using an optimal adjustment rule towards this equilibrium or desired value.

We therefore begin by postulating a simple, but fairly general, static nominal profit function of the firm which is to be maximized:

$$\max \Pi = PY^{S} - C(Y^{0}) - K(\sigma_{Y}^{2}, S, Y^{S}) - L(rB, \text{CS}.S) \qquad (2.1)$$

where P is the price of output, Y^{S} is sales, Y^{0} is production, $C(Y^{0})$ is a general function for the costs of production, including dividend payments, investment and tax as well as labour and material costs and S is the stock level. $K(\sigma_{Y}^{2}, S, Y^{S})$ represents the expected costs associated with a stock-out, which are an increasing function of the level Y^{S} and variance σ_{Y}^{2} of sales and a decreasing function of the level of stocks. $L\{rB, \text{CS}.S\}$ is the cost of holding stocks which is an increasing function of the cost of net borrowing rB (r is the net interest rate and B is net borrowing) and the direct cost of holding stocks CSS, where CS is the cost per unit of holding stocks. This structure is of course a highly stylized model of the firm. For simplicity, we have abstracted from the investment decision of the firm, and substitution effects between labour, capital and raw material inputs.

There are two identities which link the variables of the system. The first is the net borrowing identity which links the change in borrowing with the change in direct net revenue:

$$\Delta B_t = C(Y_t^{0}) - PY_t^{S} + rB_{t-1}$$

$$\Rightarrow B_t = B_{t-1}(1 + r) + C(Y_t^{0}) - P(Y_t^{S}) \qquad (2.2)$$

The second is the stockbuilding identity which defines stockbuilding as the difference between production and sales:

$$\Delta S_t = Y_t^0 - Y_t^S$$

$$\Rightarrow S_t = S_{t-1} + Y_t^0 - Y_t^S \qquad (2.3)$$

The consequence of these two identities is that, in this simple model, the firm has effectively only one choice variable when its sales are set exogenously by demand. In effect if the firm chooses the level of one of production, stocks or net borrowing, the other two are determined by identity. We are focusing here on stocks and so we shall carry out the maximization with respect to this variable, but this choice is arbitrary and unimportant.

Therefore rewrite Equation 2.3 as

$$Y_t^0 = S_t - S_{t-1} + Y_t^S \qquad (2.4)$$

Then 2.4 and 2.2 can be substituted into 2.1 to give the unconstrained profit-maximization problem

$$\begin{aligned} \max \Pi_t = {} & P_t Y_t^S - C(S_t - S_{t-1} + Y_t^S) - K(\sigma_Y^2, S_t, Y_t^S) \\ & - L[r_t\{B_{t-1}(1 + r_t) + C(S_t - S_{t-1} + Y_t^S) \\ & - P_t Y_t^S\}, \mathrm{CS}_t S_t] \end{aligned} \qquad (2.5)$$

Maximizing Π with respect to S_t yields the following first-order condition:

$$\begin{aligned} \frac{\partial C}{\partial S_t} = {} & -C'(S_t - S_{t-1} + Y_t^S) - K'(\sigma_Y^2, S_t, Y_t^S) \\ & - L_1 C'(S_t - S_{t-1} + Y_t^S) - L_2 \mathrm{CS}_t = 0 \end{aligned} \qquad (2.6)$$

In static equilibrium (where $S_t = S_{t-1}$) this would yield a general solution for S_t of the form

$$S_t = f(\underset{+}{Y_t^S}, \underset{+}{\sigma_{Yt}^2}, \underset{-}{B_{t-1}}, \underset{-}{r_t}, \underset{-}{\mathrm{CS}_t}) \qquad (2.7)$$

where the sign under each variable suggests the sign of its comparative static effect.

Note that when the firm is unconstrained in its net borrowing position we have a negative relationship between stocks and B, and between stocks and the rate of interest (r) on net borrowing. A number of recent studies (e.g. Melliss, 1986; Ireland and Wren-Lewis, 1988) have postulated a positive effect on the grounds that the firm is constrained in its net borrowing position. This proposition can also be illustrated in our simple model. If net borrowing B is constrained to be less than B^* where B^* is the solution to 2.2 when S^* is the solution to 2.7, then the constrained stock level equation can be derived from 2.2 and 2.4 as

$$S_t = S_{t-1} - Y_t^S + C^{-1}\{B_t^* - B_{t-1}(1 + r_t) + P_t Y_t^S\} \qquad (2.8)$$

where $C^{-1} > 0$ so that $\partial S_t/\partial B_t > 0$. That is, when the firm is constrained in its net borrowing an increase in borrowing is reflected in an increase in its ability to finance and hold stocks. In general, therefore, if the firm is unconstrained in its borrowing, then equilibrium is defined by 2.7, while if it is constrained it is defined by 2.8. In a statistical sense 2.8 is nested within 2.7, and so we shall base our estimation on 2.7 allowing the parameter estimates to constitute a test between the constrained and the unconstrained model.

It is convenient at this stage in the development of the model to mention two further problems: the derivation of equations for real stocks and the problem of sales as a determinant of stocks. On the first point, the model derived in Equations 2.1–2.7 is explicitly nominal as it is based on optimizing a constrained nominal profits function. However, it can be assumed that Equation 2.7, which defines the static equilibrium for nominal stock levels, is homogeneous of degree one in prices. The function can thus be redefined to express the equilibrium or target value for real stocks. What is excluded by this assumption is the proposition that the price level (or price inflation) may affect real stocks. It can be argued that the level of prices or changes in prices can affect stockholding owing to price misperceptions by firms and/or non-neutralities in the corporation tax system. For simplicity these possibilities are not explored here. One exception to this, however, arises with the cost of stockholding variable we use, which allows for differential tax treatment on stock appreciation (see section 2.4 and the data definitions).

The second point is an important empirical issue, which can conveniently be confronted in this section. It is that the theory developed so far distinguishes between sales and output. In the empirical section (section 2.4), stockbuilding equations are estimated which depend upon expected output (and its conditional variance). The reasons for using output are pragmatic. The studies alluded to in section 2.1 typically use output as the scale variable. Also, no data on manufacturing sales are available, and so a proxy for the variable has to be used. The practice we adopt is to proxy sales by output. One implication is that the use of output induces measurement error into the structural equation which is based on sales. We accept this state of affairs, essentially as there is no alternative which avoids introducing measurement errors of some kind in the stocks equation. Sales data might be recovered from the identity above ($\Delta S = Y^0 - Y^S$ where Y^0 is output and Y^S is sales) by 'stock adjusting' output. This is implied in the derivation of 'stock-adjusted' production series by the Central Statistics Office (CSO) (CSO, 1976, 'The measurement of industrial production'), but the published data on production and output refer to net output of the sector, which is meant to approximate value added, by subtracting factor inputs. It is clear that sales data cannot be reconstructed from net output, since information on sectoral inputs is not available. Nevertheless, some model builders use a sales proxy by stock adjusting net output (e.g. HM Treasury, 1982, p. 155), although this also clearly induces measurement error into their stocks equation. For this reason we have elected not to do this, and in all the empirical work reported here sales are replaced by an index of manufacturing production.

2.2.2 Costs of adjustment

Having determined the static equilibrium we turn now to the introduction of dynamics into the model. We define the appropriate solution to 2.7 or 2.8 to be the expected desired stock level S^*, and we postulate a dynamic cost-minimization problem which imposes costs in deviating from S^* and also costs of adjustment in terms of both the first and second derivative. Thus the cost function to be minimized is

$$\min E\left[\sum_{t=1}^{\infty} \{a(S_t - S_t^*)^2 + b(S_t - S_{t-1})^2 + c(\Delta S_t - \Delta S_{t-1})^2\} | \Omega_t\right] \tag{2.9}$$

That is, we minimize the expected value of the whole future stream of costs conditional on the current information set Ω_t.

The appropriate Euler condition for this problem can then be stated as

$$\begin{aligned} -aS_t^* + (a + 2b + 6c)S_t - (b + 4c)S_{t+1} + cS_{t+2} \\ -(b + 4c)S_{t-1} + cS_{t-2} = 0 \end{aligned} \tag{2.10}$$

or

$$B(L)S_t = aS_t^*$$

where

$$B(L) = cL^{-2} - (b + 4c)L^{-1} + (a + 2b + 6c) - (b + 4c)L + cL^2 \tag{2.11}$$

and a suitable transversality condition is

$$\lim_{T\to\infty} S_T = \bar{S}_T$$

A solution for 2.10 can be defined by factorizing

$$B(L) = \lambda_3(1 - \lambda_1 L - \lambda_2 L^2)(1 - \lambda_1 L^{-1} - \lambda_2 L^{-2})$$

where

$$\begin{aligned} c &= -\lambda_2\lambda_3 \\ b + 4c &= (\lambda_1 - \lambda_2\lambda_1)\lambda_3 \\ a + 2b + 6c &= (1 + \lambda_1^2 + \lambda_2^2)\lambda_3 \end{aligned} \tag{2.12}$$

Hence, we can write 2.10 as

$$S_t(1 - \lambda_1 L - \lambda_2 L^2) = \frac{(a/\lambda_3)S_t^*}{1 - \lambda_1 L^{-1} - \lambda_2 L^{-2}} \tag{2.13}$$

which on further rearrangement yields

$$S_t = \lambda_1 S_{t-1} + \lambda_2 S_{t-2} + (a/\lambda_3) \sum_{i=0}^{\infty} \gamma_i S_{t+i}^* \tag{2.14}$$

The γ_i are implied by a set of non-linear restrictions on λ_1 and λ_2, so that the model has essentially only two free parameters (λ_1 and λ_2) and the determinants of S^*. The restrictions on the γ_i can be obtained by applying the method of undetermined coefficients.

2.2.3 Introducing a measure of the variance of output

In our derivation of S^* one of the main determinants is the expected conditional variance of Y which is not directly observed. The conventional assumption is either that σ_y^2 is constant or that it varies solely with the level of output. In our view this assumption is far from satisfactory; σ_y^2 is unlikely to be constant and it undoubtedly changed during the recession in manufacturing output in the early 1980s which was largely unexpected. It is also unlikely to be positively related to output; indeed, the fall in output during the recession might well be expected to increase uncertainty rather than reduce it. Therefore a more sophisticated measure of uncertainty would seem to be necessary. Given the recent work by Pagan and Ullah (1988) on constructed measures of uncertainty we have decided to adopt the GARCH-M model to incorporate risk into the desired stockbuilding equation. This procedure is outlined below.

2.2.4 The GARCH-M procedure

Engle *et al.* (1987) suggest an extension of Engle's (1982) autoregressive conditional heteroscedasticity (ARCH) model to allow the conditional first moment of a time series to become a function of the conditional second moment which itself follows an ARCH process. Thus suppose that X_t is a vector of variables affecting S_t:

$$S_t = \alpha' X_t + \delta h_t + \varepsilon_t \tag{2.15}$$

where

$$h_t = E(\varepsilon_t^2 | \Omega_{t-1}) = \gamma_0 + \sum_{i=1}^{N} \gamma_i \varepsilon_{t-i}^2 + \phi \tag{2.16}$$

The likelihood function for this model is defined as

$$\log L = \sum_{t=1}^{T} \left(- \log h_t - \frac{\varepsilon_t^2}{h_t} \right) \tag{2.17}$$

and so the model comprising 2.15 and 2.16 can be estimated jointly by maximum likelihood procedures.

We make two further extensions to the model given by 2.15 and 2.16. The first follows Bollerslev (1986) in generalizing the ARCH process to include lagged terms in the conditional variance in the ARCH equation 2.16 which becomes

$$h_t = \sum_{i=1}^{P} \beta h_{t-i} + \sum_{i=1}^{N} \gamma_i \varepsilon_{t-i}^2 + \phi \tag{2.18}$$

and the model is then termed a generalized ARCH in mean process or GARCH-M. The second is to generalize the system to be a two-equation system by including an equation for output Y^0. This then allows us to enter the conditional variance of the output equation into the stocks equation as our uncertainty term. Therefore our model has the general form

$$S_t = \alpha_1' X_t + \delta h_{22t} + \varepsilon_t \tag{2.19}$$

$$Y_t^0 = \alpha_2' Z_t + V_t \tag{2.20}$$

where the conditional covariance matrix is H:

$$H_t = \begin{bmatrix} h_{11t} & h_{12t} \\ h_{12t} & h_{22t} \end{bmatrix}$$

$$= \beta(L) \begin{bmatrix} h_{11t} & h_{12t} \\ h_{12t} & h_{22t} \end{bmatrix} + \gamma(L) \begin{bmatrix} \varepsilon_t \varepsilon_t & \varepsilon_t V_t \\ \varepsilon_t V_t & V_t V_t \end{bmatrix} + \begin{bmatrix} \phi_{11} & \phi_{12} \\ \phi_{12} & \phi_{22} \end{bmatrix} \tag{2.21}$$

The likelihood function for this system (conditional on the initial conditions) is proportional to

$$\log L = \sum_{t=1}^{T} (-\log|H_t| - w_t' H_t^{-1} w_t) \tag{2.22}$$

where $w_t = (\varepsilon_t, V_t)$. Maximizing this function with respect to the parameters α_1, α_2, δ, $\beta(L)$, $\gamma(L)$ and ϕ then produces a simultaneous estimate of our complete model.

2.2.5 The restrictions of the rational expectations hypothesis

In the preceding discussion we considered the way that we might estimate an equation for S^* which includes a term in the conditional variance of output. The question remains as to how we can build this term into our dynamic model of stock behaviour (Equation 2.14). The association between the equation which determines S^* and a co-integrating relationship in the sense of Engle and Granger (1987) should be clear by this point. If we were following the Engle and Granger two-step estimation procedure we would use the residuals from the S^* equation in a dynamic model in first differences to estimate a standard ECM. If we had a well-determined equation for all the expected variables in our Equation 2.14 we could substitute out the expectations for the current information set, and then parameterize the model in the form of a standard ECM but also incorporating the full non-linear restrictions imposed by the REH assumption and the model. In fact we do not have a good idea of the expectation formation mechanism and so we are extremely reluctant to put the model into the 'decision rule' form, as this would mix the forward–backward restriction of 2.14 with the less plausible models of expectation formation and effectively lose these restrictions. Therefore we seek to find another parameterization of 2.14 which will not lose these restrictions but which also allows us to make explicit use of the co-integrating regression on S^*.

To do this we begin by restating 2.14:

$$S_t = \lambda_1 S_{t-1} + \lambda_2 S_{t-2} + (a/\lambda_3) \sum_{i=0}^{\infty} \gamma_i S^*_{t+i} \tag{2.23}$$

We then begin by reparameterizing this equation into

$$S_t = \lambda_1 S_{t-1} + \lambda_2 S_{t-2} + (a/\lambda_3) \sum_{i=1}^{\infty} d_i \Delta S^*_{t+i} + aeS^*_t \tag{2.24}$$

where $e = 1/(1 - \lambda_1 - \lambda_2)$ and $d_i = e - \gamma_0 - \ldots - \gamma_{i-1}$. Then by further reparameterizing we obtain

$$\Delta S_t = (\lambda_1 - 1 + \lambda_2 + ae)S_{t-1} - \lambda_2 \Delta S_{t-1} + (a/\lambda_3) \sum_{i=1}^{\infty} d_i \Delta S^*_{t+i}$$
$$+ (a/\lambda_3)e\Delta S^*_t + (a/\lambda_3)e(S^*_{t-1} - S_{t-1}) \tag{2.25}$$

The first term $(\lambda_1 - 1 + \lambda_2 + ae)S_{t-1} = 0$ as $a = (1 - \lambda_1 - \lambda_2)^2$ from 2.12 and $e = 1/(1 - \lambda_1 - \lambda_2)$; hence this term can be written as $-(1 - \lambda_1 - \lambda_2) + (1 - \lambda_1 - \lambda_2)$ and so we arrive at a parameterization which is similar to the standard ECM except that it has lead terms in the differences of the variables as well as lags:

$$\Delta S_t = -\lambda_2 \Delta S_{t-1} + a \sum_{i=1}^{N} d_i \Delta S^*_{t+i} + ae\, \Delta S^*_t + ae(S^*_{t-1} - S_{t-1}) \tag{2.26}$$

The final term is the error-correction term, and we can use the residuals from the co-integrating regression here in exactly the same way as in the Engle–Granger procedure. The future terms in ΔS^* can be constructed using the fitted values from the co-integrating regression, although as these will be subject to an REH error these variables are instrumented in estimation.

Our procedure is as follows: we first investigate co-integrating equations for the level of stocks, and then build the residual and forecast from this equation into our GECM (2.26) which incorporates the full set of non-linear REH restrictions.

2.3 A LONG-RUN INVESTIGATION

In this section we shall concentrate on the determinants of the desired long-run stock level S^* by focusing our investigation on a search for a satisfactory co-integrating vector. Given the poor performance of virtually all the formal models of inventory behaviour (e.g. Wallis *et al.*, 1987), it is not surprising that the very simple models involving only stocks and output fail co-integration tests decisively. Our earlier theory suggested a role for a range of financial effects, some measure of the cost of stockholding and the variance of output in addition to the level of output. Given the difficulties of estimating models involving variance terms which were outlined in the last section, we shall confine our attention here to investigating models which lack this term. In the next section we shall introduce the variance term and then go on to investigate the full dynamic model.

The empirical exercises undertaken here concentrate upon the manufacturing sector. Stocks of finished goods and work in progress are aggregated to give a model for the UK manufacturing sector as a whole.

Before considering evidence for co-integration the orders of integration of the variables used in later regressions are established. The Dickey–Fuller (DF) and augmented Dickey–Fuller (ADF) statistics for the levels and differences of candidate variables, are shown in Table 2.1. By and large these show that the variables are probably $I(1)$, and so can serve as potential candidates in a co-integration exercise.

We report in Tables 2.2 and 2.3 the results of using these variables to test for the existence of co-integrating vectors for stocks, liquidity and bank borrowing. There are two aspects of these results for stocks which should be emphasized. One is that the equation can be thought of as a levels equation between stocks and its long-run determinants in a single-equation framework. The first equation is an example of this. However, the remaining equations introduce another aspect, namely that the determinants of long-run stock behaviour depend upon the long-run determinants of liquidity. Table 2.2 gives the results for variables in natural units, and a parallel set of results for logarithmic versions are provided in Table 2.3.

The results for Table 2.2 are discussed first. The first result for stocks shows that it is not possible to obtain a co-integrating equation based only upon the scale variables Y and UNIU and the cost of stockholding. However, the second example shows that a reasonably satisfactory equation can be based on output in manufacturing Y, the cost of stockholding CS, liquidity L, retained earnings UNIU and bank advances CBOR. The ADF statistic marginally fails, although this appears to be due to problems induced by the extra differencing used in the ADF test. The DF appears to have a serially uncorrelated error, suggesting that the ADF may be inappropriately weighted against acceptance. However, the behavioural interpretation of this equation is, to say the least, unclear. One possible

Table 2.1 Dickey-Fuller and augmented Dickey-Fuller statistics (1970 Q1 to 1987 Q4)

		Level		*Difference*	
		DF	*ADF*	*DF*	*ADF*
Manufacturers' stock level	*S*	−1.7	−1.46	−5.6	−3.5
Cost of stockholding	CS	−1.99	−1.2	−8.4	−4.4
Banks' base rate	RCBR	−2.23	−2.16	−7.8	−4.7
Manufacturing output	*Y*	−2.06	−2.09	−8.9	−4.2
ICCs' undistributed profits	UNIU	−0.18	0.77	−12.8	−4.4
Liquidity	*L*	0.42	−0.6	−6.8	−3.6
ICCs' bank borrowing	CBOR	−0.35	−1.57	−6.16	−3.61
Three-month interbank rate	RINT	−2.14	−2.73	−6.99	−4.2
Gross domestic product	GDP	0.35	0.42	−8.0	−3.87
Inflation	INF	−1.39	−1.53	−4.68	−4.10

Table 2.2 Stocks and liquidity equations (1970 Q1 to 1987 Q4)

Constant	*Y*	*CS*	*GDP*	*L*	*UNIU*	*CBOR*	*RCBR*	*RINT*	*INF*	R^2	*DF*	*ADF*
Stocks S												
20444	−0.04	−1.2	—	—	0.31	—	—	—	—	0.54	−2.5	−2.4
21558	0.002	−0.8	—	−0.22	0.51	0.08	—	—	—	0.57	−3.9	−2.6
18891	0.01	−0.6	—	—	0.10	—	0.89	−0.70	2.2	0.73	−3.1	−3.0
18910	0.02	−0.6	—	—	0.08	—	0.98	−0.76	—	0.73	−3.3	−3.2
Liquidity L												
16635		0.59	—	—	1.97	—	−2.1	1.8	—	0.77	−3.6	−2.2
−62772		0.09	1.9	—	−0.79	—	−2.7	2.2	—	0.9	−3.9	−2.2
Lending RLEND												
−26565		1.8	1.27	—	—	—	−1.9	1.4	—	0.73	−3.1	−2.4
−36953		1.1	1.4	—	—	—	−3.4	3.1	1.5	0.70	−3.9	−1.9

Table 2.3 Stocks and liquidity equations in logarithms (1970 Q1 to 1987 Q4)

Constant	*LY*	*CS*	*LL*	*LUNIU*	*LCBOR*	*LGDP*	*RCBR*	*RINT*	*INF*	R^2	*DF*	*ADF*
*Log stocks LS**												
9.6	0.012	−0.003	—	0.02	—		0.04	−0.03		0.76	−3.2	−3.3
9.57	0.12	−0.062	−0.16	0.07	0.025		0.02	−0.018		0.84	−4.5	−5.0
Log liquidity LL												
−23.9		−0.002		−0.024		3.17	−0.118	0.10		0.88	−3.2	−2.2
Log lending RLEND												
−14.9		0.002				1.92	−0.08	0.07	3.7	0.69	−3.8	−1.9

[a]Variables prefixed L are in logarithms.

interpretation is that net liquidity LCBOR is the appropriate variable, with the interpretation that decreases in net liquidity (as bank borrowing increases) are usually associated with interest charges that are higher than usual as banks charge higher rates to overborrowed customers. However, according to this view, net liquidity should have a positive sign as it proxies (inversely) this borrowing cost. Evidently the sign implied by the second equation for stocks in Tables 2.2 and 2.3 is negative. Furthermore the sizes of the two components of net liquidity are not equal in absolute magnitude, reflecting the finding that net liquidity is not in fact $I(1)$. Consequently we have opted for the last two equations as being more acceptable in terms of their underlying behaviour. The fourth equation is perhaps preferable as its DF test statistics are both marginally better than those of the second equation. The third equation uses the inflation rate, thus implying, in an unrestricted way, that relative real interest rates influence stock levels.

The interest rate effects suggest that as borrowing rates rise stockbuilding increases, whereas as lending rates rise stockbuilding falls. In other words this is suggestive of a substitution effect; as the cost of acquiring liquidity, measured by the net internal rate RCBR − RINT rises, then liquidity will tend to fall and stocks rise. The liquidity equations also show parameter estimates consistent with the substitution effect. Hence, as the cost of stockholding rises, liquidity increases, but it falls when the net internal rate rises. Overall, however, the equations appear not to meet co-integration criteria, and the ADF is below the acceptable value. Unlike the case of the stocks equations, those for liquidity have a residual correlogram which has a slowly dampened AR(2) behaviour.

Finally, the lending equation shows a similar form of behaviour to the liquidity equations, although here the equations are somewhat more successful in meeting co-integration criteria than were the liquidity equations. (Their residual correlograms appear damped, for example, again indicating that the ADF statistics may be misleading.)

The logarithmic versions of the equations produce the same overall conclusion, not surprisingly, although the co-integration properties of the logarithm of stocks L*S* are somewhat better than those in Table 2.2. Since the overall findings are so similar to the earlier results they are not discussed any further.

At this stage of the analysis it must be conceded that none of the co-integrating vectors presented in Tables 2.2 and 2.3 is convincing. Even if we confine ourselves to considering stocks, which has by far the best results, the picture is far from persuasive. In Table 2.2 the ADF statistic barely reaches −3.2 even in the case where there are five variables in the regression. Perhaps more worryingly the output effect is apparently quite small and in one case is even perversely signed. In an equation which is not in logarithmic form it is often misleading to interpret the size of the coefficients, but this point is reinforced in Table 2.3 where, despite more

Table 2.4 Disaggregating the cost of stockholding effect

Constant	*Y*	UNIU	RCBR	RINT	PSDOT	ZONE	ZTWO	CORP	R^2	*DF*	*ADF*
17301.1	0.096	—	709.17	−564.8	−8752.4	378.1	1417.36	41.61	0.89	−4.3	−4.6
18031.4	0.030	0.05	599.22	−484.1	−7449.2	364.1	1465.49	42.93	0.90	−4.2	−4.3
18722	—	—	705.91	−562.2	−8734.8	268.0	1582.54	39.73	0.89	−4.3	−4.5
18891.9	0.087	—	658.72	−503.1	−7882.9	785.3	1407.41	—	0.89	−3.9	−4.4

acceptable ADF statistics, the output elasticity is still very low. In fact output could generally be removed from the regressions without greatly affecting the properties of the equation. This is one area of concern; another is the cost of stockholding variable which is a highly restricted combination of stock relief legislation, interest rates, the rate of change of the stock deflator PSDOT and the corporation tax rate CORP, and it is possible that the form of this restriction is inappropriate. We investigate this possibility in Table 2.4 by replacing CS with its component parts PSDOT and CORP and the dummy variables ZONE and ZTWO used to compute the two periods of stock relief legislation. This increases the size of the ADF statistics, although it must be borne in mind that the critical value also increases quite rapidly as the number of variables in the regression increases. However, both the effect of the stock deflator and the corporation tax rate take the opposite sign to their implicit effect as defined by the cost of stockholding definition. In the light of the earlier remarks it is also interesting to note that the output effect is completely unimportant, and that the third equation in Table 2.4 actually drops output altogether with little detrimental effect to the performance of the model.

If we are to accept this result, then output has no effect on the behaviour of stockbuilding at all. This is a surprising conclusion in view of earlier work which has found output or expected output to be one of the main determinants of inventory behaviour (e.g. Hall *et al.*, 1986). Figures 2.1 and 2.2 show the actual level of both stocks and output and the stock-to-output ratio respectively. It is clear from Fig. 2.2 that the behaviour of the stock-to-output ratio is quite erratic and that its behaviour seemed to change discretely in 1980. Figure 2.1 shows the separate movement of both stocks and output; up to 1981 or 1982 a positive correlation between the two is fairly evident, especially at the time of the 1980 fall in both stocks and output. This explains the earlier finding of a strong output effect. Since 1982, however, output has recovered, rising steadily from the end of 1982 onwards, but there has been no upward movement in stock levels. In effect the positive correlation has vanished and this is the result presented in the earlier statistical work. The simple theoretical exposition in section 2.2 assigned an important role to the uncertainty of output, however, and intuitively at least we might think that the period 1982–7 was one of falling uncertainty as output followed a more steady trend path. If this is correct, then we see that there is no reason to expect a rise in stock levels over this period.

In this section we have examined a broad range of variables which might be thought to determine stock levels. No combination of these variables is able both to satisfy our theoretical expectation of the signs of the effects and to pass co-integration tests convincingly. Perhaps more surprisingly, given past empirical results, no sizeable effects were found from manufacturing output, and the demand side of the model seems to have lost all

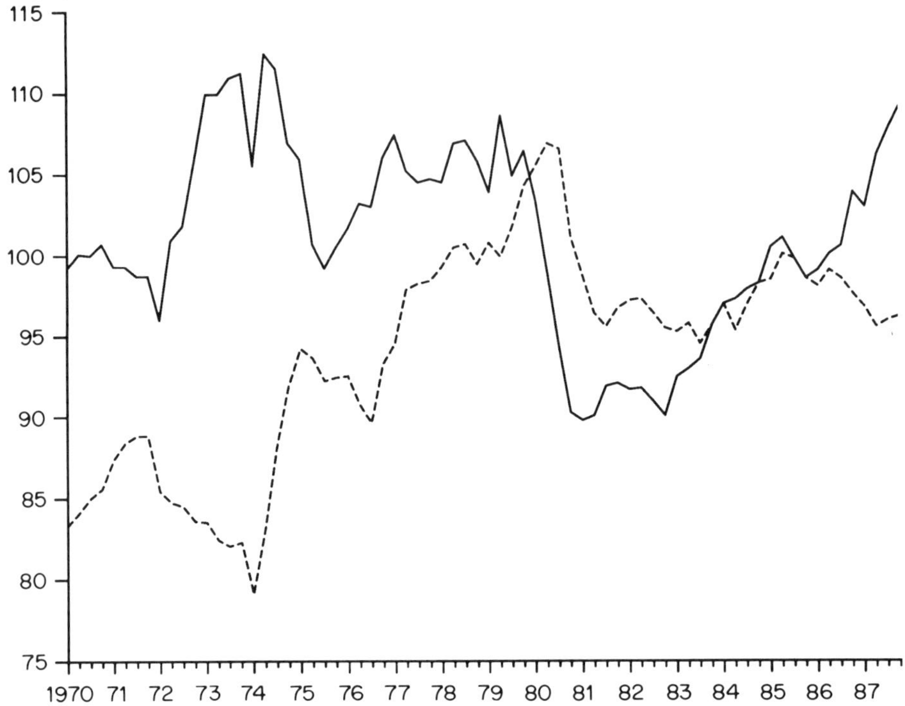

Fig. 2.1 The level of stocks (– – –) and output (——).

explanatory power. One explanation of both these findings would be that an important determinant of inventory behaviour is the variance of output, not the level, and as this has been omitted we cannot find a well-behaved co-integrating vector. We explore this possibility in the next section by using the GARCH-M formulation to introduce this risk term into the model.

2.4 EMPIRICAL RESULTS FOR THE GARCH MODEL

We proceed to implement the modelling strategy outlined in section 2.2, estimating an explicit dynamic model with time-varying variance terms. The first stage is to consider an equation for the long-run stock level based on 2.7 using the GARCH-M procedure.

Although the exposition of the GARCH model in 2.21 gives a very general model, in fact it is common practice to impose a number of simplifying assumptions on the structure of the GARCH process. We therefore assume that both $B(L)$ and $\gamma(L)$ are restricted to being first-order

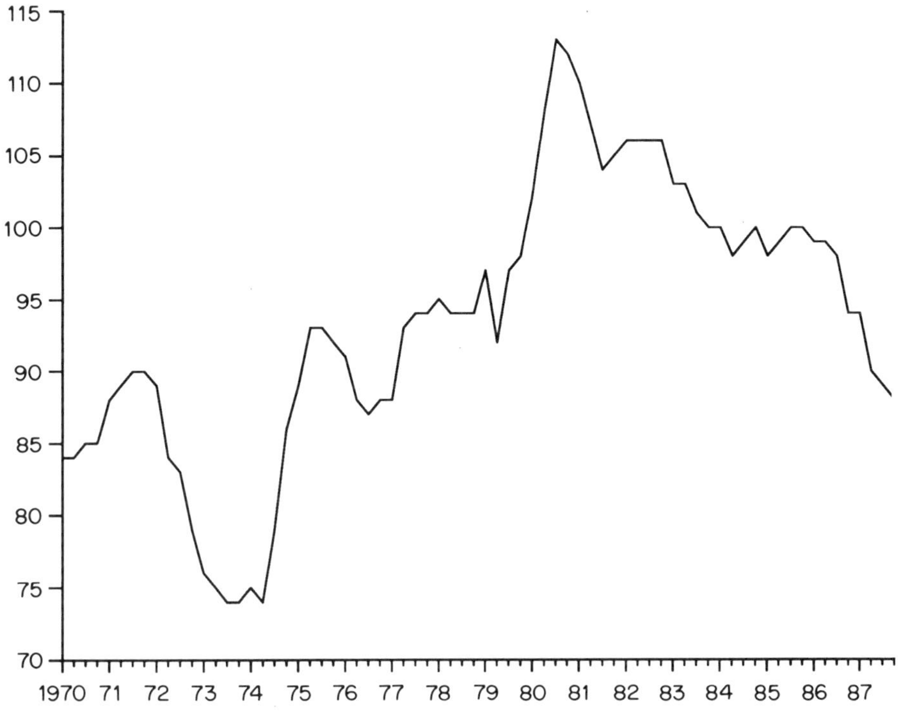

Fig. 2.2 Stock-to-output ratio.

polynomials and that they are scalars rather than matrices. The model for output is postulated to be a simple fourth-order autoregressive model, but we shall not present the estimated parameters of this equation as they have no direct interest from the point of view of this chapter.

The estimated model for our first version of the long-run stocks equation is given below (t statistics in parentheses):

$$S = \underset{(7.8)}{20374} - \underset{(0.3)}{0.08}Y + \underset{(5.6)}{0.007}\sigma_Y^2 - \underset{(6.7)}{0.22}L + \underset{(8.5)}{10.7}\text{RINT} - \underset{(8.8)}{64.2}\text{CS} + \underset{(6.9)}{0.5}\text{CBOR}$$

The GARCH parameters are as follows:[1]

[1]The GARCH equation must produce an estimate of the covariance matrix which is positive semi-definite; in a general formulation this is not necessarily the case. The restricted terms B and γ obey the restriction as long as they are positive, although the constants may not obey it. As a result we actually use the following parameterization as our constant matrix

$$\begin{bmatrix} \phi_{11} & \phi_{12} \\ \phi_{12} & \phi_{22} \end{bmatrix}' \begin{bmatrix} \phi_{11} & \phi_{12} \\ \phi_{12} & \phi_{22} \end{bmatrix}$$

β	0.8	(31.4)
γ	0.12	(5.7)
ϕ_{11}	147.9	(4.7)
ϕ_{12}	10.4	(0.5)
ϕ_{22}	122.9	(4.2)

The stock equation diagnostics are

$$\text{SE}= 718 \qquad \text{BJ}(2) = 3.6 \qquad \text{ADF} = -3.7$$

where BJ is the Berra–Jarque test for normality of the residuals. The correlogram is

$$0.65 \quad 0.52 \quad 0.44 \quad 0.29 \quad 0.18 \quad 0.20 \quad 0.19 \quad 0.08$$

Within the framework of co-integration analysis estimation is plagued by the problem of the non-standard form of the distributions of the parameter estimates. This model is, if anything, even more non-standard than the usual co-integrating regression in that it is based on a GARCH estimation procedure and involves a variance term. The use of the usual diagnostic statistics must therefore be treated with some caution.

The equation seems to perform well, however; all the coefficients are of an appropriate sign and magnitude, while the parameter on the variance term is significantly different from zero (bearing in mind the problems of inference when some of the variables are non-stationary), suggesting that the variance effect is important. The GARCH parameters suggest that time variation in the covariance matrix is important as β and γ are both significant with an estimated fairly long memory.

If we now use this first-stage regression in a dynamic GECM model as given in 2.26 we obtain the following estimates for the two parameters λ_1 and λ_2 (the non-linear two-stage least-squares estimation method is used):

$$\lambda_1 = \quad 1.22\ (9.01)$$

$$\lambda_2 = -0.38\ (3.2)$$

with SE = 262.1, DW = 2.3, BP(1) = 1.9, BP(4) = 3.5, BP(6) = 7.8 and BP(12) = 18.7 (where BP(N) is the Box–Pierce statistic with N degrees of freedom).

To give some idea of the validity of the REH restriction we estimated a version of the model which did not incorporate it. This had a poorly determined forward convolution and the standard error of the unrestricted model actual rose to 335.6. A quasi-likelihood ratio test of the restriction was $\chi^2(7) = 4.8$. Therefore the REH restriction would seem to be an absolute improvement.

The second version of the model is estimated using the logarithm of the variables, rather than the level; also it does not use the Treasury cost of stockholding variable but rather the components of the variable. The estimated model then takes the form

$$\ln S = \underset{(81.9)}{8.9} + \underset{(9.2)}{0.2}\ln Y + \underset{(0.5)}{1.98}\sigma_Y^2 + \underset{(2.0)}{0.05}(\text{RCBR} - \text{RINT})\ \underset{(9.5)}{0.06}\text{ZONE}$$

$$+ \underset{(7.25)}{0.05}\text{ZTWO}$$

The GARCH parameters are as follows:

β	0.39	(6.1)
γ	0.29	(1.4)
ϕ_{11}	−0.007	(1.5)
ϕ_{12}	−0.009	(2.0)
ϕ_{22}	0.012	(3.2)

The stock equation diagnostics are

$$\text{SE} = 0.02 \qquad \text{BJ}(2) = 0.18 \qquad \text{ADF} = -3.2$$

and the correlogram is

$$0.73 \quad 0.51 \quad 0.29 \quad 0.13 \quad -0.06 \quad -0.25 \quad -0.35 \quad -0.30$$

This equation again seems to perform fairly well. There may be slightly more doubt about the co-integration properties of the model and the variance term has a low t statistic, but otherwise this version is fairly satisfactory.

Again, we can use this model to estimate an unrestricted GECM model for stocks which yields the following results (the non-linear two-stage least-squares estimation method is used):

$$\lambda_1 \quad 1.11\ (7.6)$$

$$\lambda_2 \quad -0.30\ (2.2)$$

with SE = 0.01005, DW = 2.1, BP(1) = 0.3, BP(4) = 3.0, BP(6) = 3.6 and BP(12) = 5.0.

The standard error of the unrestricted model was 0.01005 which is slightly lower than that of the restricted model, but clearly the reduction in fit due to the restrictions is very small. A quasi-likelihood ratio test of the restrictions was $\chi^2(7) = 7.05$ which again easily accepts the restriction.

Both models perform well, although the lack of significance of the variance term in the second model may suggest that the logarithmic specification is incorrect for the output equation at least (it removes the upward trend in the variance). A striking feature of both models is the relatively small size of the root of the dynamic process; in the first model it

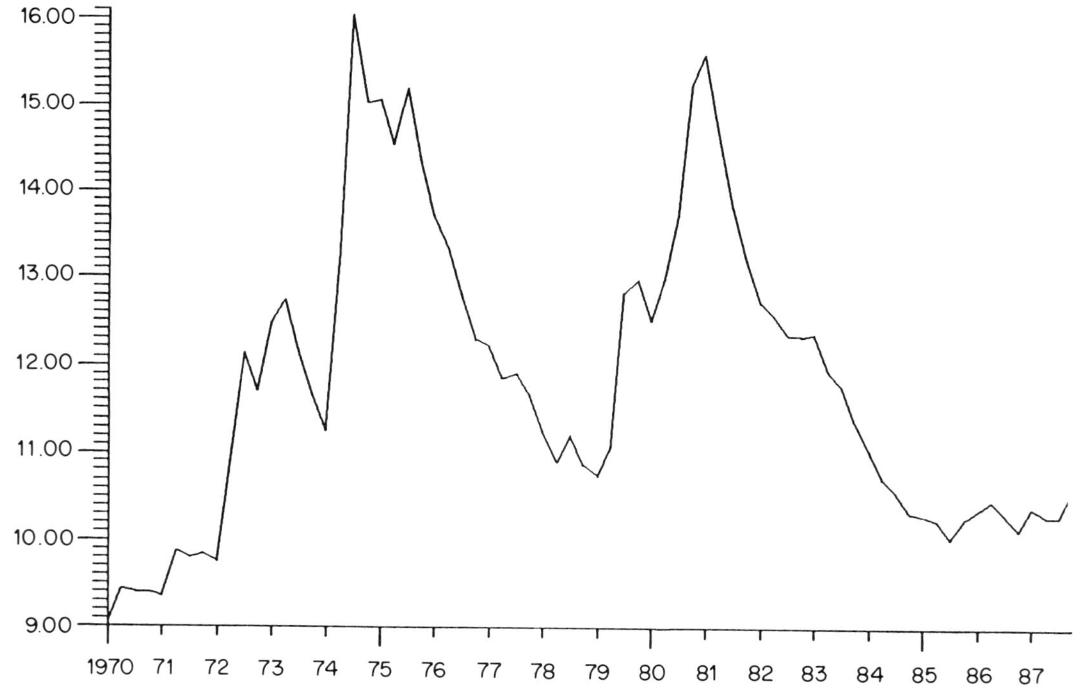

Fig. 2.3 The conditional standard error of output.

is 0.84 while in the second model it is 0.81, both much lower than the usual finding. Finally in Fig. 2.3 we present an estimate of the conditional standard error of output produced by the first model. It is obvious that both the post-oil crisis recession and the post-1979 recession are periods of unusually high uncertainty about the level of output.

2.5 CONCLUSIONS

A theoretical model of inventory behaviour which suggests a range of important financial and cost variables as well as an effect from the variance of output has been outlined in this chapter. The co-integration properties of variables excluding the variance of output were explored in section 2.3 but the equations have inadequate theoretical and statistical properties. Output variance effects were introduced into the model in section 2.4 using the GARCH-M procedures outlined in section 2.2. The results of this are encouraging; the variance of output seems to be an important determinant of the inventory decision and we find plausible effects from cost and financial variables. Finally dynamic models are estimated which incorporated the full set of backward–forward restrictions implied by the optimization model under the REH. We find that these models perform satisfactorily in general, and that the REH restrictions are accepted by the data.

DATA DEFINITIONS

RINT	3 month interbank rate (*Financial Statistics*, Table 13.15)
CS	cost of stockholding (Kelly and Owen, 1985)
S	stock level: manufacturer's work in progress and finished goods 1980 prices (*Economic Trends*, Table 13)
Y	real manufacturing production (*Economic Trends*, Table 16)
RCBR	clearing banks' base rate (*Economic Trends*, Table 39)
CBOR	real bank borrowing by industrial and commercial companies (*Financial Statistics*, Table 8.4, deflated by the GDP deflator)
UNIU	undistributed income of industrial and commercial companies adjusted for net unremitted profits
L	real liquidity (calculated from *Financial Statistics*, Table 8.4, deflated by the GDP deflator)
GDP	real gross domestic product (whole economy average measure)
INF	inflation (annual growth in GDP deflator)
PSDOT	rate of change of the stocks deflator

REFERENCES

Bollerslev, T. (1986) Generalised autoregressive conditional heteroscedasticity. *Journal of Econometrics,* **31**, 307–27.

CSO (Central Statistics Office) (1976) *The Measurement of Changes in Production, Studies in Official Statistics No. 25,* HMSO, London.

Engle, R. F. (1982) Autoregressive conditional heteroscedasticity with estimates of the variance of United Kingdom inflation. *Econometrica,* **50**(4), 987–1007.

Engle, R. F. and Granger, C. W. J. (1987) Co-integration and Error Correction: Representations, Estimations and Testing. *Econometrics,* **55**(2), 251–276.

Engle, R. F., Lilien, D. M. and Robbins, R. P. (1987) Estimating time varying risk premium in the term structure: the ARCH-M model. *Econometrica,* **55**(2), 391–407.

Hall, S. G., Henry, S. G. B. and Wren-Lewis, S. (1986) Manufacturing stocks and forward looking expectations in the UK. *Economica,* **53**, 447–66.

Henry, S. G. B. and Wren-Lewis, S. (1984) The aggregate labour market in the UK: some experiments with rational expectations models, in *Contemporary Macroeconomic Modelling* (eds P. Malgrange and P. Muet), Blackwell, Oxford.

HM Treasury (1982) Listing of macroeconomic model, in *HMSO Macroeconomic Manual,* HMSO, London.

Ireland, J. and Wren-Lewis, S. (1988) Buffer stock money and the company sector, NIESR Discussion Paper.

Kelly, C. and Owen, D. (1985) Factor prices in the Treasury model, GES Working Paper No. 83.

Mellis, C. (1986) HM Treasury Macroeconomic Model 1986, HMT GES Working Paper No. 90.

Nickell, S. (1984) An investigation of the determinants of manufacturing employment in the United Kingdom. *Review of Economic Studies,* **51**, 529–57.

Pagan, A. and Ullah, A. (1988) The econometric analysis of models with risk terms, Centre for Decision Science and Econometrics, Ontario, Technical Report No. 16.

Sargent, T. J. (1978) Estimation of dynamic labour demand schedules under rational expectations. *Journal of Political Economy,* **88**, 1009–44.

Wallis, K. F., Fisher, P. G., Longbottom, J. A., Turner, D. S. and Whitley, J. D. (1987) *Models of the UK Economy: A Fourth Review by the ESRC Macroeconomic Modelling Bureau,* Oxford University Press, Oxford.

3

Interest elasticity of consumers' expenditure

M. J. DICKS

3.1 INTRODUCTION

In this chapter some new evidence is presented on the subject of the interest elasticity of consumers' expenditure based on UK data. We find that, although the issue is by no means settled, the weight of evidence does seem to favour what Boskin (1987) calls a 'modest positive interest elasticity of private saving'. Moreover, interest rate effects appear to have increased (in both size and significance) during the 1980s, a period in which competition in UK financial markets has increased as a result of the Government's policy of deregulation. This liberalization has led to a weakening of the liquidity constraints which previously restricted households' choice and, although this will have had the effect of permitting consumers to move closer to their desired (life-cycle) levels of expenditure (since they may now find it easier to borrow through periods when income is temporarily low, thus maintaining a smoother consumption profile over time), at the same time the proportion of households that are likely to react to changes in interest rates will have risen. Our findings suggest that the latter effects may dominate, at least in the short run, implying that the leverage of monetary policy may have been strengthened as a result of deregulation of the financial markets.

The chapter is organized as follows. Section 3.2 serves to motivate our work and introduce the subject by illustrating the results of previous research carried out in both the UK and the USA. Next, in section 3.3, we show how the previous Bank model of consumers' expenditure on durables (as described by Patterson *et al.* (1987)) can be improved. Although the resulting specification arguably outperforms consumption equations of the same vintage used in the other main macromodels, it does still have problems regarding the stability of its parameters—particularly those pertaining to the interest rate and other financial variables. This is illustrated by estimating the model using recursive least squares. In section 3.4 we consider how the previous Bank model of consumers' expenditure on non-durables (again as reported by Patterson *et al.* (1987)) might be improved. Interestingly, the resulting specification also suggests that interest rate effects have become more important during the 1980s. Finally, in section 3.5, we present our conclusions.

3.2 PREVIOUS RESEARCH IN THE USA AND THE UK

Throughout much of the early 1970s the view in both the USA and the UK was that the effects of interest rate changes on consumption were likely to be small owing to offsetting income and substitution effects (e.g. Ferber's (1973) survey of the consumption literature). By the late 1970s, however, some research was beginning to hint at strong interest rate effects. Thus, Boskin (1978) reports an elasticity of −0.4. More recently the case for consumption's being interest elastic has been taken up forcefully by Summers (1982, 1984). Although he admits that, at first glance, such a view appears to fly in the face of many previous empirical studies, he claims that there are good reasons for his view. Apart from the standard problems of errors in variables[1] and mis-specification[2] most empirical work holds wealth constant when attempting to measure the effect of changes in interest rates on savings. Thus, for example, the fact that Boskin finds a wealth elasticity close to 3 for savings means that, if the interest elasticity of wealth is 0.5 then the total interest elasticity of savings is close to 2, which is within the range suggested by Summers. One problem with estimating these interest rate effects, however, is deciding how expectations should be treated. Thus Summers (1982), for example, finds that a simple life-cycle model which fails to distinguish between transitory and permanent effects implies a short-run interest elasticity of just 10%.

Blinder and Deaton (1985) attempt to avoid the problem of unobserved expectations by generating one-period-ahead forecasts from vector autoregressions for income, prices etc. They find a strong (but fragile, in the sense of depending upon the precise specification of the model) effect from nominal interest rates (a semi-elasticity of −2.3) in a 'surprise' consumption function,[3] but a much weaker effect in their 'no-surprise' model (a semi-elasticity of −0.8). Interestingly, they also find that interest rate effects

[1]For example, the 'correct' interest rate term should include real expected after-tax returns on equities, housing, durable goods and financial saving.

[2]For example, age and population variables are rarely included in empirical studies.

[3]That is, a model in which only 'surprises' in permanent income affect current consumption, once lagged consumption is controlled for.

cannot be detected using a sample period which excludes the 1980s. This, they suggest, is due to the relatively small variance in interest rates during the 1960s and early 1970s. They also report that it is nominal and not real interest rates which matter, a result they find hard to explain, although Hubbard (Blinder and Deaton, 1985) suggests that it may simply be due to the fact that durable goods are excluded from the model. Sims (Blinder and Deaton, 1985) suggests that the problem lies rather with the way inflation is predicted, which may lead to overly variable inflation forecasts. Blinder and Deaton's (1985) findings are, however, consistent with recent research carried out for the UK by Attfield *et al.* (1988) who found that 'preliminary investigations . . . suggested that the real rate performed unsatisfactorily'.

Muellbauer and Bover (1986) have recently extended previous research by Bean (1986) by considering not only the possibility that some households are liquidity constrained but also the implications of aggregation over both retired and non-retired households and over time. The importance of their work is that they find that aggregation may induce a negative correlation between interest rates and the constant in a consumption equation. This not only suggests that the evidence in favour of a 'big' interest rate elasticity needs to be treated with caution, but also provides some justification for the type of consumption function which has proved popular amongst UK econometricians. These are the error-correction models first popularized by Sargan (1964) and used, with considerable success, by Davidson *et al.* (1978) to model consumers' expenditure on non-durables. Although these models have been extended to permit a role for wealth (e.g. Hendry and von Ungern-Sternberg, 1981; Patterson 1984a) they rarely permit the identification of any explicit (substitution) effect from interest rates. Recent research by Harnett (1988) shows that, on those few occasions where significant effects have been claimed in this type of consumption function (e.g. Davis 1982), these results are very sensitive to both the chronology of the data (i.e. whether 1980-based or 1975-based data are used) and to the sample period used. Moreover, they have generally been applied only to non-durables expenditure and thus ignore what is likely to be the far more interest-sensitive element. Both Cuthbertson (1980) and Davis (1984) have discovered significant interest rate effects on durables expenditure using UK data, as have Mankiw (1982, 1985), Bernanke (1984) and Bar-Ilan and Blinder (1988) for the USA. It would appear that the conclusion that must be drawn from existing research is that the interest elasticity of consumers' expenditure is negative, although perhaps of moderate size. However, one important caveat needs to be made to these conclusions concerning institutional factors. Bernheim and Shoven (1985) have pointed out that in the USA there is virtually an automatic negative interest elasticity in the personal saving rate because defined benefit pension plans (e.g. pension funds based on final salary) will be able to meet their required rate of return with lower contributions when real interest rates rise. (Obviously the size of this effect will depend upon the extent to which the funds hold variable-rate deposits.) Thus, as Boskin (1987) mentions, in 1984 there was a decrease of almost $30 billion in contributions to private defined benefit pension plans in the USA following the rise in interest rates. Since it is by no means clear that similar effects would hold in this country, the remainder of this chapter is concerned with re-examining the response of consumers' expenditure in the UK (both on durables and non-durables) to changes in interest rates.

3.3 MODELLING CONSUMERS' EXPENDITURE ON DURABLE GOODS

The role of interest rates in the main UK macroeconomic models has been surveyed by Easton (1985). Most of the models then included direct interest rate effects in their equations for consumers' expenditure on durable goods, but there was much less consensus as to whether or not there should be a similar term in the non-durables equations. In part these differences may have reflected alternative views of how the economy works, although they may also have been due to the fact that all the models are subject to periodic review so that any analysis is just a snapshot of one particular version of them. Several strands of analysis have been examined in recent research carried out in the Bank, each of which is pertinent to the question of how strong a role interest rates might have in determining consumers' expenditure. In the first Patterson (1988b) examines a generalization of the Hendry and von Ungern-Sternberg (1981) framework, by allowing for the possibility that disaggregated (by asset) wealth-to-income ratios are a function of rates of return (instead of assuming that they are constant in the long run). The second recognizes that changes in interest rates affect consumers who are liquidity constrained and that these effects may well vary over times as, for example, competition in the mortgage and savings markets changes. In the remainder of this section and the next we consider the developments which have so far been made to the Bank's short-term model as a result of this research programme.

3.3.1 The previous Bank model of consumers' expenditure on durable goods

We begin by considering the model as reported by Patterson *et al.* (1987) (which we refer to as the previous Bank model). This was last re-estimated more than 3 years ago (Davis, 1984; Edwards, 1984). Real consumers' expenditure on durable goods (CD) is measured relative to its average value over the previous four quarters (for brevity, we refer to this as a 'dagger' function). CD is modelled as a function of real household disposable income adjusted for inflation losses on net liquid asset holdings YDLH, the flow of mortgage lending ML deflated by the price of consumer durables PCD, real interest rates RR measured as the logarithum of one plus the clearing banks' base rate minus the annual inflation rate of consumer prices, real net liquid assets RNLAJ measured relative to income and the effective minimum deposit rate on durables RMD. Both the income and net liquid asset terms are measured using moving-average or 'dagger' functions. Hence the durable consumption function is given by

$$
\begin{aligned}
\ln \text{CD} = \quad & \ln \text{CDD} \\
& + \beta_1 A(L)(\ln \text{YDLH} - \ln \text{YDLD}) \\
& + \beta_2(\ln \text{CDD} - \ln \text{YDLD}) \\
& + \beta_3\ \Delta(\ln \text{RNLAJD} - \ln \text{YDLD}) \\
& + \beta_4 B(L) \ln (\text{ML}/\text{PCD}) \\
& + \beta_5 B(L)\text{RR} \\
& + \beta_6\ \Delta\text{RMD} \\
& + \beta_7 + \text{dummy variables}
\end{aligned}
$$

where

$$\ln \text{CDD} = 0.25 \sum_{i=1}^{4} \ln \text{CD}_{-i}$$

$$\ln \text{YDLD} = 0.25 \sum_{i=1}^{4} \ln \text{YDLH}_{-i}$$

$$\ln \text{RNLAJD} = 0.25 \sum_{i=1}^{4} \ln \text{RNLAJ}_{-i}$$

$$A(L) = \sum_{i=0}^{2} (3 - i)L^i$$

$$B(L) = \sum_{i=0}^{2} L^i$$

and L^i is the lag operator (i periods).

A number of problems exist with the model. First, if it is viewed in the Hendry and von Ungern-Sternberg (1981) framework, then we might expect to see the level rather than the change in the ratio of real net liqiud assets to income as an explanatory variable (i.e. there should be an integral control term).[4] Previous research has certainly found such a role for wealth in

[4]Davis (1984) originally included the level term. However, when the model was re-based (later the same year), it was found that only the change in the ratio turned out to be significant.

non-durable consumption functions. Patterson (1984a), for example, suggests that both liquid and illiquid assets have a role to play as integral control mechanisms[5] (although it should be emphasized that he finds that it is necessary to adjust income for depreciation of the stock of durables in order to identify these effects). This implies that any failure to meet desired long-run consumption-to-income ratios will have an impact on some part of the household sector's balance sheet. If it is also true that households try to maintain a consistent ratio of durables expenditure to income in the long-run, then clearly the same result must hold in durable consumption functions (i.e. failure to meet desired expenditure can only lead to households either building up or running down other assets).

A related problem is that, since durables are long lived, households may choose to vary expenditure without much affecting their consumption of durable services (which can be met largely from their existing stock of durables). This suggests that it might be better to model the stock of consumer durables (rather than the flow) as the Treasury has recently chosen to do (Allum, 1986). Nevertheless, it should be pointed out that even though such an approach might entail moving away from a flow-based equation, past research suggests that the data do not firmly reject this sort of model. (Indeed, the logarithms of consumers' expenditure of durables and households' inflation-adjusted incomes are co-integrated, which suggests that, even though durables consumption and expenditure are unlikely to coincide, assuming that they do not so may not be very harmful.) A second is that the work carried out by the Treasury has resulted in an equation which explains changes in durable stocks using a lagged stock term as one of the explanatory variables, i.e. they run the regression

$$\Delta S_t = aS_{t-1} + bZ_t \tag{3.1}$$

where S_t is the stock of durables at the time t and Z_t is a vector of additional explanatory variables. However, since stocks and flows are linked by the identity

$$S_t = (1 - d)S_{t-1} + E_t \tag{3.2}$$

where E_t is expenditure on durables and d is the fixed depreciation rate, 3.1 can be rearranged to give

$$E_t = (a + d)S_{t-1} + bZ_t \tag{3.3}$$

Clearly, 3.3 implies that we can re-estimate the Treasury model using the *flow* of durables expenditure as the dependent variable, provided that we keep a lagged value of the stock of durables on the right-hand side and are willing to accept that the rate of depreciation is constant over time (probably a reasonable assumption as a first approximation). Such an

[5]Of course, we could appeal to liquidity constraints as another reason for including net liquid assets (e.g. Cuthbertson, 1980).

approach can therefore be used to gauge the advantages of using a stock-based model.[6]

The term in mortgage lending in the previous model specification is intended to capture the effects of credit rationing in the mortgage market, complementarity between expenditure on durables and housing (often households choose to buy furniture at the same time as they buy a house, for example) and perhaps also net cash or equity withdrawal. During the 1980s deregulation and financial innovation has led to large changes in the financial behaviour of the personal sector (Dicks, 1987), with the result that building societies now typically attempt to meet the demand for mortgage funds, taking the structure of interest rates as given, rather than try to protect existing borrowers from rises in the mortgage rate. This weakening of the liquidity constraints which previously restricted households' choice has led to a rise in both sides of the personal sector balance sheet. As regards liabilities, the growth of mortgage lending has been boosted in recent years by increased net cash withdrawal (defined as the amount by which the net increase in the stock of loans for house purchase exceeds the private sector's net expenditure on the sources of supply of housing). This excess lending must, directly or indirectly, have been used for purposes other than housing investment, such as consumption or increasing holdings of financial assets. Since, during the 1980s, it has occurred on such a large scale (being broadly equal to 3.5% of total consumers' expenditure over the period 1982–4 according to Bank estimates (Drayson, 1985; see also Appendix A3.1), it is possible that part of the explanation behind the large coefficient on mortgage lending in the durables equation is increased cash withdrawal. It is important to note, however, that most net cash withdrawn is likely to have been used for purposes other than consumption. Holmans (1986) has considered in detail the gross flows of funds which lie behind the (net) estimates made by the Bank, and has concluded that equity withdrawal[7] comprises mainly payments to last-time sellers and that money borrowed by moving owner-occupiers in excess of that needed to purchase their new homes was around one-third of the net cash-withdrawal figures during the early 1980s (i.e. only £2 billion per annum or thereabouts).[8] Nevertheless, it is likely that some cash extraction has occurred through owner-occupiers trading down or 'topping up' their mortgages. Moreover, the removal of mortgage lending guidance at the beginning of 1987 may also have stimulated this type of borrowing.

[6]In fact, when we did try including a lagged stock term in our preferred specification we found that it was insignificant. This could, of course, simply imply that the assumption that d is constant is incorrect.

[7]A slightly different concept from that used by the Bank, as it is defined as the sum of expenditure on house purchase by first-time buyers plus lending to moving owner-occupiers net of loans redeemed on the houses sold plus new money put in by moving owner-occupiers less purchase of new houses.

[8]Moreover, a fraction of this could have been used for home improvements.

3.3.2 Attempts to replicate the previous Bank equation

Table 3.1, model A, shows the previous Bank model, as reported by Patterson *et al.* (1987), together with a version of the same equation that has been estimated using current data (model B). Model B is based on an identical sample period to that used by Edwards (1984) and has broadly similar coefficients.[9] An *F* test to see whether the previous equation's coefficients can still be accepted by the new data takes a value of 1.0, compared with 95% critical value of close to 1.9. A comparison of the coefficients for the two models suggests that the main problem still concerns the effects of changes in liquid assets on durables expenditure. However, as Table 3.2 shows, the model forecasts fairly well. Indeed, when we compare it with the other main macromodels (see the parameter stability tests in Table 3.4 below) it turns out that the Bank's model forecasts as well as does the National Institute's model although less well than that used by the London Business School.

A problem arises in comparing the forecast errors for the years 1984 and 1985 with the average residuals over the sample period, since model A may provide a poor description of past data.[10] Hence, we have calculated the root mean square percentage errors (RMS%Es) for both the Bank model

Table 3.1 The Bank model (dependent variable ln CD)

	Coefficient (t value)	
Explanatory variables	*A*	*B*
ln CDD	1[a]	1[a]
ln (CDD/YDLD)	−0.674 (5.1)	−0.709 (5.4)
A(*L*) ln (YDLH/YDLD)	0.240 (4.4)	0.252 (4.4)
B(*L*) ln (ML/PCD)	0.077 (5.1)	0.079 (4.6)
B(*L*) ln RR	−0.166 (2.3)	−0.182 (2.4)
Δ ln (RNLAJD/YDLD)	1.019 (1.1)	0.997 (1.0)
Δ ln RMD	−0.176 (3.4)	−0.164 (3.0)
*D*681	0.166 (3.3)	0.158 (3.0)
*D*731	0.109 (2.2)	0.110 (2.1)
*D*792	0.228 (4.6)	0.280 (5.5)
Constant	−3.329 (4.8)	−3.459 (5.1)
R^2	0.738	0.734
SEE	0.047	0.049
DW	1.6	1.7
Sample period	1966 Q3 to 1981 Q4	1966 Q3 to 1981 Q4

Definitions of terms used are given at the end of the chapter.
[a]Constrained.

[9]Note also that it still contains one term (the change in the ratio of net liquid asset income) which is insignificant.
[10]Implying that the forecast tests would be very easy to pass.

Table 3.2 Diagnostic statistics of Bank model

Test statistics	*Comparison values*	*Model B*
Normality of errors		
Shapiro–Wilk W statistic	Reject if below 0.9546	0.95
Skewness	Reject if outside (±0.62)	−0.99
Kurtosis	Reject if outside (1.76, 4.24)	5.41
Autocorrelation		
Residual correlogram	Correlation	
	lag 1	0.13
	lag 2	−0.19
	lag 3	−0.12
	lag 4	−0.21
Ljung–Box(4)	$\chi^2(4) = 9.49$ at 95% level	7.34
LM test for autocorrelation	$\chi^2(4) = 9.49$ at 95% level	8.35
Modified LM test	$F(4, 48) = 2.57$ at 95% level	1.87
Heteroscedasticity		
Peak test	Cumulative probability that the linear model is wrong	0.85
Parmeter stability[a]		
Static forecast test (1984 Q1 to 1985 Q4)	$\chi^2(8) = 15.5$ at 95% level	5.4
Dynamic forecast test (1984 Q1 to 1985 Q4)	$\chi^2(8) = 15.5$ at 95% level	6.5

[a]For an equation estimated up to the end of 1983.

(model A) and for a similar model which has been estimated using data up to the end of 1983 (model C). Model A overpredicts the growth of consumption in seven out of eight quarters studied (both static and dynamic forecasts), but its dynamic forecast is little worse than its static forecast (with RMS%Es of 0.49 and 0.48 respectively). Model C, however, performs slightly better, with RMS%Es around one-fifth smaller on the dynamic test (at 0.40) and one-tenth better on the static test (at 0.44), implying that even if we cannot improve on the functional form of the existing model it would at least be worthwhile re-estimating the coefficients using more recent data.[11] Since the same problems evident with this previous specification of the Bank's equation are still apparent in specifications based on more up-to-date data, however (see Tables 3.3 and 3.4), then such a fallback should only be resorted to if new models forecast very inaccurately.

Table 3.2 shows that the Bank's equation suffers from a number of problems. First, the tests for normality of the residuals are not accepted—even the Shapiro–Wilk statistic is very close to the 95% significance level.

[11]An added advantage of model C is that its tendency to overpredict its weaker.

Second, tests for autocorrelation are only just passed at 95% significance levels. These tests turn out to be particularly sensitive to the sample periods used. For example, using the same coefficients as in model A but with the sample ending in mid-1984, the relevant LM test takes a value of 9.2 compared with the 95% critical value of 9.5. Fourth-order autocorrelation seems to be the main problem (see also Table 3.4).

These results suggest that there is a need to reconsider the dynamic structure of the Bank equation, despite the encouraging results from the forecast tests. A second problem that we need to keep in mind is the role of mortgage lending in the equation. The long-run solution to the previous model (i.e. the steady state durable consumption function) is given by the expression

$$\ln \mathrm{CD} = \ln \mathrm{YDLH} - 4.93 + 0.342 \ln (\mathrm{ML}/\mathrm{PCD}) - 0.737 \ln \mathrm{RR} + 0.113 g_{\mathrm{y}} - 0.782 g_{\mathrm{m}}$$

where g_{y} and g_{m} are the rates of growth of real household income and real mortgage lending respectively. An elasticity of close to 0.3 for the flow of mortgage lending is too high to be explained by complementarity of housing and durables spending, and so tends to be attributed to net cash or equity withdrawal (as already noted above). It would certainly be valuable to distinguish between the two effects if that were possible, especially given that we know that it has become easier to extract equity from the housing market recently. We also need to examine the income elasticity, which is constrained to equal unity (through the use of the error-correction term). Again it is important to see how high the income elasticity is when freely estimated; theory suggests that it ought to be somewhat higher for durable than for non-durable goods. A third problem (probably connected with that of autocorrelation mentioned above) is the use of the moving-average 'dagger' functions. These may have altered the dynamic properties of the model and are clearly worth examining more closely. Before attempting to examine these problems further, however, we first compare the previous Bank model with those used in the other main macromodels.

3.3.3 Other models of durables consumption

For ease of comparison we have re-estimated the model used by the Bank, the National Institute for Economic and Social Research (NIESR), the London Business School (LBS) and the Treasury (HMT) on a common data set.[12] These are shown in Table 3.3 (designated 'ours'), together with the coefficients reported in the various model manuals (designated 'model'). All the models use much the same explanatory variables, the most important of

[12]In practice, since this work was carried out new models will no doubt have been adopted for use in the other main macromodels. Nevertheless, this section serves to illustrate the techniques used in Bank research.

Table 3.3 Comparison of Bank model with other models (dependent variable ln CD)

	Model		Ours		Adjusted ours	
	Coefficient	*(t value)*	*Coefficient*	*(t value)*	*Coefficient*	*(t value)*
Bank						
ln CDD	1	(—)	1	(—)		
ln (CDD/YDLD)	−0.674	(5.1)	−0.635	(5.3)		
$B(L)$ ln (ML/PCD)	0.077	(5.1)	0.064	(5.1)		
$B(L)$ ln RR	−0.166	(2.3)	−0.220	(3.5)		
$A(L)$ ln (YDLH/YDLD)	0.240	(4.4)	0.261	(4.9)		
Δ ln (RNLAJD/YDLD)	1.019	(1.1)	1.373	(1.5)		
Δ ln RMD	−0.176	(3.4)	−0.146	(2.7)		
*D*681	0.166	(3.3)				
*D*731	0.109	(2.2)	0.127	(2.5)		
*D*791	0.228	(4.6)	0.288	(5.8)		
Constant	−3.329	(4.8)	−3.026	(5.6)		
NIESR						
ln CD_{-1}	0.501	(5.1)	0.442	(4.1)		
Δ ln RPDI	0.778	(2.9)	0.887	(3.2)		
Δ ln $RPDI_{-1}$	0.367	(1.4)	0.599	(2.2)		
Δ ln $RPDI_{-1}$	0.717	(4.1)	0.792	(4.4)		
DHP	−0.005	(5.3)	−0.004	(5.0)		
*D*681	0.110	(2.6)				
*D*682	−0.271	(6.0)	−0.264	(5.7)		
*D*683	0.014	(0.3)	0.003	(0.1)		
*D*731	0.094	(2.2)	0.101	(2.2)		
*D*732	−0.151	(3.3)	−0.124	(2.6)		
*D*792	0.222	(5.3)	0.261	(6.2)		
*D*793	−0.133	(2.9)	−0.189	(3.7)		
Constant	−3.42	(3.2)	−3.75	(3.4)		

Table 3.3 Contd.

	Model		*Ours*		*Adjusted ours*	
	Coefficient	*(t value)*	*Coefficient*	*(t value)*	*Coefficient*	*(t value)*
LBS						
$\ln CD_{-3}$	0.181	(3.9)	0.304	(4.9)	0.215	(4.7)
ln RPDI	1	(—)	1	(—)	1	(—)
$\ln (CD/RPDI)_{-1}$	0.605	(7.7)	0.382	(3.8)	0.569	(7.3)
RMD	−0.997	(4.1)	−0.007	(2.8)	−0.007	(4.1)
RMD_{-1}	−0.002	(1.1)	−0.003	(1.2)	−0.002	(1.1)
$\ln (KZJ/PC)_{-1}$	1.22	(3.0)	1.544	(2.5)	1.405	(3.3)
RRL	−0.386	(2.9)	−0.339	(1.8)	−0.399	(3.0)
*D*681	0.110	(2.6)				
*D*682	−0.263	(6.0)	−0.206	(3.2)	−0.243	(5.2)
*D*731	0.105	(3.7)	0.111	(2.6)	0.115	(3.8)
Constant	−2.45	(6.2)	−3.98	(5.6)	−2.804	(5.3)
*D*792					0.235	(5.4)
*D*793					−0.248	(5.1)
HMT						
$\ln CD_{-1}$	0.608	(7.0)	0.907	(10.7)	0.978	(13.6)
$\Delta_4 \ln RPDI$	1.361	(6.9)	0.555	(1.7)	0.400	(1.4)
$\ln (CD/RPDI)_{-4}$	−0.854	(7.8)	0.096	(0.6)	0.022	(0.2)
$\Delta_4 \ln (NFIN_{-4}/PC_{-3})$	0.292	(4.1)	0.719	(2.3)	0.617	(2.5)
$\Delta_4 \ln (NFIN_{-1}/PC)$	0.225	(1.9)	0.533	(2.5)	0.167	(0.9)
$\Delta_4(PEXP - RBLPE)$	0.004	(—)	0.004	(—)	0.004	(—)
Constant	−5.260	(8.0)	0.98	(1.0)	0.234	(0.3)
*D*731					−0.172	(0.8)
*D*732					0.267	(2.2)
*D*792					−0.312	(3.6)
*D*793					0.234	(4.0)

Definitions of terms used are given at the end of the chapter.

Table 3.4 Diagnostic statistics of the models in Table 3.3

	Bank		NIESR		LBS		HMT		LBS (adjusted)	HMT (adjusted)
	Model	*Ours*	*Model*	*Ours*	*Model*	*Ours*	*Model*	*Ours*		
Sample period	1966 Q3 1981 Q4	1968 Q2 1983 Q4	1967 Q1 1984 Q1	1968 Q2 1983 Q4	1967 Q3 1981 Q4	1968 Q2 1983 Q4	1968 Q2 1978 Q4	1966 Q2 1983 Q4	1968 Q2 1983 Q4	1968 Q2 1983 Q4
R^2	0.738	0.951	—	0.965	—	0.924	0.862	0.836	0.962	0.908
SEE	0.047	0.048	0.041	0.042	0.040	0.060	0.049	0.088	0.043	0.072
DW	1.6	1.52	—	2.00	2.08	2.36	1.72	0.24	2.18	1.87
Tests for normality of errors										
Shapiro–Wilk W statistic (value less than 0.9550 rejects normality)		0.9531		0.9694		0.9100		0.9150	0.8966	0.8654
Skewness (range of comparison, ±0.62)		−0.98		−0.52		0.32		−0.86	0.15	−1.86
Kurtosis (range of comparison, 1.8–4.2)		5.5		3.9		8.3		7.0	3.80	12.14
Autocorrelation										
Ljung–Box (95% significance level, 9.5)		6.5		3.4		7.7		9.9	11.8	8.3
Modified F test (95% significance level, 2.6)		1.5		0.7		1.8		2.4	2.7	1.8
Parameter stability (1984 Q1 to 1985 Q4)										
Static test (95% significance level, 15.5)		3.1		5.0		1.4		1.2	3.2	1.7
Dynamic test (95% significance level, 15.5)		3.9		6.9		1.3		—	3.8	—
RMS%E										
Static test		0.40		0.43		0.40		0.40	0.32	0.4
Dynamic test		0.41		0.51		0.32		—	0.43	—
Heteroscedasticity										
Peak test (95% significance level, 3.8)		0.70		0.85		0.69		0.25	0.69	0.09
F test for linear restriction (95% significance level, 4.0)		1.09		—		0.0		5.1	0.0	3.0

which are incomes, the effective minimum deposit rate on durables spending, interest rates and a number of dummy variables to pick up the effects of Budget changes made in 1968, 1973 and 1979. The Bank model is the only one to contain terms in mortgage lending and the ratio of net liquid assets to income, although both the LBS and Treasury models contain financial terms. The former can perhaps be criticized for entering the equation with zero lag, because of possible simultaneity problems which this might entail. Moreover, lending is measured relative to the price of durable goods PCD, whereas the total consumers deflator PC is used to convert all other variables in the equation to real terms. Hence, it is not clear if relative price movements (between PCD and the price of non-durable goods and services PCND) are not being picked up in the lending term. A second point to note is that households' inflation-adjusted income YDLH is used in the Bank model instead of the more conventional RPDI. This makes the durable and non-durable consumption functions easier to interpret, although the use of YDLH entails accepting that inflation has the same effect on both durable and non-durable expenditure. This may be part of the reason why we have found it so difficult to estimate a significant coefficient on the ratio of net liquid assets to income. Other problems evident with the Bank model (which are common with those found earlier using a shorter sample period) are that it fails to pass one of the relevant tests for autocorrelation (the Ljung–Box test), has errors which may not come from a normal distribution and forecasts less well than some of the other models we consider.

The NIESR model has a much simpler form that the Bank model, with no role for interest rates, lending or liquid assets in the equation. Despite the apparently simple dynamics there is little evidence of autocorrelation, heteroscedasticity or problems of non-normal errors. However, although the parameters appear fairly stable, the equation predicts the period 1984–5 less accurately than any of the other models we consider. This suggests that the use of a very simple dynamic structure impairs the dynamic predictive ability of the model (indicated in a comparison of the RMS%Es of the dynamic and static forecast tests).

The LBS model uses a simple error-correction structure, but without an integral control mechanism. However, like the Bank model, it does include the change in a liquid assets term—in the LBS case real building society shares and deposits are used. In addition, changes in real interest rates affect demand. Finally dummy variables play a role in the equation, and when the relevant dummies are included coefficients on all the other variables are very much closer to those reported in the LBS manual (see adjusted LBS in Table 3.3). However, the equation suffers from autocorrelated errors. Despite this both the LBS equations perform better than the other models at predicting recent changes in expenditure, with RMS%Es at around three-quarters of those of the best alternative model.

The final model to consider is the HMT model. This is the oldest of the models, which may in part explain why we had great difficulty replicating their equation. Because of these difficulties the model has not been emphasized in making comparisons, as our results indicate a model which performs rather poorly.

3.3.4 Results

In this section we present the results of estimating a new durables equation using broadly similar variables to those adopted in the previous Bank equation. Both the LBS and NIESR models suggest that use of the 'dagger' functions does not help to improve either the fit or the forecasting ability of the model. Moreover, they suggest that the income elasticity should not be constrained to equal unity (see Table 3.7 below for the relevant long-run elasticities) and that RPDI is probably as useful a measure of income as YDLH (although this proposition has not been tested directly).

In deriving the new model we have deliberately refrained from using current mortgage lending as an explanatory variable, because of problems of simultaneity. We have, however, included a number of wealth terms,[13] but with little success. Only a term in real net liquid assets proved to be useful, together with the (lagged) flow of mortgage lending. We also attempted to split lending for house purchase between that used for housing investment and net cash withdrawal, but found that in such a model neither flow could be identified as significant (see Appendix A3.1). Finally, relative price terms were included (unsuccessfully) and YDLH was replaced by RPDI. Since the latter change increased the standard error of the equation very slightly, but otherwise made little difference to the specification, we decided to retain YDLH in our model.

The resulting specification (Table 3.5) does not suffer from as many problems as the previous model specification, although it is still far from perfect (Table 3.6) It does not suffer from autocorrelation, has errors which pass the tests for normality and has fairly stable parameters (passing the Hendry forecast tests for the period 1984 Q1 to 1985 Q4). To avoid putting too much weight on recent data, which are likely to be revised significantly, we have also estimated a similar model using data up to the end of 1980. The forecasts for the subsequent 5 years indicate a better performance than for the period 1984–5. The relevant RMS%Es over the longer period forecast (at 0.38 and 0.41) are around a quarter less than for the shorter period (at 0.51 and 0.58). The main reason for this seems to be the fall in ('actual') consumption which occurred in the third quarter of 1984 and which is not well predicted by the model. All this reduction is due to lower spending on vehicles, reflecting the fact that non-seasonally adjusted durables spending rose by just 4% in the third quarter of 1984,

[13]Including gross and net liquid assets, gross illiquid assets, gross physical assets, net financial wealth and net wealth, plus ratios of these terms to income.

Table 3.5 The new CD specification (dependent variable ln CD)

	Coefficient	*(t value)*
ln CD	0.219	(2.9)
A(L) ln YDLH	1.074	(6.8)
ln RR	−0.656	(5.0)
ln RMD	−0.005	(5.3)
ln $(ML/PC)_{-1}$	0.125	(3.7)
ln $(NLAJ/PC)_{-1}$	0.206	(2.4)
*D*681	0.147	(3.9)
*D*682	−0.210	(5.4)
*D*731	0.108	(2.9)
*D*732	−0.132	(3.5)
*D*764[a]	0.117	(3.2)
*D*792	0.264	(7.2)
*D*793	−0.113	(2.7)
Constant	−8.032	(6.1)
R^2	0.988	
SEE	0.036	
DW	1.8	
Sample period	1963 Q3 to 1985 Q4	

Definitions of terms used are given at the end of the chapter.
[a]We found that this dummy was necessary, although it had not been adopted in the past. It may be associated with the Mini-Budget of December 1976 and/or the sharp rise in car prices (by Ford and Chrysler).

compared with the rise of close to 30% in the third quarters of 1982 and 1983. This suggests that either demand for cars may have been (temporarily) boosted with the introduction of the A and B number plates or that the 1984 'actual' may be revised upwards at some time in the future.

Table 3.7 shows the relevant elasticities for the new model,[14] indicating a more acceptable (higher) income elasticity of 1.4, a slightly larger (absolute) interest rate elasticity (−0.84) and a weaker effect from lending (0.16, as against 0.34 in the previous model specification). In the past we have justified the inclusion of mortgage lending as representing complementarity (houses and durable goods) and net cash or equity withdrawal. Even with these two effects, however, a long-run elasticity of 0.34 seems high, given that we could not identify a strong effect from a model-based proxy for net cash withdrawal (when other lending for house purchase was included as a separate regressor). In an attempt to identify complementarity separately we have tried including both levels and changes in the number of owner-occupied houses and a proxy for the number of houses sold in the latest quarter[15] together with the net cash-withdrawal term. Of all the terms used only the proxy for the number of houses sold in the last quarter was

[14]Re-estimated up to the end of 1985.
[15]Defined as the flow of mortgage funding divided by average house prices.

Table 3.6 Diagnostic statistics of the new CD specification

Test statistics	*Comparison values*	*New model*
Normality of errors[a]		
Shapiro–Wilk W statistic	Reject if below 0.9607	0.9859
Skewness	Reject if outside (±0.54)	−0.05
Kurtosis	Reject if outside (1.92, 4.08)	2.78
Autocorrelation[a]		
Residual correlogram	Correlation	
lag 1		0.06
lag 2		0.03
lag 3		−0.24
lag 4		−0.15
Ljung–Box(4)	$\chi^2(4) = 9.49$ at 95% level	7.4
LM test for autocorrelation	$\chi^2(4) = 9.49$ at 95% level	6.8
Modified LM test	$F(4, 64) = 2.53$ at 95% level	1.45
Heteroscedasticity[a]		
Peak test	Cumulative probability that the linear model is wrong	0.21
Parameter stability		
Static forecast test[a]		
1984 Q1 to 1985 Q4	$\chi^2(8) = 15.5$ at 95% level	11.6
	RMS%E	0.51
1981 Q1 to 1985 Q4[b]	$\chi^2(20) = 31.4$ at 95% level	13.3
	RMS%E	0.38
Dynamic forecast test[a]		
1984 Q1 to 1985 Q4[b]	$\chi^2(8) = 15.5$ at 95% level	14.3
	RMS%E	0.58
1981 Q1 to 1985 Q4[b]	$\chi^2(20) = 31.4$ at 95% level	15.43
	RMS%E	0.41

[a]All these tests are based on a model estimated using data up to the end of 1983. This sample period was used throughout (in testing down). Forecast tests were *not* used to choose between specifications since our earlier comparison of the four main models suggested that even poorly specified models would be likely to have 'reasonable' RMS%Es (of around 0.5).
[b]A shorter sample period was tried to see how well the model might forecast over a longer period.

Table 3.7 Long-run elasticities

	Elasticity with respect to		
Model	*Income*	*Interest rates*	*Mortgage lending*
Current Bank model	1.00	−0.74	0.34
NIESR	1.44	—	—
LBS	1.85	—	—
HMT	1.85	—	—
New specification	1.38	−0.84	0.16

significant. However, once this variable was included it was not possible to find an effect from net cash withdrawal. These results suggest that simple proxies for equity or net cash withdrawal are not very useful indicators of how much lending is 'leaking' into consumption. Clearly, more work needs to be done if we are to model this sort of behaviour satisfactorily.

3.3.5 Interest rate effects

In addition to checking that the coefficients relating to our preferred specification have not changed significantly in recent years (by re-estimating the equation using a sample period extended to the end of 1985) we have tried splitting the sample in 1974. In the first subperiod neither the interest rate nor income terms are well identified, whilst lending plays a stronger role. In the second subperiod only the interest rate term is poorly identified, although the coefficient on lending has halved in value. The relevant F test rejects stability, taking a value of 2.6 compared with the 95% significant vaue of 2.1; however, the 99% significant value is 2.8. To some extent instability of the equation might be expected when there have been a number of changes in the environment. In particular, we might expect the effects of mortgage leanding on consumption to have changed in recent years given the increased competition which has resulted from the banks entering the market.

In order to investigate the stability of the various parameters we have tried estimating the preferred model using recursive least squares. The main problem appears to lie with the interest rate coefficients. In particular that on ln RR is positive in a sample ending in the early 1970s but negative on more recent samples. In addition, the coefficient on RMD appears to have risen (closer to zero) over time, whilst that on real net liquid assets has fallen. This suggests that interest rates are becoming a more important factor in determining when people buy durables and when deposit requirements/liquid asset accumulation are becoming less relevant. Of course, this means that if we believe that this process is going to continue we might expect the trends in the coefficients (which are found using recursive ordinary least squares (OLS)) to continue also. As an example, we have estimated a similar model to that of Table 3.5 but where RMD and RNLAJ are first multiplied/divided by a time trend suitably scaled so as to ensure a rate of increase/decrease broadly commensurate with trends identified in the recursive OLS regressions. In addition, a dummy variable taking a value of zero throughout the 1960s and unity elsewhere was used to ensure that RR could only affect durables expenditure in the 1970s and 1980s. We found that these adjustments made identification of a net liquid assets effect very hard,[16] although otherwise the specifications were broadly

[16]Probably reflecting the fact that one cannot hope to have two time trends in the same equation!

similar to those found earlier. Obviously, if this type of model were used in a forecast somewhat different results would be obtained than with a fixed-coefficients model (such as that presented in Table 3.5).

3.4 MODELLING CONSUMERS' EXPENDITURE ON NON-DURABLE GOODS AND SERVICES

3.4.1 The previous Bank model of consumers' expenditure on non-durables

We begin by considering the properties of the previous equation (as reported by Patterson *et al.* (1987)). This modelled consumers' expenditure as a function of households' real disposable income (adjusted for the erosion of their net liquid assets by inflation) and real net financial wealth. The adjustment of the conventional measure of personal disposable income is, of course, just one of the adjustments needed if we are to approximate more closely the Hicksian concept of income. As yet no attempt has been made to allow for depreciation of the stock of durables (as suggested by Patterson (1984a)). Neither, as yet, have we tried disaggregating income in order to permit changes in the distribution of income to affect consumption (e.g. Borooah and Sharpe, 1984), although preliminary work indicates that it is possible to distinguish between the effects of labour and non-labour income.

The precise specification of the non-durable consumption function is given by

$$\begin{aligned}
\ln \mathrm{CND} = {} & \ln \mathrm{CNDD} \\
& + \beta_1(\ln \mathrm{YDLH} - \ln \mathrm{YDLD}) \\
& + \beta_2 \Delta(\ln \mathrm{YDLH} - \ln \mathrm{YDLD}) \\
& + \beta_3(\ln \mathrm{CNDD} - \ln \mathrm{YDLD}) \\
& + \beta_4(\ln \mathrm{RNFWJD} - \ln \mathrm{YDLD}) \\
& + \text{dummy variables}
\end{aligned}$$

where

$$\ln \mathrm{CNDD} = 0.25 \sum_{i=1}^{4} \ln \mathrm{CND}_{-i}$$

and

$$\ln \mathrm{RNFWJD} = 0.25 \sum_{i=1}^{4} \ln \mathrm{RNFWJ}_{-i}$$

The terms used in the specification suggest that consumers' expenditure on non-durables is influenced by changes in incomes (with a positive effect), the acceleration in income (with the consumption-to-income ratio falling when the rate of growth of income rises), lagged values of the consumption-to-income ratio (with a negative effect) and lagged values of the net ratio of financial wealth to income (with a positive effect). Finally, allowance is made for the Budgets in 1968, 1973 and 1979 which were thought to have led to some expenditure's being brought forward owing to anticipated changes in indirect tax. As in the old durables equation all the variables used in the equation are measured relative to their one-year moving averages, as suggested (for some variables, at least) by Hendry and von Ungern-Sternberg (1981). One problem with the use of these 'dagger' functions, however, is that they imply implausible dynamic responses (Dicks, 1985). As regards income the problem is not that consumption reacts slowly to a change in income (since the median lag is just one-quarter thanks to the large impact response), but that it goes on reacting (slowly) for a very long time afterwards (with the next quarter of the total long-run response taking a further 36 quarters to work through). Given that the equation has an integral control mechanism, which is generally justified as ensuring that consumption-to-income and wealth-to-income ratios return to their long-run targets, it might be thought preferable to have an equation with shorter response times to changes in income. This means that, as regards wealth, we would expect the rational lags to indicate slower response times than to changes in income. Here again, however, the specification seems implausible since the median lag is 46 quarters, whilst the response function implies quarterly impacts which first rise, than fall and then rise again before finally beginning to decrease in the longer run.

The steady state solution of the equation, given constant growth in real incomes, is given by the expression

$$\ln \mathrm{CND} = \ln \mathrm{YDLH} - 0.565 + 0.33 \ln(\mathrm{RNFWJ}/\mathrm{YDLH}) - 40.13 g_y + 21.03(g_y - g_w) \quad (3.4)$$

where g_y and g_w are the rates of growth of real income and real wealth respectively.[17] Making the usual implicit assumption that the wealth-to-income ratio should be held constant, since this is what consumers plan to do in the long run (Patterson, 1984b), we can ignore the last term in 3.4. One problem (highlighted by Patterson (1988a)) with using an error-correction term to ensure a unit income elasticity of consumers' expenditure on non-durables is that, when taken together with our new equation for consumers' expenditure on durables (which has an elasticity greater than unity),[18] this implies an elasticity of total consumption to income of 1.045. In other words the aggregate consumption-to-income ratio (or the savings ratio) depends upon the level of income and hence is unbounded. One way

[17]Note that the coefficient on g_y reported by Patterson *et al.* (1987) is slightly incorrect.
[18]See section 3.3.

of ensuring an aggregate elasticity of unity is to constrain each of the two 'component' equations (i.e. for non-durables and durables) to have unit elasticities. It is possible, however, to constrain the equations in such a way that if the ratio of durables spending to total consumers' expenditure remains at its average level (measured over some past interval), then an aggregate unit elasticity can be imposed. (Of course a local constraint of this nature does not imply a global constraint.) In this situation it might seem preferable to estimate the durables and non-durables expenditure equations jointly, although it is easy to show that it is possible to keep the current durables equation intact (with its income elasticity greater than unity) by restricting the elasticity on the non-durables equation to ensure an elasticity of total consumers' expenditure to income of unity (see Appendix A3.2 for details).[19] Such an approach implies that we would be treating spending on durables as consumption and not as savings (which many economists would find hard to accept), but at least it would be consistent in the sense that the alternative (of treating durables expenditure as savings) would imply that it would also be necessary to adjust income for depreciation of the stock of durables.

Further problems with the previous model specification have emerged in recent years through its use as part of the main short-term model in the Bank's bi-annual forecasts. The equation has generally underpredicted consumption of non-durables over the past few years, with nine out of the last ten static residuals (up to 1987 Q2) being positive. No doubt much of the problem is due to the poorer quality of recent estimates of personal incomes and/or consumption, since the discrepancies between the traditional savings ratio and one based on the financial accounts has widened in recent years. As a result, the balancing item required to bring the two savings measures in line has risen from close to £5.5 billion in both 1983 and 1984 to £11 billion in 1985 and £16.5 billion in 1986. The latter figure accounts for some 85% of total savings as indicated by the traditional measure, highlighting the scale of the problem. Our recent research suggests that the main problem with the real-side estimates could lie with the income figures rather than the consumption figures since there are discrepancies between the growth rates of average earnings (as measured by the Department of Employment) and the CSO's (National Accounts) estimates of income from wages and salaries. If it is the income estimates which are wrong then this would also help explain the 'unexpectedly' high income tax receipts of recent years, although it would, in addition, lead to a larger gap between the income and expenditure measures of gross domestic product (GDP).

Before turning to a consideration of how the previous model specification

[19]Of course this is only a short-term solution to the problem. But then we ought also to examine the long-run properties of a change in wealth on total consumption. To do this we would need to estimate a more complex system of equations than one containing simply two consumption functions.

might be improved, we first re-estimated the previous equation using more up-to-date data.[20] We have deliberately chosen not to use the data for the last 2 years because of the problems with estimates for recent years

Table 3.8 The previous CND specification (dependent variable ln CND)

	Original estimates		*New estimates*	
Explanatory variable	*Coefficient*	*(t value)*	*Coefficient*	*(t value)*
ln CNDD	1	(—)	1	(—)
ln (YDLH/YDLD)	0.37522	(12.4)	0.37399	(14.3)
Δ ln (YDLH/YDLD)	−0.13492	(3.8)	−0.15571	(5.4)
ln (CNDD/YDLD)	−0.03889	(1.0)	−0.01782	(0.6)
ln (RNFWJD/YDLD)	0.01272	(3.9)	0.01353	(4.5)
Constant	−0.02196	(3.1)	−0.02154	(3.7)
*D*681A	0.01270	(2.2)	0.01399	(3.9)
*D*731A	0.02128	(3.7)	0.01998	(3.9)
*D*79A	0.01655	(3.9)	0.01887	(3.7)
R^2	0.786		0.818	
SEE	0.006		0.0056	
DW	1.6		1.62	
Sample period	1967 Q4 to 1984 Q2		1967 Q4 to 1985 Q2	

Definitions of terms used are given at the end of the chapter.

Table 3.9 Diagnostic statistics of the previous CND specification

	Original estimates	*New estimates*
Normality		
Shapiro–Wilk	—	0.9870
Skewness	—	−0.0005
Kurtosis	—	3.0298
Autocorrelation		
Ljung–Box, $\chi^2(2)$	—	6.01
LM test, $\chi^2(4)$	9.9	6.27
Modified LM test, $F(4, 59)$	—	1.43
Heteroscedasticity		
LM test, $\chi^2(2)$	—	1.96
Parameter stability		
Static 'Hendry' forecast test		
$\chi^2(\ \ )$	3.8(6)	30.60(8)
RMS%E	—	36.86

[20] We do not compare our model with those used by the HMT, LBS etc. since this was done by Davis (1982).

described above. Nevertheless our results, shown in Tables 3.8 and 3.9, do provide a useful benchmark against which we can test other specifications. The second column of Table 3.8 shows the previous specification (as first reported by Edwards (1985)).[21] Although the error-correction term was then found to be insignificant it was not felt necessary to test the implied unit elasticity of CND to income, presumably since the then current CD equation also (mistakenly) had a unit elasticity. According to Bollerslev and Hylleberg (1985) the unit elasticity of the error-correction form of the non-durables consumption function is refuted by the data. This may, of course, still be consistent with Hendry's notion of equilibrium being that of 'all change ceasing' (Hendry, 1983), which is not an assertion about behaviour in the long run.[22] A second problem with the specification was its evidence of serial correlation, with the model just failing the relevant LM test at the 95% significance level. This result is all the more surprising since one of the original justifications for using the 'dagger' functions was that it might help remove the problem of autocorrelated errors which had been found to be evident in most of the macromodels (Davis, 1982).

Although there have been significant revisions to much of the data since 1985 our attempt at replicating the equation has been fairly successful (see third column of Table 3.8). The most noticeable development is the change in the size and significance of the error-correction term (which has halved in size). Interestingly if the equation is re-estimated using a sample period ending in 1987 Q2 the error-correction term becomes significant again, although its coefficient is now very close to zero. Harnett (1988) reports the results of running recursive least-squares programs to gauge the variability of error-correction terms in similar consumption functions. In his work the recursive estimates reported are for a simple error-correction model (which does not include a role for liquid assets or other forms of wealth) and also for a more complex model (including wealth, unemployment and interest rates). When seasonally unadjusted data are used, the coefficient on the error-correction term varies from -0.075 to -0.13 in the first model and from -0.135 to -0.245 in the second model. For some samples the coefficient is not significantly different from zero.

Another problem evident from Table 3.9 is the equation's poor performance in the forecast test. Note that although the sample period used originally to estimate the current specification ended in 1984 Q2, all the testing down carried out to find this final equation used a sample period six quarters shorter. Hence the original Hendry forecast test (which was passed comfortably) was a true test of the equation's forecasting capabilities, even though in more recent years the equation appears (at first blush) to have broken down (although, as we mentioned above, this could be due to the

[21] Although it is fairly similar to that suggested by Davis (1982).

[22] For a fuller discussion of these issues see Harnett (1988).

poor quality of the data in recent quarters). We examine this question again later (section 3.4.3).

3.4.2 The theoretical model underlying the consumption function

The Bank's CND equation can be interpreted as part of an extended error-correction system with consumption changing to eradicate disequilibrium in the target net ratio of financial assets to income and the derived target ratio of consumption to income (as outlined by Hendry and von Ungern-Sternberg (1981)). The main theoretical advance of this work on that of Davidson *et al.* (1978) was to recognize that, if consumers wish to maintain their consumption-to-income ratios constant in the long run, then the integral of past discrepancies between consumption and income would influence their wealth holdings and hence, possibly, their behaviour. For this reason a term in real net liquid assets was included in their regression work.[23] The recognition that cumulated savings might play an important role in expenditure equations was not a new development (e.g. Townend, 1976), but the theoretical underpinnings had not been clearly set out in applied work until Hendry and von Ungern-Sternberg's work. More recent research (e.g. Patterson, 1984a) has suggested that both liquid and illiquid financial wealth may play a role in explaining consumers' expenditure, although when only the former is contained in the equation it is found that the simulation properties of the short-term model are less plausible than when net financial wealth is included (Jenkinson, 1985).

This brings us to a further important consideration: the role of interest rates in determining consumption. Patterson (1988b) has generalized the Hendry–von Ungern-Sternberg framework to allow for the possibility that disaggregated wealth-to-income ratios are a function of rates of return. Anyhow, changes in interest rates will clearly affect consumers who are liquidity constrained (for the theoretical underpinnings of this type of approach see Jackman and Sutton (1982) and Stiglitz and Weiss (1981, 1987).[24] For these reasons it would seem reasonable to expect some role for interest rates, although for non-durables expenditure the empirical evidence is somewhat mixed. For example, Easton (1985) reports that, of the five main macromodels, only the Treasury and the Liverpool models then included an explicit role for interest rates in their non-durables equation.[25] The LBS model, however, considered only total and durable consumption (with non-durables given by identity), implying an interest rate effect on non-durables since each of their consumption functions included interest

[23]Of course other justifications for including such a variable, such as the existence of liquidity constraints, are possible (e.g. Flemming, 1973; Pissarides 1978).

[24]Surveys of the literature are contained in Hubbard and Judd (1986) and Zeldes (1985).

[25]Of course, the situation will have changed since then.

rate effects (which are not offsetting). The models were generally driven primarily by real personal disposable income (and in some cases this is adjusted for inflation), although the Liverpool model is something of an exception given its equilibirum approach (Easton, 1985, pp. 46–8). In addition, all the models use one or more wealth variables, usually either net liquid assets or net financial wealth.

Our own previous research (e.g. Dicks, 1985) had suggested that it was easy to improve on the previous model specification by using $\Delta_4 \ln \text{CND}$ as the dependent variable and keeping the error-correction framework. Harnett (1988) also reports a number of similar equations, although his preferred model equation is based on current-price seasonally unadjusted data. Both lines of research find a role for interest rates (and for unemployment also in the case of Harnett (1988)). One problem with the use of Δ_4 equations, however, is that if consumers' expenditure estimates are poorly seasonally adjusted (which they are!), they will tend to keep their (incorrect) quarterly pattern in the future. If we are using these models simply to forecast what the CSO estimates will look like next year (and not what the estimates will look like in 10 years' time), then of course this will not be a problem. Nevertheless, to avoid problems of this nature, we have kept to a levels equation.[26] In testing down we have allowed for the possibility of long lags on income and wealth (up to eight quarters) but assumed shorter lags on the dependent variable and interest rates (up to four quarters).

3.4.3 Results

In Tables 3.10 and 3.11 we report the results obtained by testing down from a general specification. We found that the data preferred a negative coefficient on $\ln \text{YDLH}_{-2}$ and therefore we used $\Delta \ln \text{YDLH}_{-1}$ instead. We also found that a $\Delta \ln \text{YDLH}$ term was significant. The first column of the tables shows a specification in which the long-run income elasticity has been constrained to be equal to unity so that it can be compared with the previous model equation. The second column reports our preferred specification in which the elasticity has been constrained to equal 0.946, thus giving us an overall (local) unit elasticity (i.e. of total consumption to income). This restriction is easily accepted by the data.[27]

In addition we have constrained the coefficients on the dummy variables to ensure that they have no long-lasting effect. Again, the tests for these restrictions are easily passed. However, this second group of restrictions does make some difference to the model, for they ensure that the *t* value on

[26]We have also tried estimating a Δ_1 equation in which the income elasticity is restricted to be less than unity. This turned out to fit the data slightly less well than our levels model, although it also included both interest rates and net financial wealth (which were both found to be significant).

[27]Although, interestingly, the freely estimated elasticity is greater than unity.

Table 3.10 Some new CND specifications (dependent variable ln CND)

Explanatory variable	*Unit elasticity with respect to income*	*Preferred specification (elasticity 0.946) with respect to income*
$\ln CND_{-1}$	0.58655 (7.4)	0.53402 (6.7)
$\ln CND_{-2}$	0.31808 (4.4)	0.34013 (4.7)
$\Delta \ln YDLH$	0.11337 (3.1)	0.11587 (3.0)
$\Delta \ln YDLH_{-1}$	0.19634 (6.7)	0.19570 (6.4)
ln YDLH	0.09537 (2.5)	0.11905 (—)
$\ln (RNFWJ/YDLH)_{-1}$	0.01072 (4.0)	0.00770 (2.8)
ln RR	−0.05749 (2.5)	−0.06142 (2.7)
Constant	−0.02448 (4.0)	0.04969 (2.1)
*D*681	0.01473 (3.0)	0.01661 (4.8)
$D681_{-1}$	−0.01914 (3.9)	−0.01661 (—)
*D*731	0.01821 (3.7)	0.01519 (4.4)
$D731_{-2}$	−0.01198 (2.5)	−0.01519 (—)
*D*792	0.02500 (5.1)	0.01823 (5.1)
$D792_{-2}$	−0.00987 (1.9)	−0.01823 (—)
R^2	0.997500	0.996614
SEE	0.004768	0.004805
DW	2.1352	2.0645
Sample period	1967 Q4 to 1985 Q2	1967 Q4 to 1985 Q2

Definitions of terms used are given at the end of the chapter.

Table 3.11 Diagnostic statistics for new CND specifications

Normality		
Shapiro–Wilk	0.973	0.982
Skewness	0.358	0.252
Kurtosis	3.484	3.022
Autocorrelation		
Ljung–Box, $\chi^2(4)$	3.3830	3.7145
LM test, $\chi^2(4)$	3.5637	3.6261
Modified LM test, $F(4, 53)$	0.7002	0.7131
Heteroscedasticity		
LM test, $\chi^2(2)$	3.5176	1.8020
Parameter stability		
Static 'Hendry' forecast test		
$\chi^2(8)$	16.96	18.82
RMS%E	0.07	0.07
Tests for restrictions		
Elasticity restricted, $F(1, 57)$	0.5708	0.5360
Dummies restricted, $F(3, 60)$	(—)	1.669

the constant rises above 2 (i.e. without these restrictions, but with the elasticity constrained to be less than unity, the constant in the new equation is insignificant). Patterson (1985) has shown that the original research by Davidson *et al.* (1978) was wrong to exclude the constant from their work, since the imposition of a unit long-run elasticity on a non-durables consumption equation in which income has not been adjusted for depreciation of the stock of durables implies that either there are no durables or that if they exist then they have infinite lives. One way of making an allowance for depreciation in the steady state is to include an intercept, even if it is collinear with the error-correction term. The first column of Table 3.10 indicates a significant negative constant, as we would expect if depreciation of the durables stock had not been taken into account. Once we recognize that the constrained elasticity is too high, however, by taking account of durables expenditure also and ensuring that the total consumption-to-income elasticity is unity (locally), then we find that the constant is insignificant (and could be dropped). Since we have not adjusted incomes for depreciation, our results hint that it is the fact that the elasticity of durables expenditure is above unity, and not the failure to adjust incomes for depreciation, which is the real reason why we need to keep a constant in a non-durables consumption function when its elasticity is constrained to unity (as in the Davidson *et al.* (1978) model).

The new equation clearly fits the data better than the previous model does, even if the latter is re-estimated to take account of revisions to the data (compare the standard errors in Tables 3.8 and 3.10). In part, this is simply because of the new explanatory variable (interest rates) included in the new model. Previous research (Harnett, 1988) had shown that including an interest rate term as a regressor when using a sample which covers the 1960s and 1970s would not have given similar results (with the interest rate term then being positive). We have tried checking this result for our preferred equation by splitting the sample at the end of 1977 and re-estimating the model for each of the subperiods. The interest rate term was found to be small and insignificantly different from zero in the first period (t value 1.4) although it was correctly signed. By contrast not only was the t value during the second subperiod well above 2 but the coefficient was broadly twice the magnitude of that estimated for the sample as a whole. Clearly this result implies that further work is needed if we are to understand why interest rate effects appear to be becoming more important, particularly given that we found that much the same story was true of durables expenditure. One possible reason, suggested by Dicks (1987), is that greater competition in the markets for personal sector saving and borrowing has resulted in reductions in liquidity constraints which can be correlated with changes in interest rates. For this reason it might be better to try including new proxies for credit rationing in the equation. To this end we have tried using measures of mortgage rationing and net cash withdrawal in the non-durables equation (based on the same approach as Wilcox (1985)). Neither variable turned out to be significant.[28]

The results of the diagnostic tests of the new equation (Table 3.11) show no evidence of non-normality, autocorrelation or heteroscedasticity. When it comes to the out-of-sample stability tests, however, the new model fails the Hendry forecast test. Like the old model the new specification underpredicts consumption in each of the last eight quarters. The questions raised earlier regarding the quality of recent estimates seem to have been borne out in the sense that the new equation, when confronted with the 'data' for the first time, finds that consumption appears consistently too high given the income figures. In a sense this is comforting, for in testing down we have allowed for the possibility of a faster response from changes in income than does the earlier specification[29] and we have found some change (see below). It does mean that, if we do disbelieve the National Accounts, then we need to spend more time examining the question of what the 'true' levels of consumption and income are.

The rational lags for the new model have changed significantly from those of the old model. Clearly the $\Delta \ln \mathrm{YDLH}_{-1}$ term implies a small impact effect (in the third quarter) which is negative, although otherwise the response function is close to triangular in shape. However, the stronger effects in the first and second quarters ensure that the cumulative effects work through much faster. Hence, whilst in the old model half the full long-run effect of a change in income takes under 6 months to work through and the next quarter of the total effect takes a further 8.5 years, in the new model half the total effect works through slightly more slowly (in close to a year) but the next quarter takes a mere 18 months longer. As for the rational lags regarding wealth, the median lag for the new model is only 10 quarters, compared with 11 years for the old model—again a significant change.

Next we consider the steady state solution to the new equation. This is given by the expression

$$\begin{aligned}\ln \mathrm{CND} = {} & 0.946 \ln \mathrm{YDLH} + 0.331 + 0.061 \ln (\mathrm{RNFWJ}/\mathrm{YDLH}) \\ & - 0.488 \ln \mathrm{RR} - 6.051 g_{\mathrm{y}} + 0.651 (g_{\mathrm{y}} - g_{\mathrm{w}})\end{aligned}$$

The income elasticity is only slightly less than in the old model. The wealth-to-income elasticity looks very small on the new equation, although it is clear that rather more work needs to be done if we are to understand what 'sensible' long-run properties should be imposed in this respect. Finally, the interest elasticity (at close to 0.5) is, though smaller than for the

[28] We have also tried adding other housing market variables to the model but without success—neither the house price earnings ratio nor the flow of (real) mortgage lending was significant.

[29] The usual reason given in the past for the old equation's apparent breakdown.

durables equation, much higher than most previous studies had suggested. Moreover, running the equation through recursive least squares suggests (as it did for the durables equation) that these effects vary over time in both size and significance.

3.5 CONCLUSIONS

In this chapter we have presented some results which suggest that interest rates play a significant role in helping to explain changes in consumers' expenditure on both durable and non-durable goods. Moreover, our research suggests that interest effects vary over time in both size and significance, hinting that changes in liquidity constraints may be playing an important role. Such a conclusion implies that the leverage of monetary policy is also likely to vary over time.

DATA DEFINITIONS

CD	consumers' expenditure on durables (real)
CDD	$(CD_{-1} \times CD_{-2} \times CD_{-3} \times CD_{-4})^{0.25}$
CND	consumers' expenditure on non-durable goods and services (real)
CNDD	$(CND_{-1} \times CND_{-2} \times CND_{-3} \times CND_{-4})^{0.25}$
Dxxy	dummy variable for 19*xx*, quarter *y*
D-P	hire purchase dummy used in NIESR model (similar to RMD)
KHBB	stock of mortgage loans from banks (nominal)
KHPG	stock of mortgage loans from public sector (nominal)
KHPV	stock of mortgage loans from other financial institutions (nominal)
KZJ	stock of personal sector deposits with building societies (nominal)
KZNA	stock of mortgage loans from building societies (nominal)
LM	Lagrange Multiplier
LHBB	flow of KHBB
LHPG	flow of KHPG
LHPV	flow of KHPV

LZNA	flow of KZNA
ML	LHBB + LHPG + LZNA + LHPV
NFIN	NFWJ + KZNA + KHBB + KHPG + KHPV
NFWJ	personal sector net financial wealth (nominal)
NLAJ	personal sector net liquid assets (nominal)
PC	consumers' expenditure deflator: all items (1980 = 1)
PCD	consumers' expenditure deflator: durables (1980 = 1)
PCND	consumers' expenditure deflator: non-durables (1980 = 1)
PEXP	proxy for expected rate of inflation (%)
RBLPE	RCBR + 5
RCBR	clearing banks' base rate (%)
RLA	local authority three-month rate (%)
RMD	effective minimum deposit rate on durables (%)
RNFWJ	NFWJ/PC
RNFWJD	$(\mathrm{RNFWJ}_{-1} \times \mathrm{RNFWJ}_{-2} \times \mathrm{RNFWJ}_{-3} \times \mathrm{RNFWJ}_{-4})^{0.25}$
RNLAJ	NLAJ/PC
RNLAJD	$(\mathrm{RNLAJ}_{-1} \times \mathrm{RNLAJ}_{-2} \times \mathrm{RNLAJ}_{-3} \times \mathrm{RNLAJ}_{-4})^{0.25}$
RPDI	real personal disposable income (1980 £million)
RR	$1 + (\mathrm{RCBR}/100) - (\ln \mathrm{PC}_{-1} - \ln \mathrm{PC}_{-5})$
RRL	$\Delta_2 \ln \left\{ \left[\frac{\mathrm{RLA} - \{(\mathrm{PC}/\mathrm{PC}_{-2})^2 - 1\} \times 100}{100} \right] \lambda + 1 \right\}$
YDLD	$(\mathrm{YDLH}_{-1} \times \mathrm{YDLH}_{-2} \times \mathrm{YDLH}_{-3} \times \mathrm{YDLH}_{-4})^{0.25}$
YDLH	real household disposable income (adjusted for the effects of inflation eroding the value of persons' net liquid assets stock) (1980 £million)

APPENDIX A3.1: ESTIMATES OF NET CASH WITHDRAWAL

In this appendix we give details of how estimates of net cash withdrawal (NCW) can be obtained using published data. NCW is defined as

$$\mathrm{NCW} = \mathrm{ML} - \mathrm{HI} - \mathrm{CHS} + \mathrm{SC} + \mathrm{CG}$$

where ML is the net new loans for house purchase, HI is private sector housing investment (both new dwellings and improvements), CHS is dwellings purchased from the public sector (i.e. council house sales), SC is private sector slum clearance and CG is government capital grants to the private sector for housing improvements. The sources of data are as follows: ML, *Financial Statistics*, Table 9.3 Central Statistical Office, Her Majesty's Stationery Office; HI, *Economic Trends*, *National Accounts*, Table 14 Central Statistical Office, Her Majesty's Stationery Office; CHS, *Housing Construction Statistics*, Part 2, Tables 2.12 and 2.13 Department of the Environment, Her Majesty's Stationery Office; SC *Housing Construction Statistics*, Part 2, Tables 2.2 and 2.25 Department of the Environment, Her Majesty's Stationery Office; CG, *United Kingdom National Accounts*, Table 9.4 Central Statistical Office, United Kingdom National Accounts Annual, The CSO Blue Book, Her Majesty's Stationery Office.

APPENDIX A3.2: THE AGGREGATE CONSUMERS' EXPENDITURE LONG-RUN ELASTICITY WITH RESPECT TO INCOME

We can write consumption functions for non-durables (CND) and durables (CD) as

$$\text{CND} = K_1 Y^{\alpha} \tag{A3.1}$$

$$\text{CD} = K_2 Y^{\beta} \tag{A3.2}$$

where Y is income and we would expect $\alpha < 1$ and $\beta > 1$. We next define total consumption C as the sum of its components:

$$C = \text{CND} + \text{CD} \tag{A3.3}$$

Clearly we can write the aggregate income elasticity as the sum of the individual elasticities:

$$\begin{aligned} E_{cy} &= \frac{Y}{C}\frac{\mathrm{d}C}{\mathrm{d}Y} \\ &= \frac{Y}{C}\left(\frac{\mathrm{dCND}}{\mathrm{d}Y} + \frac{\mathrm{dCD}}{\mathrm{d}Y}\right) \\ &= \frac{Y}{C}\,(K_1 \alpha Y^{\alpha-1} + K_2 \beta Y^{\beta-1}) \end{aligned} \tag{A3.4}$$

which, using A3.1 and A3.2, gives

$$E_{cy} = \frac{\alpha\text{CND} + \beta\text{CD}}{C} \tag{A3.5}$$

Our current CD equation implies that $\beta = 1.59$ (evaluated assuming that the wealth-to-income ratio is held constant) and our CND equation implies that $\alpha = 1$. Given that CD/C has averaged 8.32% between 1955 and 1986 then, on average over this period, the aggregate elasticity of C to Y implied by our model has been 1.049.

In order to ensure that the aggregate elasticity average unity over this period we can substitute the current model estimate for β in A3.5 and calculate a 'target' value of α using the mean ratio of durables to total consumption. This gives a figure of 0.946 for α which would need to be imposed on our non-durables equation.

REFERENCES

Allum, P. (1986) Consumers' expenditure on durable goods, HM Treasury Academic Panel Paper.

Attfield, C., Demery, D. and Duck, N. (1988) More surprises in the consumption function, University of Bristol Discussion Paper.

Bar-Ilan, A. and Blinder, A. (1988) The optimality of usually doing nothing, NBER Working Paper, No. 2500.

Bean, C. (1986) The estimation of 'surprise' models and the 'surprise' consumption function. *Review of Economic Studies*, **53** 407–516.

Bernanke, B. (1984) Permanent income, liquidity, and expenditure on automobiles: evidence from panel data. *Quarterly Journal of Economics*, **99** 587–614.

Bernheim, D. and Shoven, J. (1985) Pension funding and saving, *NBER Working Paper* No. 1622.

Blinder, A. and Deaton, A. (1985) The time series consumption function revisited. *Brookings Papers on Economic Activity*, **2**, 465–521.

Bollerslev, T. and Hylleberg, S. (1985) A note on the relation between consumers' expenditure and income in the United Kingdom. *Oxford Bulletin of Economics and Statistics*, 7(2), 153–170.

Borooah, V. K. and Sharpe, D. R. (1984) Aggregate consumption and the distribution of income in the United Kingdom: an econometric analysis. *Economic Journal*, **96**, 449–466.

Boskin, M. (1978) Taxation, saving, and the rate of interest. *Journal of Political Economy*, **86**, 53–527.

Boskin, M. (1987) Deficits, public debt, interest rates and private saving: perspectives and reflections on recent analyses and on US experience, in *Private Saving and Public Debt* (eds M. J. Boskin, J. S. Flemming and S. Gorini), Blackwell, Oxford.

Cuthbertson, K. (1980) The determination of expenditure on consumer durables. *National Institute Economic Review*, **94**, 62–72.

Davidson, J., Hendry, D., Srba, F. and Yeo, S. (1978) Econometric Modelling of the aggregate time-series relationship between consumers' expenditure and income in the UK. *Economic Journal*, **88**, 661–92.

Davis, E. (1982) The consumption function in macroeconomic models: a comparative study, Bank of England Technical Paper No. 1.

Davis, E. (1984) A recursive model of personal sector expenditure and accumulation, Bank of England Technical Paper No. 6.

Dicks, M. (1985) Non-durable consumption (CND), Bank of England mimeo.

Dicks, M. (1987) The financial behaviour of the UK personal sector, 1976–85. *Bank of England Quarterly Bulletin*, **27** 223–33.

Drayson, S. (1985) The housing finances market: recent growth in perspective. *Bank of England Quarterly Bulletin*, **25**, 80–91.

Easton, W. W. (1985) The importance of interest rates in five macroeconomic models, Bank of England Discussion Paper No. 24.

Edwards, A. (1984) Re-estimation of durable consumption, Bank of England mimeo.

Edwards, A. (1985) Non-durable consumption, Bank of England mimeo.

Ferber, R. (1973) Consumer Economics: a survey, *Journal of Economic Literature*, **11**, 1303–42.

Flemming, J. (1973) The consumption function when capital markets are imperfect. *Oxford Economics Papers*, **25**, 160–172.

Harnett, I. (1988) An econometric comparison of personal sector consumption in the United Kingdom and the United States, Ph.D. Thesis, Nuffield College, Oxford.

Hendry, D. F. (1983) Econometric modelling: the consumption function in retrospect. *Scottish Journal of Political Economy*, **30**(3), 193–220.

Hendry, D. F. and von Ungern-Sternberg, T. (1981) Liquidity and inflation effects on consumer expenditure, in *Essays in the Theory and Measurement of Consumer Expenditure* (ed. A. Deaton), Cambridge University Press, Cambridge.

Holmans, A. E. (1986) Flow of funds associated with house purchase for owner-occupation in the United Kingdom 1977–1984 and equity withdrawal from house purchase finance, Government Economic Service Working Paper No. 92.

Hubbard, R. G. and Judd, K. L. (1986) Liquidity constraints, fiscal policy and consumption. *Brookings Papers on Economic Activity*, **1** 1–60.

Jackman, R. and Sutton, J. (1982) Imperfect capital markets and the monetarist black box: liquidity constraints, inflation and the asymmetric effects of interest rate policy. *Economic Journal*, **92**, 103–28.

Jenkinson, N. (1985) Testing the new consumption function, Bank of England mimeo.

Mankiw, G. (1982) Hall's consumption hypothesis and durable goods. *Journal of Monetary Economics*, **10**, 417–26.

Mankiw, G. (1985) Consumer durables and the real interest rate. *Review of Economics and Statistics*, **67**, 353–62.

Muellbauer, J. and Bover, O. (1986) Liquidity constraints and aggregation in the consumption function under uncertainty, University of Oxford Applied Economics Discussion Paper No. 12.

Patterson, K. D. (1984a) Net liquid assets and net illiquid assets in the consumption function: some evidence for the UK. *Economic Letters*, **14**, 339–95.

Patterson, K. D. (1984b) Some properties of consumption functions with integral correction mechanisms. *Manchester School*, **52**, 347–62.

Patterson, K. D. (1985) Income adjustments and the role of consumers' durables in some leading consumption functions. *Economic Journal*, **94**, 237–54.

Patterson, K. D. (1988a) The aggregate consumption elasticity with respect to income, Bank of England mimeo.

Patterson, K. D. (1988b) Modelling consumption and asset decisions, Bank of England mimeo.

Patterson, K. D., Harnett, I., Robinson, G. and Ryding, J. (1987) The Bank of England quarterly model of the UK economy. *Economic Modelling*, **4**, 398–629.

Pissarides, C. A. (1978) Liquidity constraints in the theory of consumption. *Quarterly Journal of Economics*, **82**, 279–96.

Sargan, D. (1964) Wages and prices in the UK: a study in econometric methodology, in *Econometric Analysis for National Economic Planning* (eds P. Hart, G. Mills and J. Whittaker), Colston Paper No. 16, Colston Research Society, London.

Stiglitz, J. E. and Weiss, A. (1981) Credit rationing in markets with imperfect competition. *American Economic Review*, **71**, 393–410.

Stiglitz, J. E. and Weiss, A. (1987) Macro-economic equilibrium and credit rationing, NBER Working Paper No. 2164.

Summers, L (1982) Tax policy, the rate of return and savings, NBER Working Paper No. 995.

Summers, L. (1984) The after tax rate of return affects private savings, NBER Working Paper No. 1351.

Townend, J. (1976) The personal saving ratio. *Bank of England Quarterly Bulletin*, **16**, 53–73.

Wilcox, J. (1985) A model of the building society sector, Bank of England Discussion Paper No. 23.

Zeldes, S. (1985) Consumption and liquidity constraints: an empirical investigation, Wharton School Working Paper.

4

Measuring the risk of financial institutions' portfolios: some suggestions for alternative techniques using stock prices

S. G. HALL AND D. K. MILES

4.1 INTRODUCTION

Financial intermediaries in many countries are subject to special forms of regulation over the structure of their balance sheets. In the UK regulation of banks has involved the supervisor, the Bank of England, issuing guidelines on the adequacy of capital funds and on the risks of large and connected exposures to particular borrowers. The Financial Services Act has resulted in new forms of regulation for a wide range of non-bank financial intermediaries. Analysis of the risks of portfolios held by market-makers, securities dealers and other intermediaries who take open positions will form a key part of the job of the new teams of regulators. Draft guidelines on minimum levels of capital, or maximum leverage, are already being produced by these new regulatory bodies.

Non-financial corporations are not subject to these types of regulation. This raises the question as to what is special about financial firms. There is a large and rapidly growing literature on this topic. (See Chant (1987), Goodhart (1987) and Marquand (1987) for good reviews of the issues involved.) What is often argued is that information problems and externalities, whilst not unique to the financial sector, are sufficiently more serious there to warrant special supervision. Many of the information problems arise from the difficulty which individual customers of a financial institution may have in evaluating the risk involved in a transaction. This can give rise to incentives for financial intermediaries to take more risks than customers would choose. It has long been argued that such information problems also create an environment in which bank runs may occur (but for a counter view see Kaufman (1987)).

The externalities argument starts from the observation that financial institutions are heavily interlinked. The failure of one institution will have repercussions for other institutions. Whilst this is no less true for non-financial institutions, a common argument is that such interdependences are particularly important in financial markets and that the default of one institution—even if it did not *directly* affect a large part of the financial system—might, by undermining confidence, come to trigger a system-wide problem. This contagious undermining of confidence is really dependent upon the existence of information problems and so the externalities and information problems are rather hard to isolate.

There is much academic debate about both the scale and importance of these, supposedly unusual, features of financial markets and about the appropriate response to them. However, the significance of forms of market failure has appeared sufficient for governments over much of the world to construct special regulatory systems for financial intermediaries. What these systems have in common is an analysis of the riskiness of financial institutions. In particular great attention has been paid to the adequacy of financial institutions' own capital funds in reducing default probabilities to acceptably low levels. The recent proposals on the convergence of bank regulation across the major economies, for example, represent a detailed scheme for relating adequate capital to the riskiness of institutions' asset portfolios (Bank for International Settlements, 1987; Bank of England, 1988).

Indeed, an analysis of the risk of institutions' portfolios is crucial to the current system of supervision of financial intermediaries. In this chapter we discuss some of the formidable problems with conventional methods for measuring portfolio risk and suggest some new techniques. We begin in section 4.2 by considering the relation between risk, leverage and defaults. The problems in empirically measuring risk are discussed, and a method for estimating default probabilities is presented in section 4.3. Results from applying this technique to the risk faced by large UK banks are presented in section 4.4. Extensions to the basic model are considered in sections 4.5 and 4.6. A summary and conclusion are offered in section 4.7.

4.2 RISK LEVERAGE AND DEFAULTS

Financial intermediaries' capital represents funds available to absorb losses on the balance sheet. Since the regulator's main aim is to monitor the risks of insolvency, it is natural that the adequacy of capital should be the prime focus of attention. Adequacy can only be judged relative to the volatility of the value of an institution's assets and liabilities. It is for this reason that a massive amount of effort has gone into measuring the risks of losses on intermediaries' portfolios. (Much of the work done in this difficult area has addressed the volatility of the price of, or the returns on, institutions' assets.) However, estimating the risk of the value of assets and liabilities is difficult. There are three particularly hard problems to face in analysing the risk on portfolios:

1. The number of different classes of assets and liabilities is large and is changing.
2. Many balance sheet items do not have market prices, and so analysis of the volatility of the value of such items is particularly hard.
3. The variability of asset returns is likely to change, often dramatically, over time.

The first problem is particularly difficult. Suppose that we can aggregate assets and liabilities held by an institution into J classes. Let the prices of the assets and liabilities be denoted by P_j ($j = 1, 2, \ldots, J$). The value of capital can be written as

$$K = \sum_{j=1}^{J} P_j X_j$$

where X_j is the amount of the jth asset or liability held; X_j is negative for liabilities and positive for assets. The variance of the value of the portfolio—the variance of the capital—is then

$$\sum_{j=1}^{J} \sigma_{p}^{2} X_j^2 + \sum_{\substack{j=1 \\ j \neq k}}^{J} \sum_{k=1}^{J} \sigma_{P_j p_k} X_j X_k$$

where σ_j^2 is the variance of the jth asset, or liability, price and $\sigma_{p_j p_k}$ is the covariance of prices between the jth and kth items on the balance sheet.

If there are as few as 10 classes of asset and liability there are 55 variances and covariances to calculate (10 variances and 45 covariances). The number of variances and covariances goes up roughly in line with the square of J; the number is $J(J + 1)/2$. Because of the scale of the problem the empirical analysis of the variance of the value of capital, which under certain assumptions is a highly informative measure of volatility,[1] has usually proceeded by focusing on the individual variances of a small class of broadly defined balance sheet items. Covariances are often ignored. Furthermore, analysis of the variability is sometimes only carried out on the asset side of the balance sheet. A ranking of the variability of asset prices is then produced, from which a set of weights is defined to calculate minimum acceptable levels of capital.

In the UK much work both within the Bank of England (on the volatility of banks' and securities dealers' portfolios) and outside the Bank by The

[1] If asset prices are normally distributed about their expected values the variance is a complete measure of risk.

Securities Association (TSA) and the Securities and Investment Board (SIB) has been performed along these lines. Charts showing the variances of various asset prices have been produced to inform the capital adequacy debates. One feature of these charts is the frequent dependence of the measures of volatility on the time period used for the calculation. This presents a particularly tough problem for the regulator.

One way around the three problems associated with measuring volatility noted above is to use the market's valuation of an institution's balance sheet to infer its expectations of the volatility of the value of the underlying portfolio of assets and liabilities. For example, several US studies use the price of the stock of regulated banks to measure the value of the insurance provided by Federal deposit guarantees, which in turn is related to their risk of default (Marcus and Shaked, 1984; Ronn and Verma, 1986; Pennachi 1987). These authors use the insight that the value of deposit insurance can be related to the price of a hypothetical put option offered by the insurer; the measurement of the changing volatilities of the value of bank assets is not their primary concern. Our aim here, rather than to measure the value of the explicit and implicit insurance offered by regulation, is to devise techniques to measure these time-dependent volatilities and to use share prices to do so.

Of course we cannot get something for nothing and the crucial assumption upon which the approach of using share price data to measure risk rests is that the market is efficient at evaluating companies. In the light of the stock market crash of October 1987 we have to be sceptical about the validity of such an assumption. However, provided that we do make the market efficiency assumption, we can proceed by making a further, but far less controversial, assumption that the valuation of a company depends in part upon the perceived risk associated with the company's balance sheet and upon an evaluation of the price of risk, i.e. the compensation that the market requires to accept an increase in risk.

4.3 MEASURING RISK USING STOCK PRICES

We begin by assuming that the market values an institution efficiently. If we denote an institution's share price at time t as Q_t this implies

$$Q_t = \sum_{j=1}^{J} \frac{P_{jt}X_{jt}}{N} \tag{4.1}$$

where N is the number of shares (assumed constant) and ΣP_jX_j is the market value of the assets and liabilities, as above. Since for many institutions there will be items on the balance sheet which do not have market prices there will not usually be a means of testing the validity of 4.1. However, assuming the validity of Equation 4.1 will allow us implicitly to value balance sheet items for which secondary market prices do not exist.

Basically the idea behind the proposed technique is that if Equation 4.1 holds and if we can model how the market assesses the expected value of a financial intermediary, we can use the variability in actual market valuations around their expected values to estimate the market's perceptions of the volatility of the institution's underlying portfolio. To implement the technique requires some theory about how share prices are determined.

The most widely used theory of how equilibrium prices of assets evolve is the capital asset pricing model (CAPM) originally developed almost 30 years ago (Sharpe, 1964; Lintner, 1965; Markowitz, 1952). According to this theory the return on an asset, in our case a share of the financial institution, depends on the safe rate of interest and the expected or perceived risk of the asset. In periods when no dividends are paid the return on a share in an institution is just the capital gain. Thus, we can write

$$\frac{E(Q_t - Q_{t-1})}{Q_{t-1}} = R_{st} + \mathrm{rp}_t \tag{4.2}$$

where R_s is the safe rate of return over one period (e.g. a Treasury bill yield) measured at the beginning of the period, rp_t is the risk premium at time t and E is the expectations operator. Expectations are formed at the end of $t - 1$ when it is assumed that R_{st} is known. We shall initially draw no distinction between true mathematical expectations and the market's expectations. Thus, implicit in our definition of market efficiency is the assumption of rational expectations.

The risk premium can be expressed as the price of risk multiplied by the perceived amount of risk for which compensation is required. The price of risk, denoted λ_t, is dependent on the preferences of shareholders. The amount of risk needs to be carefully defined. In stock market equilibrium only certain types of risk are costly. 'Costly risk' is the risk in the return on the institution's shares for which the shareholders will require compensation. This is often referred to as the non-diversifiable risk. The CAPM has the implication that this measure of risk, which is *not* the same as risk from a regulatory perspective, is that part of the conditional variability in the institution's share price which is correlated with the return on an efficiently diversified market portfolio. (We return to this point below.) Denoting the expected non-diversifiable risk as $E(\mathrm{ND})_t$ we therefore have

$$\mathrm{rp}_t = \lambda_t E(\mathrm{ND})_t$$

If, on the whole, the market gets it right, the actual return on the institution's shares between $t - 1$ and t will equal the expected return, given by Equation 4.2, plus some random mistake which is on average zero. Denoting this mistake e_t we now have

$$\frac{Q_t - Q_{t-1}}{Q_{t-1}} = R_{st} + \lambda_t E(\mathrm{ND})_t + e_t \tag{4.3}$$

The value of capital at time t is, by Equation 4.1, Q_tN. Therefore at the end of period $t - 1$, when Q_{t-1} can be observed, the expected value of capital at time t can be derived by rearranging 4.2 to give

$$E(Q_tN) = Q_{t-1}N\{1 + R_{st} + \lambda_t E(\mathrm{ND}_t)\} \tag{4.4}$$

The variability of Q_tN about its expected, or average, value depends on e_t since, by 4.3, we have

$$Q_tN = Q_{t-1}N\{1 + R_{st} + \lambda_t E(\mathrm{ND}_t) + e_t\} \tag{4.5}$$

Thus

$$Q_tN - E(Q_tN) = Q_{t-1}Ne_t \tag{4.6}$$

Equation 4.6 is the one-step-ahead forecast error made by the market on the assumption that the CAPM is used to predict prices. By assumption the CAPM is the true model of share prices, and so Equation 4.6 gives rational expectation forecast errors.

Now we can immediately write down the conditional variance, as measured at $t - 1$, of the value of capital at time t, i.e. $E\{[Q_tN - E(Q_tN]^2\}$. This is $(Q_{t-1}N)^2\sigma_{e_t}^2$ where $\sigma_{e_t}^2$ is the variance of e at time t. This is a variability measure relevant to a regulator. It is the variability in the market value of the capital funds around the market's expected value. *If* the assumption of market efficiency is valid, this simple measure will be equal to the sums of the variances and covariances of the individual balance sheet items given earlier. This is because the conditional variance of the financial institution's portfolio can be expressed in terms of the conditional variability and covariability of individual assets and liabilities or, more directly, in terms of the conditional variance of the value of the total portfolio. Assuming stock market efficiency, we can estimate the conditional variance of the value of the total portfolio by estimating the differences between the expected value of the market valuation and the actual market value over time. Strong market efficiency implies that actual stock market valuations equal the value of the underlying portfolio. The conditional variance of market valuations around their expected values, i.e. $(Q_{t-1}N)^2\sigma_{e_t}^2)$, is therefore equal to the conditional variance of the underlying portfolio. This is the beauty of the technique. If a measure of $\sigma_{e_t}^2$ can be derived, and if e_t is approximately normally distributed, a natural measure of the adequacy of capital then suggests itself:

$$\frac{Q_{t-1}N}{(Q_{t-1}N)\sigma_{e_t}} = \frac{1}{\sigma_{e_t}}$$

This expression[2] shows the number of standard deviations that the value of

[2]Strictly speaking, the expression should also take account of the expected return over the period. This is not, in practice, significant over short periods since *expected* returns over short periods are small.

capital represents at time $t - 1$. When capital is exhausted the institution is insolvent. Therefore if $1/\sigma_{e_t}$ were around 3 the probability of bankruptcy by end t would be around 1 in 1000. It is because of the potential for harmful and widespread knock-on effects from the bankruptcy of one financial organization that regulators want to be able to measure this probability.

We now outline a method for estimating σ_{e_t}. Under the CAPM we can rewrite Equation 4.2 as

$$\frac{E(Q_t - Q_{t-1})}{Q_{t-1}} = R_{st} + \beta_t E(\mathrm{RM}_t - R_{st}) \tag{4.7}$$

where RM_t is the return on an efficient market portfolio and β_t is the expected conditional covariance between the returns on the institution's share and on the market portfolio divided by the expected conditional variance $\sigma^2\mathrm{RM}_t$ of the return on the market portfolio. β_t is the 'beta' as usually defined in the theory of finance. (We could think of the return on the market portfolio RM_t as being, for example, the return from holding a value-weighted market index like the FT 500.) Now the CAPM also predicts that the expected return on the market portfolio depends on its risk. This risk is its variance since, by definition, no variability on the return from the efficient market portfolio is diversifiable. Therefore the costly, or non-diversifiable, risk of the market portfolio is just its variance. Thus

$$E(\mathrm{RM}_t) = R_{st} + \lambda_t E(\sigma^2\mathrm{RM}_t) \tag{4.8}$$

where

$$\lambda_t = \frac{E(\mathrm{RM}_t - R_{st})}{E(\sigma^2\mathrm{RM}_t)}$$

and $\sigma^2\mathrm{RM}_t$ is the variance of the returns on the market portfolio. λ_t is the price of risk, i.e. the required excess in the return on the market portfolio over the risk-free rate divided by the amount of risk.

Now, if expectations are on average correct but subject to a random error v_t, we can write 4.8 as

$$\mathrm{RM}_t = R_{st} + \lambda_t E(\sigma^2\mathrm{RM}_t) + v_t \tag{4.9}$$

and so

$$E(\sigma^2\mathrm{RM}_t) = E(v_t^2)$$

Adding the random noise term e_t to 4.7 and recalling the definition of β_t gives

$$\frac{Q_t - Q_{t-1}}{Q_{t-1}} =$$

$$R_{st} + \frac{E[\mathrm{cov}\{(Q_t - Q_{t-1})/Q_{t-1}, \mathrm{RM}_t\}]E(\mathrm{RM}_t - R_{st})}{E(v_t^2)} + e_t$$

From 4.9 $E(\mathrm{RM}_t - R_{st}) = \lambda_t E(v_t^2)$ and we also know that

$$E\left\{\mathrm{cov}\left(\frac{Q_t - Q_{t-1}}{Q_{t-1}}\right), \mathrm{RM}_t\right\} = E(v_t e_t)$$

Putting all this together we have the following two-equation system:

$$\mathrm{RM}_t = R_{st} + \lambda_t E(v_t^2) + v_t \tag{4.10}$$

$$\frac{Q_t - Q_{t-1}}{Q_{t-1}} = R_{st} + \lambda_t E(v_t e_t) + e_t \tag{4.11}$$

To estimate the unknown parameters we need to specify a process whereby expectations of variances and covariances are formed. Engle *et al.* (1987) outline just such a process and describe how the unknown parameters of the system can be estimated from observable data. Their technique draws upon the idea that the variability in the return on an asset tends to follow patterns. Mandlebrot noted as far back as 1963 that in looking at the change in asset prices 'large changes tend to be followed by large changes—of either sign—and small changes tend to be followed by small changes . . .'. If this is so an autoregressive conditional heteroscedasticity (ARCH) process can be fitted to the variances and covariances of Equations 4.10 and 4.11. The simple ARCH model suggests equations of the form

$$E(v_t^2) = \alpha_0 + \alpha_1(v_{t-1}^2) + \alpha_2(v_{t-2}^2) + \ldots \alpha_n(v_{t-n}^2) \tag{4.12}$$

$$E(v_t e_t) = \Psi_0 + \Psi_1(v_{t-1}e_{t-1}) + \Psi_2(v_{t-2}e_{t-2}) + \ldots \Psi_n(v_{t-n}e_{t-n}) \tag{4.13}$$

where $\alpha_0, \alpha_1, \ldots, \alpha_n$ and $\Psi_0, \Psi_1, \ldots, \Psi_n$ are parameters. A special case of 4.12 and 4.13 is where $\alpha_1, \alpha_2, \ldots, \alpha_n = 0$ and $\Psi_1, \Psi_2, \ldots, \Psi_n = 0$ when the variances and covariances would be constant over time. The procedure outlined by Engle *et al.* (1987) shows how to estimate all the unknown parameters of the system simultaneously by maximum likelihood methods. (To use their procedure it is much simpler if we can assume that the price of risk λ_t is constant, i.e. $\lambda_t = \lambda$ for all t. In our preliminary estimation work we have made this assumption.)[3]

A third ARCH equation for $E(e_t^2) = E(\sigma_{et}^2)$ is also estimated to give the market's perception of the total expected risk, both diversifiable and

[3]The assumption of a constant price of risk is restrictive. However, we believe that over the relatively short period used for estimation the variability in the price of risk is likely to be small relative to the changes in both the perceived risk of holding shares and the safe rate of interest. The price of risk is a 'deep parameter' in the sense that it depends upon the preferences of individual shareholders; a usual assumption in economics is that parameters of utility functions are unchanging. Changes in the distribution of wealth allied with variability in attitudes to risk across individuals would, of course, be sufficient to cause variability in the market price of risk.

non-diversifiable, of the institution's portfolio in period t as perceived at $t - 1$. This equation is

$$E(e_t^2) = \delta_0 + \delta_1(e_{t-1}^2) + \delta_2(e_{t-2}^2) + \ldots + \delta_n(e_{t-n}^2) \qquad (4.14)$$

$E(e_t^2)$ is the key variable for determining the risk of the financial institution's portfolio. Notice that $E(e_t^2)$ does not enter into the equation for the return on the institution's share; it is only the non-diversifiable element of the total share price volatility which is relevant in defining equilibrium returns. However, for the supervisor of the financial institutions it is the risk of default which is crucial. This depends on the *total risk* of the institution's portfolio regardless of whether, from the shareholders' point of view, much of this risk may be diversifiable; shareholders and regulators of financial institutions do not have common interests. However, both the market and the regulator are concerned about the volatility in the value of the financial institutions' portfolios. Indeed our technique depends crucially upon this being so. What is important to note is that the relevant type of volatility is not the same for regulators and shareholders.

What the estimation technique rests upon is the simple idea that if the random or unexpected element in the return on an asset rises in one period this increases the perceived risky or random element in the near future. It takes a period of less volatile returns to bring people's perceptions of underlying volatility back down. This is an intuitively plausible idea and probably accords well with post-crash events since it seems almost certain that people's ideas of the riskiness of stocks has increased dramatically compared with pre-crash.

What the technique outlined does allow us to do is to calculate $E(\sigma_{e_t}^2)$, i.e. to derive a measure of the market's perception of the variance of the value of capital and to model how it changes over time. This itself is potentially highly informative, especially if changes in $\sigma_{e_t}^2$ can be linked to changes in the structure of the balance sheet. Indeed, the ARCH model provides a natural way of testing hypotheses about precisely how changes in balance sheet structure, or in regulation or macroeconomic policy, influence the perceived volatility of the value of financial intermediaries' capital. We now describe preliminary results on the volatility of the value of the four big UK banks.

4.4 RESULTS

Monthly data on the share prices of Barclays, Midland, National Westminster and Lloyds over the period 1975.6–1987.9 were used to define one-month rates of return. Adjustments were made for ex dividend days using reported per share dividend payments. We used the (value-weighted) FT 500 index to construct a proxy for the return on the market index RM_t.

The one-month Treasury bill rate was used for the safe rate R_{st}. The most general version of the five-equation system which we estimate can be written

$$\text{RM}_t = a_0 + a_1 R_{st} + a_2 E(v_t^2) + v_t \tag{4.15}$$

$$\frac{Q_t - Q_{t-1}}{Q_{t-1}} = b_0 + b_1 R_{st} + b_2 E(v_t e_t) + e_t \tag{4.16}$$

$$E(v_t^2) = \alpha_0 + \alpha_1(v_{t-1}^2) + \alpha_2(v_{t-2}^2) + \ldots + \alpha_n(v_{t-n}^2) \tag{4.17}$$

$$E(v_t e_t) = \Psi_0 + \Psi_1(v_{t-1}e_{t-1}) + \ldots + \Psi_n(v_{t-n}e_{t-n}) \tag{4.18}$$

$$E(e_t^2) = \delta_0 + \delta_1(e_{t-1}^2) + \ldots + \delta_n(e_{t-n}^2) \tag{4.19}$$

where a_i, b_i, α_i, Ψ_i and δ_i ($i = 0, 1, 2, \ldots$) are coefficients to be estimated.

Comparing 4.15 and 4.16 with 4.10 and 4.11, and assuming λ_t is constant, gives the following restrictions implied by the CAPM:

(a) $a_0 = b_0 = 0$
(b) $a_1 = b_1 = 1$
(c) $a_2 = b_2$ (>0)

Further restrictions are as follows:

(d) $E(e_t^2)$ should not help explain $(Q_t - Q_{t-1})/Q_{t-1}$.
(e) Expected variances (or covariances) only, and no other expected moments, are sufficient measures of risk for which compensation is required.
(f) The errors e_t, v_t are normally distributed (an assumption needed to justify both the CAPM and the estimation technique) and serially uncorrelated.

We tested each of these assumptions by relaxing, in turn, the restrictions implicit in Equations 4.10 and 4.11, i.e. we take as our null the case where $a_0 = b_0 = 0$, $a_1 = b_1 = 1$ and $a_2 = b_2$ and test the restrictions (a)–(e) in turn. We also test for non-normality and serial independence of errors—condition (f). For all specifications we initially use a much restricted version of the general forms of the ARCH processes 4.17–4.19. We restrict the order of the highest lag in the ARCH equations to be 8 and impose a linearly declining pattern on the coefficients. Thus our estimated version of 4.17 is

$$v_t^2 = \hat{\alpha}_0 + \hat{\alpha}_1 \left\{ \sum_{i=1}^{8} c_i(v_{t-i}^2) \right\} + \text{error} \tag{4.20}$$

where

$$c_i = \frac{9 - i}{36}$$

i:	1	2	3	4	5	6	7	8
c_i:	0.22	0.19	0.17	0.14	0.11	0.08	0.06	0.03

This restricted version of the ARCH process is similar to that used by Engle *et al.* (1987) who argue that a parsimonious specification generally proves to be statistically acceptable and is more likely to be economically sensible. They found that unrestricted versions often threw up some negative parameters, and in their application the likelihood of the unrestricted versions was ill behaved.

The test of the significance of the ARCH element of the conditional variances/covariances is simply a test of the significance of $\hat{\alpha}_1$ in 4.20. In our preliminary regressions we have also restricted the coefficients on the weighted averages of past variances and covariances for the three ARCH equations for a particular bank to be equal. We denote the common parameter $\hat{\alpha}_1$; it is the weight given to past forecast errors in estimating the future variability of asset returns. Thus, we estimate four parameters for each bank: the price of risk $\hat{\lambda}$; the weight $\hat{\alpha}_1$ given to past variances (covariances) in estimating future variances (covariances); two constants for the ARCH processes denoted $\hat{\alpha}_0$, for the market variances v_t^2, and $\hat{\delta}_0$, for the bank specific variances e_t^2.

Table 4.1 shows the results from the restricted equations. Table 4.2 shows the tests of the restrictions. The price of risk is consistently estimated as being significantly positive, the hypothesis of time-varying variances and covariances is strongly confirmed (all estimates of $\hat{\alpha}_1$ are highly significant), errors on individual bank returns do not appear to deviate from being normally distributed and serial correlation does not seem significant. Tests of only up to eighth-order serial correlation are shown in Table 4.2. Tests of up to first- and fourth-order serial correlation showed no sign of mis-specification. Tests of the other strong CAPM restrictions give mixed results. In general the hypothesis that it is only the variances of market returns that matter is not rejected. However, there are signs that conditional variances do add information in predicting returns on individual assets;

Table 4.1 Results of the restricted equations

	$\hat{\lambda}$	$\hat{\alpha}_1$	$\hat{\alpha}_0$	$\hat{\delta}_0$	*Log likelihood*
Midland	2.225	1.748	$2.5(10^{-7})$	$9(10^{-10})$	−1.969
	(3.1)	(33.3)	(0)	(0)	
Barclays	2.174	1.096	0.254	0.100	24.564
	(2.8)	(20.5)	(8.8)	(12.9)	
NatWest	4.219	0.693	0.527	0.139	5.220
	(4.5)	(16.7)	(17.1)	(16.1)	
Lloyds	1.723	0.810	0.520	0.153	−48.477
	(1.9)	(15.1)	(12.0)	(11.7)	

Estimation period, 1976.2–1987.8; number of observations, 139. The t statistics are given in parentheses.

Table 4.2 Tests of restrictions of the CAPM models

	L_1	L_2	L_3	L_4	L_5	L_6	L_7
Midland	23.67	4.46	4.55	26.81	0.82	1.21	7.82
Barclays	0.66	10.80	5.90	0.03	0.80	1.39	8.50
NatWest	18.40	14.32	10.40	9.66	15.68	1.41	8.43
Lloyds	12.19	8.69	1.12	4.65	3.07	1.50	8.85

L_1, likelihood ratio test of no constants in CAPM equations.
L_2, likelihood ratio test that coefficients on safe rate equal unity.
L_3, likelihood ratio test of equality of price of risk coefficients in market return and individual bank return.
L_4, likelihood ratio test that $E(e_t^2)$ is irrelevant in predicting return on bank share—a test that the expected covariance, and not the expected variance, of the bank return is relevant.
L_5, likelihood ratio test that the expected conditional variance of the market return, and not other moments, is relevant in predicting the market return. This is a test that $y = 1$ where $E(v_t^2)^y$ is entered as an explanatory variable for RM_t.
L_6, test of normality of errors on bank return (e_t); this is the Bera and Jarque normality test.
L_7, Box–Pierce test for up to eighth-order serial correlation of bank return errors.

L_1, L_2, L_6 are distributed χ_2^2 under null: 95% critical value, 6.00; 97.5% critical value, 7.38.
L_3, L_4, L_5 are distributed χ_1^2 under null: 95% critical value, 3.84; 97.5% critical value, 5.02.
L_7 is distributed χ_8^2 under null: 95% critical value, 15.51; 97.5% critical value, 17.53.

conditional covariances with the market return would appear not to be a sufficient statistic for risk. In three out of four cases the restriction of no constants in the equations is rejected. This may reflect mismeasurement of the safe rate of return. In one case, NatWest, the hypothesis of a common price of risk for the market and bank returns—a crucial restriction—is clearly rejected; for the other banks the restriction cannot be clearly rejected.

4.5 EXTENSIONS: A GARCH SPECIFICATION

There are two potentially serious problems with the specifications of the CAPM models discussed above. First, we have severely restricted the form of the ARCH equations for expected variances and covariances. Only eight lags of squares and cross-products of residuals are used in updating the variance–covariance matrix of returns. This almost inevitably leads to implausibly high variability in estimated market betas. Second, we have not imposed a common price of risk across the models estimated for the four banks. The price of risk is a market variable and should be common across all assets.

The first problem, restricting the memory of agents in forecasting asset volatility, can be handled by making today's expected variances and covariances depend on yesterday's expectations. This gives a generalized ARCH (or GARCH) process[4] of the form

$$E(v_t^2) = \alpha_1 E(v_{t-1}^2) + \alpha_2 v_{t-1}^2 \tag{4.21}$$

Unravelling 4.21 shows that the expected variance at time t depends on the complete history of past residuals with declining weights placed on past squares and cross-products of errors. The equation has a natural interpretation in terms of Bayesian updating. At the end of each period the variance forecast is updated in the light of the *ex post* variability of the asset return within that period. The weight attached to the news is α_2. If no weight is attached to news α_2 is zero and the expected conditional variance is a constant. Clearly for 4.21 to make sense we require $\alpha_1, \alpha_2 \geq 0$.

We re-estimated the CAPM models of share prices using this GARCH specification. We restricted the coefficients α_1 and α_2 (from Equation 4.21) to be common for the variances and covariances of different assets. That is, we assume that the market attaches the same relative weights to past random forecast errors (v_{t-j} and e_{t-j}, $j = 1, ,2, \ldots$) in forming expectations of current conditional variances and covariances across all assets. This restrictive assumption makes the highly non-linear estimation far simpler. There is also some plausibility in the idea that individuals adopt similar forecasting rules for what are similar forecasting problems.

We also imposed the equality of the price of risk across all assets. This gives a very tightly parameterized version of the CAPM model with only three unknown parameters: the price of risk $\hat{\lambda}$ and the parameters $\hat{\alpha}_1$ and $\hat{\alpha}_2$ from the updating equations for conditional variances and covariances (see 4.21). The results from estimating the five-equation model (four banks and the market rate) are shown in Table 4.3.

Table 4.3 Results from estimating the five-equation model

$\hat{\lambda}$	$\hat{\alpha}_1$		$\hat{\alpha}_2$		*Log likelihood*
2.287	0.89		0.20		−86.503
(3.74)	(134.1)		(11.9)		
	L_1	L_2	L_3	L_4	
Market returns	1.48	3.47	4.95	17.45	
Midland Bank	2.01	5.79	6.03	7.44	
Barclays	2.75	4.22	5.48	8.78	
NatWest	22.21	6.78	8.23	11.88	
Lloys Bank	10.46	0.35	2.89	8.15	

L_1, Bera–Jarque test statistic for normality of errors: $\sim\chi^2$ under null.
L_2, Box–Pierce test for up to first-order serial correlation of errors: $\sim\chi_1^2$ under null.
L_3, Box–Pierce test for up to fourth-order serial correlation of errors: $\sim\chi_4^2$ under null.
L_4, Box–Pierce test for up to eighth-order serial correlation of errors: $\sim\chi_8^2$ under null.

[4]The GARCH specification was first analysed by Bollerslev (1986).

The three parameters are highly significant, each with the expected sign. The coefficient $\hat{\alpha}_2$ on news is far enough from zero to reject strongly the hypothesis of constant variances and covariances. The price of risk is very close to the average of the prices shown in Table 4.1. The estimate of just over 2 is also close to the average of several US studies (see, in particular, Merton (1980) and the references cited therein). The relatively high value of $\hat{\alpha}_1$ implies that a significant weight is given to past residuals even beyond 12 periods. The mean lag in the conditional variance–covariance equation is 10 months. This gives a correspondingly smoother path for risk measures.

There now appear some signs of serial correlation with the GARCH specification. For each of the four banks there is some evidence of negative first-order serial correlation in residuals. There are still no signs of higher-order correlation for the banks and no indication of error correlation at any order for the market returns. There now also appears some evidence of non-normality in the distribution of residuals. This is not surprising given the finding of Bollerslev and Engle that estimation of the GARCH specification often produces residuals apparently following distributions with fat tails. (See Bollerslev (1985) and Bollerslev and Engle (1986) where results are reported from the estimation of single-equation GARCH models, assuming that residuals follow Student's t distribution. In a multi-equation system, maximum likelihood estimation of a GARCH in mean process with errors following Student's t distribution is more difficult.)

Figures 4.1–4.4 show time series for each bank of $1/\{E(\sigma^2_{e_t})\}^{1/2} = 1/\{E(e^2_t)\}^{1/2}$. These measures are generated using the parameters of the expectation formation mechanisms for variances and covariances reported in Table 4.3. As we noted above the measures show the number of standard deviations that the value of capital represents for each bank at each period. Alternatively, the measures show the number of standard deviations away from its expected value that the value of the bank's portfolio would need to be to result in insolvency. This is a natural measure of bankruptcy risk.

The figures reveal that our measure of the one-period-ahead chances of insolvency are minute. Even allowing for the possibility that residuals come from a distribution with fatter tails than a normal distribution, the probability of being seven standard deviations below the expected return is infinitesimal. However, probabilities of insolvency over time periods further than one month into the future will increase significantly and could be calculated using the GARCH equations to forecast $E(e^2_{t+j})$ dynamically for $j > 1$. Given the size of $\hat{\alpha}_1$ and $\hat{\alpha}_2$ and the fact that the probability of insolvency over, say, a 5 year horizon depends on the chances of perhaps only one of 60 monthly residuals being very strongly negative, the odds of bankruptcy can quickly become significant.

Figures 4.1–4.4 are best seen as indicative of trends in risk; they suggest that there has been significant variation in risk over the past decade.

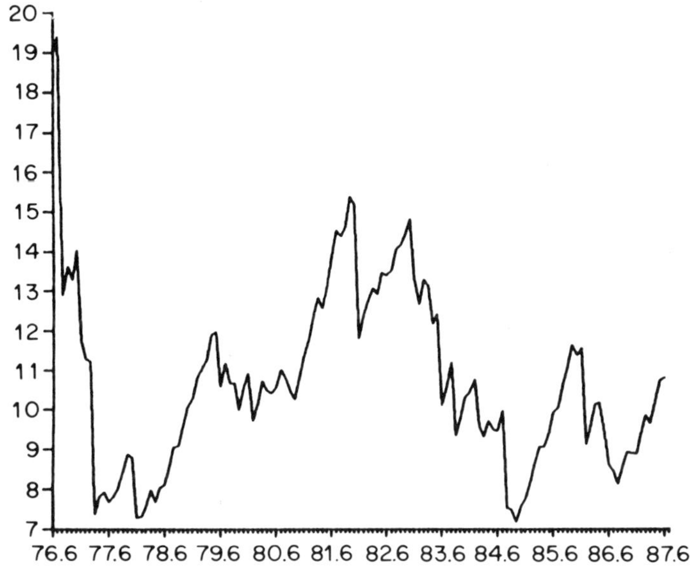

Fig. 4.1 Midland 1/SE.

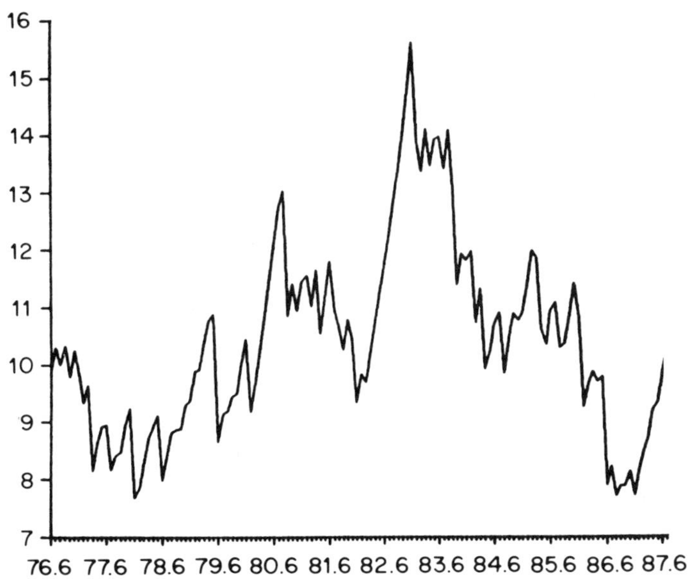

Fig. 4.2 Barclays 1/SE.

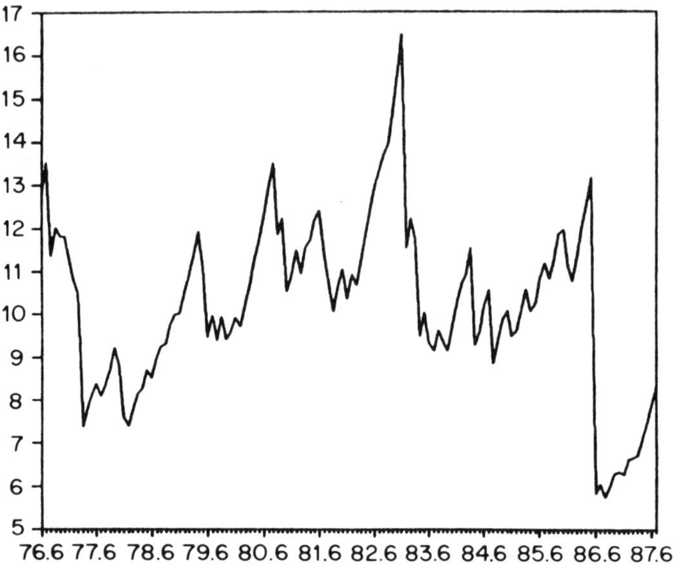

Fig. 4.3 Natwest 1/SE.

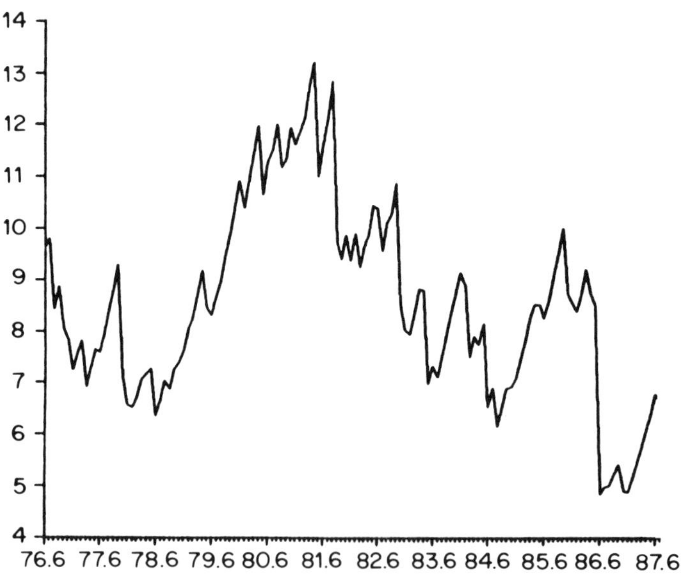

Fig. 4.4 Lloyds 1/SE.

Around 1978 and mid-1986 would appear to have been relatively risky periods for banks.

4.6 RELAXING THE RESTRICTIONS OF MARKET EFFICIENCY

A crucial assumption underlying the derivation of our meaures of the volatility of the value of financial institution's portfolios was that at each point in time the stock market value of the institution equals the market value of its portfolio of assets and liabilities.

Can this restriction be eased? Suppose that the market only gets the valuation right on average; it makes random errors. We can then replace 4.1 with the less restrictive equation

$$NQ_t = \sum P_{ij}X_{jt} + w_t \tag{4.22}$$

where $E(w_t) = 0$. We shall call w_t 'stock market noise'. It follows that

$$E(NQ_t) = E\left(\sum P_{jt}X_{jt}\right)$$

and

$$NQ_t - E(NQ_t) = \sum P_{jt}X_{jt} - E\left(\sum P_{jt}X_{jt}\right) + w_t$$

Therefore

$$E\{NQ_t - E(NQ_t)\}^2 = E(\sigma^2_{\Sigma P_{jt}X_{jt}}) + E(w_t^2) + 2E\left\{\text{cov}\left(\sum P_{jt}X_{jt}, w_t\right)\right\} \tag{4.23}$$

where

$$\sigma^2_{\Sigma P_{jt}X_{jt}} = \left\{\sum P_{jt}X_{jt} - E\left(\sum P_{jt}X_{jt}\right)\right\}^2$$

and cov $(\Sigma P_{jt}X_{jt}, w_t)$ is the covariance between the market's one-step-ahead forecast error in predicting the value of the portfolio and the stock market noise in period t. It is hard to predict what values this covariance might typically have. We assume that it is greater than or equal to zero. Using the CAPM with the ARCH processes we derived an estimate of $E(\sigma^2_{e_t})$ where

$$E(\sigma^2_{e_t}) = \frac{E\{NQ_t - E(NQ_t)\}^2}{(Q_{t-1}N)^2} \tag{4.24}$$

By 4.24, and assuming a non-negative value for the covariance term, this estimate represents an upper bound on the market's perception of the risk of the financial institution's portfolio of assets and liabilities. Thus the value of our proxy for the market's estimate of the risk of an institution's portfolio may still be informative even if the stock market does not exactly price the value of that portfolio. However, the greater is 'stock market noise' the less informative is our measure.

A second aspect of our strong definition of market efficiency is that market expectations are rational expectations. A less strict condition is

$$E_{\mathrm{mkt}}(Q_t N) = E(Q_t N) + z \tag{4.25}$$

where z is a random variable which is on average zero. In this case market expectations $E_{\mathrm{mkt}}(Q_t N)$ of market values are equal to true mathematical expectations plus noise. Plugging 4.25 into earlier formulae, and assuming once again that $Q_t N = \Sigma P_{jt} X_{jt}$, gives a condition analogous to 4.22:

$$\begin{aligned} E\{NQ_t - E_{\mathrm{mkt}}(NQ_t)\}^2 &= E\left(\sigma^2 \sum P_{jt} X_{jt}\right) + E(z^2) \\ &\quad - 2E\left\{\mathrm{cov}\left(z, \sum P_{jt} X_{jt}\right)\right\} \end{aligned} \tag{4.26}$$

Once again, if the expectations noise z is not too great, nor too variable, the derived measure is informative. On the assumption that the covariance term in 4.26 is greater than or equal to zero, the measure represents an upper bound on the true volatility of the financial institution's underlying portfolio.

4.7 SUMMARY AND CONCLUSION

What we have tried to do is to use information on stock market valuations of financial institutions to derive measures of the riskiness, or volatility, of the value of the firms' portfolios of assets and liabilities. If one is very sceptical about the market's ability to evaluate institutions' portfolios, then the derived measures might be viewed as revealing something about market perceptions but as having little to do with fundamental risk. At the other extreme is the (Hayekian) view that markets are supremely efficient at aggregating and conveying information and that market perceptions of risk are the best measures available. Either way the derived measures are, we believe, of interest. What the measures we obtained suggest is as follows.

1. Perceptions of the risk of the four UK banks have changed significantly over time.
2. The relation between the risks of a particular bank and the risks of investing more generally in the stock market (summarized by a bank's beta) is, on the whole, close—betas have a mean of around unity. Given

the size and diversified nature of the big banks' balance sheets this is not surprising; unexpected events that cause the market to change its view on the economic prospects of the UK are likely to have a significant impact upon bank valuations. At some periods the correlations between general UK risk (as measured by the risk on the market index) and the risk of banks is low however. For example, there could be shocks to sectors of the economy which are not significantly indebted to banks but which have a high weight in the FT 500 index.

3. Although there is significant variation in the perceived chances of insolvency for banks over time those chances, proxied by $1/E(\sigma)$ in the Figures, have always been seen as extremely small, at least over a one-month horizon.

What it would be interesting to consider is the determinants of bank (or other financial intermediary) risk. We aim to address this issue in future work by trying to explain the evolution of our measure of insolvency risk in terms of, for example, balance sheet structure, the level of capital or regulatory innovations. We also aim to analyse the riskiness of other institutions such as securities dealers and to assess how robust results are to different assumptions about how variances and covariances might evolve (e.g. ARCH versus GARCH). Finally, we are aware that the assumption of market efficiency, in the sense in which it is used here, is so strong that any results we derive from applying our technique have to be treated with care. Our initial feeling is that the assumption that the stock market can efficiently evaluate the risk of various assets and liabilities is such that derived measures should be used as no more than a check on the estimates which are independently made of the variability of the underlying elements of financial institutions' portfolios.

REFERENCES

Bank for International Settlements (1987) Committee on Banking Regulations and Supervisory Practices Consultative Paper on Proposals for International Convergence of Capital Measurement and Capital Standards, December.

Bank of England (1988) Proposals for international convergence of capital measurement and capital standards, Banking Supervision Division Explanatory Paper, January.

Bollerslev, T. (1985) A conditionally heteroscedastic time series model for security prices and rates of return data, University of California at San Diego, Department of Economics Discussion Paper No. 85–32.

Bollerslev, T. (1986) Generalized autoregressive conditional heteroscedasticity. *Journal of Econometrics*, **31**, 307–28.

Bollerslev, T. and Engle, R. (1986) Modelling the persistence of conditional variances. *Econometric Reviews*, **5**(1), 1–50.

Chant, J. (1987) Regulation of financial institutions—a functional analysis, Bank of Canada Technical Paper No. 45.

Engle, R., Lilien, D. and Robbins, R. (1987) Estimating time varying risk premia in the term structure: the ARCH-M model. *Econometrica*, **55**(2), 391–407.

Goodhart, C. (1987) 'Why do we need a central bank. *Oxford Economic Papers*, **39**, 75–89.

Kaufman, G. (1987) The truth about bank runs, Federal Reserve Bank of Chicago Staff Memorandum SM-87-3.

Lintner, J. (1965) The valuation of risk assets and the selection of risk investments in stock portfolios and capital budgets. *Review of Economics and Statistics*, **47**, 13–37.

Mandlebrot, B. (1963) The variation of certain speculative prices. *Journal of Business*, **36**, 394–419.

Marcus, A. J. and Shaked, I. (1984) The valuation of F.D.I.C. deposit insurance using option pricing estimates. *Journal of Money Credit and Banking*, **16**, 446–60.

Markowitz, H. (1952) Portfolio selection. *Journal of Finance*, **7**, 77–91.

Marquand, J. (1987) Financial market supervision: some conceptual issues, Bank for International Settlements, Economic Paper No. 19.

Merton, R. (1980) On estimating the expected return on the market. *Journal of Financial Economics*, **8** 323–61.

Pennachi, G. G. (1987) A re-examination of the over (or under) pricing of deposit insurance. *Journal of Money Credit and Banking*, **19**, 340–60.

Ronn, E. I. and Verma, A. K. (1986) Pricing risk-adjusted deposit insurance: an option based model. *Journal of Finance*, **41**, 871–95.

Sharpe, W. (1964) Capital asset prices: a theory of market equilibrium under conditions of risk. *Journal of Finance*, **19**, 425–42.

5

The long-run determination of the UK monetary aggregates

S. G. HALL, S. G. B. HENRY

AND J. B. WILCOX

5.1 INTRODUCTION

In this chapter we present the results of an empirical study of the demand for the monetary aggregates M0, M1, M3 and M4. A two-stage approach is adopted in the study: in the first stage the main determinants of the long-run demand for money are examined, and in the second stage we concentrate on specifying the dynamic structure.

Modelling the demand for money has received considerable attention over many years. Recently a range of new approaches have been tried. The buffer stock model has received considerable attention (e.g. Carr and Darby, 1981; Cuthbertson, 1986; Cuthbertson and Taylor, 1987), the estimation of complete systems has been considered by Davidson (1987) and Davidson and Ireland (1987), a Bayesian approach to modelling the monetary aggregates has been used by Lubrano *et al.* (1986) and more 'conventional' approaches have been adopted by Hendry and Mizon (1978), Hendry (1979), Trundle (1982), Hendry and Ericsson (1983), Artis and Lewis (1984), Johnston (1984) and Patterson (1987). Despite the fact that many of these studies claim to offer structurally stable demand functions, subsequent studies often proceed by demonstrating the inadequacies of their predecessor. Indeed the whole area of monetary modelling can be characterized as one of structural breakdown. This comes as no surprise to economists actually working in the monetary sector where the anecdotal orthodoxy is that general innovations in cash management and the financial sector generally preclude the possibility of a stable money demand function of the simple textbook form.

We make use of the co-integration tools provided by Engle and Granger

(1987) and Johansen (1988), and illustrated by Hall (1986, 1988), to approach the question of modelling the monetary aggregates from a new perspective. This procedure enables us to concentrate at the first stage on testing that the set of explanatory variables used is sufficient to model the series adequately. When this procedure is used on a simple demand-for-money equation for each of the aggregates, which has only real income, prices and an interest rate as explanatory variables, the inability of this limited set of variables to capture the major movements in the series becomes transparent. Attempting to model the dynamics at this stage may merely serve to obscure this basic problem. If a valid dynamic model of money demand, of any form including an error-correction model (ECM) or a forward-looking buffer stock model, is to exist it must contain a set of variables which satisfy the tests of co-integration which are applied at the first stage. If this is not the case then the model will be subject to the Granger and Newbold (1974) spurious regression problem and we would not expect it to be structurally stable. Therefore a preliminary test for co-integration may rule out many models as inadmissible.

There are a number of practical difficulties with the approach we shall use, which is based on the Engle–Granger two-step estimation procedure. The well-known problem of small-sample bias highlighted by Banerjee *et al.* (1986) is one such problem. Another and perhaps more serious problem in our view is the problem of multiple co-integrating vectors. In general, if we are considering N non-stationary variables there may exist anything up to $N - 1$ distinct co-integrating vectors. Therefore, in anything more complex than a two-variable case we cannot know that we are dealing with a unique co-integrating vector, and using ordinary least squares (OLS) to estimate a co-integrating vector may simply produce a complex linear combination of all the distinct co-integrating vectors which exist in the system. If this happens we cannot interpret the resulting equation in any meaningful economic way. Johansen (1988) has offered a solution to both these problems by providing a maximum likelihood estimation technique for all the distinct co-integrating vectors which exist amongst a set of variables. Therefore this technique provides numerical confirmation of the OLS estimates as well as checking on the number of other co-integrating vectors which may exist. The maximum likelihood procedure is discussed in the Appendix. As the technique is still relatively new, we shall rely mainly on the conventional OLS procedures and use the new method as a test of the properties of the old method.

Below we consider the monetary aggregates M0, M1, M3 and M4. We model each of the aggregates in turn following a similar procedure for each. First we examine the possibility of forming a co-integrating regression for the aggregate using only the price level, real income and an interest rate as explanatory variables. For all the aggregates this fails to provide a co-integrating vector. This original set of variables is then augmented by a wealth term and by variables capturing financial innovation. It is shown that this larger set of variables is capable of providing a co-integrating set for each of the aggregates. Dynamic equations are also provided for each aggregate.

This chapter has the following plan. In section 5.2 we discuss the approach of co-integration and define the time series properties of the data to be used in subsequent sectors. Then each of the monetary aggregates, M0, M1, M3 and M4, is tested and examined in individual sections (sections 5.3–5.6). In the final section we make inter-aggregate comparisons and draw some general conclusions.

5.2 CO-INTEGRATION AND LONG-RUN PROPERTIES

The concept of co-integration, first proposed by Granger and Weiss (1983) and extended by Engle and Granger (1987), is fundamental to the use of the ECM formulation. In particular, the Granger representation theorem establishes that for a valid ECM to exist the set of variables must co-integrate, and if the variables do co-integrate then a valid ECM form of the data must exist. The importance of this result to general estimation procedures is that if an ECM model is estimated for a set of variables which do not co-integrate then this regression will be subject to all the well-known problems of 'spurious' regression outlined by Granger and Newbold (1974). This suggests that tests for co-integration be a necessary component of estimation exercises conducted with ECMs. Further, the 'super-convergence' proof due to Stock (1985, 1987) and generalized by Park and Phillips (1986) and Phillips and Durlauf (1986) suggests that very precise estimates of the levels terms can be obtained in the co-integrating regression (although some doubts about this, which may in fact be relevant here, are raised by Banerjee *et al.* (1986)).

We shall not attempt to summarize the background theory of co-integration here, as recent surveys are provided by Granger (1986) and Hendry (1986) and an application is described by Hall (1986). Some of the analysis will rely on the maximum likelihood approach of Johansen (1988) which is not yet widely known, and so we summarize the technique in the Appendix. Before any estimation work can properly begin within this framework we first need to establish the properties of the series we are dealing with. This is because, in principle, it is only possible for certain combinations of series to co-integrate, and so if the set of series under consideration does not fall within this set there is simply no point in proceeding with estimation. Table 5.1 presents the Dickey–Fuller (DF) and augmented Dickey–Fuller (ADF) tests for the series we shall be considering throughout this chapter. The tests for integration of order zero ($I(0)$) are tests carried out on the level of the variables, the tests for integration of

Table 5.1 The time series properties of the variables

	Test for I(0)		*Test for I(1)*		*Test for I(2)*	
	DF	*ADF*[a]	*DF*	*ADF*[a]	*DF*	*ADF*[a]
LM0[b]	−2.3	−2.4	−6.6	−1.8	−16.4	−5.7
LNM1[c]	−0.5	−0.6	−8.6	−3.8	−16.8	−7.4
LM1[b]	5.2	2.6	−7.1	−1.7	−19.0	−6.5
LM3[b]	3.1	0.9	−6.1	−2.5	−16.0	−5.9
LM4[b]	3.1	0.9	−3.6	−2.6	−14.0	−6.5
LGDP[b]	−1.2	−1.1	−11.9	−5.4		
LPGDP[b]	0.9	−0.4	−4.1	−2.6	−14.6	−4.8
LQCE[b]	0.3	0.4	−11.7	−3.7		
LCPI[b]	0.9	−0.9	−2.9	−1.7	−11.5	−5.2
LTFE[b]	−0.9	−0.6	−10.8	−4.9		
LPTFE[b]	0.7	−0.8	−2.9	−1.7	−12.6	−4.3
RTB[b]	−2.4	−2.4	−8.9	−5.3		
ΣBSSR[b]	−1.6	−1.6	−8.5	−4.6		
BDR[b]	−2.4	−2.6	−7.9	−4.5		
CONS[b]	−1.8	−1.8	−8.2	−4.6		
CC[d]	1.3	1.9	−4.9	−2.4		
CDA[d]	11.5	2.5	−1.7	0.5		
CAP[d]	2.7	0.9	−2.1	−1.9		
BSSR[b]	13.9	1.8	−1.6	−1.6		
LFW[b]	0.8	−0.7	−2.8	−2.6		
LTW[e]	0.7	1.4	−6.1	−3.1		
SND[c]	−1.2	−2.7	−4.6	−3.7		
LSM[f]	−1.6	0.7	−11.6	−3.8		

a	ADF uses fourth-order correction.
b	1963 Q2 to 1987 Q2.
c	1975 Q2 to 1987 Q2.
d	1966 Q1 to 1986 Q4.
e	1968 Q1 to 1986 Q4.
f	1963 Q1 to 1987 Q2.
LM0	log M0
LNM1	log non-interest bearing M1
LM1	log M1
LM3	log M3
LM4	log M4
LGDP	log real gross domestic product
LPGDP	log GDP deflator
LQCE	log real total consumption
LCPI	log consumer price index
LTFE	log total final expenditure
LPTFE	log TFE deflator
RTB	three-month Treasury bill rate
BSSR	building society average share rate
ΣBSSR	cumulated interest rate term defined in section 5.3
BDR	clearing banks' seven-day deposit rate
CONS	20 year consul yield
CC	number of credit cards issued
DA	number of cash dispensers in use
LCAP	log number of current accounts per head of the population
LFW	log financial wealth of the personal sector
LTW	log non-financial wealth of the personal sector
LPW	log total financial and non-financial wealth of the personal sector
LFTI	log *Financial Times* ordinary share index
SND	defined in section 5.5
LSM	log real stock market turnover

order 1 ($I(1)$) are carried out on the first difference of the variables and the tests for integration of order 2 ($I(2)$) are carried out on the second differences of the variables.

The DF and ADF tests are constructed as t tests with a non-standard distribution which is tabulated in Dickey and Fuller (1979). In broad terms the conclusions of Table 5.1 are that the measures of real output (LGDP, LQCE and LTFE) and the interest rate variables (RTB, BSSR, BDR and CONS) are clearly $I(1)$ variables. The various measures of money (M0, M1, M3 and M4) and prices (LPGDP, LCPI and LPTFE) are probably $I(2)$ variables, although they are often close to the critical value of the $I(1)$ test and so might be $I(1)$. This conforms well with our theoretical priors as it suggests that money and prices must co-integrate $I(2, 1)$, i.e. money and prices are $I(2)$ and combine to be $I(1)$, and then this series can co-integrate with the remaining variables (income interest rates etc.) to produce a stationary residual process. The implication of this is that we might well be able to work in terms of real money which is $I(1)$ rather than nominal money and prices.

5.3 AN EXERCISE FOR M0

Our starting point is to illustrate the major features of real M0 over the period end-1969 to end-1986 (Fig. 5.1). Real M0 has fallen by about 30%

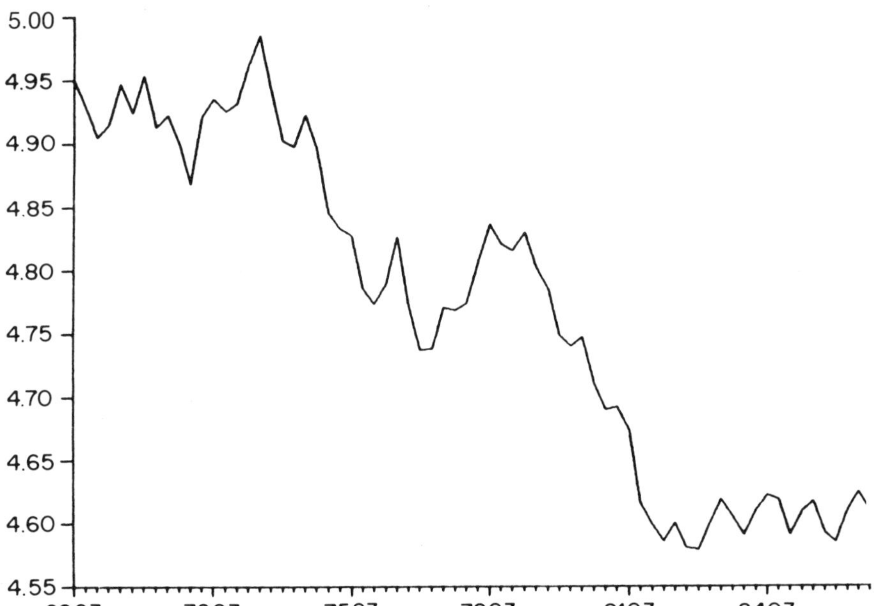

Fig. 5.1 Real M0 (logarithmic scale).

Fig. 5.2 Real consumption (logarithmic scale).

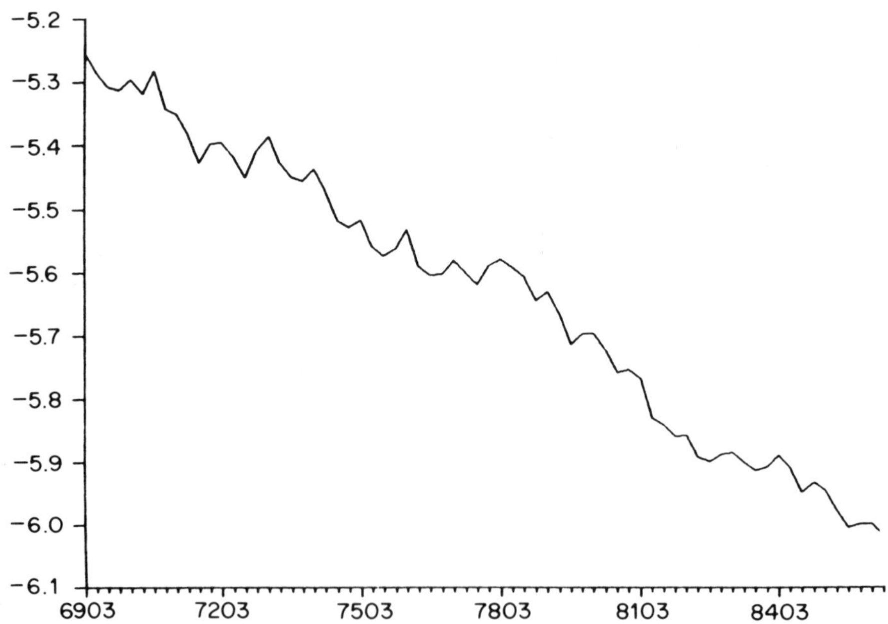

Fig. 5.3 M0 relative to consumption (logarithmic scale).

over this period, but the fall has been far from uniform. There is a correspondence between periods for which real M0 falls more rapidly and periods of sluggish growth in real consumers' expenditure (Fig. 5.2). Thus the ratio of M0 to consumption shows a smoother downward trend than that of real M0 (Fig. 5.3). The theory of the transactions demand for money suggests that the price level times the square root of real expenditure may be the appropriate deflator; M0 deflated in this way is shown in Fig. 5.4.

This casual empiricism leads us to the widely held belief that real expenditure and price movements cannot by themselves explain the demand for cash over the past 20 years. This assertion can be examined by running tests of co-integrability on the variables concerned (see Table 5.2).

When the simple unrestricted transactions demand-for-money equation is run (Equation (1) in Table 5.2), the upward trend in velocity is partly captured by an unacceptably low price elasticity. When the price elasticity is restricted to unity, the income elasticity becomes unacceptably low (Equation (2) in Table 5.2). When both the price and income elasticities are restricted (Equations (3) and (4) in Table 5.2) the equations fail the co-integrability tests even more noticeably than the first two equations.

The OLS results strongly suggest that no co-integrating vector exists amongst this set of variables. The results of the Johansen procedure for this set of variables are shown in Table 5.3. The likelihood ratio test that there

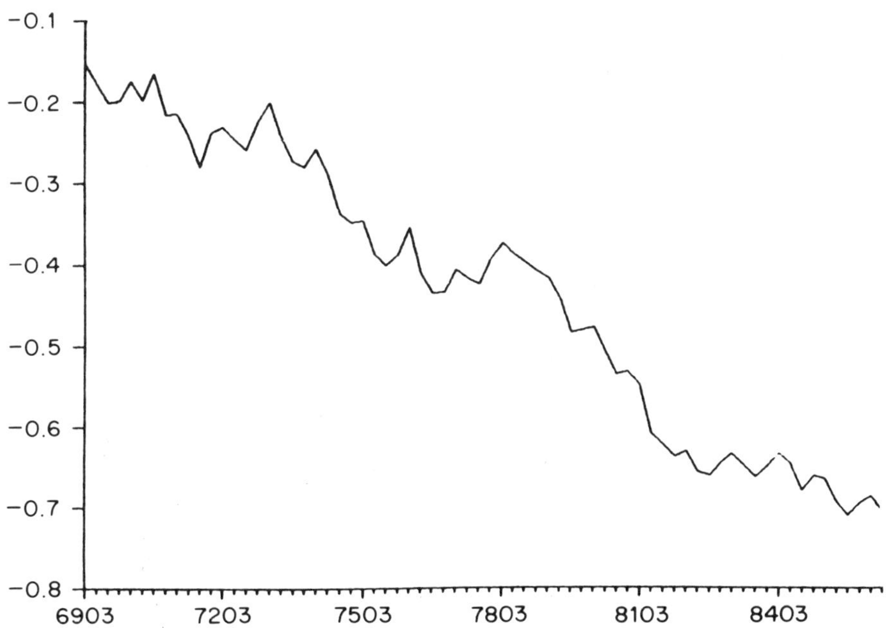

Fig. 5.4 Real M0 relative to the square root of real consumption.

Table 5.2 Tests of co-integrating vectors involving LM0

	(1)	*(2)*	*(3)*	*(4)*
LCPI	0.7	1.00	1.00	1.00
LQCE	0.47	0.88	1.00	0.50
BSSR	0.007	−0.009	−0.039	−0.031
CRDW	0.32	0.14	0.06	0.06
DF	−2.3	−1.7	1.1	0.79
ADF	−2.1	−2.6	1.3	0.87
R^2	0.99	0.71	0.12	0.13

Sample period, 1969 Q3 to 1986 Q4.
CRDW, co-integrating regression Durbin–Watson statistic.

Table 5.3

	Eigenvector			
Eigenvalue	LM0	LCPI	LQCE	BSSR
0.18	−30.27	26.67	−6.14	−0.59
0.16	−44.35	31.91	27.83	0.28
0.05	18.89	−10.14	−22.74	0.04
0.0007	−39.22	27.91	−0.53	1.57

are at most *r* co-integrating vectors gives the results shown in Table 5.4. The likelihood ratio test suggests that we are unable to reject the hypothesis that there are no co-integrating vectors. Therefore the Johansen procedure confirms the OLS suggestion that co-integration does not exist between this set of variables. It is interesting to note that the eigenvectors corresponding to the two largest eigenvalues produce parameter estimates which are similar to the OLS results in Equations (1) and (2) in Table 5.2.

5.3.1 Financial innovation and the demand for cash

The most plausible explanation for the decline in the ratio of M0 to nominal consumers' expenditure is financial innovation. Over the sample period transactions technology has changed considerably with the wide-

Table 5.4

r	*LR test*	*5% critical value*
0	30.2	38.6
1	16.0	23.8
2	3.8	12.0
3	0.05	4.2

spread introduction of cash dispensers and credit cards and a noticeable increase in the number of bank current accounts. Johnston (1984) provides a further description of these changes and attempts to assess their impact on narrow money holdings. Our next attempt to find a co-integrating solution involved the three innovation variables indicated above. The results are reported in Table 5.5.

Even with these trended innovation variables the equations fail the tests of co-integration. A further problem arises because of the logarithmic form of the innovation variables. As these variables have low values at the beginning of the sample the effect of an extra unit implied by the logarithmic form is large. An alternative possibility is to consider entering the innovation variables linearly (Table 5.6).

None of the equations in Table 5.6 passes the co-integrability tests. The equations that come closest to passing are (13), which has a perversely signed coefficient on the cash dispenser variable, and (16). In this case the Johansen procedure produces results which are at slight variance with Tables 5.5 and 5.6. If we include all three innovation variables (as in

Table 5.5 Tests of co-integrating vectors involving LM0–LCPI–LQCE

	(5)	*(6)*	*(7)*	*(8)*	*(9)*	*(10)*	*(11)*
BSSR	−0.002	0.004	0.01	−0.015	0.012	−0.015	0.011
LCC	0.08		0.02	0.001	−0.28		
LCDA	−0.11	−0.07		−0.25		−0.25	
LCAPOP	−0.78	−0.68	−1.02				−0.97
CRDW	0.64	0.48	0.45	0.27	0.15	0.27	0.44
DF	−2.9	−2.6	−2.4	−2.4	−1.5	−2.3	−2.45
ADF	−1.96	−2.1	−2.1	−2.2	−2.2	−2.2	−2.23
R^2	0.99	0.99	0.98	0.96	0.92	0.96	0.98

Table 5.6 Tests of co-integrating vectors involving LM0 – LCPI – LQCE

	(12)	*(13)*	*(14)*	*(15)*	*(16)*	*(17)*	*(18)*
BSSR	−0.0002	−0.015	0.002	0.001	−0.02	−0.05	0.0008
CC ($\times 10^{-5}$)	0.69	−3.9	0.19	—	−2.4	—	—
CDA ($\times 10^{-5}$)	−0.96	0.26	—	0.05	—	−6.2	—
CAPOP	−0.02	—	−0.02	−0.02	—		−0.02
CRDW	0.45	0.38	0.40	0.38	0.26	0.25	0.38
DF	−0.94	−2.8	−1.06	−1.1	−2.3	−2.1	−1.1
ADF	−1.13	−2.5	−1.64	−1.6	−2.5	−2.1	−1.6
R^2	0.98	0.93	0.98	0.98	0.93	0.89	0.98

Equation (12)), then the likelihood ratio tests suggest that there may be up to four co-integrating vectors in the data. The explanation for this discrepancy is that the Johansen procedure treats all the variables in a similar fashion whereas the OLS procedure normalizes on one variable (money in this case) and so treats this variable in a special way. The Johansen procedure will therefore reveal co-integrating vectors which do not involve money while the OLS procedure is barred from this. It therefore seems that a number of co-integrating vectors exist between the innovation variables and interest rates but that none of these may be the relevant one for determining money.

If we apply the Johansen procedure to a case where there is only one innovation variable (we chose CC) then we obtain the results shown in Table 5.7. The results of the likelihood ratio test that there are at most r co-integrating vectors are shown in Table 5.8. We can reject the hypothesis that there are no co-integrating vectors; there may be two co-integrating vectors in this set (12.3 is on the borderline). The coefficients implied by the first co-integrating vector are plausible and conform with the parameters given in Table 5.6 reasonably well.

Our interpretation of these conflicting results is that financial innovation is indeed a promising explanation of the movement in M0 but that our measures of innovation are not satisfactory. Therefore in the next section we turn to a more flexible alternative approach.

Table 5.7

	Eigenvector		
Eigenvalue	LM0 − LCPI − LQCE	CC	BSSR
0.302	−7.13	−0.0004	−0.52
0.15	18.17	0.0004	0.72
0.023	12.29	0.0007	−0.57

Table 5.8

r	*LR test*	*5% critical value*
0	36.5	23.8
1	12.3	12.0
2	1.6	4.2

5.3.2 An alternative approach to innovation

An alternative approach to direct measures of innovation is to attempt to model the innovation process. This approach separates two distinct interest rate effects.

1. For a given transactions technology a rise (fall) in the rate will lead to an increase (decrease) in velocity.
2. An increase in the rate provides an incentive for cash saving technology and payments methods to be introduced. Such changes are likely to be asymmetric and once implemented are unlikely to be repeated exactly or reversed, e.g. the introduction of cash dispensers. Furthermore, such changes alter the transactions technology and hence the likely magnitude of responses under 1.

We now consider a model of the effect described in 2. The money demand function considered is of the form

$$(\mathrm{LMO} - \mathrm{LCPI} - \mathrm{LQCE})_t = a + br_t + I_t + e_t$$

where I_t is a variable capturing the innovation process.

The benefits to innovation considered are those which arise from a reduced need to hold assets in the form of cash. It is assumed that the opportunity cost of holding cash is the nominal rate of interest. A general model of the process might assume that the benefits from innovating in any period can be proxied by an expected future rate of interest r^e. The costs of introducing cash saving payment methods are not explicitly modelled but are represented by a time-varying constant $A_2(t)$. Note that the gains to innovation will be positive if $r_t^e - A_2(t)$ is positive; if this term is less than or equal to zero we assume that no innovation takes place. A possible functional form relating the rate of introduction of cash savings payments methods to the expected rate of interest might be

$$\Delta I_t = \max[\{r_t^e - A_2(t)\}: 0]$$

This implies that unless the expected interest rate is above a certain minimum level no innovation takes place. This would suggest using a term of the form

$$I_t = A_1 \sum_{s=0}^{t} \max[\{r_s^e - A_2(s)\}: 0]$$

or, allowing for the possibility of other non-linearities in the response,

$$I_t = A_1 \left(\sum_{s=0}^{t} \max[\{r_s^e - A_2(s)\}^{A_4}: 0] \right)^{A_3}$$

where A_3 and A_4 allow for possible non-linearities.

A particularly simple form which assumes that the function is linear ($A_3 = A_4 = 0$), that the cost of innovation is constant ($A_2(t) = A_2$), that the expected rate can be proxied by the actual rate and that over the sample period the rate has always exceeded A_2 is

$$I_t = A_1 \sum_{s=0}^{t} (r_s - A_2) = A_1 \sum_{s=0}^{t} r_s - A_1 A_2 t$$

Table 5.9 Tests of co-integrating vectors involving LM0 – LCPI – LQCE

	(19)	*(20)*	*(21)*
BSSR	−0.0012	0.0012	—
ΣBSSR	−0.0013	−0.0008	−0.0013
Time	—	−0.004	—
CRDW	0.67	0.73	0.65
DF	−3.8	−3.8	−3.7
ADF	−2.9	−2.9	−2.8
R^2	0.99	0.99	0.99

Table 5.9 uses this restricted equation as the innovation variable. Since in this case, because the additional lags in the ADF test statistic were not significant, the sample DF statistic is relevant, these results indicate that the simple form of innovation variable provides a co-integrating vector with the logarithm of the ratio of M0 to nominal consumers' expenditure. We have estimated equations using more general forms of the innovation variable (A_4, $A_3 \neq 0$) but so far these show little improvement on Equation (21) of Table 5.9.

If we apply the Johansen procedure to the two variables LMO – LCPI – LQCE and ΣBSSR we obtain the result shown in Table 5.10. The results of the likelihood ratio test to determine that there are at most r co-integration vectors is shown in Table 5.11. This also suggests that a co-integrating vector exists and, further, if we normalize the first eigenvector on money we obtain a coefficient of −0.0013 on BSSR which is identical with the OLS estimate in Equation (21).

Given the agreement between the OLS results and the Johansen results we shall proceed to estimate a dynamic model based on Equation (21). At this

Table 5.10

	Eigenvector	
Eigenvalue	LM0 – LCPI – LQCE	ΣBSSR
0.16	58.26	0.0769
0.017	−20.28	−0.037

Table 5.11

r	*LR test*	*5% critical value*
0	13.3	12.0
1	1.14	4.2

second stage the dependent variable used is the difference of the logarithm of M0, and the explanatory variables are past changes in the logarithm of consumers' expenditure and the consumer price deflator together with the level of the interest rate. The lagged residuals RES_{t-1} from the co-integrating equation are entered into the dynamic equation and should appear with a negative sign. Initial parameter estimates suggested a restriction between the coefficients on the lagged residuals and changes in the exogenous variables; hence, the equation below contains a term of the form $\widehat{M0_t} - M0_{t-1}$ where $\widehat{M0_t}$ is the long-run equilibrium level of $M0_t$ suggested by the co-integrating equation. Following a conventional general to specific search methodology we arrive at the following dynamic equation for M0:

$$\Delta LMO = \underset{(4.4)}{0.01} + \underset{(4.1)}{0.39}\Delta LMO_{t-1} + \underset{(2.2)}{0.30}\Delta\Delta LCPI_{t-1}$$

$$+ \underset{(3.1)}{0.18}(\widehat{M0_t} - M0_{t-1}) + \underset{(6.1)}{0.05}DUM711$$

where DUM711 is a dummy variable for decimalization; 't' statistics are shown in parentheses.

$\sigma = 0.010$	$R^2 = 0.65$	DW = 2.3	
ARCH(1) = 0.09	RESET(4) = 7.0	BJ(2) = 1.7	
LM(1) = 1.86	LM(2) = 3.90	LM(4) = 4.6	LM(8) = 9.3
LB(1) = 1.52	LB(2) = 3.75	LB(4) = 4.4	LB(8) = 12.9
CHISQ(8) = 4.9	CHISQ(12) = 4.8	CHISQ(24) = 16.7	

Sample period, 1967 Q1 to 1986 Q4. See appendix A5.2 for definitions of the diagnostic test statistics.

The model, although simple, passes a wide range of diagnostic tests of its error process, functional form and stability. Given the notorious structural instability of money equations we felt that we should investigate the structural stability of this equation more methodically than is allowed by the simple forecasting test. We therefore performed recursive estimation over the period 1979 Q1 to 1986 Q4 and the resulting parameter estimates are presented in Figs 5.5–5.8. In all cases the parameters are remarkably stable and never move outside the two standard error band. A sequential one-period-ahead Chow test also never reaches the 5% critical value at any point over this period (Fig. 5.9) (see also Fig. 5.10 which shows the CUSUMSQ statistic).

5.4 A CO-INTEGRATION EXERCISE FOR M1

In this section we begin by examining the textbook model of money demand involving M1, income, interest rates and prices to see whether these

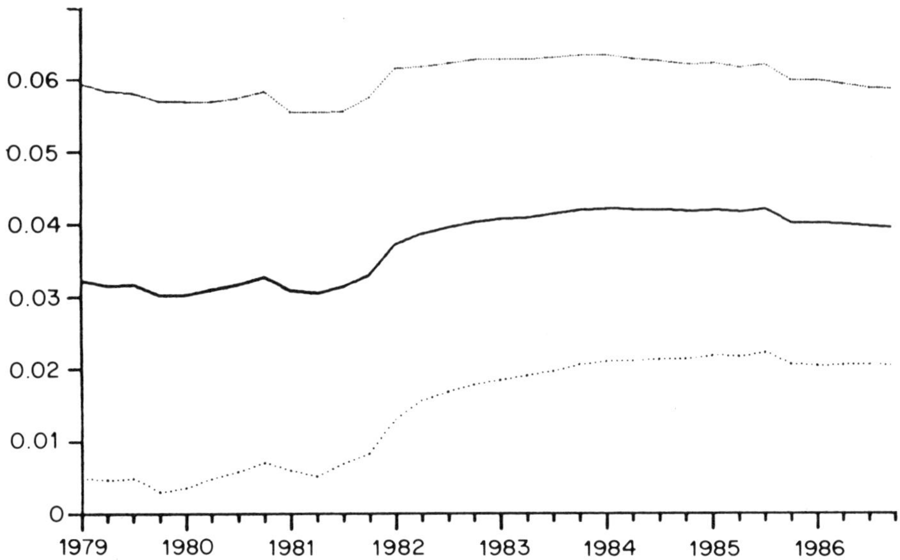

Fig. 5.5 Recursive coefficients from the dynamic M0 equation: recursive estimation time series of $\Delta LM0_{t-1}$. The dotted lines show two standard errors around the coefficient values.

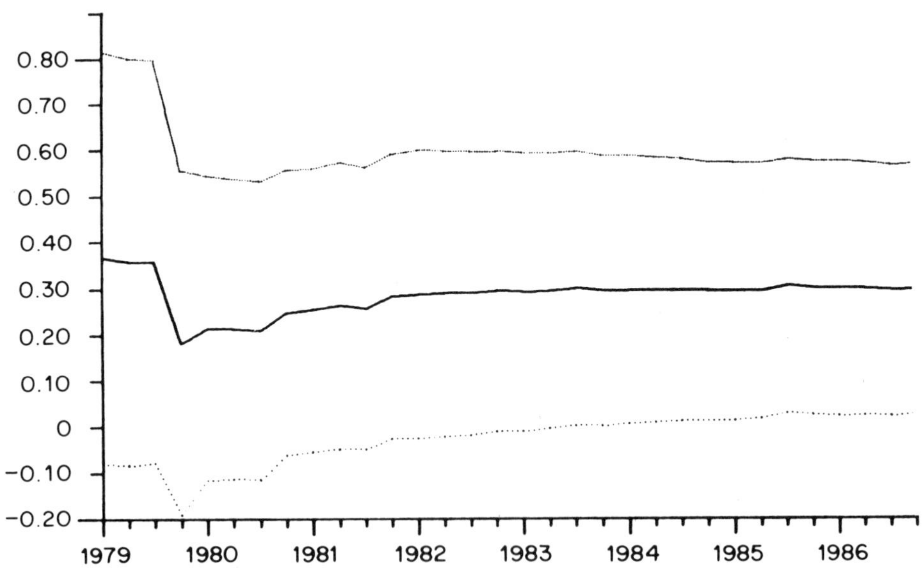

Fig. 5.6 Recursive coefficients from the dynamic M0 equation: recursive estimation time series of $\Delta\Delta LCPI_{t-1}$. The dotted lines show two standard errors around the coefficient values.

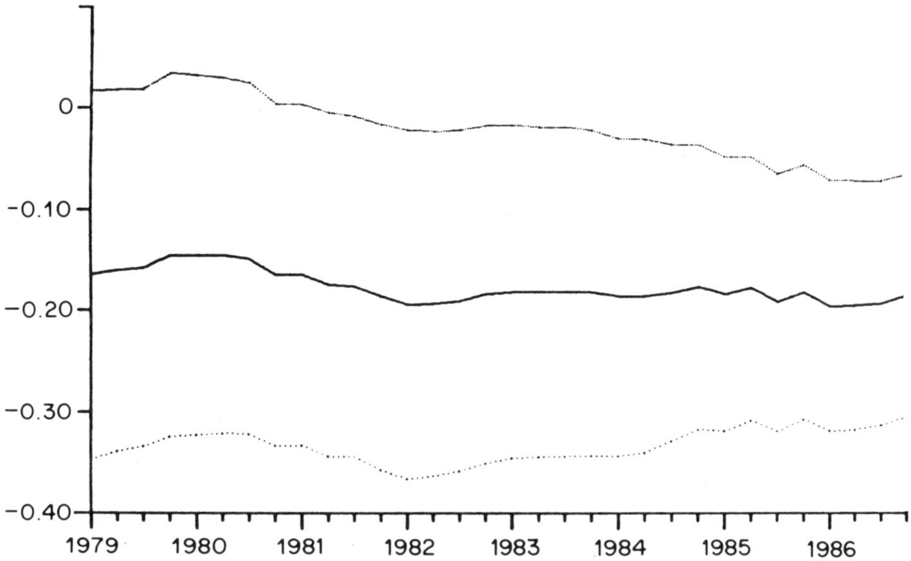

Fig. 5.7 Recursive coefficients from the dynamic M0 equation: recursive estimation time series of $\widehat{M0_{t-1} - M0_t}$. The dotted lines show two standard errors around the coefficient values.

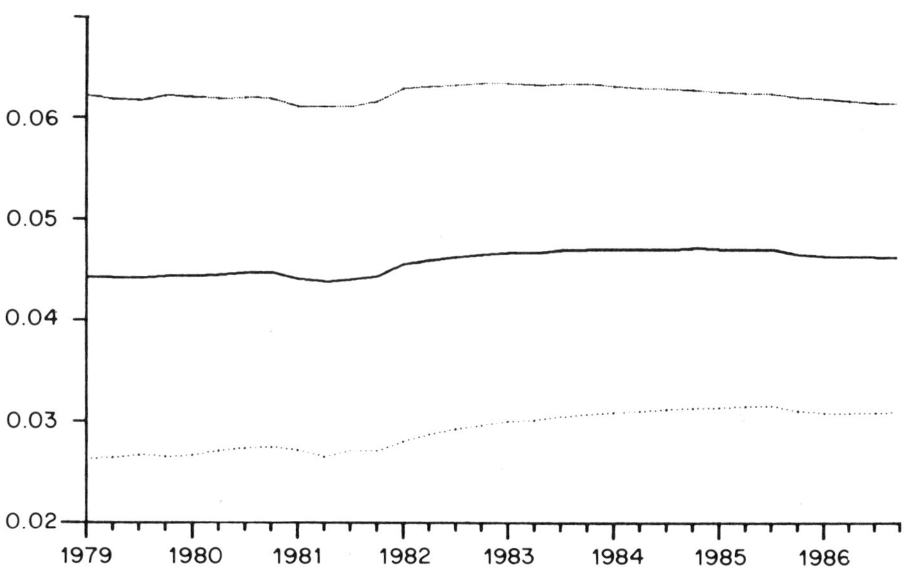

Fig. 5.8 Recursive coefficients from the dynamic M0 equation: recursive estimation time series of DUM711. The dotted lines show two standard errors around the coefficient values.

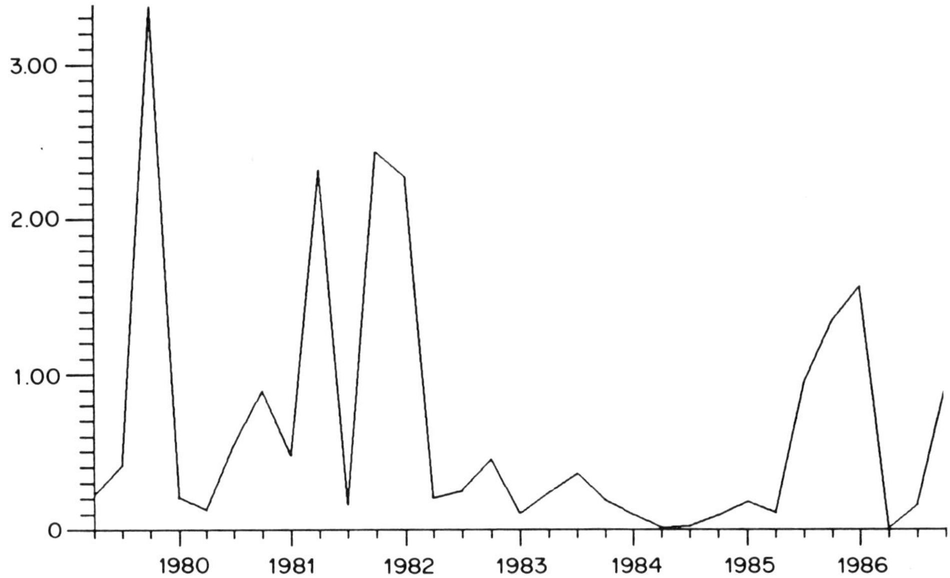

Fig. 5.9 Test statistics for recursive estimation of the dynamic M0 equation: sequential one-period-ahead Chow test.

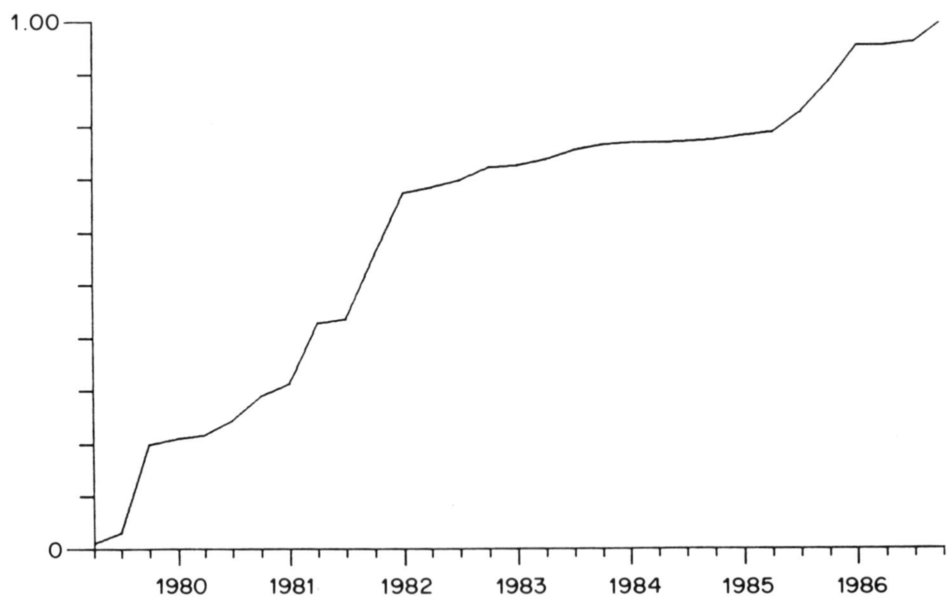

Fig. 5.10 Test statistics for recursive estimation of the dynamic M0 equation: CUSUMSQ statistic.

variables co-integrate. As the latent mapping between the conceptual model and the statistical model is unspecified, we shall consider a number of alternative definitions of both income and prices to guard against the possibility that our results are dependent on particular data definitions. As measures of real output we shall use real GDP (generally used in US studies of money demand (e.g. Baba *et al.*, 1982)), real total final expenditure (TFE) (generally used in UK studies (e.g. Hendry, 1979)) and real consumption. As measures of prices we shall use the three corresponding price deflators.

Table 5.12 presents estimates of the parameters and test statistics for a set of possible co-integrating equations. The parameter estimates are quite sensible; in the final three equations involving prices, income and interest rates, the price elasticity varies between 0.91 and 1.04, the income elasticity varies between 0.81 and 1.58 and the interest rate effect is −0.03. However, it is clear from the ADF statistics that none of these equations represents a co-integrating set of variables. Therefore we can immediately rule out any simple model which implies a long-run relationship between M1, income, prices and interest rates only. This set does not co-integrate and so we would not expect any dynamic equation based solely on this set to be stable. This then confirms the anecdotal view that innovation over the past 20 years has been crucial in the determination of money demand.

A number of studies have attempted to incorporate measures of financial innovation. Johnston (1984) used data on the number of cash-dispensing machines, the number of credit cards and the number of current accounts per head of the population in his study for the UK. Baba *et al.* (1982), when studying US money demand functions, use direct data on the interest rates on new types of interest-bearing accounts in M2. We shall begin

Table 5.12 Tests of co-integrating vectors involving M1

	(22)	*(23)*	*(24)*	*(25)*	*(26)*	*(27)*	*(28)*	*(29)*	*(30)*
LPGDP	0.96			0.84			0.88		
LPTFE		0.96			0.81			0.84	
LCPI			0.99			0.69			0.74
LGDP				0.62			0.85		
LTFE					0.70			0.91	
LQCE						1.5			1.6
RTB							−0.02	−0.03	−0.02
CRDW	0.05	0.05	0.05	0.05	0.05	0.08	0.15	0.14	0.22
DF	2.5	2.7	2.8	1.2	1.8	0.15	−0.5	−0.5	−1.6
ADF	−0.5	−0.4	−0.2	−0.05	0.08	−0.03	−0.7	−0.7	−0.9
R^2	0.97	0.97	0.97	0.97	0.97	0.98	0.98	0.98	0.99

Sample period, 1966 Q1 to 1986 Q4.

investigating the financial innovation story by including a range of variables used by Johnston and the cumulated interest rate effect used in the last section.

This is done in Equations (31)–(34) of Table 5.13 where CC, LCDA and LCAP are added to the basic money demand function which was considered in Table 5.12. We now only consider the use of LTFE and LPTFE; this choice is rather arbitrary as the data are not really able to choose between the various measures of output and prices. However, none of the subsequent results is sensitive to this choice. Three of the four regressions reported then pass the co-integration tests once the innovation variables are included. However, we would still reject these as suitable co-integrating vectors as the price elasticity has an implausibly low coefficient. If we impose a unit coefficient on the price effect (Equations (34)–(36) of Table 5.13) then co-integration can be rejected.

If we consider the time series of real M1, shown in Fig. 5.11, we can quickly gain an insight into the nature of the problem. Real M1 is virtually constant from 1963 to 1982 with no discernible trend. This pattern changes sharply in 1982 and a rapid growth in real M1 begins. None of the explanatory variables in Table 5.13 exhibits this type of behaviour and so it seems likely that some other important effect is missing. The early 1980s saw two important developments with regard to the behaviour of M1. Firstly the removal of the 'corset' in 1981 had a general effect on the monetary sector and secondly the early 1980s saw the wide-scale introduction of interest-bearing cheque accounts. During the 1970s less than 10% of M1 was interest bearing; with the rapid growth of the financial sector and the introduction of the new accounts in the early 1980s this proportion rose

Table 5.13 Testing the effect of innovation

	Dependent variable					
	LM1			LM1 − LPTFE		
	(31)	*(32)*	*(33)*	*(34)*	*(35)*	*(36)*
LTFE	0.70	1.7	0.2	−0.5	1.4	1.2
LPTFE	0.55	0.76	0.1	—	—	—
RTB	−0.008	−0.02	−0.02	−0.02	−0.03	−0.02
CC ($\times 10^{-5}$)	3.2	—	—	1.5	—	—
LCDA	—	−0.05	—	—	−0.13	—
LCAP	—	—	2.1	—	—	−0.5
CRDW	0.39	0.20	0.15	0.17	0.21	0.15
DF	−2.4	−1.2	−2.4	−0.7	−1.3	−0.4
ADF	−2.1	−0.5	−2.7	−1.9	−0.9	−0.9
R^2	0.99	0.98	0.99	0.36	0.32	0.32

Fig. 5.11 Real M1 (logarithmic scale).

rapidly, so that by the end of 1982 almost 30% of M1 was interest bearing and by the middle of 1987 65% was interest bearing. A reasonable interpretation therefore is that large amounts of this new M1 would actually represent a growth in the real M1 stock which was due, almost solely, to the growth in the new interest-bearing element.

In order to remove these effects we include a variable LM/N = LOG(M1/NIBM1) which shows the rising proportion of interest-bearing M1. At this stage we make no attempt to model the introduction of interest-bearing M1 accounts by economic variables. This is partly because the data period of the growth of these deposits is still quite short, about 5 years, and partly because data such as the number of high interest accounts are not available.

The possibility of a co-integrating vector existing between this full set of variables is considered in Table 5.14. Equation (37) in Table 5.14 performs a completely unrestricted estimate of the co-integrating vector. The tests for co-integration are all passed and the parameter values are reasonable; however, the price elasticity is a little low at 0.9. Equations (38)–(40) restrict one coefficient at a time and test for co-integration. With this full set of variables, imposing price homogeneity does not cause a breakdown of co-integration nor does the income elasticity become implausible, as was the case in Table 5.13. The remaining equations of Table 5.14 restrict the co-integrating vector to have a unit effect from LM/N and LTFE; neither restriction prevents co-integration nor does it substantially alter the remaining parameters.

Table 5.14 A co-integrating vector for M1

	Dependent variable			
	LM1 *(37)*	LM1 – LPTFE *(38)*	LM1 – LPTFE – LTFE *(39)*	LM1 – LPTFE – LM/N – LTFE *(40)*
Constant	−2.9	−4.9	−4.8	−4.8
LTFE	0.88	1.005	—	—
LPTFE	0.78	—	—	—
CONS	−0.02	−0.02	−0.02	−0.03
ΣBSSR	−0.003	−0.001	−0.001	−0.001
LM/N	0.98	1.2	1.2	—
CRDW	0.76	0.71	0.76	0.74
DF	−4.4	−4.4	−4.4	−4.2
ADF	−3.8	3.5	−3.5	−3.2
R^2	0.99	0.92	0.98	0.98

We now proceed to verify these results using the Johansen procedure. If we apply the technique to the full set of unrestricted variables the conclusion is that there are four co-integrating vectors within the set of variables. We shall not present the full matrix here, but one of the four is very similar to our final restricted equation with a near unit coefficient on LPTFE, LTFE and LM/N. We therefore repeated the Johansen procedure using the restricted variable in Equation (40). This produced the results shown in Table 5.15. The likelihood ratio test of a maximum of r co-integrating vectors is shown in Table 5.16. In this case we can reject the hypothesis that there is only one co-integrating vector ($r = 1$) in favour of two co-integrating vectors. In fact the second vector (associated with an eigenvalue of 0.17) is virtually identical with that estimated in Equation (40) of Table 5.14 and so we shall use this equation as our co-integrating vector for M1.

Having now achieved a suitable co-integrating model of the long-run determination of M1, we can use the residuals from this equation to build a dynamic model. We proceed along a conventional path of specifying a high-order dynamic model and nesting down from this general model to a parsimonious representation of the data. This should then produce a structurally stable satisfactory model for M1.

Following this procedure produces the model

$$\begin{aligned}\Delta \mathrm{LM1}_t = {} & \underset{(3.7)}{0.01} + \underset{(1.6)}{0.14}\Delta \mathrm{LM1}_{t-1} + \underset{(4.3)}{0.39}\Delta \mathrm{LM1}_{t-2} \\ & - \underset{(2.7)}{0.3}\Delta \mathrm{LTFE}_t + \underset{(2.4)}{0.36}\Delta(\mathrm{LM/N})_t \\ & + \underset{(2.0)}{0.36}(\Delta \mathrm{LPTFE}_{t-2} - \Delta \mathrm{LPTFE}_{t-4}) \\ & - \underset{(2.4)}{0.004}(\Delta \mathrm{CONS}_t + \Delta \mathrm{CONS}_{t-1}) \\ & - \underset{(3.5)}{0.20}\mathrm{RES}_{t-1}\end{aligned}$$

where RES denotes residuals from the co-integrating regression (Equation (40) of Table 5.14).

$\sigma = 0.0157$	$R^2 = 0.50$	DW = 1.98
ARCH(1) = 0.005	RESET(4) = 1.2	BJ(2) = 7.6
LM(1) = 0.04	LM(4) = 0.7	LM(8) = 8.1
LB(1) = 0.0	LB(4) = 3.0	LB(8) = 7.8
CHISQ(8) = 10.8	CHISQ(12) = 10.6	CHISQ(24) = 22.8

The sample period is 1967 Q1 to 1986 Q4

Table 5.15

	Eigenvector		
Eigenvalue	LM1 − LPTFE − LM/N − LTFE	CONS	ΣBSSR
0.202	21.7	0.013	0.034
0.17	35.9	0.046	1.38
0.03	16.3	0.023	−0.01

Table 5.16

r	*LR test*	*5% critical value*
0	37.5	23.8
1	18.6	12.0
2	2.9	4.2

The model passes a wide range of diagnostics. The ARCH statistic is close to the 5% cut-off region and easily passes the Hendry forecast test. The recursive residuals are reasonably random and the model easily passes the CUSUMSQ test over the period Q1 to 1986 Q4 (Fig. 5.12). Over this period the cumulated sum of residuals (CUSUM) is only −4.7 after 24

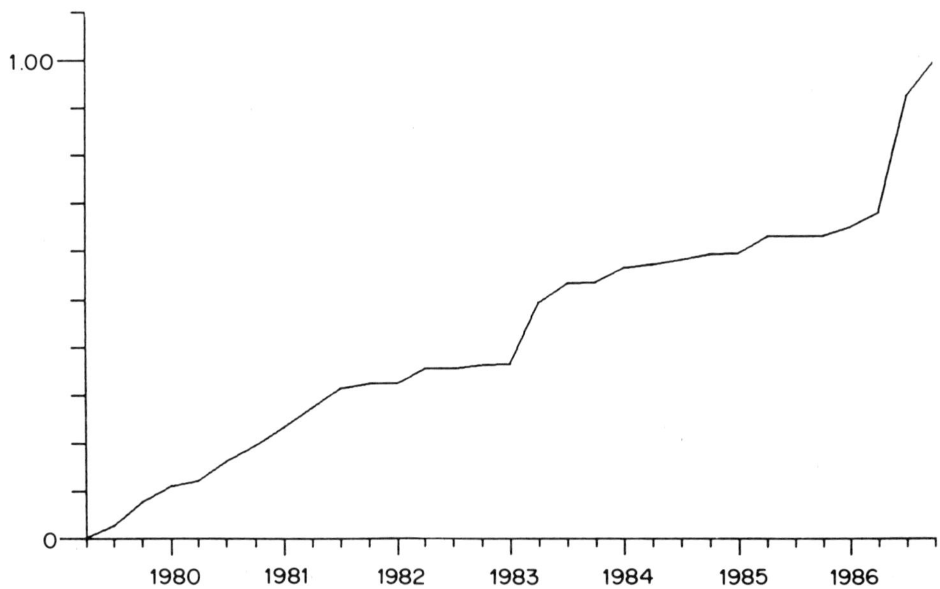

Fig. 5.12 Test statistics for recursive estimation of the dynamic M1 equation: CUSUMSQ statistic.

quarters, and a recursive one-period-ahead Chow test reaches its 5% critical value only once (Fig. 5.13). The recursive parameter estimates are all highly stable. The one failure in the sequential Chow test occurs in the third quarter of 1986; this seems to be due to a marked distortion of the money figures possibly caused by the flotation of the Trustee Savings Bank.

By using the variable LM/N in the co-integrating regression we are clearly not offering an explanation of the sharp rise of interest-bearing M1. However, we are isolating this important effect and demonstrating that co-integration is not possible if we ignore it. In order to generate some rationale for the movement in this variable we shall now present a co-integrating vector for LM/N itself. Below we use three additional variables to capture this growth of interest-bearing M1. The first is a dummy variable reflecting the introduction of the new monetary control arrangements in August 1981. The second captures the sharp increase in the size and turnover of the financial sector. In addition, a further effect may come from changes in the wealth-to-income ratio so that increased wealth might cause higher holdings of interest-bearing M1.

A suitable co-integrating regression for LM/N is

$$\begin{aligned} \text{LM/N} = 2.7 + 0.76(\text{LFW} - \text{LTFE}) + 0.04\text{LSM} \\ - 0.04\text{DUM81} + 0.003\text{BDR} \end{aligned}$$

$$\text{CRDW} = 0.87 \qquad \text{DF} = -3.5 \qquad \text{ADF} = -3.5 \qquad R^2 = 0.90$$

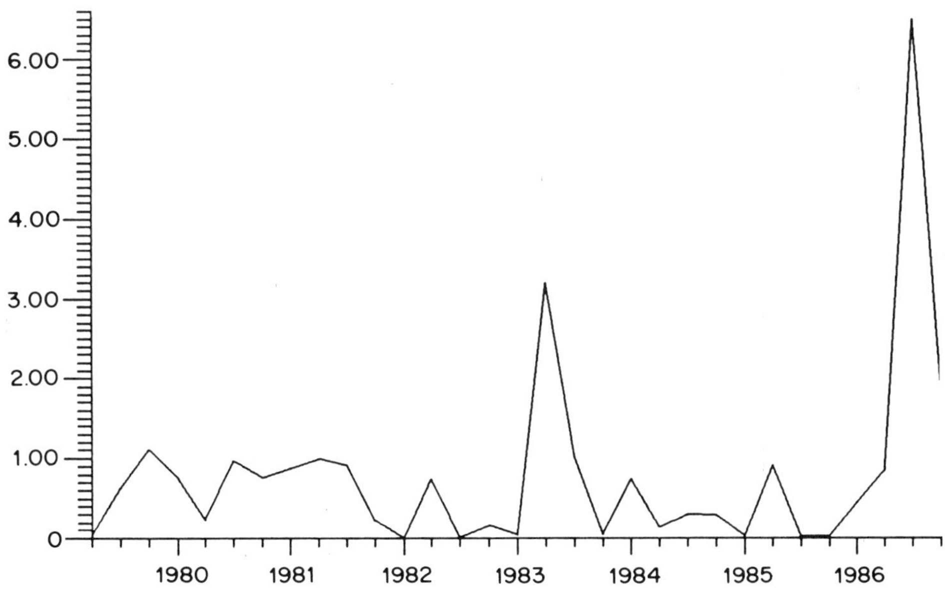

Fig. 5.13 Test statistics for recursive estimation of the dynamic M1 equation: sequential one-period-ahead Chow test.

where DUM81 is a dummy which captures the introduction of the new monetary control arrangements in August 1981. Clearly, most of the work is being done by the wealth-to-expenditure ratio. Stock market turnover has only a small effect but it must be remembered that a large part of the change in personal wealth is due to changing stock market prices. The dummy variable also captures a range of innovation effects which have appeared since 1981. We also find an important effect from the own rate of interest.

5.5 A MODEL OF M4

We now carry out a similar procedure for the broader aggregates M4 and M3, again considering first the co-integrating properties of a simple money demand equation. We begin with M4, which is the broader of the aggregates. The simple textbook model for M4 is considered in Table 5.17.

The ratio of M4 to nominal income is shown in Fig. 5.14. As might be expected the simple set of variables considered in Table 5.17 does not provide a co-integrating set. Descriptions of the movements in broad money over this period have focused on various forms of financial innovation as explanations; they have also stressed the importance of the sectoral composition of money holding (e.g. Bank of England, 1986). In this chapter we do not attempt to model the sectoral composition; however, even at the aggregate level we are able to find convincing evidence of the importance of financial innovation.

The first important omission in our initial set of explanatory variables is that none of them captures the significant changes in wealth, both financial

Table 5.17 Testing the simple model of M4 (dependent variable LM4)

	(41)	*(42)*	*(43)*
LPGDP	—	0.819	—
LPTFE	0.807	—	—
LCPI	—	—	0.80
LGDP	—	2.613	—
LTFE	2.27	—	—
LQCE	—	—	2.43
RTB	−0.011	−0.0081	−0.005
CRDW	0.25	0.34	0.665
DF	−2.11	−2.4	−3.9
ADF	−1.46	−1.3	−2.6
R^2	0.992	0.991	0.997

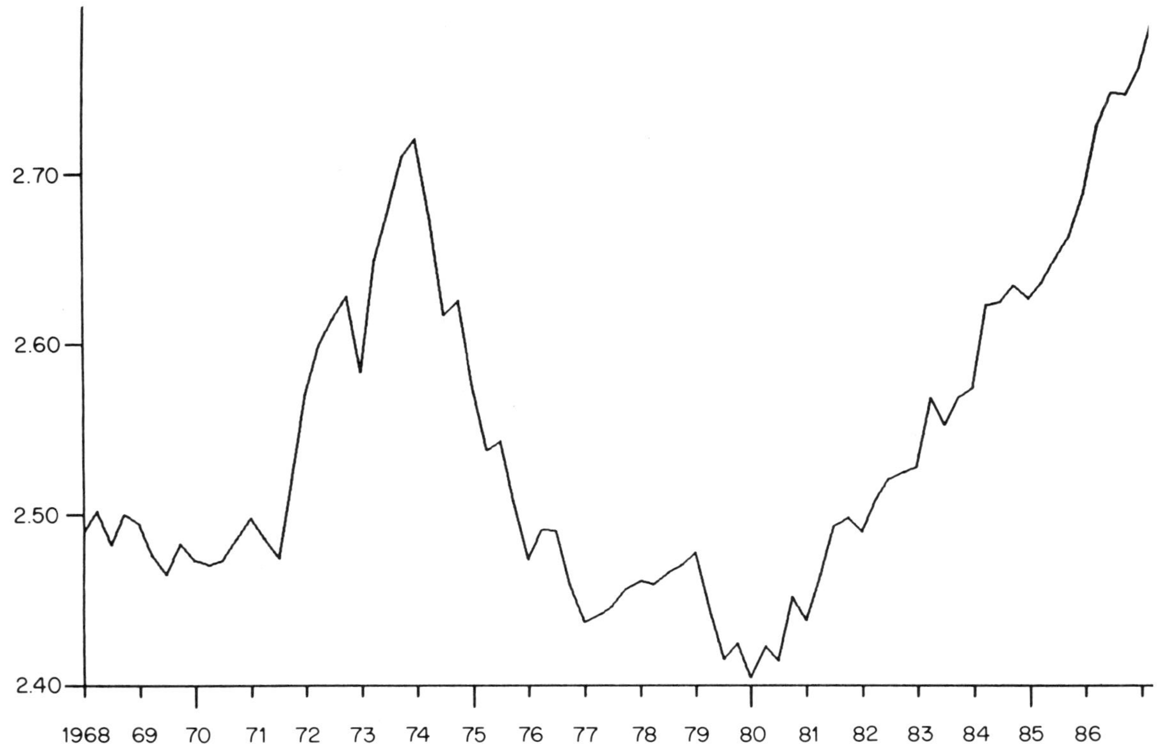

Fig. 5.14 M4 relative to GDP (logarithmic scale).

and tangible, that have occurred over the sample period. The role of wealth in many key macroeconomic relationships is at present receiving renewed attention. Although wealth might be thought the crucial scaling variable if the demand for money is seen as part of a wider portfolio decision, many demand-for-money equations have omitted such a variable (for an exception see Grice and Bennett (1984)). Wealth plays a crucial role in determining the demand for money in the equations below; this is particularly important in explaining developments since 1980 when both wealth and broad money have grown rapidly. The wealth variable we shall use is personal sector gross wealth, both financial and tangible; the latter mainly reflects the value of the owner-occupied housing stock.

A second variable added to our initial list is inflation. A number of studies have found that inflation has a significant impact on money holdings; for an example and further references on this see Taylor (1987). This effect could be due to a number of influences including the tendency for nominal rates not to move in line with expected inflation. In part, it could reflect front-end loading which occurred in debt markets during periods of high inflation and high nominal interest rates. During such periods the real value of debt fell noticeably, and the constraints associated with front-end loading could have resulted in consumers running down liquid assets to maintain consumption levels.

With one exception, variables reflecting rates of return on assets were found to be unimportant. A 2 year moving average of the quarterly change in the logarithm of stock market prices was used as a proxy for expected capital gains. Although this term proved to be unimportant, a moving average of the falls in the index proved to be useful in capturing the movements in money holdings, helping, in particular, to capture movements in liquid asset holdings following the large fall in the stock market index in the early 1970s.

It is perhaps worth commenting further on the failure to identify significant interest rate effects. To the extent that the interest rate differentials that enter are themselves stationary we should not expect them to enter the co-integrating regression. It is a little more surprising, however, that no such effects were found in the dynamic equations at the second stage. This may be a reflection of problems of measuring appropriate own and competing rates for a period of financial innovation. It may also reflect the fact that different rates are appropriate for different sectors of the economy, and a disaggregated approach may be able to identify interest rate effects.

The final variable added to the set was a dummy variable to capture the introduction of competition and credit control. With these additions it proved straightforward to form a co-integrating vector.

The results in Table 5.18 provide a plausible co-integrating vector for M4. The parameter values show only minor variation as the restriction of unit elasticity is applied. The demand for M4 has a long-run income

Table 5.18 A co-integrating vector for M4

	Dependent variables		
	LM4 *(44)*	LM4 − LPGDP *(45)*	LM4 − LPGDP − LGDP *(46)*
LPGDP	0.99	—	—
LGDP	1.07	1.05	—
Δ_4LPGDP	−0.71	−0.71	−0.71
LPW − LGDP − LPGDP	0.71	0.71	0.72
SND	−0.20	−0.20	−0.20
DCCC	0.09	0.09	0.10
CRDW	1.30	1.30	1.30
DF	−6.00	−6.00	−6.00
ADF	−5.1	−5.1	−5.0
R^2	0.99	0.99	0.96

Sample period, 1968 Q1 to1987 Q2.
PW personal sector real and financial wealth.
LFTI, logarithm *Financial Times* ordinary share index.
ND = min(ΔLFTI:0)
SND = $\Sigma_{i=0}^{7}$ ND(t − i)
DCCC has a value of zero prior to 1971 Q4 and unity thereafter.

elasticity of 0.28 and a wealth elasticity of 0.72. The inflation effect plays a powerful role with an increase of 1 percentage point in the inflation rate leading to a reduction in desired money holdings of 0.7%. The stock market term implies that if falls in the index over the previous 2 years amounted to 1% then money holdings would be 0.2% larger than if no falls in the index had occurred.

We now verify that this is indeed a co-integrating vector, as well as considering its uniqueness, by applying the Johansen procedure to this set of variables. The final equation in Table 5.18 contains five variables; the Johansen procedure suggested that there may exist two co-integrating vectors but that there are unlikely to be more than two. The test statistics are shown in Table 5.19. The eigenvalues and eigenvectors corresponding to the two significant test statistics are given in Table 5.20. In this case the

Table 5.19

r	*LR test*	*5% critical value*
0	78.9	57.2
1	42.1	38.6
2	17.7	23.8
3	7.3	12.0
4	1.14	4.2

Table 5.20

	Eigenvector				
Eigenvalue	LM4V	Δ_4LPGDP	LPW − LGDP − LPGDP	SND	DCCC
0.391	4.82	25.6	− 4.05	− 1.53	− 2.23
0.281	−92.5	−80.33	66.68	11.03	10.13

eigenvector corresponding to the second eigenvalue is almost identical with the OLS results given in Table 5.18. The eigenvector corresponding to the largest eigenvalue is quite implausible as a causal relationship for M4 and, given the large coefficient on inflation, it seems likely that this co-integrating vector is actually determining inflation. Therefore this procedure again finds a set of results which broadly support our OLS findings.

We now proceed to a dynamic model for M4 which is based on the final co-integrating regression given in Table 5.18. Once again we proceed along a conventional path of general to specific modelling, beginning with an ECM containing four lags in the differences of all the variables. The final parsimonious model is

$$\Delta LM4_t = \underset{(4.8)}{0.016} + \underset{(5.2)}{0.512}\Delta LM4_{t-1} - \underset{(2.4)}{0.15}RES_{t-1}$$

where RES denotes residuals from the co-integrating regression (Table 5.18, Equation (46)).

$\sigma = 0.0096$	$R^2 = 0.30$	DW = 1.98
ARCH(1) = 0.27	RESET(4) = 6.5	BJ(2) = 0.32
LM(1) = 0.57	LM(4) = 10.8	LM(8) = 10.7
LB(1) = 0.12	LB(4) = 2.45	LB(8) = 3.02
CHISQ(8) = 6.1	CHISQ(12) = 6.4	CHISQ(24) = 11.4

Sample period, 1969 Q1 to 1987 Q2

Recursive estimation over the period 1979 Q1 to 1987 Q2 again shows these parameters to be very stable. The CUSUMSQ statistic (Fig. 5.15) and a sequential one-period-ahead Chow test (Fig. 5.16) clearly suggest that the equation is stable.

5.6 A MODEL OF M3

We now repeat the exercise for M3 following much the same procedure as used for the other aggregates. We begin by examining the co-integrating properties of the simple textbook model for M3, involving interest rates,

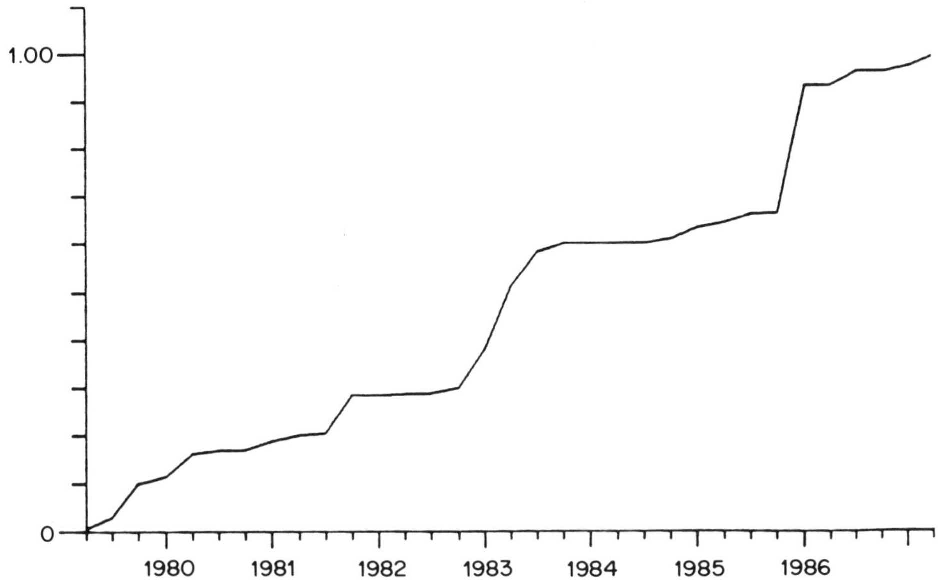

Fig. 5.15 Test statistics for recursive estimation of the dynamic M4 equation: CUSUMSQ statistic.

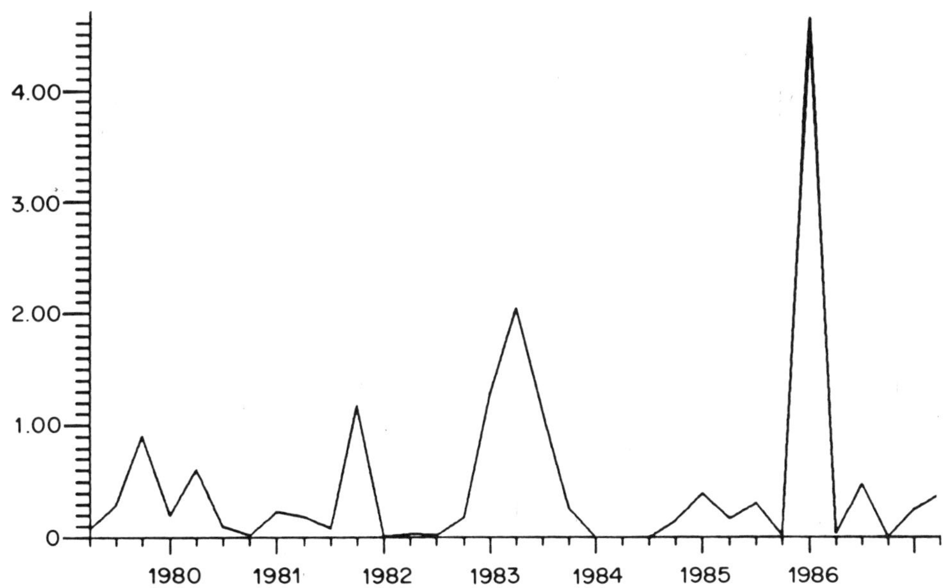

Fig. 5.16 Test statistics for recursive estimation of the dynamic M4 equation: sequential one-period-ahead Chow test.

Table 5.21 Testing the simple model of M3

	(47)	*(48)*	*(49)*
LPGDP	—	0.84	—
LPTFE	0.82	—	—
LCPI	—	—	0.74
LGDP	—	1.5	—
LTFE	1.4	—	—
LQCE	—	—	2.0
RTB	−0.005	−0.002	0.0
CRDW	0.13	0.16	0.33
DF	−1.3	−1.5	−2.9
ADF	−1.9	−1.8	−2.5
R^2	0.99	0.99	0.99

Sample period, 1968 Q1 to 1987 Q2.

output and prices. This is done in Table 5.21. This table shows, quite decisively, that again this simple set of variables does not constitute a co-integrating vector. Figure 5.17 shows the path of M3 relative to total final expenditure, and it is clear from this that there have been large changes in M3 holdings which must be explained by something other than nominal income.

The approach we take is to base our M3 co-integrating regression around that used for M4 (Table 5.22). Two additions are made to allow for innovation on the part of the building societies. The first attempts to capture the effect of the introduction of new types of accounts by the societies in 1974 and the second attempts to capture a further burst of innovation after 1981. These changes are modelled by allowing the elasticity of the demand for M3 with respect to wealth to alter during these periods. The changes are captured not by a step change in the coefficient but by an ogive which allows a more gradual adjustment.

The equation is very similar to that for M4. The inflation effect and the wealth effect are a little larger. The term describing falls in the stock market index also has a larger effect than in the M4 equation, probably reflecting the concentration of financial institutions money holdings in M3. The terms capturing innovation around 1974 and 1981 indicate a loss of market share by the banks amounting to 2% of personal sector wealth in the mid-1970s and a further 1% in the early 1980s.

If we now apply the Johansen procedure to this set of variables we obtain the results shown in Table 5.23. The likelihood ratio test showing that there are at most r co-integrating vectors is shown in Table 5.24. On the basis of this test procedure there may be five co-integrating vectors amongst these seven variables. In this case the eigenvector corresponding to the second-largest eigenvalue is very similar to the OLS result. We shall therefore

Fig. 5.17 M3 relative to GDP (logarithmic scale).

Table 5.22 A co-integrating vector for M3

	Dependent variables		
	LM3 *(50)*	LM3 − LPGDP *(51)*	LM3 − LPGDP − LGDP *(52)*
LPGDP	0.96		
LGDP	0.90	0.91	
Δ_4LPGDP	−0.74	−0.74	−0.74
LPW − LGDP − LPGDP	0.88	0.84	0.83
SND	−0.27	−0.27	−0.27
DCCC	0.94	0.08	0.08
LPW74	−0.003	−0.01	−0.02
LPW81	−0.01	−0.01	−0.01
CRDW	1.20	1.10	1.10
DF	−5.80	−5.40	−5.40
ADF	−5.1	−4.8	−4.9
R^2	0.99	0.96	0.95

$$\text{LPW74} = (\text{LPW} - \text{LGDP} - \text{LPGDP})D74$$

$$\text{LPW81} = (\text{LPW} - \text{LGDP} - \text{LPGDP})D81$$

$$D74 = 1 - \exp(-0.01t_1^2)$$

$$D81 = 1 - \exp(-0.01t_2^2)$$

t_1 and t_2 are time trends starting in 1974 Q2 and 1981 Q4 respectively.

proceed to the dynamic modelling stage on the basis of the OLS results.

Once again we use a conventional general to specific methodology to derive a dynamic model. As in the case of M4 this produced a simple dynamic model which is given below:

$$\Delta\text{LM3}_t = \underset{(4.6)}{0.016} + \underset{(4.8)}{0.48}\Delta\text{LM3}_{t-1} - \underset{(3.7)}{0.28}\text{RES}_{t-1}$$

where RES denotes the residuals from the co-integrating regression in Table 5.22, Equation (52).

$\sigma = 0.015$ $\quad R^2 = 0.32$ $\quad$ DW = 2.04

ARCH(1) = 0.18 $\quad$ RESET(4) = 4.5 $\quad$ BJ(2) = 0.84

LM(1) = 0.25 $\quad$ LM(4) = 9.5 $\quad$ LM(8) = 10.5

LB(1) = 0.05 $\quad$ LB(4) = 7.6 $\quad$ LB(8) = 8.0

CHISQ(8) = 13.4 $\quad$ CHISQ(12) = 13.6 $\quad$ CHISQ(24) = 20.3

Sample period, 1969 Q1 to 1987 Q2

Table 5.23

Eigenvalue	*Eigenvector*						
	LM3 – LPCDD – LGDP	Δ_4LPGDP	LPW – LGDP – LPGDP	SND	DCCC	LPW74	LPW81
0.62	−27.6	− 1.6	20.7	−2.5	2.3	−1.1	0.6
0.54	−35.8	−30.3	25.1	−1.1	1.4	−0.6	−0.5
0.39	33.0	53.7	30.5	8.5	−2.2	−0.2	1.2
0.34	−18.8	−43.9	22.6	2.9	4.1	−0.1	−0.8
0.22	18.4	− 2.7	−43.3	0.3	0.9	−0.4	1.9
0.08	5.9	− 6.1	2.0	0.6	−2.4	0.2	−0.2
0.002	4.7	0.1	15.3	−0.9	−3.4	1.4	−0.7

Table 5.24

r	*LR test*	*5% critical value*
0	228.8	103.0
1	155.6	78.1
2	96.2	57.2
3	58.0	28.6
4	26.4	23.8
5	7.2	12.0
6	0.2	4.2

This equation is again well behaved in terms of a wide range of diagnostic tests which include the standard structural stability tests. Recursive estimation over the period 1979 Q1 to 1986 Q4 shows that the parameters are highly stable. The CUSUM and CUSUMSQ statistics show no sign of underlying mis-specification (Fig. 5.18). Finally the sequential Chow test (Fig. 5.19) detects instability in 1987 Q1 and 1986 Q1 only (with a critical value of 4 neither failure is large).

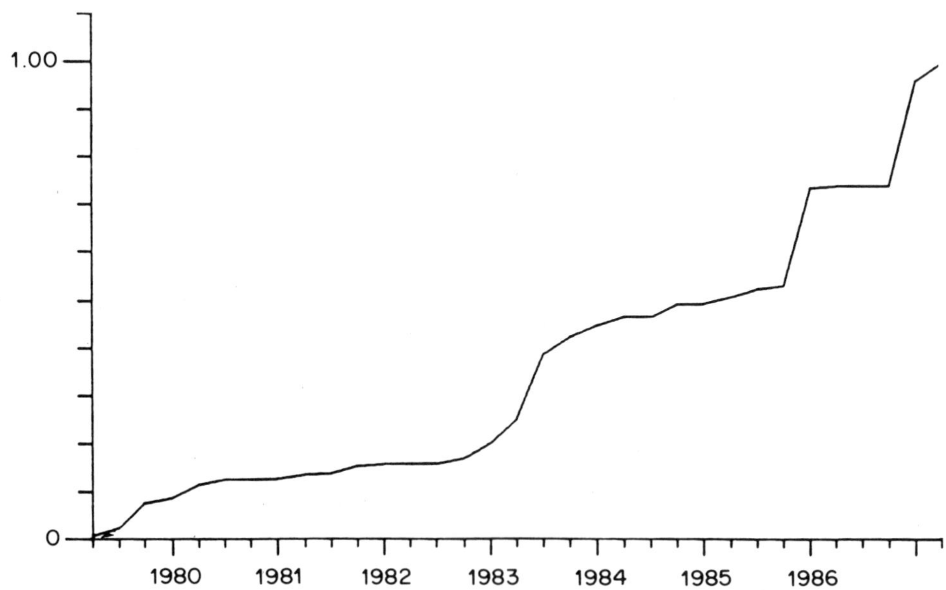

Fig. 5.18 Test statistics for recursive estimation of the dynamic M3 equation: CUSUMSQ statistic.

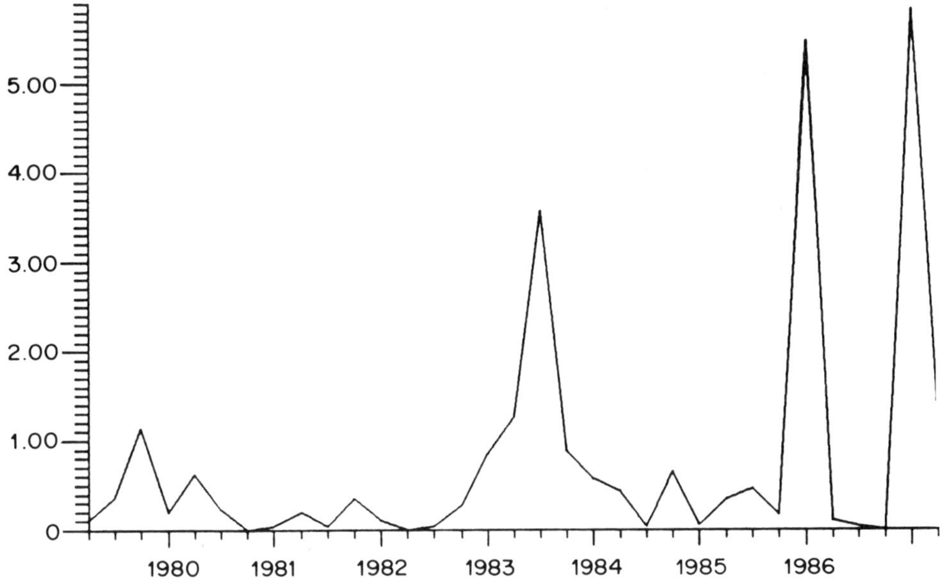

Fig. 5.19 Test statistics for recursive estimation of the dynamic M3 equation: sequential one-period-ahead Chow test.

5.7 CONCLUSION

In this chapter we have applied co-integration techniques to model a range of monetary aggregates M0, M1, M3 and M4. In each case we have been able, after some searching, to find a suitable set of co-integrating variables and to build a dynamic model which is satisfactory on a broad range of criteria.

Perhaps the most striking conclusion we have reached is that in no case does the simple textbook set of variables prove to be adequate. To practitioners this is not surprising, of course, as it is simply another way of saying that models based on this set of variables are inadequate and will be found to be structurally unstable. This is such a well-known phenomenon of monetary modelling over the last 20 years that it needs no documentation. With the perspective of co-integration theory, however, it becomes evident that the way forward is not to play with increasingly complex dynamics but rather to seek the missing components. Once this is done the dynamic model is relatively straightforward and, indeed, in the case of M0, M3 and M4 a striking feature is just how simple the resulting dynamics are.

As we move from narrow money M0 to broad money M4 it is not surprising that the types of extra effects we need to include change. At the narrow money end we need to take account of financial innovation and the move into interest-bearing M1 accounts. At the broad money end, where we are dealing with more of an asset than a medium of exchange, we need to allow for broad wealth effects.

APPENDIX A5.1: THE JOHANSEN PROCEDURE

Johansen (1988) sets his analysis within the following framework. Begin by defining a general polynomial distributed lag model of a vector of variables X as

$$X_t = \pi_1 X_{t-1} + \ldots + \pi_k X_{t-k} + \varepsilon_t \qquad t = 1, \ldots, T \qquad \text{(A5.1)}$$

where X_t is a vector of N variables of interest, the π_i are $N \times N$ coefficient matrices and ε_t is an independently identically distributed N-dimensional vector with zero mean and variance matrix Ω. Within this framework the long-run, or co-integrating, matrix is given by

$$I - \pi_1 - \pi_2 - \ldots - \pi_k = \pi \qquad \text{(A5.2)}$$

where I is the identity matrix.

π will therefore be an $N \times N$ matrix. The number r of distinct co-integrating vectors which exists between the variables of X will be given by the rank of π. In general, if X consists of variables which must be differenced once in order to be stationary (integrated of order 1 or $I(1)$) then, at most, r must be equal to $N - 1$, so that $r \leqslant N - 1$. Now we define two matrices α, β, both of which are $N \times r$, such that

$$\pi = \alpha\beta'$$

and so the rows of β form the r distinct co-integrating vectors.

Johansen then demonstrates the following theorem.

Theorem The maximum likelihood estimate of the space spanned by β is the space spanned by the r canonical variates corresponding to the r largest squared canonical correlations between the residuals of X_{t-k} and ΔX_t corrected for the effect of the lagged differences of the X process. The likelihood ratio test statistic for the hypothesis that there are at most r co-integrating vectors is

$$-2 \ln Q = -T \sum_{i=r+1}^{N} \ln(1 - \hat{\lambda}_i) \qquad \text{(A5.3)}$$

where $\hat{\lambda}_{r+1}, \ldots, \hat{\lambda}_N$ are the $N - r$ smallest squared canonical correlations.

Johansen then goes on to demonstrate the properties of the maximum likelihood estimates and, more importantly, he shows that the likelihood ratio test has an asymptotic distribution which is a function of an $(N - r)$-dimensional Brownian motion which is independent of any nuisance parameters. This means that a set of critical values can be tabulated which will be correct for all models. He demonstrates that the space spanned by β is consistently estimated by the space spanned by $\hat{\beta}$.

In order to implement this theorem we begin by reparameterizing A5.1 into the following ECM:

$$\Delta X_t = \Gamma_1 \Delta X_{t-1} + \ldots + \Gamma_{k-1} \Delta X_{t-k+1} + \Gamma_k X_{t-k} + \varepsilon_t \qquad \text{(A5.4)}$$

where

$$\Gamma_i = -I + \pi_1 + \ldots + \pi_i \qquad i = 1, \ldots, k$$

The equilibrium matrix π is now clearly identified as $-\Gamma_k$.

Johansen's suggested procedure begins by regressing ΔX_t on the lagged differences of ΔX_t and defining a set of residuals R_{0t}, and then regressing X_{t-k} on the lagged differences and defining R_{kt}. The likelihood function, in terms of α, β and Ω, is then proportional to

$$L(\alpha, \beta, \Omega) = |\Omega|^{-T/2} \exp\left\{ -\tfrac{1}{2} \sum_{t=1}^{T} (R_{0t} + \alpha\beta' R_{kt})' \Omega^{-1} (R_{0t} + \alpha\beta' R_{kt}) \right\} \qquad \text{(A5.5)}$$

If β were fixed we could maximize over α and Ω by a regression of R_{0t} on $-\beta' R_{kt}$ which gives

$$\hat{\alpha}(\beta) = -S_{0k}\beta(\beta' S_{kk}\beta)^{-1} \qquad \text{(A5.6)}$$

and

$$\hat{\Omega}_{(\beta)} = S_{00} - S_{0k}\beta(\beta' S_{kk}\beta)^{-1}\beta' S_{k0} \qquad \text{(A5.7)}$$

where

$$S_{ij} = T^{-1} \sum_{t=1}^{T} R_{it} R'_{jt} \qquad i, j = 0, k$$

Therefore maximizing the likelihood function can be reduced to minimizing

$$|S_{00} - S_{0k}\beta(\beta' S_{kk}\beta)^{-1}\beta' S_{k0}| \qquad \text{(A5.8)}$$

It can be shown that (A5.8) will be minimized when

$$\frac{|\beta' S_{kk}\beta - \beta' S_{k0} S S_{00}^{-1} S_{0k}\beta|}{|\beta' S_{kk}\beta|} \qquad \text{(A5.9)}$$

attains a minimum with respect to β.

We now define a diagonal matrix D which consists of the ordered eigenvalues $\lambda_1 > \ldots > \lambda_N$ of $S_{k0} S_{00}^{-1} S_{0k}$ with respect to S_{kk}. That is, λ_i satisfies

$$|\lambda S_{kk} - S_{k0}S_{00}^{-1}S_{0k}| = 0 \tag{A5.10}$$

Define E to be the corresponding matrix of eigenvectors so that

$$S_{kk}ED = S_{k0}S_{00}^{-1}S_{0k}E \tag{A5.11}$$

where we normalize E such that $E'S_{kk}E = I$.

The maximum likelihood estimator of β is now given by the first r rows of E, i.e. the first r eigenvectors of $S_{k0}S_{00}^{-1}S_{0k}$ with respect to S_{kk}. These are the canonical variates, and the corresponding eigenvalues are the squared canonical correlations of R_k with respect to R_0. These eigenvalues can then be used in the test proposed in A5.3 to test either for the existence of a co-integrating vector ($r = 1$) or for the number of co-integrating vectors ($N > r > 1$).

Johansen calculates the critical values for the likelihood ratio test for the cases where $m \leqslant 5$, where $m = P - r$, P is the number of variables in the set under consideration and r is the maximum number of co-integrating vectors being tested for. This limits us to testing only within sets of five or fewer variables. Johansen provides an approximation formula for the critical values, and we have used this to compute the critical values for all cases up to $m = 10$ (Table A5.1). For $m \leqslant 5$ we can compare the approximation with the numerically derived results to gauge the accuracy of the approximation.

Table A5.1 Critical values for the likelihood ratio test (95% critical value)

m	*Johansen critical values*	*Approximation values*
1	4.2	3.25
2	12.0	12.1
3	23.8	23.6
4	38.6	38.4
5	57.2	56.6
6	n/a	78.1
7	n/a	103.0
8	n/a	131.1
9	n/a	162.8
10	n/a	197.7

n/a, not available.

APPENDIX A5.2: Diagnostic test statistics

LM(i): Lagrange Multiplier test for i-th order serial correlation; $\chi^2(\text{i})$.

LB(i): Ljung-Box test for i-th order serial correlation; χ^2(i).
ARCH(1): χ^2(1) test for autoregressive conditional heteroscedasticity.
RESET(4): χ^2(4) test of functional form.
BJ(2): χ^2(2) test for normality of residuals.
CHISQ(i): χ^2(i) Hendry static forecasting test.

REFERENCES

Artis, M. J. and Lewis, M. K. (1984) How unstable is the demand for money function in the UK. *Economica,* **51**, 473–6.

Baba, Y., Hendry, D. F. and Starr, R. M. (1982) US money demand 1960–1984, Nuffield Discussion Paper No. 27.

Banerjee, A., Dolado, J. J., Hendry, D. F. and Smith, G. W. (1986) Exploring equilibrium relationships in econometrics through state models: some Monte Carlo evidence. *Oxford Bulletin of Economics and Statistics,* **48**(3), 253–78.

Bank of England (1986) Financial change and broad money. *Bank of England Quarterly Bulletin,* **26**(4), 499–507.

Carr, J. and Darby, M. (1981) The role of money supply shocks in the short-run demand for money. *Journal of Monetary Economics,* **8**, 183–200.

Cuthbertson, K. (1986) Price expectations and adjustment lags in the demand for money. *Scottish Journal of Political Economy,* **33** (4), 334–54.

Cuthbertson, K. and Taylor, M. P. (1987) Buffer Stock Money: An Appraisal, in *The Operation and Regulation of Financial Markets* (eds Goodhart, Currie and Llewellyn), Macmillan, London

Davidson, J. E. H. (1987) Disequilibrium money: some further results with a monetary model of the UK, in *The Operation and Regulation of Financial Markets* (eds Goodhart, Currie and Llewellyn), Macmillan, London.

Davidson, J. and Ireland, J. (1987) Buffer stock models of the monetary sector. *National Institute Economic Review,* August, **145**.

Dickey, D. A. and Fuller, W. A. (1979) Distribution of the estimation for autoregressive time series with a unit root. *Journal of American Statistical Association,* **74**, 427–31.

Engle, R. F. and Granger, C. W. J. (1987) Co-integration and error correction: representation, estimation and testing. *Econometrica,* **55**(12), 251–76.

Granger, C. W. J. (1986) Development in the study of cointegrated economic variables. *Oxford Bulletin of Economics and Statistics,* **48**(3), 213–28.

Granger, C. W. J. and Newbold, P. (1974) Spurious regression in econometrics. *Journal of Econometrics,* **2**, 111–20.

Granger, C. W. J. and Weiss, A. A. (1983) Time series analysis of error correcting models, in *Studies in Econometrics, Time Series and Multivariate Statistics* (eds S. Karlin, T. Amemiya and L. A. Goodman), Academic Press, New York.

Grice, J. and Bennet, A. (1984) Wealth and the demand for £M3 in the United Kingdom 1975–81. *Manchester School,* **52**(3), 239–71.

Hall, S. G. (1986) An application of the Granger and Engle two-step estimation procedure to UK aggregate usage data. *Oxford Bulletin of Economics and Statistics,* **48**(3), 229–40.

Hall, S. G. (1988) Maximum likelihood estimation of cointegrating vectors: an example of the Johansen procedure. *Oxford Bulletin of Economics and Statistics,* **51**

Hendry, D. F. (1979) Predictive failure and econometric modelling, in *Macroeconomics: The Transactions Demand for Money* (ed. P. Ormerod), Heinemann, London.

Hendry, D. F. (1986) Econometric modelling with cointegrated variables: an overview. *Oxford Bulletin of Economics and Statistics*, **48**(3), 201–13.

Hendry, D. F. and Ericsson, N. (1983) Monetary trends in the UK, Paper presented to the 22nd Meeting of the Bank of England Panel of Academic Consultants.

Hendry, D. F. and Mizon, G. E. (1978) Serial correlation as a convenient simplification not a nuisance: a comment on a study of the demand for money by the Bank of England. *Economic Journal*, **88**, 49–63.

Johansen, S. (1988) Statistical analysis of cointegrating vectors. *Journal of Economic Dynamics and Control*, **12**(2–3), 231–54.

Johnston, R. B. (1984) The demand for non-interest bearing money in the UK, Treasury Working Paper No. 28.

Lubrano, M., Pierse, R. G. and Richard, J. F. (1986) Stability of a UK money demand equation: a Bayesian approach to testing exogeneity. *Review of Economic Studies*, **53**(4), 603–34.

Park, J. Y. and Phillips, P. C. B. (1986) Statistical inference in regressions with integrated processes: Part 1, York University Discussion Paper No. 811.

Patterson, K. D. (1987) The specification and stability of the demand for money in the UK. *Economica*, **54**, 41–55.

Phillips, P. C. B. and Durlauf, S. N. (1986) Multiple time series regression with integrated processes. *Review of Economic Studies*, **53**, 473–95.

Stock, J. H. (1985) Asymptotic properties of least square estimates of cointegrating vectors, Harvard University mimeo.

Stock, J. H. (1987) Asymptotic properties of a least squares estimator of cointegrating vectors. *Econometrica*, **55**(5), 1035–56.

Taylor, M. P. (1987) Financial innovation, inflation and the stability of the demand for broad money in the United Kingdom. *Bulletin of Economic Research*, **39**, 225–33.

Trundle, J. (1982) The demand for M1 in the UK, Bank of England mimeo.

6

A capital asset pricing model with time-varying betas: some results from the London Stock Exchange

S. G. HALL, D. K. MILES AND M. P. TAYLOR

6.1 INTRODUCTION

According to the capital asset pricing model (CAPM) developed originally by Sharpe (1964) and Lintner (1965), the required excess return on a risky asset is proportional to its non-diversifiable risk, for which a sufficient statistic is the covariance of the asset return with the return on the market portfolio. In the case where this covariance is zero, the risk is completely diversifiable and the required excess return over the safe rate of return is zero. Empirical tests of the CAPM have generally yielded results unfavourable to the model in its simplest form. In particular, variables other than the covariance of the return with the market return have been found to be significant in explaining the excess return—variables ranging from the own return variance to seasonal dummies (see Jensen (1972) or Schwert (1983) for surveys).

Following doubts cast on such empirical studies by Fama (1977, Chapter 9), Roll (1977) demonstrated that a theoretically correct implementation of the CAPM is practically impossible. This is because, in the theoretical derivation of the CAPM, the market portfolio is assumed to be mean–variance efficient in the sense of Markowitz (1952). In particular, such a portfolio would involve investment in every individual existing asset with an optimal weight. In practice, researchers have generally employed stock market indices in which the weights are almost certainly suboptimal. Many assets which would be expected to be in an optimal portfolio are excluded (e.g housing, human capital). According to Roll's critique, virtually no empirical study is capable of rejecting the CAPM.

Another explanation for these empirical findings is simply that the CAPM is incorrect and that another pricing theory should be used such as the arbitrage pricing theory (APT) of Ross (1976) or the consumption-based CAPM due to Breeden (1979).

In this chapter, we pursue a third line of inquiry into the empirical failure of the CAPM—namely that the relevant distributional moments for the CAPM are not the unconditional covariances of returns, but the *conditional* covariances. Thus, asset betas—the ratio of the covariance of the asset return with the market return to the variance of the market return—may be random and time varying rather than constant as in the traditional formulation. It seems reasonable, since agents must form expectations concerning these moments, that conditional covariances, given information up to the time that the expectation is formed, should be the relevant measures of risk for the CAPM. If, in addition, excess returns are characterized by conditional heteroscedasticity (e.g. Klemkosky and Martin, 1975), time variation in asset betas is implied.

In what follows, we model the conditional heteroscedasticity of excess returns using the autoregressive conditional heteroscedasticity (ARCH) model of Engle (1982) and its generalization—the generalized ARCH (GARCH) formulation—due to Bollerslev (1986). The models are estimated on monthly UK data for the period March 1975 to June 1987. To some extent our analysis is similar to the US study by Bollerslev *et al.* (1988). However, we also test this version of the CAPM against a more general model which allows expected returns to depend on time-varying conditional covariances with consumption. We are able to reject both the traditional CAPM and the consumption-based CAPM of Breeden in favour of a model which makes the risk premiums depend on a composite measure of non-diversifiable risk.

6.2 THE CAPITAL ASSET PRICING MODEL

The Sharpe–Lintner formulation of the CAPM states that the expected or required excess return on an asset over the safe asset return is proportional to the required excess return on the market portfolio, with the factor of proportionality being equal to the asset beta:

$$E(R_i) - r = \beta_i\{E(R_m) - r\} \tag{6.1}$$

$$\beta_i = \frac{\text{cov}(R_i, R_m)}{\text{var}(R_m)} \tag{6.2}$$

where R_i and R_m are the one-period returns on the asset and the market portfolio respectively and r is the one-period safe rate of return. A natural extension of the model is to condition the moments of 6.1 and 6.2 on information available to agents at the end of period $t - 1$ when formulating required returns during period t:

$$E(R_{it}|\Omega_{t-1}) - r_{t-1} = \beta_{it}\{E(R_{mt}|\Omega_{t-1}) - r_{t-1}\} \tag{6.3}$$

$$\beta_{it} = \frac{\text{cov}(R_{it}, R_{mt}|\Omega_{t-1})}{\text{var}(R_{mr}|\Omega_{t-1})} \tag{6.4}$$

where Ω_{t-1} is the information set at time $t - 1$.

Apart from the problem of parameterizing the conditional covariances in 6.4, which we shall address in the next section, 6.3 is non-operational because of the lack of an observed series for the required or expected market rate of return one period ahead. If, however, we assume that the 'market price of risk' λ, defined as

$$\lambda = \frac{E(R_{mt}|\Omega_{t-1}) - r_{t-1}}{\text{var}(R_{mt}|\Omega_{t-1})} \tag{6.5}$$

is a constant, we have

$$E(R_{mt}|\Omega_{t-1}) - r_{t-1} = \lambda\,\text{var}(R_{mt}|\Omega_{t-1}) \tag{6.6}$$

so that parameterization of the process generating the conditional second moments will be sufficient.

If the conditional variance of the market return is a sufficient statistic for the risk attached to the market portfolio, then λ simply measures how many units of excess market return are required to compensate for one unit of market risk. It is in this sense that it measures the market price of risk. Under certain regularity conditions, Merton (1980) shows that the market price of risk is the weighed harmonic mean of investors' coefficients of relative risk aversion, with the weights given by each investor's share in aggregate wealth. Thus, in a simple representative agent model, λ would itself be the coefficient of relative risk aversion. Throughout this chapter we assume λ to be a constant. This considerably simplifies the analysis and seems reasonable given the relatively short data period—roughly 10 years—that we examine.

Using 6.3, 6.4 and 6.6, we can write

$$R_{it} = r_{t-1} + \lambda\,\text{cov}(R_{it}, R_{mt}|\Omega_{t-1}) + \varepsilon_{it} \tag{6.7}$$

$$R_{mt} = r_{t-1} + \lambda\,\text{var}(R_{mt}|\Omega_{t-1}) + \upsilon_t \tag{6.8}$$

where we have replaced expected with actual values by augmenting the right-hand side of each equation with the rational expectations forecast errors

$$\varepsilon_{it} = R_{it} - E(R_{it}|\Omega_{t-1}) \tag{6.9}$$

$$v_t = R_{mt} - E(R_{mt}|\Omega_{t-1}) \tag{6.10}$$

It is clear from 6.9 and 6.10 that the relevant conditional second moments are themselves equal to the forecast error variances and covariances:

$$\text{var}\,(R_{mt}|\Omega_{t-1}) = E(v_t^2|\Omega_{t-1}) \tag{6.11}$$

$$\text{cov}\,(R_{it}, R_{mt}|\Omega_{t-1}) = E(\varepsilon_{it}v_t|\Omega_{t-1}) \tag{6.12}$$

Equations 6.7, 6.8, 6.11 and 6.12 form the basis of the variant of the CAPM estimated in this chapter.

In the next section we suggest a tractable parameterization of the conditional second moments.

6.3 PARAMETERIZING THE CONDITIONAL SECOND MOMENTS

Engle *et al.* (1987) suggest an extension of Engle's (1982) ARCH model whereby the conditional first moment of a time series itself becomes a function of the conditional second moment, which follows an ARCH process:

$$Y_t = \alpha' x_t + \delta h_t^2 + \varepsilon_t$$

$$h_t^2 = E(\varepsilon_t^2|\Omega_{t-1}) = \gamma_0 + \sum_{i=1}^{n} \gamma_i \varepsilon_{t-i}^2 + \kappa' z_t$$

where x_t and z_t are vectors of weakly exogenous conditioning variables. Engle *et al.* (1987) term this kind of model ARCH in mean or ARCH-M.

A straightforward multivariate extension of the ARCH-M model can be applied to the CAPM formulation of the previous section as follows. We establish the following notation:

$$R_t = (R_{it} - R_{mt})'$$

$$\omega_t = (\varepsilon_t\ v_t)'$$

$$\iota = (1\ 1)'$$

$$e = (0\ 1)'$$

$$H_t = \begin{bmatrix} \text{var}\,(R_{it}|\Omega_{t-1}) & \text{cov}\,(R_{it}, R_{mt}|\Omega_{t-1}) \\ \text{cov}\,(R_{it}, R_{mt}|\Omega_{t-1}) & \text{var}\,(R_{mt}|\Omega_{t-1}) \end{bmatrix}$$

Then the ARCH-M formulation of 6.7, 6.8, 6.11 and 6.12 is

$$R_t = r_{t-1}\iota + \lambda H_t e + \omega_t \tag{6.13}$$

$$\text{vech}(H_t) = A_0 + \sum_{i=1}^{n} A_i \text{ vech}(\omega_{t-i}\omega'_{t-i}) \tag{6.14}$$

where vech( ) denotes the column-stacking operator of the lower triangular portion of a symmetric matrix and the A_i are 3×3 coefficient matrices except for A_0 which is a 3×1 coefficient vector. The system 6.13 and 6.14 describes a multivariate ARCH-M(n) model.

A further extension of the ARCH formulation, which imposes smoother behaviour on the conditional second moments, has been suggested by Bollerslev (1986). In Bollerslev's GARCH formulation, the conditional second moments are functions of their own lagged values as well as the squares and cross-products of lagged forecast errors. Thus, for example, the GARCH-M(n, p) formulation of the above model would consist of 6.13 and

$$\text{vech}(H_t) = A_0 + \sum_{i=1}^{n} A_i \text{ vech}(\omega_{t-i}\omega'_{t-i}) + \sum_{i=1}^{p} B_i \text{ vech}(H_{t-i}) \tag{6.15}$$

where the B_i are 3×3 coefficient matrices. Below, we present estimates of both ARCH-M and GARCH-M formulations of CAPM.

It should be noted that, although there now exists considerable empirical evidence that financial asset prices are characterized by ARCH behaviour (e.g. Dickens, 1987), the ARCH parameterization of the conditional second moments does not appear to have any immediate economic rationale. It should therefore be interpreted in much the same spirit as autoregressive moving-average (ARMA) time series models, i.e. as a convenient and parsimonious representation of the behaviour of time series data.

Stacking all the parameters of the system into a single vector

$$\mu = (\lambda, (A_0)', \text{vech}(A_1)', \ldots, \text{vech}(A_n)', \text{vech}(B_1)', \ldots, \text{vech}(B_p)')'$$

and applying Schweppe's (1965) prediction error decomposition form of the likelihood function, we obtain the log likelihood for a sample of T observations (conditional on initial values) as

$$L(\mu) = \sum_{t=1}^{T} \log|H_t(\mu)| - \sum_{t=1}^{T} \omega'_t H_t^{-1}(\mu)\omega_t \tag{6.16}$$

where we have assumed normality of the forecast errors.

Although the analytic derivatives of 6.16 can be computed (Engle *et al.*, 1987) variable-metric algorithms which employ numerical derivative are simpler to use and easily allow changes in specification, and this approach was applied here. Under the usual regularity conditions (Crowder, 1976), maximization of 6.16 will yield maximum likelihood estimates with the usual properties.

As they stand, the above formulations are very general and contain a large number of parameters to be estimated, which may be problematic given the non-linearities of the system. As a first step, it seems reasonable to assume that each covariance depends only upon its own past values and surprises. Accordingly, we assume that the A_i and B_i matrices are diagonal. In addition, since inversion of any GARCH model of non-zero order implies an infinitely long memory with respect to past surprises, we limit the estimated GARCH models to first order, i.e. GARCH-M(1, 1). For the ARCH-M model, we set $n = 8$ and, following Engle (1982), assume that agents linearly discount past surprises in forming expectations of future forecast error variances and, furthermore, that these discount factors are the same in each of the three ARCH equations:

$$\text{vech}\,(H_t) = A_0 + A_1\{c_i\,\text{vech}\,(\omega_{t-i}\omega'_{t-i})\} \tag{6.17}$$

$$c_i = \frac{9 - i}{36} \qquad i = 1, 2, \ldots, 8$$

or, for the GARCH model,

$$\text{vech}\,(H_t) = A_0 + A_1\,\text{vech}\,(\omega_{t-1}\omega'_{t-1}) + B_1\,\text{vech}\,(H_{t-1}) \tag{6.18}$$

Apart from estimating the ARCH-M and GARCH-M formulations of the CAPM, we also subject the CAPM specification to a range of diagnostic tests.

6.4. DATA

We used beginning-of-month data on the share prices of firms quoted on the London Stock Exchange to define one-month *ex post* rates of return. Data on dividend payments per share were used to adjust the change in share prices to give the one-month holding-period returns. Value-weighted data on the returns from companies in particular sectors were aggregated to form the returns on four portfolios. The four portfolios were for the following sectors (numbers of individual stocks in each portfolio in parentheses): mechanical engineering (58), financial (122), electrical (12) and chemical (20).

The return on the market portfolio was taken as the percentage change in the FT 500 share index (beginning month to beginning month) adjusted for dividend payments. The dividends adjustment is crude because data on the exact timing of dividend payments by each firm in the index are not easily available. Annual average (value-weighted) dividend yields of the firms in the index were used to calculate estimates of the monthly dividend yields assuming that the timing of payments was uniformly distributed throughout the year. We used the one-month yield on the UK Treasury Bill as our measure of the safe rate of interest.

Data were collected from March 1975 to June 1987. Allowing for lags this gives an estimation period beginning in December 1975, yielding 139 observations.

6.5 EMPIRICAL RESULTS

The model to be estimated comprises the CAPM equation 6.13 and the accompanying ARCH or GARCH error process 6.17 or 6.18. We shall present two sets of estimates here. First we present a set of estimates for the four sectors chemical (C), electrical (E), mechanical (M) and financial (F), based on a set of two-equation ARCH-M models. These results do not incorporate the restriction that the price of risk λ should be constant across all four sectors. We shall then present estimates for a five-equation system, comprising all four sectors and the market equation, using a GARCH-M error process. This imposes the cross-equation parameter restriction on all sectors simultaneously and also allows a free estimate of the rate at which individuals discount observed past errors rather than imposing a fixed eight-month period, as in the case of our ARCH-M estimates.

We begin, in Table 6.1, by reporting the estimates of the ARCH-M model for the four sectors estimated independently. The lower half of the table presents a range of statistical tests for normality of the errors and for serial correlation. All the models passed all the tests for normality and for absence of serial correlation in the errors. However, only one of the estimated models demonstrates a significant ARCH coefficient: A_1 for the mechanical sector is significantly different from zero while in the other three sectors it is insignificant and numerically very small, which suggests that the conditional covariance matrix of the error term may not be time varying. Apart from this result the performance of the models is fairly satisfactory.

One possible explanation of the finding of a constant conditional covariance matrix may be that the imposed linear weighting pattern over eight-months is in fact too restrictive. In particular, this weighting pattern puts a very large emphasis on the first two or three months in the lag structure; in fact the mean lag is only about two and a half months. Thus, in these estimates we are effectively forcing the model to choose between a very short memory, which produces a rapidly changing conditional covariance matrix, or a constant covariance matrix, but nothing between the two. It may be that the conditional covariance matrix is changing over time but only fairly slowly. To investigate this we need to estimate the type of lag structure in a less restrictive way. The GARCH-M model allows us to do this in a reasonably parsimonious way. Furthermore, there is an intuitive interpretation of the GARCH(1, 1) model given by 6.18: expectations of conditional moments are updated in the light of new information with the weight given to the latest outcome equal to A_1. In additon, taking advantage of the parsimony of the GARCH formulation, we also estimate all four sectors simultaneously so that the price of risk λ is constrained to be equal across all the markets.[1]

We impose the restriction that A_1 and B_1 in 6.18 are scalars rather than vectors, but that A_0 is a full vector of 15 constants. In words, we assume

Table 6.1 ARCH-M estimates of the four sectors

	Chemical		*Electrical*		*Mechanical*		*Financial*	
λ	5.0	(7.8)	4.9	(7.6)	3.1	(4.4)	5.1	(7.8)
$A_0(\varepsilon_t, \varepsilon_t)$	0.0033	(18.5)	0.0042	(23.8)	0.0002	(0.9)	0.0028	(16.3)
$A_0(\varepsilon_t, \mathrm{v}_t)$	0.0022	(8.6)	0.0007	(10.5)	0.0001	(0.3)	0.00044	(7.5)
$A_0(v_t, v_t)$	0.0023	(18.6)	0.0024	(23.5)	0.0005	(6.4)	0.0022	(15.8)
A_1	0.047	(1.4)	0.0000001	(0.00)	0.985	(6.0)	0.06	(1.7)
SK_1	0.39		0.09		−0.33		−0.01	
$KURT_1$	0.35		0.18		0.24		0.66	
BJ_1	4.64		0.44		3.1		2.6	
$LB(1)_1$	0.19		1.8		1.9		0.04	
$LB(2)_1$	1.05		1.8		2.4		1.11	
$LB(4)_1$	1.54		3.6		5.5		1.98	
$LB(8)_1$	8.00		6.8		18.1		4.5	
$LB(16)_1$	12.73		18.6		21.6		8.23	
SK_2	−0.2		−0.19		−0.19		−0.2	
$KURT_2$	0.32		0.32		0.24		0.32	
BJ_2	1.63		1.68		1.34		1.63	
$LB(1)_2$	0.32		0.33		0.31		0.32	
$LB(2)_2$	0.70		0.69		0.81		0.71	
$LB(4)_2$	3.05		3.02		3.08		3.06	
$LB(8)_2$	9.62		9.67		8.34		9.59	
$LB(16)_2$	14.59		14.58		13.49		14.6	

SK, coefficient of skewness, critical value (95%) $\approx$ 0.41.
KURT, excess kurtosis, critical value (95%) $\approx$ 0.81.
BJ, Bera–Jarque normality test ($\sim\chi^2(2)$ under null).
LB(N), Ljung–Box statistic for serial correlation ($\sim\chi^2(N)$ under null).
Subscripts 1, 2, sector equation and market equation respectively.
The numbers in parentheses are the asymptotic t ratios.

that across a range of stocks people attach the same relative importance to past events in forming expectations about volatility of prices, i.e. people use similar forecasting rules for similar forecasting problems. A common assumption made in GARCH models is that the parameter matrices are diagonal; this is not appropriate in this model as the covariance terms are central to the analysis.

When we allow unrestricted parameter matrices, the question of the positive semi-definiteness of H_t arises. This is discussed by Baba *et al.* (1987), who suggest the following restriction to impose positive semi-definiteness on the model:

$$H_t = A_0'A_0 + A_1'\omega_{t-1}\omega_{t-1}'A_1 + B_1'H_{t-1}B_1$$

where A_0, A_1 and B_1 are symmetric-parameter matrices. In our case A_1 and B_1 are scalars rather than vectors, so that we only need restrict A_0.

Estimation of this five-equation (four sectors and the market index) model by maximum likelihood then gives the following set of parameter estimates:

$$\hat{\lambda} = 3.24 \qquad (3.1)$$

$$\hat{A}_1 = 0.027 \qquad (4.1)$$

$$\hat{B}_1 = 0.956 \qquad (119.6)$$

$$\hat{A}_0 =$$

$$\begin{bmatrix} -0.006\ (7.5) & & & & \\ 0.001\ (0.9) & 0.005\ (4.0) & & & \\ -0.0004\ (0.1) & 0.0003\ (0.4) & 0.005\ (8.4) & & \\ -0.0009\ (0.5) & 0.000006\ (0.0) & -0.0005\ (1.1) & 0.003\ (2.6) & \\ -0.001\ (22.2) & 0.0002\ (0.9) & 0.0003\ (1.7) & -0.02\ (1.0) & -0.002\ (4.6) \end{bmatrix}$$

where the asymptotic t ratios are in parentheses.

Table 6.2 presents evidence on the properties of the model's five sets of residuals. In this model the estimate of the price of risk λ is reasonably close

[1] In order to interpret the GARCH CAPM model 6.13 and 6.18 for this multi-equation system, simply re-interpret some of the notation. In particular,

$$R_t = (R_{1t}\ R_{2t}\ R_{3t}\ R_{4t}\ R_{mt})'$$

$$\omega_t = (\varepsilon_{1t}\ \varepsilon_{2t}\ \varepsilon_{3t}\ \varepsilon_{4t}\ v_t)'$$

$$\iota = (1\ 1\ 1\ 1\ 1)'$$

$$e = (0\ 0\ 0\ 0\ 1)'$$

$$H_t = \text{cov}(R_t|\Omega_{t-1})$$

where the numbers in the subscripts refer to the four sectors examined.

Table 6.2 Diagnostics for multivariate GARCH residuals

	Chemical	*Electrical*	*Mechanical*	*Financial*	*Market*
SK	0.37	0.06	− 0.35	−0.18	− 0.26
KURT	0.38	0.11	0.21	0.39	0.14
BJ	4.33	0.19	3.3	1.83	1.88
LB(1)	0.33	1.49	2.0	0.05	0.63
LB(2)	0.91	1.51	2.7	0.39	0.76
LB(4)	1.37	3.77	5.6	0.94	2.33
LB(8)	6.34	7.40	18.0	2.77	7.09
LB(16)	11.08	20.03	22.2	5.50	12.42

See Table 6.1 for definitions of diagnostic test statistics.

to those in the simpler ARCH model, although somewhat lower than the average across the four sectors. Our estimates of the price of risk are also reasonably close to those obtained for US data by French *et al.* (1987), who in effect estimate only the market equation 6.8, allowing for univariate GARCH-M. They are at variance, however, with the point estimate of 0.499 obtained by Bollerslev *et al.* using US data, although their estimate does seem intuitively rather small. The residual diagnostics show that all the error processes are consistent with normality with no serious problems of serial correlation. We now find a highly significant role for the time-varying part of the error process. This is demonstrated by the t statistics on A_1 and B_1. The sum of A_1 and B_1 is close to, but below, unity which gives finite long-run forecasts for moments (Engle, 1987). The mean lag is estimated to be around 22 months, which confirms the suggestion made earlier that a much longer time horizon was needed in the ARCH process.

The estimates of the matrix of constants A_0 has the interesting property that it is almost diagonal; all the diagonal elements are significant while only one of the off-diagonal elements is significant. This suggests that the unconditional covariance matrix is actually diagonal. This amounts to the statement that agents expect a non-zero variance on all sectors even in the long run but that they do not have a prior expectation about the long-run covariances of the system. The model actually performs fairly well if the complete A_0 matrix is dropped, although this restriction is clearly rejected by the data (likelihood ratio test statistic of 77.5 ($\sim\chi^2(15)$ under the null). However, we decided to investigate the possibility of a diagonal constant matrix A_0. The likelihood ratio test for restricting the A_0 matrix to be diagonal is 6.8 ($\sim\chi^2(10)$ under the null) which is easily accepted. Therefore this form of the GARCH error process is our preferred model. The parameter estimates for the restricted model are

$$\hat{\lambda} = 3.25 \ (3.0)$$

$$\hat{A}_1 = 0.031 \ (4.8)$$

$$\hat{B}_1 = 0.955\ (142.0)$$

$$\hat{A}_0 = \begin{bmatrix} 0.004\ (5.2) & & & & \\ & 0.002\ (4.4) & & & \\ & & 0.006\ (8.8) & & \\ & & & 0.005\ (5.5) & \\ & & & & 0.005\ (8.1) \end{bmatrix}$$

where the asymptotic t ratios are in parentheses. The diagnostics for the model residuals are given in Table 6.3.

Table 6.3 Diagnostics for restricted multivariate GARCH residuals

	Chemical	*Electrical*	*Mechanical*	*Financial*	*Market*
SK	0.37	0.07	− 0.34	−0.02	− 0.26
KURT	0.38	0.11	0.22	0.4	0.15
BJ	4.37	0.2	3.3	1.8	1.86
LB(1)	0.33	1.47	2.0	0.04	0.62
LB(2)	0.92	1.50	2.7	0.4	0.75
LB(4)	1.38	3.79	5.6	0.94	2.34
LB(8)	6.34	7.42	18.0	2.78	7.11
LB(16)	11.9	20.0	22.2	5.52	12.46

See Table 6.1 for definitions of diagnostic test statistics.

The residual diagnostics again indicate that the model is free from serial correlation and has a normally distributed error process. The parameter estimates have changed very little from the unrestricted model. This model shows an important element of time variation in the determination of the covariance matrix and again the mean lag is just under 2 years.

Figures 6.1–6.4 show the time-varying betas for each of the four sectors, i.e. the ratio of the expected covariance between the sector error and the market error divided by the expected variance of the market error at each point in time (Equation 6.2). Figure 6.5 shows the expected variability of our diversified portfolio—the FT 500. These figures show that, despite the rather long lag structure, the conditional covariance matrix can still change in a fairly sudden fashion, although the actual range of the fluctuations is not very great. Figure 6.5 reveals that 1977 and 1981–2 were perceived as being particularly risky periods with the expected variances from holding the diversified portfolio around twice as high as the average for the whole period. In the 1980s there appears to have been a significant reduction in the correlation between returns in the financial sector and for the whole portfolio. Further, by the end of the period the risk from holding a financial

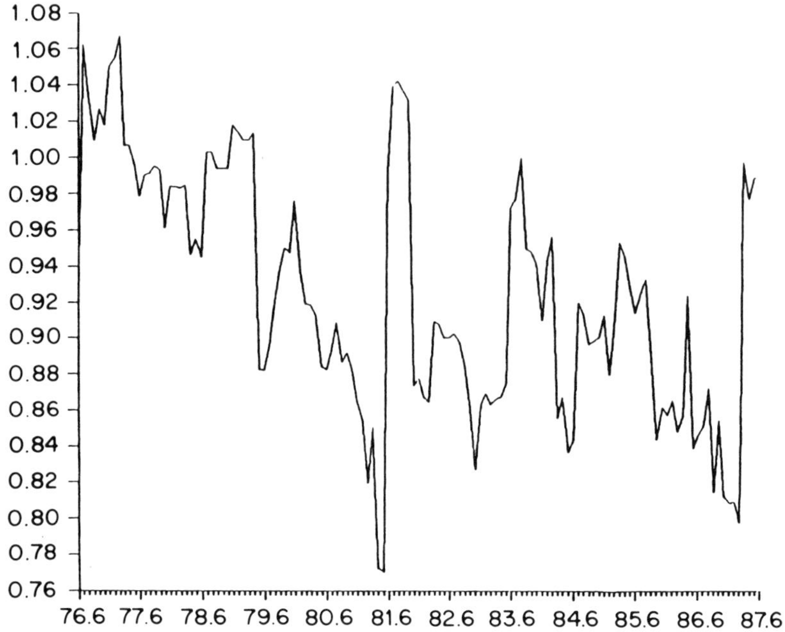

Fig. 6.1 Chemical sector beta.

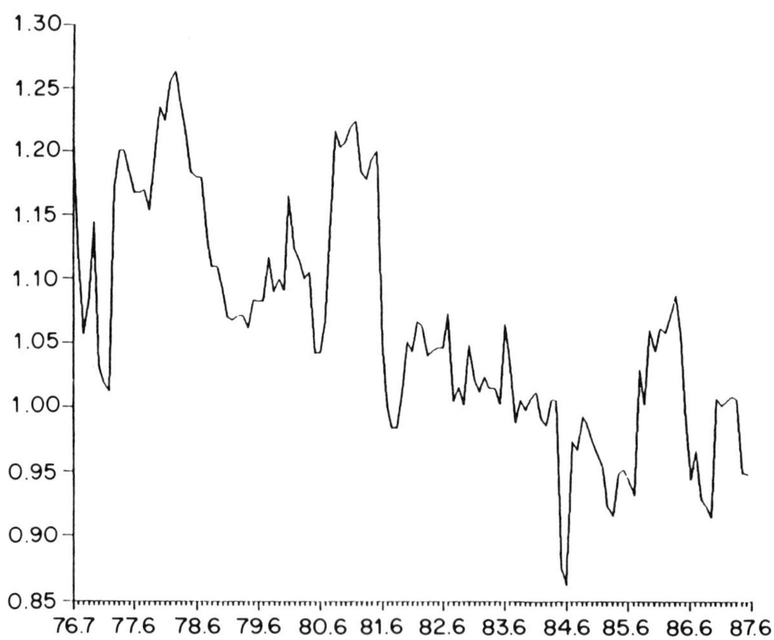

Fig. 6.2 Electrical sector beta.

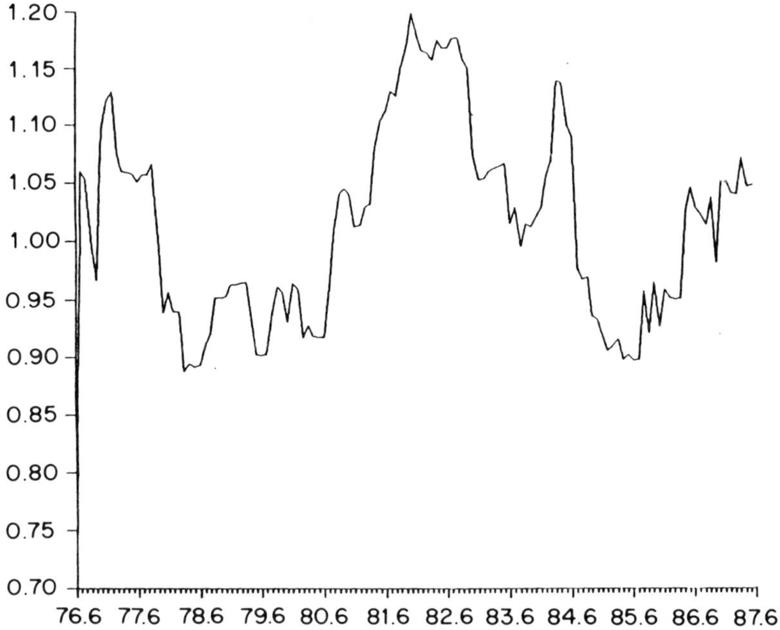

Fig. 6.3 Mechanical sector beta.

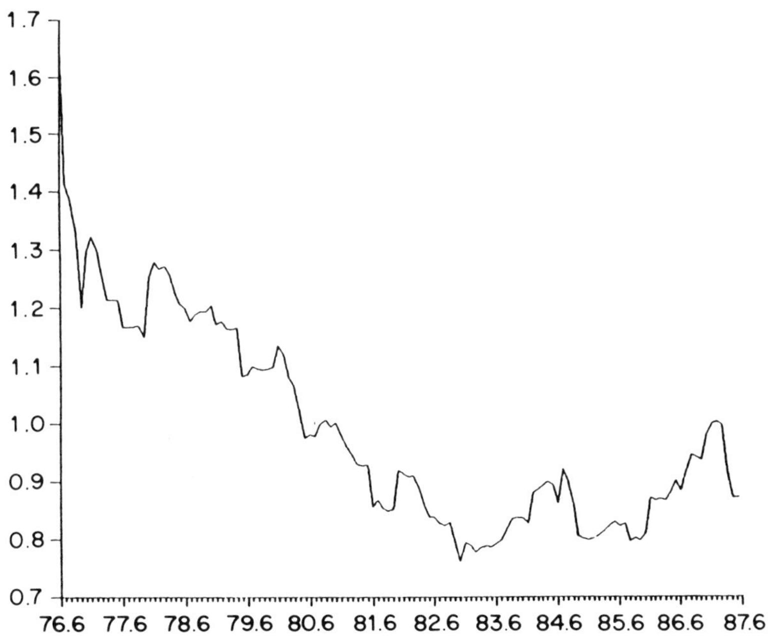

Fig. 6.4 Financial sector beta.

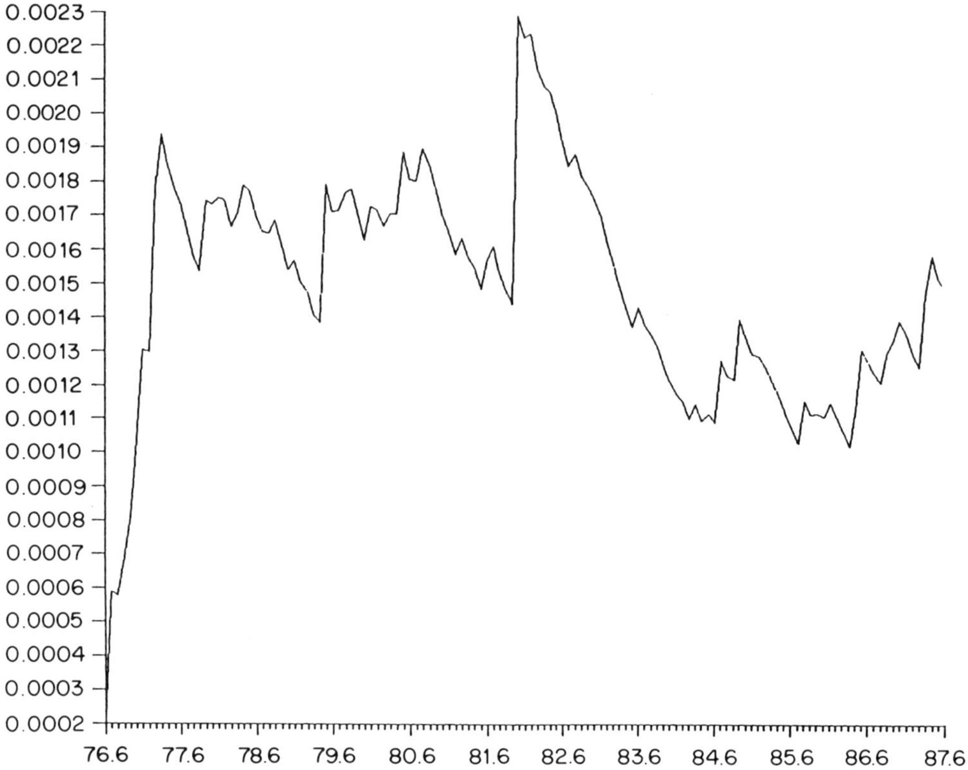

Fig. 6.5 The variance of the market rate.

sector portfolio is more easily diversified than with the other sectors. This may reflect the recent importance of shocks specific to the financial sector—e.g. less developed country (LDC) debt developments—which have little impact on the non-financial sectors of the economy.

6.6 MORE GENERAL MEASURES OF RISK

The CAPM model estimated above takes the covariance of the return on a portfolio with the market return as a sufficient measure of the risk attached to that portfolio. This is only valid if the market portfolio is *the* efficiently diversified portfolio. In practice, it is unlikely that the volatility of the stock market index is a good proxy for the risk of an efficiently diversified portfolio; we noted above that many assets in personal sector portfolios are omitted from the stock market portfolio (e.g. housing and human capital). Breeden (1979) has developed a model in which a proxy for the volatility of the (unobserved) value of the portfolio of wealth of individuals is used. His insight is that, with efficient capital markets, intertemporal optimizing decisions by individuals would make consumption expenditure closely linked to the present value of the total wealth of individuals. (Here wealth would include human capital and the expected productivity of investments at future dates.) With diminishing marginal utility of consumption, individuals will want to smooth expenditure through time, and changes in real consumption will be linked to changes in the perceived value of wealth. Indeeed, under certain strong conditions, there is an exact relation between changes in comsumption and unexpected fluctuations in the value of portfolios of assets (see Breeden (1979) for further details). A natural measure of the risk of a particular asset then becomes the covariance between the value of that asset and changes in consumption.

Breeden derives an equilibrium condition, analogous to our Equation 6.7, which we can write as

$$E(R_{it}|\Omega_{t-1}) = r_{t-1} + \lambda \operatorname{cov}(R_{it}, \Delta c_t|\Omega_{t-1}) \tag{6.19}$$

where Δc_t is the change in the natural logarithm of aggregate real consumption and λ is now a weighted average of individual coefficients of relative risk aversion whose weights depend on consumption levels. The major difference between 6.19, which we might call a consumption-based CAPM, and the model discussed in the previous section is in the measure of risk.

We estimated a general model of returns on assets using both measures of risk. This model can be written

$$R_{it} = r_{t-1} + \lambda_{\mathrm{m}} E\{\operatorname{cov}(R_{it}, R_{\mathrm{m}t}|\Omega_{t-1})\} + \lambda_{\mathrm{c}} E\{\operatorname{cov}(R_{it}, \Delta c_t|\Omega_{t-1})\} + \varepsilon_{it} \tag{6.20}$$

were λ_{m} is the price of market-related risk (which is the same as λ above) and λ_{c} is the price of consumption-related risk.

In practice, neither covariance term in 6.20 will be likely to prove a sufficient measure of risk; we can interpret the coefficients λ_{m} and λ_{c} as revealing the contribution of each proxy to predicting actual, but unobservable, perceived risk. We model expected covariances using the same GARCH(1, 1) specification as above. We need to append to our earlier model an equation describing the expected change in consumption so as to derive proxies for conditional covariances between consumption and asset prices. The Hall (1978) consumption function is in the spirit of the consumption CAPM and suggests a natural specification of Δc_t as a random walk with drift:

$$\Delta c_t = c_0 + u_t \tag{6.21}$$

where c_0 is a constant and u_t is the unexpected element of the change in consumption.

We now have a six-equation system with c_0 and the risk parameters λ_c and λ_m to estimate. As above, we impose equality of these risk parameters across equations. We also adopt a similar model of the processes generating expected variances and covariances, with key parameters A_1 and B_1 as above. Writing out the model in full we have

$$R_t = r_{t-1}\iota + \lambda_m H_t e_1 + \lambda_c H_t e_2 + w_t$$

$$\Delta c = c_0 + u_t$$

$$\text{vech}(H_t) = A_0' A_0 + A_1 \text{vech}(\tilde{w}_{t-1}\ \tilde{w}_{t-1}') + B_1 \text{vech}(H_{t-1})$$

The notation is as before except for the following:

$$e_1 = (0\ 0\ 0\ 0\ 1\ 0)'$$

$$e_2 = (0\ 0\ 0\ 0\ 0\ 1)'$$

$$\tilde{w}_t = (\varepsilon_{1t}\ \varepsilon_{2t}\ \varepsilon_{3t}\ \varepsilon_{4t}\ v_t\ u_t)'$$

and H_t is a 6×6 matrix. $\tilde{w}_t$ is a vector of residuals with the first four elements the residuals from the asset portfolios, the fifth the total stock market residual and the final element the consumption shock. As before,

$$w_t = (\varepsilon_{1t}\ \varepsilon_{2t}\ \varepsilon_{3t}\ \varepsilon_{4t}\ v_t)'$$

6.7 EMPIRICAL RESULTS FOR THE GENERAL CAPITAL ASSET PRICING MODEL

Consumption data are not available monthly and we were forced to use the percentage change in an index of real monthly retail sales as a proxy for Δc_t. Other data are as above. The estimated parameter values are as follows:

$$\hat{\lambda}_m = 4.23 \qquad (3.5)$$

$$\hat{\lambda}_c = 26.54 \qquad (3.6)$$

$$\hat{A}_1 = 0.083 \qquad (5.1)$$

$$\hat{B}_1 = 0.390 \qquad (5.7)$$

$$\hat{c}_0 = 0.0026 \qquad (3.0)$$

$\hat{A}_0 =$

Chemical	Electrical	Mechanical	Financial	Market	Consumption
0.34 (5.6)					
0.15 (2.7)	0.31 (6.6)				
0.19 (3.0)	−0.0003 (0.01)	0.21 (4.8)			
0.02 (0.4)	0.26 (7.5)	0.28 (8.6)	0.12 (1.5)		
0.13 (10.1)	0.14 (9.6)	0.14 (9.3)	0.13 (8.1)	0.24 (14.2)	
0.00 (0)	0.001 (0.2)	−0.004 (0.1)	−0.002 (0.2)	0.01 (2.2)	0.11 (11.7)

where the asymptotic t ratios are in parentheses. The diagnostics for the model residuals are given in Table 6.4.

Table 6.4 Diagnostic tests on general model residuals

	Chemical	*Electrical*	*Mechanical*	*Financial*	*Market*
SK	0.42	0.08	−0.33	−0.05	−0.19
KURT	0.40	0.17	0.27	0.62	0.31
BJ	5.19	0.33	3.14	2.41	1.56
LB(1)	0.13	1.52	1.37	0.03	0.33
LB(2)	1.47	1.59	1.55	1.27	0.79
LB(4)	2.13	3.66	5.10	2.16	3.01
LB(8)	8.42	6.87	17.74	4.41	9.53
LB(16)	13.52	19.33	21.58	8.16	14.65

See Table 6.1 for definitions of diagnostic test statistics.

Both λ_m and λ_c are positive and significantly different from zero; our empirical versions of both the original Sharpe–Lintner CAPM and the consumption CAPM can therefore be rejected in favour of a more general model where the two different measures of risk are both relevant. It is notable that in this extended CAPM model the parameters of the GARCH process are significantly different from those in the earlier models. The weight attached to past history is smaller than in earlier models, whilst the martix of constants A_0 reveals a large number of significant off-diagonal elements implying that unconditional covariances are generally well determined and significantly different from zero. Nonetheless A_1 and B_1 are both significantly different from zero, revealing clear signs of time variations in conditional variances and covariances and hence in risk premiums. Model residuals from the portfolios of assets appear consistent with the hypotheses that they follow serially uncorrelated and normally distributed processes.

6.8. CONCLUSION

In this chapter we have estimated versions of the CAPM which allow expectations of the risk characteristics of portfolios to change over time. The results suggest that perceptions of risk are time varying, but that agents update their perceptions relatively slowly; memories are long and a fairly small weight is placed on the most recent random element in returns. Despite this, and because of the high volatility of one-month returns, natural measures of perceived risk—betas—do show significant short-term variation. Extended versions of the CAPM which allow different measures of undiversifiable risk were estimated and suggested that, whilst significant time variation in risk premiums still exists, no single measure of risk appears adequate.

REFERENCES

Baba, Y., Engle, R. F., Kraft, D. F. and Kroner, K. F. (1987) Multivariate simultaneous generalized ARCH, University of California at San Diego mimeo.

Bollerslev, T. (1986) Generalized autoregressive conditional heteroskedasticity. *Journal of Econometrics*, **31**, 307–28.

Bollerslev, T., Engle, R. F. and Wooldridge, J. M. (1988) A capital asset pricing model with time-varying covariances. *Journal of Political Economy*, **96**, 116–31.

Breeden, D. T. (1979) An intertemporal asset pricing model with stochastic consumption and investment opportunities. *Journal of Financial Economics*, **7**, 265–96.

Crowder, M. J. (1976) Maximum likelihood estimation for dependent observations. *Journal of the Royal Statistical Society, Series B*, **38**, 45–53.

Dickens, R. (1987) The ARCH model as applied to the study of international asset market volatility, Bank of England Technical Paper No. 13.

Engle, R. F. (1982) Autoregressive conditional heteroskedasticity with estimates of the variance of UK inflation. *Econometrica*, **55**, 987–1008.

Engle, R. F. (1987) Multivariate GARCH with factor structures—cointegration in variance, Paper presented at a Conference on Time-varying Variances in Money and Finance, University of California at San Diego, April 1987.

Engle, R. F., Lilien, D. and Robins, R. (1987) Estimating time varying risk premia in the term structure: the Arch-M model. *Econometrica*, **55**, 391–407.

Fama, E. F. (1977) *Foundations of Finance*, Blackwell, Oxford.

French, K. R., Schwert, G. W. and Stambaugh, R. F. (1987) Expected stock returns and volatility. *Journal of Financial Economics*, **19**, 3–29.

Hall, R. (1979) Stochastic implications of the life cycle–permanent income hypothesis: theory and evidence. *Journal of Political Economy*, **86** 971–88.

Jensen, M. (1972) Capital markets: theory and evidence. *Bell Journal of Economics and Management Science*, **3**, 77–102.

Klemkosky, R. and Martin, J. (1975) The adjustment of beta forecasts. *Journal of Finance*, **30** 1123–8.

Lintner, J. (1965) The valuation of risk assets and the selection of risky investments in stock portfolios and capital budgets. *Review of Economics and Statistics*, **4**, 13–37.

Markowitz, H. (1952) Portfolio selection. *Journal of Finance*, **7**, 77–91.

Merton, R. (1980) On estimating the expected return of the market: an exploratory investigation. *Journal of Financial Economics*, **8**, 323–61.

Roll, R. (1977) A critique of the asset pricing theory's tests. *Journal of Financial Economics*, **4**, 129–76.

Ross, S. (1976) The arbitrage theory of capital asset pricing. *Journal of Economic Theory*, **13**, 341–60.

Schweppe, F. (1965) Evaluation of likelihood functions for Gaussian signals, *IEEE Transactions on Information Theory*, **11**, 61–70.

Schwert, G. W. (1983) Size and stocks returns, and other empirical regularities. *Journal of Financial Economics*, **12**, 3–12.

Sharpe, W. (1964) Capital asset prices: a theory of market equilibrium under conditions of risk. *Journal of Finance*, **19**, 425–42.

7

An empirical model of companies' debt and dividend decisions: evidence from company accounts data

G. CHOWDHURY AND D. K. MILES

There is no consensus amongst economists on the key determinants of companies' financial decisions. Despite the vast amount of econometric work undertaken, much of it in connection with large macromodels, there is still no agreement on, for example, the impact of changes in tax rates, of capital expenditure or of expected profit flows upon debt finance, dividend payments and new equity issues.[1]

Whilst there is no generally accepted model (either theoretical or empirical) of company financial behaviour, no-one doubts the relevance of analysing financing decisions. In the UK it is particularly important to have an idea of the key determinants of company finances at a time when the environment in which the financing decisions are taken is rapidly changing. Recent changes in the system of company taxation may have a profound impact on the way in which firms finance their expenditure and upon their dividend policy. At the same time the role of banks as the key financial intermediaries between lenders (historically the personal sector) and borrowers is likely to alter both as a result of these tax changes and, more importantly, because of the major institutional developments now taking place in the City of London. Such institutional developments may well

This chapter is an extended version of a paper appearing in *Applied Economics*, 1989.

[1]For an indication of the type of applied work undertaken on company finances and the very different conclusions drawn from it see, for example, Modigliani and Miller (1958), Dhrymes and Kurz (1967), Fama (1974), Bain *et al.* (1975), Castanias (1983), Smirlock and Marshall (1983), Poterba and Summers (1984), Cuthbertson (1985), Edwards *et al.* (1985), Anderson (1986), Chowdhury *et al.* (1986) and King (1986).

result in significant changes in the relative costs of different forms of finance. Quite how companies will respond to all these developments is hard to predict without a model of their behaviour.

Chowdhury *et al.* (1986) estimate a model of companies' short-term financing decisions (choices between liquid asset accumulation, trade credit and short-term bank debt), taking as given dividends, longer-term debt flows and new equity issues. It was argued that the short-term financing flows, in total, acted as a buffer and the 'strategic' financing flows (dividends, longer-term debt flows and new issues) reflected choices made at a higher level in a hierarchy of decisions. In this chapter, we aim to push the modelling effort back up the hierarchy using the same source of disaggregated data.

The advantages of using company-specific data were discussed by Chowdhury *et al.* (1986) and will not be repeated here. We were sufficiently encouraged by the results of that research to continue the project of modelling company financing decisions believing that insights might be gained which, for various reasons,[2] could not be uncovered with aggregate data. Consequently, in the work presented here we extend the earlier study. We deal with company decisions relating to dividends and external debt. Data are drawn from the published accounts of a sample of 653 UK companies to estimate a model of these 'strategic' financial decisions. Each of the companies reported in every year between 1969 and 1984.

In section 7.1 we consider the theory of company financial decisions. In section 7.2 the broad trends in financing patterns revealed by our sample are assessed, and in section 7.3 we develop a model of debt and dividend flows. In section 7.4 the issues involved in the estimation of this model are considered. In section 7.5 the results of estimating the model are discussed.

7.1 THE THEORY OF COMPANY FINANCES

Companies' actual financing decisions present the economic theorist with major problems. The two dominant, but incompatible, themes in the theoretical literature on company finance are that financial decisions are irrelevant (Modigliani and Miller, 1958; Miller, 1977; Miller and Scholes, 1978; Auerbach and King, 1983; King, 1986) and that the interaction of the personal and company tax systems make extreme financing rules (e.g. finance all expenditure by debt, or pay zero dividends in all periods) optimal (Modigliani and Miller, 1963; Stiglitz, 1969, 1973; King, 1974, 1977). Neither theory is consistent with observed behaviour.

[2]The two major advantages of company-specific data are that they allow issues of aggregation bias to be ignored because the data describe the actions taken by the agent which economic theory focuses upon, i.e. the firm, and that the massive increase in the number of observations over that available at the aggregate level allows models of greater complexity to be estimated with more precision than is usually the case in applied research.

Attempts have been made to prove rigorously that either bankruptcy costs, combined with uncertainty, or principal–agent aspects of the manager–shareholder relation can imply that financial policy 'matters' and that internal solutions (use of non-debt finance and non-zero dividend payments) generally exist (Ross, 1977; Brennan and Schwartz, 1978; Chen, 1978; Kim, 1978; Bhattacharya, 1979). However, there are problems with these models. First, the conditions which might make dividends act as a useful signal to shareholders about the state of the firm do not obviously hold. For example, it is far from clear that firms who do not possess the attribute which the signal is supposed to reveal should find it prohibitively costly to pay dividends, nor is it obvious that no other tax-efficient means of revealing the attribute is available. Second, the direct costs of bankruptcy, which might be expected to be significant if they are to explain why nearly all companies have a financing structure very far from the extreme forms predicted by some models, appear to be relatively small (Warner, 1977).[3]

Other theories which aim to explain why companies do not follow extreme financial policies and regularly pay dividends whilst avoiding very high debt-to-equity ratios are not wholly convincing. Feldstein and Green (1980) consider four other theories which appear to be in accord with the facts but find problems with each of them.

1. The idea that shareholders prefer a steady stream of dividends to lumpy payments when shares are sold (which would provide income if firms retained profit rather than paid dividends) implicitly relies upon a level of transaction costs associated with share sales which seems implausible.
2. The argument of Miller and Scholes (1978) that shareholders can offset tax on dividends against tax-deductible interest payments cannot explain the UK experience where interest costs are not deductible.
3. The bird in the hand argument, that shareholders distrust management and fear that retained profit might be wasted, is fallacious. As Edwards (1984) points out, if a firm reduces its dividend, its shareholders can immediately sell shares and do not need to leave their funds in the corporate sector.
4. King (1977, 1986), Auerbach (1979) and Bradford (1979) have argued that dividend payments are consistent with equilibrium even when, for tax reasons, retentions might seem preferable. This is because, under certain conditions, the market value of a pound of retained earnings is less than a pound. This is the so-called trapped equity model. The theory relies upon the assumption that funds can never be distributed to shareholders except as dividends. Take-overs and mergers, however, provide one means of transferring funds to shareholders, and it is only if the costs of these transactions are sufficiently high that the argument holds (King, 1986).

[3]The adverse effect on the reputations, and more immediately on the jobs, of managers who run companies which become bankrupt may, however, provide a major incentive to avoid bankruptcy.

The model which Feldstein and Green themselves develop depends upon shareholder risk aversion, differences in tax rates across investors and uncertainty over the profitability of firms. If the returns on investments made by different firms in different states of the world are not perfectly correlated, risk-averse shareholders will want to hold shares in the different firms. Shareholders with low or zero rates of tax on dividend income ('institutions') will favour dividend payments against retentions, whilst others facing relatively low rates of capital gains tax ('households') will favour retentions. If the firm aims to maximize its share price, it will balance the demands for its stock from institutions and households by paying some dividends and retaining part of its distributable income. The problem with this model is that once firms are allowed to offer different commodities, as is the case with risk-averse shareholders and different patterns of returns across companies, the hypothesis that shareholders will be unanimous in favouring share price maximization is without foundation. Indeed, it has been shown (Auerbach and King, 1983) that in a wide range of models the conditions which are necessary for shareholders to be unanimous in supporting the share price maximization imply that, if tax rates vary across investors, shareholders will be segmented into two groups: one specialized in equity and one in debt. The relative wealths of these groups determine the aggregate financial structure of the corporate sector but each firm will be *indifferent* to its financial policy (a Miller equilibrium).

Attention has been paid in a series of recent papers to the phenomenon of tax exhaustion[4] (De Angelo and Masulis, 1980; Auerbach, 1984; Mayer, 1986). Tax exhaustion has been common in the UK, and the increasing probability that a firm might become tax exhausted as a result of an extreme financial policy implies that a non-trivial internal optimum for the financing decisions can generally be shown to exist. These models do not rely upon bankruptcy or transaction costs nor upon the use of dividends (or other quantifiable company decision variables) to act as a signal of underlying performance. Rather, they rely upon the ability of firms to perceive the tax advantages of following certain strategies and upon perceptions of the probabilities of becoming or staying tax exhausted.

Whilst not doubting the theoretical consistency of these tax-related models, we do not believe that they can constitute a complete theory of company financial behaviour. Companies as corporate bodies have been in existence for well over 100 years issuing debt and equity and paying dividends all the while. Tax exhaustion is a relatively recent phenomenon and cannot therefore explain away the puzzles of corporate finance.

It seems almost inevitable to us that in fact no single theory of company financial decisions can explain the behaviour over time of a large group of

[4]A company is tax exhausted when it cannot offset a tax deductible expense against its tax liability because that liability is zero.

companies. An empirical model which is to have any hope as an explanation of behaviour will, of necessity, reflect several diverse influences acting on companies. What we can hope to do in constructing an empirical model is to assess the relative significance of, for example, changes in the system of company taxation and in the riskiness of a specific company's trading environment, or of changes in current and expected future profitability, in determining its finances.

7.2 TRENDS IN FINANCING

Our data source comprises the published accounts of 653 UK companies who have each reported in every year from 1969 to 1984 (including reports published in 1985 Q1). The sample was selected by applying filters to all those companies which have continuously supplied accounts to DATASTREAM over the 16 year period. The filters applied were the same as those described by Chowdhury *et al.* (1986); they exclude companies whose activities are predominantly overseas, companies for which the sources/uses statement on the DATASTREAM tape contained apparent errors, financial companies and trust funds. The resulting sample of firms have a total capital employed which is equivalent to 40% of that of all UK industrial and commercial companies (ICCs). Comparison of the total profits flows of this sample with Central Statistics Office (CSO) aggregates is difficult because this sample of firms does not distinguish foreign profits, which are excluded in the aggregate figures. Making a crude adjustment for this[5] suggests that the sample again accounts for just under 40% of the total. The companies are drawn from a wide range of sectors of the economy and vary enormously in size. For example, capital employed, varies from several billion pounds (Shell, General Electric and ICI) to less that £500,000 for some firms.

Table 7.1 represents an aggregated constant-price sources/uses statement for the firms in our sample. It shows the aggregate flows of profit, tax payments, investment and stockbuilding, dividend payments, new equity issues and quick finance. (Quick finance here is defined as net trade credit received minus net additions to the stock of liquid assets.)

The variability in the aggregate flows of debt, new equity and quick finance is apparent. Quick finance is particularly volatile, varying, for example, from −£0.67 billion to over £1 billion between 1978 and 1979 and falling to near zero in the following year. This would seem to be consistent with the hypothesis that quick finance acts as a buffer in the short run. Dividend payments (fourth column), in aggregate, appear less volatile than the other financial flows (fifth, sixth and seventh columns).

Table 7.2 shows the relative contributions of debt and equity in more detail. In nearly all years debt (defined here as issues of new loan capital

[5] By scaling down each company's reported profit by the ratio of domestic sales to total sales.

Table 7.1 Aggregate flow of funds of sample of 653 companies (£million, 1980 prices)[a]

	Profits	*Investment*[b] *and Tax*	*Dividends*[c]	*New equity*	*Total debt*	*Quick finance*
1969	12483	12909	2449	1125	2602	−764
1970	12395	13484	2478	942	2644	94
1971	13208	12704	2439	587	1763	−313
1972	15360	17281	1877	2339	4166	−2591
1973	18326	19500	2251	578	3695	−840
1974	18442	23373	1813	143	4812	1908
1975	15528	15174	1390	998	1411	−1259
1976	17806	17606	1462	1140	1791	−1633
1977	14637	14586	1481	727	1349	−653
1978	16074	15977	1585	558	1605	−678
1979	16040	18243	2200	608	2519	1241
1980	13206	13478	1822	564	1525	−49
1981	13744	14100	1582	930	2370	−1400
1982	13761	14029	1692	450	1829	−381
1983	15073	13362	1749	1084	127	−1259
1984	16526	18933	1977	1133	3055	−55

[a]Subject to small errors in individual accounts and to rounding the rows will add up: columns 2 − 3 = 4 − 5 − 6 − 7.
[b]Includes stockbuilding and acquisition of non-liquid financial assets.
[c]Comprising almost entirely ordinary dividends.

Table 7.2 Debt and equity flows

	Total of debt and new equity raised (£80 million)	*Of which new equity (%)*	*(Percentage of sample raising funds from new issues)*	*Of which debt (%)*	*(Percentage of sample raising funds from debt)*	*Percentage of sample raising both debt and equity finance*
1969	3727	30.2	(19.0)	69.8	(37.1)	14.2
1970	3586	26.3	(16.5)	73.7	(35.5)	12.4
1971	2350	25.0	(20.1)	75.0	(32.8)	12.2
1972	6505	36.0	(25.4)	64.0	(51.8)	17.2
1973	4273	13.5	(23.9)	86.5	(60.8)	18.2
1974	4955	2.9	(17.8)	97.1	(60.9)	13.6
1975	2409	41.4	(21.3)	58.6	(39.8)	8.7
1976	2931	38.9	(19.8)	61.1	(53.2)	12.2
1977	2076	35.0	(23.1)	65.0	(49.0)	12.6
1978	2163	25.8	(27.1)	74.2	(52.1)	17.5
1979	3127	19.4	(27.7)	80.6	(60.5)	19.3
1980	2089	27.0	(26.3)	73.0	(49.5)	16.1
1981	3300	28.2	(30.3)	71.8	(50.4)	18.1
1982	2279	19.7	(28.3)	80.3	(54.7)	17.6
1983	1211	89.5	(31.5)	10.5	(50.5)	16.5
1984	4188	27.0	(38.0)	73.0	(57.4)	25.7

plus the flow of all short-term debt) was well over twice the size of new equity issues. The table shows that, whilst around half the companies used debt as a source of funds in a given year, the proportion of companies that issued equity was generally around a quarter.

The relation between stocks of debt and the total value of the capital employed of the sample is shown in Table 7.3. The weighted average (by company size) of the gearing ratio was similar at the end of the period to what it was at the beginning. Throughout the period variability (in aggregate) is low with the ratio never falling below 20% and only marginally exceeding 25% in the peak year of 1972. The third column shows the unweighted average of company-specific gearing ratios for each year. The contrast is interesting. The unweighted average gearing ratios are significantly lower than the weighted averages and have also increased markedly over the whole period. This implies that smaller firms have consistently had lower gearing than larger firms, but that the gearing of small firms has tended to rise and that of large firms has tended to fall. Thus the coefficient of variation of the company gearing ratios has fallen.

Table 7.3 Gearing

	Total debt/total capital employed[a]		
	Weighted average (%)	*Unweighted average %*	*(Coefficient of variation)*[b]
1969	22.6	1.05	(1.22)
1970	23.7	10.9	(1.20)
1971	24.2	12.4	(1.05)
1972	25.2	16.0	(0.82)
1973	24.9	16.7	(0.87)
1974	26.0	17.9	(0.91)
1975	25.0	15.9	(0.87)
1976	24.1	15.6	(0.86)
1977	22.6	14.4	(0.88)
1978	21.3	13.6	(0.90)
1979	20.8	14.2	(0.82)
1980	21.0	14.7	(0.83)
1981	21.4	14.7	(0.85)
1982	22.0	16.1	(0.82)
1983	20.7	16.2	(0.78)
1984	1.5	17.0	(0.77)

[a]Capital employed is measured at historic cost.
[b]Defined as

$$\frac{\{\Sigma_{i=1}^{N}(g_{it} - g_t)^2/N\}^{1/2}}{g_t}$$

where g_{it} is the gearing for firm i in period t and g_t is the average gearing across all N firms in t.

The stock of debt held by the sample of firms represents between 40% and 45% of the stock issued by all UK companies, whilst the proportion of the aggregate capital employed accounted for by the sample was just under 40%. This suggests that average gearing is marginally higher for our sample of companies than for all ICCs. This is consistent with the idea that larger companies, who are more heavily represented in the sample than in the economy generally, have, on average, higher gearing than smaller firms.

Figure 7.1 and Table 7.4 give a more detailed picture of the dividend flows for our sample of companies. The figure shows the pay-out ratios for each year and reveals that there has been significant variability in the ratio of dividends[6] to available internal funds (profits net of tax). Comparing the dividend pay-out ratio with the measure of the rate of return suggests that in years when profits have been high (1972–3, 1976, 1983–4) the pay-out ratio has fallen and in years when profitability is relatively low (1970, 1980, 1981) the ratio rises. This is consistent with the notion that shareholders prefer a smooth path of payments and that dividend payments reflect the longer-term prospects of the company.

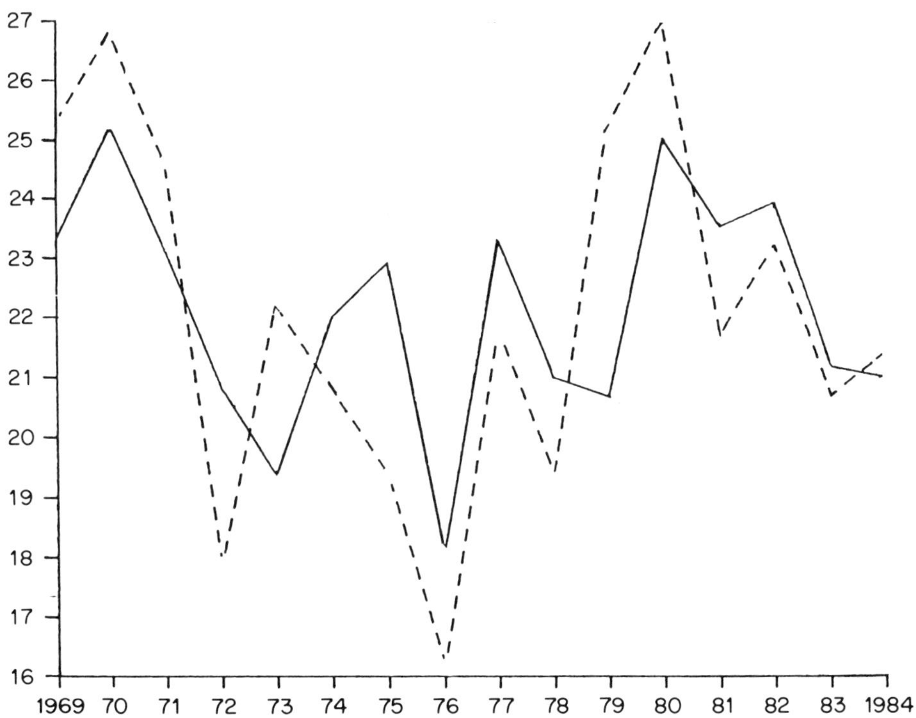

Fig. 7.1 Dividend pay-out ratio (– – –) and profitability (inverse profit rate, ——) (weighted averages; profits net of tax).

[6]Dividends paid after April 1973 have been grossed up for pre-payment of tax by companies.

Table 7.4 Dividend payments

	Proportion of companies which pay a dividend (%)	*Proportion of companies which cut total dividend payments (in nominal terms)(%)*
1970	96.8	12.0
1971	97.0	10.9
1972	96.5	28.9
1973	98.2	22.5
1974	98.6	47.2
1975	97.4	33.8
1976	98.3	9.0
1977	97.9	12.4
1978	99.1	9.0
1979	98.5	12.1
1980	98.0	28.2
1981	95.1	33.4
1982	93.1	22.8
1983	93.1	22.8
1984	91.7	11.0

Despite this it is apparent from Table 7.4 that companies are not unwilling in certain circumstances to *cut* dividends even in nominal terms. In 1974, for example, nearly half the companies in the sample reduced their dividends from the level in the previous year. This is not necessarily inconsistent with the idea that dividends act as a signal of a company's performance. Shareholders, although unaware of many aspects of the health of their particular company, no doubt have a good feel for the state of companies in general. If dividends do act as a signal, they do so only to reveal company-specific factors which differ from the norm. To cut dividends along with the other companies does not show that a firm is performing unusually poorly.

Whereas, at times, quite a number of companies bring themselves to cut dividends, they do seem very reluctant to pay no dividend. The proportion of firms in our sample paying some dividend has never fallen beneath 90% and has usually been around 97%. Since 1979, however, there has been a significant increase in the proportion of firms paying no dividend. This may be linked to the abolition of dividend controls (see below).

The stylized facts which emerge from the company accounts can be summarized briefly as follows: companies have financed the larger part of their requirement for outside funds by debt, but have also relied upon new equity issues for a sizeable proportion of the total. Indeed a small but significant number of firms have consistently issued both debt and equity in the same financial year. Nearly all companies pay dividends, the level of which, relative to funds available for distribution, moves anticyclically.

As noted above, these stylized facts are not consistent with some of the key results in the theory of corporate finance, and the phenomenon of tax exhaustion has been presented as a possible explanation. Tax exhaustion has been common for the companies in our sample. There is no exact way of knowing whether a company is tax exhausted (at the margin) from its published accounts. However, a company which counts a part of its current Advanced Corporation Tax (ACT) payment as irrecoverable is certainly tax exhausted and expects to remain so for some considerable time. Table 7.5 shows the proportion of companies in our sample with irrecoverable ACT. It also shows estimates made by the Institute of Fiscal Studies (IFS) of the proportion of firms not able to claim ACT in a sample of some 400 companies reporting between 1969 and 1981. (Companies with irrecoverable ACT are a strict subset of those firms that have unrecovered ACT.) The second column of the table shows that by the early 1980s about a third of the sample were, and expected to continue to be, tax exhausted. The third column suggests that there have also been a significant proportion of companies which, although not certain that any ACT paid would never be recovered, were nonetheless currently tax exhausted. Given that tax exhaustion has been and still is widespread, the desire to avoid becoming tax exhausted might therefore be a major determinant of firms' financing decisions.

Table 7.5 Tax exhaustion

	Proportion of sample with irrecoverable ACT[a] (%)	*IFS estimate of proportion of companies not able currently to claim ACT offset*(%)
1969	—	—
1970	—	—
1971	—	—
1972	—	—
1973	8.6	29.7
1974	5.2	48.0
1975	4.1	40.0
1976	4.4	36.8
1977	9.8	37.0
1978	16.8	38.1
1979	22.5	42.7
1980	32.8	47.6
1981	33.4	52.8
1982	33.5	
1983	27.1	
1984	20.1	

[a]Firms who do not foresee being able to offset ACT paid on dividends currently distributed against mainstream corporation tax liability. This is a sufficient, but certainly not necessary condition for being tax exhausted.

7.3 A MODEL OF COMPANY FINANCIAL DECISIONS

The source/uses identity of a company can be written

$$P_t - T_t - I_t - S_t = D_t - \Delta B_t - E_t - Q_t \qquad (7.1)$$

where P_t is the profit earned in period t, T_t is the tax, I_t is the investment, S_t is stockbuilding, D_t is dividends paid, ΔB_t is the flow of new debt finance with residual maturity exceeding 1 year (B_t is the stock of debt), E_t is new equity issues and Q_t is the flow of net trade credit received plus short-term debt finance (maturity under 1 year) minus net acquisitions of liquid assets.

We call D_t, ΔB_t and E_t strategic financing flows. Q_t is quick finance and conforms to the definition in Chowdhury *et al.* (1986). We assume that the strategic finanical flows are simultaneously determined and that the elements of Q_t are determined conditional on these flows. Q_t in total acts as a buffer. We assume that the factors which determine issues of longer-term (or strategic) debt are different from those which influence decisions about overdraft finance and other short-term debt. The shorter maturity debt is part of quick finance, the determinants of which were investigated by Chowdhury *et al.* (1986). In this chapter we model strategic debt flows and payments of dividends. New equity issues are not modelled directly and because of the buffer role for quick finance no specific equity issues equation is implied by our estimates. Any factors which affect equity issues, however, will almost certainly influence debt and dividend flows.

It is far from clear, either theoretically or empirically, whether financing decisions are made conditional upon company profits and investment flows or are simultaneously determined. In their classic paper Modigliani and Miller (1958) showed that under strong conditions the financing and investment decisions were independent. The existence of tax advantages to certain financing strategies does not, in itself, alter this result. However, real and financial decisions are not independent if the possibility of tax exhaustion is a major concern of companies. If risks of bankruptcy matter, then once again the independence of financing and investment decisions is, in theory, unlikely. When both time lags and costs of adjustment are considered, however, it does seem plausible that profits and investment are determined prior to current debt and dividend flows. Profits are the result of employment, production and pricing decisions of the firm and of economy-wide developments outside its scope; they are likely to be predetermined with respect to current financial flows. This is not to say that the balance sheet structure of firms does not impact upon pricing and output decisions, but rather that such feedbacks are not immediate: decisions on the productive activities of the company (including investment) require more time because the costs of implementing them, and especially of subsequently reversing them, are likely to be higher than with financing decisions. It also seems likely that tax payments, which are a function of past profit and expenditure decisions,[7] are predetermined with respect to current financial flows.

We therefore consider it reasonable to assume hierarchical decision-making with company income and capital expenditure determined at a higher point than financial flows in a decision tree. If this is so, it is valid in estimation to condition dividends and the flow of debt finance upon post-tax profits, investment and those variables which reflect the relative advantages of equity, retentions and debt.[8] However, we do not believe that stockbuilding can be taken as (weakly) exogenous with respect to dividend payments, strategic debt issues or capital issues. We believe that the level of stocks, whilst being more costly to change rapidly than elements of quick finance, may well be simultaneously determined with, and perhaps dependent upon, the other longer-term financial flows.

We assume that decisions about strategic debt and dividends are made simultaneously and will to a large extent depend upon the same factors. As a starting point for estimation we therefore include a common set of explanatory variables for the two equations. The explanatory variables are listed in Table 7.6. They fall in to seven categories:

1. taxation
2. bankruptcy/risk
3. cost of funds (relative interest rates)
4. adjustment costs/expectations
5. the scale of flows
6. external controls
7. leasing

7.3.1 Taxation

The models in King (1977) and Mayer (1986) imply the relevance of both tax rates (corporation tax, income tax, imputation rate and capital gains tax rate)[9] and measures of the tax-paying status of the firm (proxies for the likelihood of current and future tax exhaustion). There are serious problems in measuring the tax position of the individual firm. The clearest indicator of tax exhaustion is whether a company counts a part of its ACT as irrecoverable. This is included in a 0, 1, form.

[7]With one exception, namely when ACT is paid but not recovered in which case tax paid and current dividends are simultaneously determined (see below).

[8]An indirect test of the validity of the assumption that investment is independent of financial flows is feasible using tests of statistical exogeneity (see below). The empirical evidence on the independence of investment decisions and financing decisions is mixed: Fama (1974) and Smirlock and Marshall (1983) find that the decisions are independent; Dhrymes and Kurz (1967) find that they are not.

[9]The way in which these tax rates determine the financial policy of a firm, in restricted models, is summarized by Chowdhury *et al.* (1986, p. 20).

Table 7.6 Variables used in estimation[a]

Dependent variables		
	D	Gross payments of dividends
	ΔB	Change in the stock of debt (residual maturity exceeding 1 year)
Explanatory variables		
1. Tax variables	CTX	Rate of mainstream corporation tax
	IMPT	Imputation rate (zero pre-1973)
	MTAX	Estimate of the economy-wide average marginal income tax rate of shareholders
	ZTAX	Estimate of average effective capital gains tax rate
	EXH	Tax exhaustion dummy variable: 1 if company reports non-zero irrecoverable ACT, otherwise 0
	CTEX	(EXH).(CTX)
	IMEX	(EXH).(IMPT)
2. Bankruptcy/risk proxies	SDBT	Stock of all debt
	SHTD	Stock of debt with residual maturity 1 year or less
	INCG	Income gearing (interest payments divided by total income less tax)
	VARY	Square of change in the pre-tax rate of return (a measure of volatility of income)
	LIQA	Stock of liquid assets
	FINA	Stock of other financial assets
3. Cost of funds	GILT5	Nominal rate of interest on 5 year gilts
	INTK	Three-month interbank interest rate (deviation from GILT5)
	RBNK	Clearing banks' base rate of interest (deviation from GILT5)
	DIYL	Dividend yield, FT all industrial shares (deviation from GILT5)
	CTGIL	(GILT5).(CTX)
	INFL	Annual rate of change of retail price index
	CTINF	(CTX).(INFL)
4. Expectations/costs of adjustment	NULC	Whole economy index of competitiveness based on relative unit labour costs
	INVE	Planned future investment
	GRTH	Growth in capital employed (year on year)
	(Also SDBT, SHTD, lags of PRF and DIV)	

Table 7.6 Contd.

5. Variables to determine the scale of flows	PRF	Company gross trading income (net of stock appreciation) plus non-trading income
	INVT	Expenditure on physical assets (includes stockbuilding)
	ACQS	Expenditure on non-physical assets
	INTL	Interest payments
	TAX	Total tax payments
6. External controls	DCON	0, 1 dummy for periods of dividend controls
	CCC	0, 1 dummy for introduction of competition, credit control
	CORSET	0, 1 dummy for operation of corset
7. Leasing	RLEAS	Nominal interest rate on 7 year leases (mid-point of highest and lowest)—deviation from GILT5
	HIRL	Rental payments on hired capital goods

Data for all variables not derived from company accounts are aligned so as to conform with the company's report date.
[a]All stock and flow data are nominal values. Interest rates are also nominal.

7.3.2 Bankruptcy/risk

The stock of debt, relative to capital employed, and the level of income gearing,[10] all lagged, are, plausibly, related to the probability of bankruptcy. These variables are significant in many studies which use discriminant analysis to assess probabilities of bankruptcy (Marais, 1979). The stock of debt with residual maturity of less than 1 year is also included since it seems likely that the level of such debt will be more closely linked to the dangers of cash-flow crises than the level of longer-term debt. The volatility of income is clearly relevant to the assessment of default risks, and the square of the change in the rate of return on capital is included as a (crude) measure of the recent variability of profits. Risks of bankruptcy are likely to be inversely related to stocks of liquid assets held. The lagged stock of highly liquid assets (cash, bank deposits and Treasury bills) is included in the specifications, and stocks of less liquid financial assets (e.g. gilts) are entered separately.

7.3.3 Cost of funds (relative interest rates)

The impact of interest rates is not obvious, given that dividend and debt flows are modelled conditional upon company income and investment.

[10]Interest payments as a proportion of profits net of tax.

Three nominal interest rates are included: banks' base rate, the 3 month interbank rate and a 5 year gilt rate. The first two rates are entered as deviations from the gilt rate which is included as a level. Since most debt has a maturity of less than 5 years, and since the cost of servicing equity might be more closely linked to a longer-term rate, we might expect debt to be more attractive when a short-term rate (bank rate or the interbank rate) falls relative to a longer-term rate. A more direct measure of the cost of issuing equity is the yield on equity of the FT 500. This is included along with the dividend yield (both measured as deviations from the long-term rate on 5 year gilts).

The tax advantage of the interest deductibility of debt is linked to the level of interest rates as much as to the rate of tax; therefore the product of the long-term nominal interest rate and the corporate tax rate is included. Inflation (the annual rate of change of the retail price index (RPI)) is also included. If anything, this is expected to have a negative impact upon flows of debt and dividends since unused tax losses and allowances can only be carried forward in nominal terms, thus making tax exhaustion more costly when inflation rises.

7.3.4 Adjustment costs/expectations

Adjustment costs imply that lagged dependent variables will be significant in estimated relationships. The lagged stock of debt is included in both equations, as are the first two lags of dividend payments. Longer lags of dividends are included since these flows might be slow to adjust to changes in a company's environment if shareholders prefer a smooth flow of disbursements.

No attempt has been made explicitly to model expectations of future available income. Two lags of profits, tax and interest payments are initially included. It is likely that the estimated effect of these lags is in part due to the impact of those flows on expectations of future profitability. The future health of a company might, however, depend on current competitiveness and will probably be highly correlated with future investment plans. Both variables can be measured[11] and are included.

7.3.5 The scale of flows

Investment, company profits and interest and tax payments determine the scale of flows. Endogeneity between interest payments and debt flows and

[11]Most companies show their commitments to future investment in their reports. This variable is taken as our proxy for expected investment.

between tax payments and dividends is clearly a problem. The endogeneity of tax payments can be avoided (in principle) by subtracting unclaimed ACT from total payments; the tricky part is in identifying unclaimed (as opposed to irrecoverable) ACT. Initially we make the assumption that all unclaimed ACT is irrecoverable. Current interest payments are clearly simultaneously determined with debt flows and are excluded from all specifications. Investment has been disaggregated into physical investment and acquisitions of non-physical assets. The endogeneity of both flows is questionable and is tested.

7.3.6 External controls

Controls on bank lending and on dividend payments were in force for much of the period used for estimation: 1971–84. The bank lending controls (the 'corset') probably had significantly less impact than did dividend controls and we have attempted to allow for any corset effects in a fairly crude way with 0, 1, dummies. Any effects from the introduction of competition and credit control are also handled in this way. We considered it essential to try and model the impact of dividend controls with care, and an iterative estimation technique was used to this end (see below).

7.3.7 Leasing

The rise of leasing in the 1970s presented a problem. It seems likely that the decision on whether to lease assets, or to finance additions to the usable capital stock directly by debt or new issues (or increasing retentions), is made simultaneously with the decisions about the flows of debt and dividends. This means that whilst the decision over the change in the usable capital stock (i.e. net investment plus net new leases) might be independent of (or at least made prior to) decisions about financing, the level of direct investment is not. Ideally, the solution is to add the flow of new leases to direct investment and to include among the explanatory variables in the model the determinants of the relative attractiveness of the direct acquisition of capital and of leasing. These determinants might be the company's tax status (tax exhausted or tax paying) and the level of leasing rates relative to borrowing costs. There is no (new) problem involved in proxying these determinants. The problem is in identifying from company accounts the flow of new leases; for most of the period leasing agreements written are not directly reported in company accounts. However, interest payments on rented capital are reported and we include this variable in the equations along with leasing rates and time trends. Between them these act as crude proxies for leasing.

7.4 ESTIMATION TECHNIQUE

The model that we estimate can be written

$$D_{it} = \alpha_i + \sum_{k=1}^{K} Z_{itk}\beta_k + U_{it} \qquad i = 1, \ldots, N \tag{7.2}$$

$$\Delta B_{it} = \gamma_i + \sum_{j=1}^{J} X_{itj}\psi_j + W_{it} \qquad t = 1, \ldots, T \tag{7.3}$$

where D_{it} is the dividends paid by firm i in period t, ΔB_{it} is the flow of debt finance for firm i in period t, Z_{itk} is the value of the kth observable explanatory variable, relevant to the dividends decision, for the ith firm in the tth period, X_{itj} is the value of the jth observable explanatory variable, relevant to the debt finance decision, for the ith firm in the tth period, U_{it} and W_{it} are error terms, N is the number of firms, T is the number of time periods, α_i and γ_i are the firm-specific time-invariant unobservable determinants of dividends and debt respectively, and β_k and ψ_j are the slope coefficients measuring the responses of dividends to Z_k and debt to X_j.

In principle, it would be possible to estimate firm-specific slope coefficients on all, or some, of the elements of Z and X. In practice, this is not feasible as there are only 14 annual observations on each firm. This severely limits the number of explanatory variables which could be estimated, and interpretation of results would be extremely difficult with over 600 different estimates of each slope parameter.

Several assumptions can be made about the unobserved firm-specific effects, the most straightforward of which is that they are non-stochastic. This gives the fixed effects model. In this case the 'within', or covariance, estimator is efficient and consistent, provided that the errors satisfy the usual assumptions for the validity of ordinary least squares (OLS). The within estimator is obtained by performing OLS on the model transformed into deviations from the company-specific means. This is equivalent to applying least squares to the pooled data using N-step dummy variables for the intercept terms.

An alternative assumption for the firm-specific effects is that they are a random sample drawn from some distribution: the 'random effects' model. Models of this type are associated with the generalized least-squares (GLS) estimator of Balestra and Nerlove (1966) which is equivalent to a weighted combination of the within and 'between'[12] estimators, with weights inversely related to the variances of the two estimators. If the model is correctly specified and the α_i and γ_i are generated stochastically, then the GLS estimator is efficient, having a smaller variance than either the within or between estimators, although the gains may be negligible with such a large data set. Moreover, it is likely that the unobservable firm effects are

[12]The 'between' estimator is OLS on the company-specific averages of the variables.

correlated with some of the measured explanatory variables. Under these circumstances the within estimator is to be preferred as it remains consistent whereas the GLS estimator is, in general, inconsistent.

In addition to company-specific dummies, we have also included time dummies in the equations. The time dummies pick up the effect of factors specific to a particular year but which have a common impact on all firms within that year.

Problems are posed by the inclusion of lagged dependent variables. The within estimator is inconsistent as N increases with T fixed, with bias of order $1/T$. In this study $T = 14$, which is reasonably large for panel data, and so we expect the bias to be small. The GLS estimator is consistent, provided that the firm-specific effects are independent of the measured explanatory variables, only under further strong conditions.[13] These considerations led us to rely mainly on the within estimator. However, we do compare the results of within estimation with those of GLS estimation. A Hausman (1978) test is used to indicate whether there is correlation between the unobserved firm effects and the measured explanatory variables.

The size of firms in our sample varies greatly and it would be surprising if errors from regressions using the levels of variables were homoscedastic. Heteroscedasticity would lead to inefficiency in our estimates and would bias inferences. To avoid this problem we have estimated equations in ratio form, dividing flow and stock variables from company accounts by a factor reflecting the scale of the company: adjusted total liabilities lagged 1 year.[14] In these equations interest rates, dummy variables, tax rate terms, income and capital gearing and the other variables measured in common units across firms enter unscaled. Company-specific effects are proportional to the scaling factor.

We have assumed that all the explanatory variables are weakly exogenous. Weak exogeneity is, we believe, a plausible assumption—but one which can, in principle, be tested. Exogeneity tests (Hausman, 1978) require the estimation of equations for variables whose exogeneity is in question. With around 40 explanatory variables the scale of this problem is vast, and estimating a string of subregressions for all 40 variables was not seriously considered. However, we did investigate the exogeneity of investment expenditure and of tax payments, and the results are reported below.

Tests of structural stability of the estimated equations are important in assessing their value in explaining company behaviour. Three such tests were undertaken. First, the sample was split arbitrarily into two groups of

[13]If either the first observation on the dependent variable is independent of the individual effect *or* it is fixed.

[14]Adjusted total liabilities consist of the firm's total liabilities (including all debt, total share capital and reserves) purged of provisions for tax and certain other long-term contractual debt of a firm.

companies and parameter equality restrictions were tested. Second, the sample was split systematically into companies of above and below average size and also split by reference to growth performance and similar tests were undertaken. These tests help to assess whether the same model can be used to explain the behaviour of different firms. Third, we used the total sample of companies but only over a shorter time period to see whether the model was stable over time.

7.4.1 Estimation of the impact of dividend controls

Allowing for the impact of dividend controls is difficult but crucial. Two points about the controls give a hint about how to model their effect. First, many companies exceeded the statutory limit.[15] Second, the limit may well have provided a norm for payments so that some companies may have paid a higher dividend than they would have done otherwise.[16] The costs of deviating from the statutory limit, in either direction, may therefore have been significant but they were clearly not infinite.

One way to model the impact is to assume that firms have a loss function which penalizes deviations in dividend payments both from the statutory limit and from that level of dividends which the firm would pay in the absence of dividend controls. Assuming that the costs are symmetric and quadratic gives a single-period loss function L of

$$L = \eta(D^* - D)^2 + \delta(D^c - D)^2 \qquad \eta, \delta \geq 0 \tag{7.4}$$

where D denotes dividend payments, D^* is the optimal level of dividends if no controls are in force and D^c is the maximum dividend payable under the controls. Minimizing L gives a necessary condition for an optimum:

$$D = (1 - \lambda)D^* + \lambda D^c \tag{7.5}$$

where $\lambda = \delta/(\delta + \eta)$. When there are no controls, clearly $D = D^*$.

The parameters of interest which we aim to estimate are those which describe the relation between the Z variables of Equation (7.5) and D^*, i.e.

$$D^* = Z\beta \tag{7.6}$$

(in an obvious notation). Combining 7.5 and 7.6 gives

$$D = (1 - \lambda)Z\beta + \lambda D^c \tag{7.7a}$$

when controls are in force and

$$D = Z\beta \tag{7.7b}$$

[15]See Bank of England (1980), especially Chart A.

[16]A cartoon from *Financial Weekly* (6 July 1979), which appeared shortly after the abolition of controls, shows the chairman of a company announcing to the other board members: 'Fortunately, since there is no longer any dividend control, we can get away without paying anything.' As noted above, the proportion of firms paying no dividend has increased steadily since 1979.

when controls are not in force. Combining 7.7a and 7.7b and adding a random error u gives

$$\widetilde{D} = (1 - \lambda)Z\beta + \lambda\widetilde{D}^{c} + u \tag{7.8}$$

where $\widetilde{D} = D$ in control periods and $\widetilde{D} = (1 - \lambda)D$ in off periods, and $\widetilde{D}^{c} = D^{c}$ in control periods and $\widetilde{D}^{c} = 0$ in off periods.

We aimed to estimate 7.8 by an iterative technique which involved first estimating 7.7a using data from on periods, constructing $\widetilde{D}$, using the first-round estimate of λ and then estimating 7.8 directly. This gives a second-round estimate of λ and the procedure can be repeated until convergence.

There is a special case when the procedure breaks down but in which a much simpler technique works. This is when the control bites to the same extent in all on periods. This would occur if the authorities consistently set D^{c} equal to $Z\beta - c$, where c is a constant. In this case Z and D^{c} are perfectly correlated, but the dividends equation can then be written

$$D = Z\beta - c\lambda(\text{DCON}) + u$$

where DCON is a simple 0, 1 dummy for off, on periods. We used both the iterative technique and the simpler more restricted specification.

In addition to these attempts to allow for variations in the extent to which controls bite during the on periods, we attempted to estimate the extent of any catch-up following the abolition of restrictions. We included in our specifications a measure of the cumulative difference between actual dividends and what we estimate dividends would have been with no controls (denoted CUMUL). This measure of the backlog of dividends payments takes on non-zero values only after 1979 Q2. Since we were uncertain both as to the extent and the timing of any catch-up effect we tested various hypotheses. In particular we considered whether any catch-up took place only in the first period after controls were lifted or if the backlog of dividends was paid off gradually. We did not constrain catch-up effects to equal the cumulative impact of controls from the on periods.

7.5 RESULTS

There are 9142 sample observations, the product of T (14) and N (653). Initially, the Z and X sets of variables were identical although testing down proceeded independently on each equation.

Attempts to estimate the dividend equation by the iterative method outlined above did not give encouraging results. Correlation between the maximum dividend payable D^{c} and the other explanatory variables was sufficiently high to give poorly defined coefficients on D^{c}. Starting with a value for λ of 0.1 the system slowly converged towards a negative coefficient on D^c which was both theoretically implausible and not well defined statistically. Similar results occurred with other starting values. Estimated equations with the simple 0, 1 dividend control dummy worked far better, lending some support to the hypothesis that the bite of dividend controls, which we estimate to have been significant, changed little between 1973 and abolition in 1979.

Hausman tests for all specifications of both dividends and debt equations decisively rejected the null hypothesis that the firm effects were uncorrelated with the other explanatory variables.[17] This results suggests that the disaggregated equations we estimate are unlikely to be replicated at the aggregate level because of the inability to allow for these company-specific factors (Pakes, 1983).

A comparison of R^2 values suggested that entering tax and interest rate effects linearly, as opposed to logarithmically, was superior although in both cases the differences were very small. It was also clear than proxying gearing risks with interest payments relative to capital employed, rather than relative to income, was superior and that using the dividend yield on equities gave a marginally better fit that using the total yield.

In the common general model it was apparent that the effect of leasing rates, of competitiveness, of base rates and of the corset (as proxied by a 0, 1 dummy) were weak and poorly defined in both the debt and dividend equations. Omitting these variables from each equation proved easily acceptable. The resulting models are shown in column 1 of Tables 7.7 and 7.8. It is clear that the exclusion restrictions which these two equations suggest might be acceptable are different: the majority of the tax rate variables and the interest rate terms are individually insignificant in the debt equation whilst most of these coefficients are reasonably well defined in the dividends equation.

Imposing statistically acceptable restrictions to each equation separately resulted in the specifications shown in column 2 of Table 7.7. and 7.8. In general, coefficients are well determined, especially on variables from the companies' own accounts where variability across firms is much larger than for tax and interest rates where variability across companies arises only from differences in company year ends.

Lagrange multiplier tests for first-order residual correlation suggested no sign of dynamic mis-specification.[18] Tests of the stability, over time and across companies, of these two restricted models were undertaken. To assess stability over time the equations were estimated over the first 12 time periods only (1971–82) and a Chow test was performed. A second Chow

[17]Under the null the test statistic is distributed $\chi^2(k)$, where the degree of freedom k is equal to the number of slope parameters. The values of the statistic for the specifications in columns 2 of Tables 7.8 and 7.9 were 3200 and 586. (The critical 95% values are around 60.)

[18]For Lagrange multipler tests of first-order serial correlation in the error the F statistics were 0.428 and 0.471 for dividends and debt respectively. The 95% significance level is 1.0.

Table 7.7 The dividend equations (dependent variable, flow of gross dividend payments)

		Common general model (1)		*Preferred restricted model (2)*	
Tax variables	CTX	−0.120	(9.6)	−0.117	(9.7)
	ZTAX	1.09	(0.1)		
	IMPT	0.070	(5.5)	0.070	(5.6)
	MTAX	−0.640	(0.2)	−0.479	(9.4)
	EXH_{-1}	−0.011	(1.7)	0.021	(1.6)
	(CTX).(EXH_{-1})	0.022	(1.7)	0.021	(1.6)
	IMEX	0.009	(5.1)	0.009	(5.0)
Bankruptcy/ risk	SDBT	−0.015	(5.1)	−0.018	(9.2)
	SHTD	−0.004	(1.2)		
	VARY	−0.01	(1.3)		
	$VARY_{-1}$	−0.03	(2.3)	−0.028	(2.5)
	LIQA	−0.002	(0.6)		
	FINA	0.005	(4.6)	0.005	(4.7)
Cost of funds	GILT5	−0.007	(8.1)	−0.007	(8.1)
	INTK	−0.006	(1.7)	0.0007	(1.9)
	DIYL	−0.002	(4.9)	−0.002	(5.0)
	CTGIL	0.010	(6.8)	0.010	(6.7)
	INFL	−0.00003	(1.0)		
	CTINF	−0.0008	(1.5)		
Scale of flows	PRF	0.091	(48.2)	0.091	(48.6)
	PRF_{-1}	−0.0008	(2.4)	−0.008	(2.4)
	PRF_{-2}	−0.015	(4.2)	−0.015	(4.2)
	TAX	0.122	(24.6)	0.122	(25.1)
	TAX_{-1}	0.016	(2.4)	0.015	(2.3)
	INVT	0.006	(7.7)	0.006	(7.8)
	ACQS	−0.060	(14.5)	−0.056	(14.7)
	$INTL_{-1}$	−0.018	(0.9)		
	HIRL	−0.034	(4.5)	−0.035	(4.6)
Expectations and adjustment	INVE	−0.011	(7.3)	−0.011	(7.3)
	$GRTH_{-1}$	−0.0008	(2.8)	−0.0008	(2.8)
	DIV_{-1}	0.293	(19.6)	0.295	(19.9)
	DIV_{-2}	0.100	(6.7)	0.100	(6.7)
External controls	CCC	0.022	(7.8)	0.022	(15.7)
	DCON	−0.009	(3.0)	−0.009	(3.0)
t2m4t3m5.6t4m3	CUMUL	−0.360	(21.6)	−0.357	(21.7)
$(\text{Capital employed})^{-1}$		$-0.4(10^{-4})$	(0.1)		
R^2		0.824		0.825	
Residual sum of squares		1.50249		1.50343	
Standard error		0.0133412		0.013341	
Durbin–Watson		1.89		1.89	
Degrees of freedom		8440		8447	

Within estimator with time dummies; company-specific variables scaled by inverse of capital employed. *t* statistics are given in parentheses.

Table 7.8 The debt equations (dependent variable, flow of debt)

		Common general model (1)	*Preferred restricted model (2)*
Tax variables	CTX	−0.001 (0.1)	0.026 (2.1)
	ZTAX	26.00 (0.3)	
	IMPT	0.02 (0.4)	
	MTAX	−3.40 (0.3)	
	EXH_{-1}	−0.022 (0.7)	
	$(CTX).(EXH_{-1})$	0.040 (0.7)	
	IMEX	0.016 (1.9)	
Bankruptcy/ risk	SDBT	−0.195 (15.2)	−0.195 (15.3)
	SHTD	0.283 (17.9)	0.283 (18.0)
	VARY	−0.089 (2.5)	−0.088 (2.5)
	$VARY_{-1}$	−0.023 (0.5)	
	LIQA	−0.021 (1.8)	−0.021 (1.8)
	FINA	−0.001 (0.2)	
Cost of funds	GILT5	−0.004 (0.9)	
	INTK	0.001 (0.7)	
	DIYL	−0.001 (0.5)	
	CTGIL	0.003 (0.4)	
	INFL	−0.003 (1.9)	
	CTINF	0.004 (1.7)	
Scale of flows	PRF	−0.162 (18.8)	−0.161 (19.3)
	PRF_{-1}	0.025 (1.7)	0.023 (1.7)
	PRF_{-2}	−0.009 (0.5)	
	TAX	0.193 (8.5)	0.191 (8.6)
	TAX_{-1}	−0.048 (1.6)	−0.056 (2.0)
	INVT	0.264 (75.1)	0.264 (75.4)
	ACQS	0.119 (6.7)	0.119 (6.8)
	$INTL_{-1}$	−0.136 (1.5)	−0.136 (1.6)
	HIRL	0.125 (3.6)	0.125 (3.6)
Expectations and adjustment	INVE	0.002 (0.3)	0.002 (10.8)
	$GRTH_{-1}$	0.002 (1.8)	
	DIV_{-1}	−0.04 (0.6)	
	DIV_{-2}	0.074 (1.0)	
External controls	CCC	−0.005 (0.4)	−0.006 (1.3)
	DCON	−0.005 (0.3)	
	CUMUL	0.157 (2.1)	0.151 (2.1)
$(\text{Capital employed})^{-1}$		−0.004 (2.5)	−0.003 (2.5)
R^2		0.498	0.500
Residual sum of squares		31.19489	31.2342
Standard error		0.060808	0.06077
Durbin–Watson		1.66	1.66
Degrees of freedom		8440	8459

Within estimator with time dummies; company-specific variables scaled by inverse of capital employed. *t* statistics are given in parentheses.

Table 7.9 Tests of stability: statistics[a] distributed as F under null with 95% critical value approximately 1.0

	Dividends	*Debt*
Estimate over 1971–82 using all 653 companies	0.660	4.04
Estimate using 500 randomly selected companies over 1971–84	0.780	0.760

[a]Statistics are

$$\frac{(\mathrm{RSS}^{\mathrm{T}} - \mathrm{RSS}^{\mathrm{S}})/d}{\mathrm{RSS}^{\mathrm{S}}/\mathrm{df}}$$

where $\mathrm{RSS}^{\mathrm{T}}$ is the residual sum of squares from full sample regression, $\mathrm{RSS}^{\mathrm{S}}$ is the sum of squares from the subset of the sample, d is the difference in degrees of freedom and df is the number of degrees of freedom for subsample regression.

test, to assess stability across companies, was performed by selecting a random sample of 500 of the firms (according to alphabetic ordering of names) and comparing the result of estimating the model with this sample, over all 14 periods, with the full sample. With so many degrees of freedom these tests are particularly stringent, but, as Table 7.9 shows, three out of the four test statistics are acceptable and consistent with the hypothesis that the parameters of the equations are stable. The Chow test suggested some instability over time for the debt model even though the individual coefficients did not appear to change significantly in the subperiod regression.

7.5.1 The results in detail

We consider the impact upon the debt and dividend decisions of flows of receipts and expenditure, of balance sheet structure, of tax and interest rates and of dividend controls.

(a) Flows of receipts and expenditure

As expected, in the short run higher profits increase the payment of dividends and encourage firms to repay some of their debt (Table 7.10). At the margin an extra £1 of income increases dividends by around 9p in the short run and by nearly 12p in the long term. An extra £1 of income is predicted to reduce the stock of debt by 16p in the short run. Although high current profit flows reduce the need for debt finance, higher company income in the recent past (the first lag) seems to increase a firm's confidence in being able to service more debt. In the dividends equation there are also sign reversals on the lags of income flows; this is plausible since a fall in

Table 7.10 The effects of changes in receipts and expenditures on dividends and strategic debt

	Dividend payments[a]		*Stock of strategic debt*[a]	
	Short run	*Long run*	*Short run*	*Long run*
Gross profits	9[b]	12	−16[b]	−70
Investment	0.5[b]	1	26[b]	135
Financial assets	−6[b]	−9	12[b]	60
Tax payments	12[b]	23	19[b]	71
Interest payments	—	—	−14	−70

[a]Pence per additional £1 of expenditure/receipt.
[b]Estimate statistically significant at the 95% level. Long-run responses are calculated, and so their standard errors are not applicable.
The sample average of dividend payments is £2.1 million and of stock of strategic debt is £14.9 million.

current profits conditional on past levels (i.e. a negative coefficient on lag income) is likely to reduce marginally the payments of dividends as expectations of future prospects are revised down.

Investment expenditure has a powerful impact upon debt flows and a small, though very well defined, impact upon dividend payments. Over a quarter of the extra funds needed to fund capital expenditure, at the margin, is met by new debt issues. A very much smaller proportion (12%) of the cost of acquiring non-physical assets is met by heavier borrowing. Higher investment appears to increase the flow of dividends slightly; Lee and Chang (1985) suggest one reason for this. They argue that companies wishing to invest heavily will need to persuade both shareholders and suppliers of debt that the firm is likely to be profitable; paying higher dividends may give such a sign. Higher acquisitions of non-physical assets, however, reduce the payments of dividends significantly—by almost 6p for each extra £1 spent in the short run. This seems plausible since a company's holdings of non-physical assets, e.g. shares in other companies, are a substitute for the firm's owners holding such assets (and therefore company acquisitions are a substitute for dividend payments) in a way that physical assets are not. However, it does suggest that, just as physical investment may not be (weakly) exogenous with respect to debt flows, non-physical investment may not be (weakly) exogenous in the dividends equation.

Although there are severe problems involved in undertaking exogeneity tests, since these involve estimating a well-specified subsidiary equation for each variable whose exogeneity is in doubt, we attempted these tests with physical and non-physical investment. It proved hard to find meaningful subsidiary equations for either flow, and consequently the tests are weak. Including residuals from the subsidiary regressions in both the debt and dividend equation (Hausman, 1978) gave mixed results. Physical investment appeared exogenous with respect to dividends but not with respect to debt flows, while non-physical investment seemed exogenous with respect to debt but not to dividends. Instruments for the flows of investment were sufficiently poor that instrumental variable estimation gave implausible results.

The estimated model suggests that firms which expect to undertake higher investment in future periods, other things being equal, reduce current dividend payments. The effects are not large (at most 2p for each £1 of planned future expenditure) but are statistically precise. They suggest that the expectations of a higher requirement for funds in the future encourages firms to pay out less now but not to alter significantly their use of debt finance. In turn this suggests that the expectation of higher future investment may encourage firms to build up liquid assets in the short term.

The impact of tax and interest payments upon financial flows is powerful although in some cases puzzling. Higher tax payments, in the short run, need to be financed and the flow of debt, at the margin, increases by 19p for each extra £1 going to the Revenue. In the longer term higher tax payments represent a reduction in available income (and thus the ability to service debt) and increase the company's incentive to issue less debt, slightly offsetting the direct short-term effect. The scale of debt servicing costs is more directly measured by the lags of interest payments, higher levels of which are predicted to reduce the flow of debt and the level of dividend payments.

One puzzle here is that higher tax payments, both current and lagged, appear to increase the level of dividends, and by large amounts. There are two plausible arguments for this finding. First, it seems likely that one of the best indicators of whether a company is tax exhausted is its actual level of tax payments: a company with high payments is less likely to be tax exhausted and consequently more likely to be able to offset ACT, thus giving an incentive to distribute income. The second argument is that we have not taken proper account of the endogeneity of total tax payments by only subtracting irrecoverable (as opposed to unrecovered) ACT.[19] If this is so, instrumenting current tax payments should at least reduce the coefficient in the dividends equation. In fact, when we attempted to instrument tax payments this did not happen and an exogeneity test suggests that tax payments were weakly exogenous with respect to dividends. We conclude that the tax exhaustion story is the more plausible.

Although the leasing rate proved insignificant in both equations, the flow of rental payments on hired capital was clearly relevant. The higher are rental payments, for given levels of profit, the lower are dividend payments and the greater is the reliance upon debt finance.

Company size (as measured by the reciprocal of capital employed) had a significant effect on debt flows with larger firms, other things being equal,

[19]This argument would not explain the positive impact of past tax payments on current dividends.

borrowing more than small firms. This is consistent with the evidence presented in section 7.4 for higher gearing for larger companies.

(b) Risk and dynamic adjustment

Rewriting the debt equation in stock terms gives a lagged dependent variable with a coefficient of around 0.8. The dividends equation has well-defined effects from the first two lags of dividends with the sum of the coefficients being around 0.4. Thus the equations display significant lags with a major part of the effect of a change in a current dated variable still to come through after 2 years. This slow response is plausible in the case of dividends but more surprising with debt. However, the coefficients on the stock of debt are very well determined in both equations, with higher stocks reducing both debt flows and dividend payments. In the case of dividends it is the stock of total debt (short term plus long term) which is negatively linked to payments. A 1 percentage point rise in total debt is predicted to reduce the flow of dividend payments by around 8% in the following period. The maturity composition of total borrowing is important in determining the impact of the balance sheet position upon flows of medium- and longer-term debt. Higher outstanding stocks of short-term debt encourage issues of longer-term debt as companies aim to reschedule their portfolio and increase average debt maturity. However, higher stocks of longer-term debt reduce the attractiveness of funding current requirements by more debt issues; this is a plausible correction mechanism and one which yields a long-run solution to the debt equation.

Companies feel more able to pay higher dividends if their holdings of less liquid financial assets are high. A £1 rise in holdings of gilts and shares, for example, will increase dividends by around 1p in the long run. Whilst dividends did not seem to be significantly affected by holdings of more liquid financial assets (cash, deposits, Treasury bills), there was a clear impact of liquid assets stocks upon borrowing. An increase of £1 in stocks of liquid assets was predicted to reduce the stock of debt by around 10p in the long run. Less liquid financial assets had no significant effect in the debt equation.

Variability in earnings, (proxied by VARY) has a well-determined negative impact upon both flows. The effect of a permanent 20% rise in this (rather crude) measure of risk is to reduce the stock of debt by around 0.5%. The flow of dividend payments falls by only 0.2%. Rapid growth has a further negative impact on dividends with a rise in the rate of change of total capital employed from 10% to 15% reducing dividends by 0.25% in the long run. Such an increase in growth, if sustained, would increase reliance upon debt significantly with capital gearing predicted to be around 4% higher. This seems intuitively plausible with firms likely to be more confident about their ability to service debt the higher is recent growth.

(c) *Interest rate and tax rate effects*

The pattern of responses to tax and interest rate effects revealed by the equations of Tables 7.7 and 7.8 is complex. Coefficients on the tax rates, and especially on the corporation tax rate, are well defined and, in the case of dividends, the effects of interactive terms between tax and interest rates and between tax rates and the tax exhaustion dummy are significant.[20]

It is difficult to untangle the net effect of isolated interest rate or tax rate changes because of these interactive terms. Table 7.11 shows the long-run semi-elasticities of dividend payments to changes in tax and interest rates. We have calculated the impact of tax rates by setting interest rates at their average levels over 1971–84, and vice versa. We also considered alternative assumptions in assessing the impact of the interactive effects.

The results proved very sensitive to the point at which the semi-elasticity is calculated and need to be interpreted with great care. At average levels of interest rates, changes in the corporation tax rate have only a small net effect upon dividend payments. When the 5 year gilt rate is as little as 1 percentage point beneath its mean level, however, a reduction in the tax rate from 0.50 to 0.40 is predicted to increase the level of dividend payments by 0.8% in the long run.

Table 7.11 Effects of tax and interest rate changes on dividends[a]

	Long-run change in dividends (%)
Cut in corporate tax rate from 0.50 to 0.40	
(a) with GILT5 at average rate (11.2%)	+2.4
(b) with GILT5 at 10%	+7.9
(c) with GILT5 at 12%	−1.4
Cut in imputation rate from 0.33 to 0.30	−10.1
Cut in marginal income tax rate from 0.30 to 0.29	−10.1
Company becomes tax exhausted	
(a) at average tax rates	+4.0
(b) at current tax rates	−7.1
Gilt rate (5 year) up 1.0%	
(a) at average tax rates	−9.2
(b) at current tax rates	−15.1
Interbank rate up 1% (relative to GILT5)	+3.2
Dividend yield up 1% (relative to GILT5)	−9.2

[a]The table shows the impact of changing tax and interest *rates*, holding the levels of tax payments and interest payments constant. They therefore represent substitution effects.

[20]This contrasts with the recent finding of Edwards *et al.* (1985) that in a model of dividends, estimated using company accounts data, tax effects were poorly determined when time dummies were included.

This reflects the net result of a powerful negative effect of the level of the tax rate and an offsetting positive effect of the product of the tax and interest rate. That these two effects are offsetting is not implausible; given the time lags (sometimes as long as several years) between the accrual of a tax-deductible expense and its use, the higher is the discount rate then the lower should be the impact of a particular tax rate. Clearly this can be offset by a higher level of the tax rate.

Cutting the corporation tax rate from 0.5 to 0.4 is estimated to reduce the stock of debt by about 10% in the long run. It should be noted that this tax rate coefficient is not very well determined. Nonetheless the qualitative result that dividend and debt flows tend to respond in different directions to corporate tax rate changes is noteworthy. Changes which make debt relatively less desirable (a cut in rates), and therefore make equity finance relatively more attractive, encourage higher dividend payments. This might be due to a desire by the firm to make its equity more attractive to suppliers of funds.

As expected, reductions in the imputation rate reduce dividends; the effect is powerful. Reductions in shareholders' estimated average marginal income tax rates have an offsetting and this is, somewhat implausibly, even stronger; we are doubtful that the coefficient purely reflects tax changes because the MTAX variable is very stongly trended (downwards) and could be picking up the influence of any trended omitted variables.

At current tax rates a company which becomes tax exhausted is predicted to reduce dividends by 7.0%. It is puzzling that at higher rates tax exhaustion seems to have less effect on dividends.

Increases in long-term interest rates appear to reduce dividend payments substantially whilst increases in short rates relative to long rates raise the pay-out ratio. This result proved to be unstable across split sample regressions and we are wary of any firm conclusions.

In summary, dividend payments seen more sensitive than debt flows to tax and interest rates, and to the tax-paying status of the company. The net effect of changes in tax rates upon dividend payments is often highly sensitive to the point of departure, and exact quantitative predictions about the effects of the major tax changes announced in the 1984 Budget cannot sensibly be made. Nonetheless, the model does suggest that the kind of reduction in the company tax rate which has occurred since 1984, and the probable reduction in the extent of tax exhaustion, might cause a significant long-term reduction in debt gearing and an increase in dividends.

(d) Dividend and lending controls

The introduction of dividend controls appears to have had a very large impact upon dividend payments. Ths impact effect is estimated to have reduced payments by around 20%; the longer-term effect is twice as large.

This evidence is consistent with that presented by Poterba (1984) who estimated that gross dividends paid by companies may have been reduced by up to 50% as a result of controls. No significant effect of dividend controls upon borrowing was found.

The results suggest that the cumulative divergence between actual dividend payments and desired payments which dividend controls caused was more than made up for in the post-1979 period. The catch-up period was lengthy, and we could easily reject the hypothesis that the lost dividends were recouped within 1 or even 2 years. We estimate that around a third of the backlog of real dividends was paid off in each of the years following the abolition of controls; thus over 150% of the estimated effect was regained by 1984. The fact that companies appear to have more than made up for the effect of dividend controls may, in large part, just reflect shareholders' discount rates. The average lag between controls biting and firms paying back the 'lost' dividends is just over 6 years. With a real discount rate of 5% shareholders would need to receive, in real terms, almost 140% of the total 'lost' dividends to feel no worse off. Our estimates suggest that companies actually paid more than would have been necessary to compensate shareholders at a discount rate even as high as 5%. Firms were apparently keen to more than make up for the relatively low pay-out ratios of the 1970s. This in turn might reflect worries about the re-introduction of controls at some point in the future.

Although dividend controls appeared to have no significant impact on debt financing, the payment of extra dividends in the post-control period appears to have marginally reduced reliance on debt. This is a puzzle. However, the effect is not very well defined and the exclusion of the relevant variable has no impact on the other coefficients in the debt equation.

The corset appeared to have no discernible effect upon either debt or dividends though the introduction of competition and credit control did.[21]

(e) Diversity in responses across companies

The stability tests reported above summarize the effect of estimating the equations over sub-periods and over random subsamples of companies. We also tested whether there were systematic differences in behaviour between different types of company by splitting the sample first according to company size and then by reference to the rate of growth of the firm's capital employed. Table 7.12 shows the results of testing for equality of slope parameters across those subsamples.

[21] There is a problem, however, in interpreting the CCC dummy since it is almost perfectly correlated with the time dummy for 1971 and the latter had to be dropped to allow matrix inversion.

Table 7.12 Tests of parameter equality (across large/small and fast-growth/slow-growth firms)

	Dividends		*Debt*	
	Test 1	*Test 2*	*Test 1*	*Test 2*
Split by company size	0.37	3.64	0.534	2.93
Split by company growth rate	2.92	20.00	5.08	8.87

Test statistic 1, under the null, is

$$\frac{(\mathrm{RSS}^{\mathrm{T}} - \mathrm{RSS}^{\mathrm{SM}})/\{\mathrm{RSS}^{\mathrm{SM}}/(\mathrm{NS} - K)\}}{\mathrm{NL}} \approx F(\mathrm{NL}, \mathrm{NS} - K)$$

Test statistic 2, under the null, is

$$\frac{(\mathrm{RSS}^{\mathrm{T}} - \mathrm{RSS}^{\mathrm{SM}} - \mathrm{RSS}^{\mathrm{LG}})/K}{(\mathrm{RSS}^{\mathrm{SM}} + \mathrm{RSS}^{\mathrm{LG}})/\mathrm{NL} + \mathrm{NS} - 2K} \approx F(K, \mathrm{NL} + \mathrm{NS} - 2K)$$

where NS is the number of small (low-growth) company observations,[a] NL is the number of large (high-growth) company observations,[a] $\mathrm{RSS}^{\mathrm{T}}$ is the residual sum of squares using the whole sample, $\mathrm{RSS}^{\mathrm{SM}}$ is the residual sum of squares using small (low-growth) firms, $\mathrm{RSS}^{\mathrm{LG}}$ is the sum of squares using firms of above average size (growth rate) and K is the number of slope parameters.

Both statistics can be used to test the same null hypothesis of parameter equality. The 95% (99%) critical value for test 1 is approximately 1(1) and for test 2 is 1.4(1.6).

[a]Equal to the number of such firms multiplied by $T - 1$ where T is the number of time periods.

The most significant differences in behaviour across companies, in terms of differences in key parameters, occurred when the sample was split into above and below average company size, although the test statistics more clearly reject the hypothesis of coefficient equality across firms with different growth rates. The important differences in behaviour between large and small firms are common to the debt and dividend equations. Small companies appear more concerned about capital gearing and variability in company income, reducing dividend payments and debt finance by significantly more than larger firms when these measures of risk rise. Larger firms appear to pay out more of their income in dividends than smaller firms. The larger companies also finance more of their investment expenditure from debt (39% against 26%). Coefficients on tax rates, interest rates and tax payments also seem to differ across companies, with larger firms generally responding more to changes. However, some of these tax and interest rate effects are not very well determined in the subregressions although the semi-elasticities remain large and highly sensitive to the point at which they are calculated.

Differences in behaviour between companies of above and below average growth are much less easy to summarize and it is difficult to draw any conclusions that are simultaneously general and interesting. It is clear that there are certain differences between companies, but this is only to be expected with such a large sample. Spliting the sample by growth performance did suggest some problem with coefficients on the acquisition of non-physical assets and on current tax payments as these change dramatically between the two types of firm. This suggests to us that endogeneity problems may remain, despite the weak evidence to the contrary reported above.

7.6 CONCLUSIONS

Our aim has been to estimate the determinants of the debt and dividend payments decisions of companies. In constructing a model of these key financial decisions we have been able to judge between different, and sometimes mutually exclusive, theories of company finance. We have also assessed how behaviour appears to vary across companies. Along with the non-linear nature of the basic model, these differences across firms mean that the results could not be obtained using aggregate data. It also means that no simple conclusions about aggregate behaviour emerge, although the assessment we make of the relative strength of different theories does make possible some broad judgements on aggregate developments.

Four types of model, which often overlap, were identified at the outset: those that generate irrelevance results for finance decisions; those that focus on the tax incentives for favouring certain forms of finance; theories that stress the smoothing and signalling role of dividends; theories which make a firm's attention to the risks of default and bankruptcy the dominant factor in its debt and dividend behaviour. We have found evidence that there is some truth in three of these theories, although the irrelevance propositions find little support. We have constructed models with well-defined coefficients which fit the past well, given the nature of the data. Measures of capital and income gearing and proxies for income variability have proved significant and suggest that considerations of risk are central to financing decisions.

Long lags of company income and of dividend payments were found to be relevant in determining current flows, suggesting that the smoothing of payments is a common phenomenon. Powerful effects of changes in tax rates and in interest rates were apparent, although the interaction of the two made it difficult to derive simple predictions about the impact of changing rates. One thing was clear, namely that the effect of relative prices is made considerably more complex by the existence of tax exhaustion. However, the difficulties that we have had in accurately measuring tax exhaustion mean that we cannot claim to have modelled the effect of the tax systems with great precision; more work is called for here.

We estimate that dividend controls had a major impact upon dividend payments both during and after their period of operation. We also found that there was a significant overlap between the factors influencing debt and dividends. The advantage of estimating the two company financial decisions alongside one another lies in being able to assess the extent of this overlap. Where there are factors which influence debt flows but not dividends (the maturity structure of the stock of debt, the level of past interest payments and the extent of liquid asset holdings), or dividends but not debt (interest rates, some tax rates), it is plausible that equity issues might absorb the impact of an isolated change in one of the other flows. Thus far we have not directly estimated a model of equity issues, primarily because of the problems of using least-squares estimation with so many zero entries amongst the new issues data. However, we do believe that this data set could be used in future work to throw more light upon companies' use of equity finance.

REFERENCES

Anderson, G. (1986) Modelling dividend behaviour: an application of the Tobit model to panel data, McMaster University Economics Working Paper.

Auerbach, A. J. (1979) Wealth maximisation and the cost of capital. *Quarterly Journal of Economics*, **93**, 431–46.

Auerbach, A. J. (1984) The dynamic effects of tax law asymmetries, NBER Working Paper No. 1152.

Auerbach, A. J. and King, M. A. (1983) Taxation, portfolio choice and debt-equity ratios: a general equilibrium model. *Quarterly Journal of Economics*, **97**, 587–609.

Bain, A., Day, D. and Wearing, A. L. (1975) *Company Financing in the United Kingdom*, Martin Robertson, Oxford.

Balestra, P. and Nerlove, M. (1966) Pooling cross section and time series data in the estimation of a dynamic model—the demand for natural gas. *Econometrica*, **34**, 595–612.

Bank of England (1980) Dividend payments: some recent trends. *Bank of England Quarterly Bulletin*, **20**(1), 33–42.

Bhattacharya, S. (1979) Imperfect information, dividend policy and 'the bird in the hand' fallacy. *Bell Journal of Economics*, **10**, 259–70.

Bradford, D. (1979) The incidence and allocation effect of a tax on corporate dividends, NBER Working Paper No. 349.

Brennan, M. and Schwartz, E. (1978) Corporate income taxes, valuation, and the problem optimal capital structure. *Journal of Business*, **51**, 103–14.

Castanias, R. (1983) Bankruptcy risk and optimal capital structure. *Journal of Finance*, **38**, 1617–35.

Chen, A. H. (1978) Recent developments in the cost of debt capital. *Journal of Finance*, **33**, 863–77.

Chowdhury, G., Green, C. J. and Miles, D. K. (1986) An empirical model of company short-term financial decisions: evidence from company accounts data, Bank of England Discussion Paper No. 26.

Cuthbertson, K. (1985) Sterling bank lending to UK industrial and commercial companies. *Oxford Bulletin of Economics and Statistics*, **47**, 91–113.
De Angelo, H. and Masulis, R. W. (1980) Optimal capital structure under corporate and personal taxation. *Journal of Financial Economics*, **8**, 3–29.
Dhrymes, P. and Kurz, M. (1967) Investment, dividends and external finance behaviour of firms, in *Determinants of Investment Behaviour* (ed. R. Ferber), Columbia University Press, New York.
Edwards, J. S. S. (1984) Does dividend policy matter. *Fiscal Studies*, **5**, 1–17.
Edwards, J. S. S., Mayer, C. P., Pashardes, P. and Poterba, J. (1985) The effects of taxation on corporate dividend distributions, IFS Working Paper No. 78.
Fama, E. (1974) The empirical relationship between the dividend and investment decisions of firms. *American Economic Review*, **64**, 304–18.
Feldstein, M. and Green, J. (1980) Why do companies pay dividends, Harvard Institute of Economic Research Discussion Paper No. 736.
Hausman, J. A. (1978) Specification tests in econometrics. *Econometrica*, **46**, 251–73.
Kim, E. H. (1978) A mean variance theory of optimal capital structure. *Journal of Finance*, **33**, 45–73.
King, M. A. (1974) Taxation and the cost of capital. *Review of Economic Studies*, **41**, 21–35.
King, M. A. (1977) *Public Policy and the Corporation*, Chapman and Hall, London.
King, M. A. (1986) Taxes, takeovers and the stock market, Paper presented at a NERA Seminar, May.
Lee, C. F. and Chang, H. S. (1985) Interactions of dividends and investment—a test for the John and William signalling equilibrium model, University of Illionis Working Paper, September.
Marais, D. A. J. (1979) A method of quantifying companies' relative financial strength, Bank of England Discussion Paper No. 4, July.
Mayer, C. P. (1986) Corporation tax, finance and the cost of capital. *Review of Economic Studies*, **53**, 93–112.
Miller, M. H. (1977) Debt and taxes. *Journal of Finance*, **32**, 261–75.
Miller, M. H. and Scholes, M. S. (1978) Dividends and taxes. *Journal of Financial Economics*, **6**, 333–65.
Modigliani, F. and Miller, M. H. (1958) The cost of captial corporation finance and the theory of investment. *American Economic Review*, **53**, 261–97.
Modigliani, F. and Miller, M. (1963) Corporate income taxes and the cost of capital: a correction. *American Economic Review*, **53**, 433–42.
Pakes, A. (1983) On group effects and errors in variables in aggregation. *Review of Economics and Statistics*, **75**(1), 168–73.
Poterba, J. (1984) Public policy and corporate dividend behaviour: the postwar British experience, MIT Working Paper No. 339.
Ross, S. (1977) The determination of financial structures: the incentive signalling approach. *Bell Journal of Economics*, **8**, 23–40.
Smirlock, M. and Marshall, W. (1983) An examination of the empirical relationship between the dividend and investment decisions: a note. *Journal of Finance*, **83**, 1659–67.
Stiglitz, J. E. (1969) A re-examination of the Modigliani–Miller theorem. *American Economic Review*, **59**, 784–93.
Stiglitz, J. E. (1973) Taxation, corporation financial policy and the cost of capital. *Journal of Public Economics*, **2**, 1–34.

8

Modelling the flow of funds with an application to the demand for liquid assets by the UK personal sector

D. G. BARR AND K. CUTHBERTSON

8.1 INTRODUCTION

The impacts of changes in financial variables on the real sector are major issues in monetary economics. Broadly speaking, changes in financial variables may arise from government policy, from external events and from changes in behaviour by the private sector. Fiscal policy and open-market operations by the authorities cause changes in domestic interest rates which are also strongly influenced by changes in foreign interest rates. Innovation in the provision of financial services initiated either by government legislation (e.g. Financial Services Act 1986) or by marketing considerations (e.g. entry of banks into the home loans market) may also lead to a re-allocation of portfolios and a change in relative interest rates.

In the theoretical literature we could reasonably take the view that the determination of asset prices is governed by two seemingly contradictory approaches, i.e. by 'structural' or 'reduced-form' models. Applied work on the term structure takes a 'reduced-form' approach. For example, in the expectations hypothesis long rates are viewed as depending on expected future short rates, and the determinants of the 'liquidity premium' are often omitted or simply modelled as an additive *ad hoc* set of variables (Modigliani and Sutch, 1967; Modigliani and Shiller, 1973). The market segmentation and preferred habitat theories are rather loosely formulated and therefore difficult to test in any precise manner. In the structural approach, asset demand and supply functions are estimated and the model is 'solved' for asset prices. However, the equilibrium returns generated by the structural approach will yield an implicit relationship between long rates and short rates. Furthermore, in the structural approach it is clear that the exogenous determinants of asset demands and supply functions can be viewed as influencing the liquidity premium. Hence the two approaches are really complementary.

It is generally accepted that the structural approach in the form of a portfolio balance model is a useful way of analysing the flow of funds and the determination of asset prices. Flow of funds models are essentially structural models of the movement of funds between government, commercial companies, people, the overseas sector and financial institutions. Such models are very diverse. A number of macroeconometric models of the financial sector have been built up in a somewhat piecemeal fashion (e.g. Spencer and Mowl, 1978; Mayes and Savage, 1980; Wallis, 1984; Patterson *et al.*, 1987) or are highly aggregative (Minford *et al.*, 1980). In general such models provide a reasonable 'fit' to the data but theoretical restrictions are limited to little more than an examination of the 'right signs' on certain coefficients. Adding-up constraints are usually met implicitly by a set of 'missing equations' whose structure often remains unexplored. Almost by construction such a piecemeal approach does not consider cross-equation restrictions familiar in microtheory such as homogeneity and symmetry of the coefficients on the 'price' vector.

The Brainard–Tobin (1968) approach fulfils the minimum requirement of adding up, but the long-run asset demands are somewhat *ad hoc* and are often not based on a choice theoretic model (Backus *et al.*, 1980; Green, 1984; Owen, 1986; Cohen, 1987). The mean–variance model has been widely used to model subsystems of the financial sector, notably the banking sector (Parkin *et al.*, 1970; White, 1975; Courakis, 1975, 1980; Berndt *et al.*, 1980). However, the theoretical problems associated with this approach (Keating, 1985; Courakis, 1988) are formidable and attempts to circumvent them can produce implausible outcomes. At an empirical level the mean–variance model and Brainard–Tobin type models have met with very mixed success.

In comparison with the empirical performance of systems models, single-equation studies of the demand for assets, particularly aggregate money variables, could be said to have fared better (Hendry, 1979, 1985; Rose, 1985; Baba *et al.*, 1988). This is in large part due to the application of error-feedback and 'general to specific' modelling strategies (Hendry, 1983; Hendry *et al.*, 1984) and the use of single-equation co-integration techniques (Granger, 1986; Hall, 1986; Hendry, 1986) has given new insights and impetus to the error-feedback approach.

In this chapter we wish to examine both the theoretical basis of the portfolio balance approach to modelling the flow of funds and general to specific estimation strategies that may yield reasonable search procedures in a systems framework. The modelling strategy propounded here has been applied, using a specially constructed consistent stock-flow matrix for financial data (Barr *et al.*, 1989), to produce a flow of funds (FOF) model for the UK financial system. In the FOF project we have modelled the main financial asset and liability decisions of the personal, company, monetary and overseas sectors and other financial intermediaries (OFI) (Barr and Cuthbertson, 1989a–f) using a variety of econometric methods and testing procedures. In this chapter we provide illustrative results using this approach to model the demand for liquid assets by the UK personal sector. The rest of this chapter is organized as follows. In section 8.2 we examine the applicability of alternative theories of the demand for assets to modelling the flow of funds and argue in favour of adopting an approach based on neoclassical consumer demand theory. Of the several approaches available we suggest a development of the Almost Ideal Demand System (AIDS), originally due to Deaton and Muellbauer (1980), to represent long-run asset demands. In section 8.3 we discuss the issues of dynamic adjustment, modelling expectations and econometric problems in a systems framework and in section 8.4 we present our illustrative empirical results. In section 8.5 we present illustrative simulation properties of the model and we end with a brief summary.

8.2 THEORETICAL MODELS

The development of theories of the demand for assets has proceeded in a number of directions. Friedman (1956) argued that the demand for assets should be based on axioms of consumer choice. He focused on the demand for money and presents a fairly long list of possible arguments of this function (i.e. a vector of expected returns, wealth and income) with 'signs' to be determined primarily by the data. Friedman eschews the idea of approaching the theory of demand for assets by considering *explicit motives* for holding assets. He did not present an explicit model of consumer choice and hence his model contains few *a priori* and potentially refutable restrictions. This perhaps accounts in part for the development of the 'motives approach' which resulted in numerous models which can be classified under the broad headings of transactions, precautionary and risk-aversion (or, more usually, mean–variance) models. In contrast with Friedman (1956) such models yield precise functional forms and strong a priori restrictions. However, transactions models apply only to narrow money and there appears to be no independent role for inflation (e.g. Baumol, 1952; Tobin, 1956) unless real assets are introduced into the choice set (e.g. Feige and Parkin, 1971). On theoretical grounds the applicability of such models to firms is open to doubt (Sprenkle, 1969) and different models yield widely different a priori restrictions, e.g. the income elasticity in Baumol (1952) is 0.5, while in Akerlof and Milbourne (1980) it may be negative. Precautionary demand models appear difficult to test because in principle we require a measure of the variance of transactions (Miller and Orr, 1966). The mean–variance model (Tobin, 1958; Merton, 1973; Courakis, 1988) considers the demand for a set of assets, and several versions of the model allow tests of symmetry and homogeneity. However, narrow (non-interest bearing) money is dominated (Tsiang, 1972) by other 'capital certain' assets (e.g. building society deposits). Broad money, which is also predominately 'capital certain', cannot be separately identified from other liquid assets. All capital certain assets (or liabilities) are homogeneous in this model and hence it does not explain the choice between these assets which are a major element of the flow of funds.

We wish to argue that, from a theoretical standpoint, it is useful to approach the demand for assets in the context of neoclassical demand theory rather than by considering explicit 'motives' for holding money. We aruge that this approach is tractable and allows the basic axioms of rational choice to be tested. It is a natural extension of Friedman's (1956) ideas but incorporates technical aspects which post-date his contribution. To illustrate this approach we show how a particular model of consumer demand, namely the AIDS model, can be adapted to the demand for assets.

8.2.1 Separability and two-stage budgeting

The decision as to which portfolio of assets to hold is nested within the very general decision concerning labour supply, consumption and saving (Tobin, 1969). A fully specified model would identify, for example, the interrelationship between the demand for any particular asset and the willingness to supply labour. Such a model would probably be intractable, and as a result modelling has developed by assuming that some groups of decisions are taken 'independently' of others. For example, the Keynesian consumption function takes income as given and is not concerned explicitly with either labour supply or portfolio allocation.

This separation is an essential part of the FOF model. It is assumed that the portfolio allocation decision is independent of all others. A consequence of this assumption is that the total size of the portfolio at the start of any decision period can be taken to be exogenous (i.e. the labour supply and saving decisions are independent of the choice between assets). This notion of separability (or two-stage budgeting) also provides a method of delineating the 'size' of the portfolio allocation model *per se*. Separability implies that we can consider, for example, that the personal sector makes decisions on saving, then borrowing, and then splits gross wealth between capital certain (liquid) assets and risky assets (e.g. gilts, foreign). Separability implies that the choice within the set of liquid assets depends only on returns on the liquid assets and total wealth held in liquid assets. If separability holds in an appropriate form we can ignore asset returns on risky assets when considering the choice between alternative liquid assets.

This may reduce collinearity problems. At the outset we shall apply the principle of separability to reduce our model to a more manageable size, although it is beyond the scope of this chapter to discuss non-parameteric tests of separability (Varian, 1983; Swofford and Whitney, 1986).

Separability is also useful when dealing with rationing. If a set of assets is assumed to be weakly separable from the rationed assets (e.g. personal sector money holdings from rationed mortgage loans for the 1960s and 1970s), then all we need to do is to deduct the expenditure on the rationed goods (mortgages) from total expenditure and model the demand for this set as a separate system. Alternatively we can include some explicit measure of rationing other than price (e.g. collateral). Finally, in applied demand analysis it is usual to assume that preferences are weakly *intertemporally* separable. Demand in the current period then depends only on initial endowments (wealth) and expected prices over a single period. We invoke this assumption in the present chapter—intertemporal models for consumer demand theory have been investigated by Weissenberger (1986) and Rossi (1987).

The basic model used in this study is the AIDS model due to Deaton and Muellbauer (1980), although we modify it in various ways. In particular, we assume a quasi-separable utility function, from which the following separation of the associated cost function can be derived:

$$C(u, p^a, p^b, p^c) = C\{u, C_a(u, p^a), C_b(u, p^b), C_c(u, p^c)\}$$

where a, b, c denote groups of assets, C_a etc. are the subcost functions and p^i is the vector of prices of 'goods' in group i (i = a, b, c). The cost function denotes the *minimum* cost of attaining a specified utility level u. (This is equivalent to the familiar optimum at which u is the maximum utility available from specified expenditure equal to C.) By separating the cost function according to groups a, b and c each subcost function can be minimized (and, in a very loose sense, a form of subutility function maximized). The global cost can then be minimized given that each subgroup is allocated optimally. This procedure is analogous to two-stage budgeting (although further restrictions are needed to ensure this outcome—see below).

Assuming that the first-stage allocation between groups has occurred, we can take the total wealth given to each group as the budget constraint for an optimal allocation within the group. The advantage of this separation from an econometric point of view is that it allows the demand functions within each subgroup to depend (directly) only on those rates of return in the same group (i.e. there are fewer explanatory variables to be considered). However, this does not imply that the shares are totally independent of the other rates since these will influence the allocation of total wealth between the subgroups. Consequently, unless there are no wealth effects (the notional subutility functions are homothetic) the shares will depend indirectly on the excluded rates.

A word of caution is in order here concerning the two-stage budgeting procedure proposed. Weak separability is necessary and sufficient for the second stage (i.e. lower-level decisions) of two-stage budgeting, which is the main area of application discussed below. However, weak separability has some drawbacks. First, it places quite severe restrictions on the degree of substitutability between goods in different groups (Pudney, 1981). For example, whole groups will be substitutes or complements of each other. The second problem is potentially more serious, however. In modelling the upper-level decisions (i.e. the choice between the broad groups a, b, c etc.) it would be extremely useful to be able to establish the maximization problem in terms of *group* price and quantity indices (rather than having to utilize *all* prices that the consumer faces), since this would considerably reduce the number of parameters to be estimated for the upper-level equations. However, strictly speaking, this is only possible under highly restrictive assumptions. If preferences are homothetic, which implies that all expenditure elasticities are unity or equivalently that the budget shares *within* each group are independent of total group expenditure, then group price indices can be legitimately used in determining the upper-level allocations. If preferences are *not* homothetic then group price indices can be used provided that the utility function is strongly separable and has the generalized Gorman polar form. However, the former implies additivity between groups:

$$u = u_a(q_a) + u_b(q_b) + \ldots$$

Additivity is restrictive in that inferior goods are ruled out, goods can only be substitutes given that inferior goods are not allowed and expenditure elasticities are proportional to price elasticities. None of these restrictive assumptions seems attractive in modelling asset demands. The problem then is that the group price indices P_a, say, are given by $P_a = P_a(u_a, p^a)$ and are dependent on u_a, which in turn depends on *all* other prices outside the group. One possibility is not to invoke homotheticity and to assume that P_a does not vary very much with u_a and hence most of the 'explanation' of P_a is the subset of prices p^a. Given the other approximations involved in empirical studies this may be a reasonable expedient to adopt if homotheticity is not found to hold in the data. Having aired the above problems we now return to discuss the second-stage or lower-level demand functions.

To derive the demand functions within each subgroup we proceed by analogy with consumer demand theory and then present the model in terms of financial asset demands. Initially we deal only with the determinants of long-run static equilibrium asset demands. Considerations of dynamic adjustment are discussed in section 8.3.

8.2.2 Consumer demand theory

Neoclassical demand theory is usually based either on maximization of utility subject to an expenditure constraint or the equivalent 'dual' of minimizing cost to achieve a given level of utility. For expositional clarity we assume weak intertemporal separability and consider only a one-period decision. The general consumer maximization problem is therefore

$$\max u = u(q_1, \ldots, q_n) \tag{8.1}$$

subject to

$$\sum_{i=1}^{n} \tilde{p}_i q_i = C \tag{8.1a}$$

or

$$\min C(\tilde{p}, u) \tag{8.2}$$

subject to

$$u = \bar{u} \tag{8.2a}$$

where u is utility, q_i is the quantity of (real) goods i, $\tilde{p}_i$ is the price of good i and C is the total nominal expenditure.

Approaching the problem via the dual is mathematically more tractable and has the added advantage that we can state the problem without recourse to the underlying utility function if we so wish. The axioms of rational choice in consumer demand theory (i.e. the existence of consistent preferences) are met provided that we choose a cost function that is concave and homogeneous of degree one in prices.[1] Of the several flexible functional forms available we select the PIGLOG (price-independent generalized logarithmic) which, in common with others (e.g. indirect translog (Christensen *et al.*, 1975)), is a second-order approximation but has the advantage of desirable aggregation properties and yields long-run equilibria in the levels of the variables. (The latter is important when we consider co-integration in section 5.3.) Within the PIGLOG class we choose the AIDS cost function

$$\ln C = \alpha_0 + \sum_{l}^{n} \alpha_i \ln \tilde{p}_i + 0.5 \sum_{i}\sum_{j} \gamma^{*}_{ij} \ln \tilde{p}_i \ln \tilde{p}_j$$

$$+ \beta_0 u \prod_{k} \tilde{p}_k^{\beta k} \tag{8.3}$$

Using Sheppard's lemma

$$s_i = \frac{d(\ln C)}{d(\ln \tilde{p}_i)} \tag{8.4}$$

[1]It is also usually assumed that the cost function is continuous in prices and that the first and second derivatives with respect to prices exist.

we obtain the goods expenditure shares s_i as[2]

$$s_i = \alpha_i + \sum_{j=1}^{n} \gamma_{ij} \ln \tilde{p}_j + \beta_i \ln\left(\frac{C}{P^*}\right) \tag{8.5}$$

where

$$\ln P^* = \sum_{1}^{n} s_i \ln \tilde{p}_i \tag{8.5a}$$

$$\gamma_{ii} = \gamma_{ii}^* \tag{8.5b}$$

$$\gamma_{ij} = 0.5(\gamma_{ij}^* + \gamma_{ji}^*) \tag{8.5c}$$

$$s_i = \frac{\tilde{p}_i q_i}{C} \tag{8.5d}$$

The adding-up constraint 8.1a implies

$$\sum_i \alpha_i = 1 \qquad \sum_i \gamma_{ij} = 0 \qquad \sum_i \beta_i = 0 \tag{8.6}$$

Homogeneity requires

$$\sum_j \gamma_{ij} = 0 \tag{8.7}$$

Symmetry and negativity (of the Hicksian demand functions) are direct consequences of the axioms of rational choice. From 8.5c we see that symmetry implies[3]

$$\gamma_{ij} = \gamma_{ji} \tag{8.8}$$

Negativity arises from the concavity of the cost function and implies that the matrix of coefficients

[2]From 8.3 and 8.4

$$s_i = \alpha_i + \gamma_{ii} \ln \tilde{p}_i + \sum_{i \neq j} \gamma_{ij} \ln \tilde{p}_j + \beta_i \left(\beta_0 u \prod_k \tilde{p}_k^{\beta k}\right) \tag{a}$$

From 8.3

$$\beta_0 u \prod_k \tilde{p}_k^{\beta k} = \ln C - \ln P^{**} \tag{b}$$

where

$$\ln P^{**} = \ln C - \left(\alpha_0 + \sum \alpha_i \ln \tilde{p}_i + \sum_i \sum_j \gamma_{ij}^* \ln \tilde{p}_i \ln \tilde{p}_j\right) \tag{c}$$

If the $\ln \tilde{p}_i$ variables are reasonably collinear, Deaton and Muellbauer (1980) show that

$$\ln P^{**} \approx \ln P^* = \sum s_i \ln \tilde{p}_i \tag{d}$$

Hence using (b) and (d) in (a) we obtain our share equation 8.5 in the text.

[3]Note that adding up and symmetry imply homogeneity (although homogeneity and adding up do not imply symmetry).

$$k_{ij} = \gamma_{ij} + \beta_i\beta_j \ln\left(\frac{C}{P^*}\right) - s_i\delta_{ij} + s_is_j \qquad (8.8a)$$

where δ_{ij} is the Kronecker delta, is negative semi-definite.

Thus our systems approach implicitly imposes data admissibility in the form of adding-up constraints and the additional theoretical constraints of symmetry, homogeneity and negativity.

8.2.3 Asset demands

To motivate the application of consumer demand theory to asset demands suppose that we make the reasonable assumption that there exists a utility function defined over the *expected* (one-period-ahead) value of *real* assets a^{τ}_{it+1}:[4]

$$u = u(a^{\tau}_{1t+1}, a^{\tau}_{2t+1}, \ldots, a^{\tau}_{nt+1}) \qquad (8.9)$$

The budget (wealth) constraint then becomes

$$\sum_i p^{\tau}_{it} a^{\tau}_{it+1} = W^{\tau}_t \qquad (8.9a)$$

where

$$p^{\tau}_{it} = \{(1 + r_{it})(1 - g_{zt})\}^{-1} \qquad (8.10)$$

Z_t is the aggregate goods price index, W_t is the nominal wealth, W^{τ}_t is real wealth ($= W_t/Z_t$), r_{it} is *expected* (proportionate) nominal return on asset i between t and $t + 1$ (including any capital gains), g_{zt} is *expected* (proportionate) rate of goods price inflation between t and $t + 1$, and p^{τ}_{it} is the real price (i.e. approximately equal to the inverse of the expected real interest rate $r_{it} - g_{zt}$). The real price can be viewed as a real discount factor. The higher is the expected own yield r_{it} and the lower the expected rate of inflation, the lower is the real price, i.e. the lower is the opportunity cost of holding this asset (in real terms).

Comparing 8.9 and 8.9a with the equivalent equations 8.1 and 8.1a from consumer demand theory we can reformulate the above model in terms of a cost function which, by Sheppard's lemma, yields asset share equations

$$s_{it} = \alpha_i + \sum_j \gamma_{ij} \ln p^{\tau}_{jt} + \beta_i \mathrm{RW}_t \qquad (8.11)$$

where

[4] We can argue that, ultimately, utility depends only on current and future consumption. However, in the absence of fully contingent binding contracts, agents must hold some asset stocks when saving takes place, and it is reasonable to assume that agents are not indifferent to the composition of their assets. Hence asset holdings represent purchasing power over future consumption goods. Any factors not in the wealth constraint that influence the composition of such assets will implicitly be captured in the parameters of the utility function 8.9

$$s_{it} = \frac{a_{it}}{W_t} \qquad (8.11a)$$

$$\mathrm{RW}_t = \ln\left(\frac{W^\tau}{P^{*\tau}}\right)_t \qquad (8.11b)$$

$$\ln P_t^{*\tau} = \sum_i s_{it} \ln p_{it}^\tau = \ln P_t^* + g_{zt} \qquad (8.11c)$$

8.2.4 Transactions variable

The perceived cost of achieving a given level of utility may depend in part on which assets are most useful for undertaking transactions (Weale, 1986). For example, this may be important for (gross) liquid assets and capital certain liabilities. In terms of the AIDS cost function (Equation 8.5) we require an additional term

$$\phi \ln\left(\frac{e_{t+1}}{Z_{t+1}}\right) \qquad (8.12)$$

where e_{t+1} is the expected level of nominal transactions in period $t + 1$ and Z_{t+1} is the expected price level at $t + 1$. Thus the cost of achieving a given level of utility depends on the level of *future* transactions.

Using Sheppard's lemma our asset demand (share) equations become

$$s_{it} = \alpha_i + \sum_j \gamma_{ij} \ln p_{jt}^\tau + \beta_i\left\{\ln\left(\frac{W}{Z}\right)_t - \phi\ln\left(\frac{e_{t+1}}{Z_{t+1}}\right) - \ln P_t^* - g_{zt}\right\}$$

$$(8.13)$$

The terms in real wealth $\ln(W/Z)_t$ and real transactions $\ln(e_{t+1}/Z_{t+1})$ can be reparameterized into a wealth-to-transactions (or wealth-to-income) ratio and a separate real transactions term. It seems reasonable when using discrete time periods to use future expected transactions when deciding on the allocation of assets at the end of the period rather than the more conventional current and lagged values. A further testable restriction concerns the wealth and expenditure coefficients, the ratio of which equals ϕ for each equation. A further nested test is $\phi = 1$: the cost function is homogeneous with respect to the level of transactions. In this case Equation 8.13 reduces to

$$s_i = \alpha_i + \sum_j \gamma_{ij} \ln p_{jt}^\tau + \beta_i \ln\left(\frac{W_t}{e_{t+1}P_t^*}\right) \qquad (8.14)$$

$e_{t+1}P_t^*$ is the discounted present value of future (nominal) transactions and hence $\ln(W_t/e_{t+1}P_t^*)$ is the current-period logarithm of the ratio of wealth to expected income.

8.2.5 Summary

The consumer demand approach and in particular use of the AIDS model applied to asset demands allows the basic axioms of rational choice to be utilized to reduce the parameter space. The approach appears to be less restrictive than the inventory, precautionary and mean–variance models yet utilizes a theoretically coherent structure. In principle, the consumer demand approach can be applied to capital certain as well as capital uncertain assets and liabilities.

8.3 DYNAMIC ADJUSTMENT AND ECONOMETRIC ISSUES

Our long-run AIDS share equations 8.11 can be represented in vector notation:

$$s_t^* = \Pi X_t \tag{8.15}$$

where s_t^* is the $k \times 1$ vector of equilibrium asset shares, X_t is the $m \times 1$ vector of independent variables and Π is the $k \times m$ matrix of long-run parameters.

If we include only own lags, in a system of asset demand equations then we must implicitly accept that all assets adjust at the same time (Smith, 1975). To avoid this problem cross-lagged terms must also be included (Brainard and Tobin, 1968). The latter can be rationalized by generalizing the quadratic cost of adjustment function of Christofides (1976):

$$L^* = (s - s^*)_t' C_1 (s - s^*)_t + (\Delta s_t') C_2 (\Delta s_t) - (\Delta s_t) C_3 (\Delta s_t^*) \tag{8.16}$$

where the C_i ($i = 1, 2, 3$) are conformable adjustment matrices. Minimizing L^* with respect to s_t we obtain the generalized error feedback equations (EFEs)

$$\Delta s_t = \Pi^* \Delta X_t + L(s - s^*)_{t-1} \tag{8.17}$$

where the disequilibria in $k - 1$ asset shares at time $t - 1$ influence the current-period adjustment of any particular asset share. Since $\Sigma_1^k (s_i - s_i^*)_{t-1} = 0$, only the $k - 1$ independent disequilibrium shares are required in 8.17, i.e. L is $k \times (k - 1)$ (Anderson and Blundell, 1983). The adding-up restrictions imply that the columns of Π^* and L sum to zero. In addition on intuitive grounds we might expect the diagonal elements of L to be negative. However, this is not required for dynamic stability. As long as the eigenvalues of the appropriate adjustment matrix have modulus less than unity, the system is dynamically stable.[5]

[5] If the disequilibrium term for asset 1 is excluded then the estimated adjustment matrix is

$$L = (1_2, 1_3, \ldots, 1_k) \qquad k \times (k - 1)$$

The dynamics of the full model can be written

$$s_t = (I_k + L^*) s_{t-1}$$

where S_t is $k \times 1$, $L^* = (i, 1_2, 1_3, 1_k)$ is $k \times k$, $i = (1, 0, \ldots, 0)$ is $k \times 1$ and I_k is the $k \times k$ identity matrix. One of the eigenvalues of $I_k + L^*$ is unity and stability requires that the other $k - 1$ eigenvalues are negative.

The above adjustment equation could be further generalized by including additional lagged own and cross shares, i.e. terms in Δs_{t-j} and ΔX_{t-j}, although the dynamics are then not consistent with the quadratic cost-of-adjustment function. Indeed, we can also interpret 8.17 merely as a reasonably parsimonious method of incorporating dynamics while maintaining the adding-up restrictions but without alluding to the cost function 8.16. We feel that quadratic costs are very unlikely to apply to adjustments in financial assets (e.g. costs are unlikely to rise with the size of the transaction undertaken) and we therefore interpret Equation 8.17 merely as a convenient method of characterizing sluggish adjustment.

Several methods are available to obtain a parsimonious set of dynamic share equations. First, we can substitute for s^* from 8.11 in 8.17, producing a general ADL model, and then test down. Second we can reparameterize the ADL (autoregressive distributed lag) model into an error-feedback formulation as in 8.17 and test down using a non-linear estimator (Bewley, 1979). Third we can estimate the long-run shares $s^* = \Pi X$ using co-integration tests to search for a suitable co-integrating set of X variables. The lagged asset disequilibria $(s - s^*)_{t-1}$ are substituted in 8.17 and a search over the short-run parameters Π^* and L is then undertaken.

The first two methods require a search procedure over a very large number of parameters and the long-run solution alters as one moves to the preferred specification. Also we cannot be sure that the resulting long-run parameters form a co-integrating vector. Although the co-integration technique suffers from small-sample bias (and non-uniqueness (Johansen, 1988)), it has the major advantage that any sensible long-run co-integrating vector is held fixed while searching over the short-run parameters. For this reason we have found the co-integration technique to be most useful. However, we have also used the ADL and non-linear techniques on the equation reparameterized in error-feedback form but we do not report these results here (e.g. Barr and Cuthbertson, 1989a).

The long-run co-integrating regressions 8.15 for the k asset shares are run on ordinary least squares (OLS) which yields super-consistent parameter estimates. The lagged residuals from $k - 1$ of these regressions, i.e. $(s_j - \hat{s}_j^*)_{t-1}$, are then included in the EFE (see Equation 8.17).

Any cross-equation restrictions in the system of equations for the *co-integrating* regressions can be imposed under Zellner's SUR model but with a fixed-diagonal variance–covariance matrix obtained from running OLS on each equation separately. This method of implementing SUR is equivalent to OLS on each equation separately except for the imposition of any cross-equation constraints on the long-run parameters.

An IV (instrumental variables) estimator may be required when estimating the EFEs because of possible simultaneity between asset prices (yields) and shares. Thus when estimating the EFE, three-stage least squares (3SLS) can be applied with a fixed variance–covariance matrix obtained from two-stage least squares (2SLS) on each equation. This produces consistent estimators if there is no serial correlation in the system of equations (Zellner and Theil, 1962).

Any hypothesis testing on the EFE using quasi-likelihood ratio tests (e.g. symmetry of the 'price' coefficient matrix) requires the variance–covariance matrix to be held fixed over the restricted and unrestricted system of equations and the same set of instruments to be used in each equation (Gallant and Jorgenson, 1979). Small-sample adjustments to the asymptotic test statistics are usually advisable (Pudney, 1981; Bewley, 1983).

Expected capital gains (e.g for capital uncertain assets) can be treated in a number of ways. Auxiliary equations could be run for each of the expected returns using OLS and the predictions used as instruments for the unobservable expectations (Feige and Pearce, 1976). However, in view of the possibly large number of expectations terms it may be easier to use the errors-in-variables method.[6] Like the previous method this may introduce an MA(1) error into the share equations (Pesaran, 1987). Cochrane–Orcutt type estimation using IV distorts the RE (rational expectations) orthogonality conditions. Systems estimators which are generalizations of Hansen (1982) and Cumby *et al.*, (1983) have not yet been developed and therefore serial correlation corrections in the system remain problematic (Berndt and Savin, 1975). We therefore use 3SLS in our second-stage EFE 8.17, and in general serial correlation is not found to be an acute problem.

8.4 DATA AND EMPIRICAL RESULTS FOR THE PERSONAL SECTOR

The basic data used are taken from the flow of funds table in *Financial Statistics* with adjustments made for classification changes. Benchmark stocks are obtained from a variety of published sources, and stock figures are constructed for the personal, company, overseas and public sectors with a detailed breakdown for the financial sector (into banks, various non-bank financial intermediaries, Life Assurance and Pension Funds). The constructed stock figures use consistent revaluation indices across sectors and the accounting identities continue to hold for all the stock data. Thus the personal sector data used in this study are derived from a full stock-flow-consistent set of accounts (which is described more fully by Barr *et al.*, (1989)). The data are seasonally unadjusted but seasonal dummies are not reported. The rates of return used are discussed below, together with detailed definitions of the asset classifications.

[6]The instruments used in the 3SLS regressions are 'prices' lagged one, two and three periods, the lagged change in real wealth and expenditure, and their lagged levels, the lagged shares and any time trends. Alternative subsets of these instruments did not qualitatively alter the results.

Financial innovation and the emergence of new financial assets and liabilities create problems in terms of data classification. After 1982 there was increasing provision and marketing of high-interest checking accounts, reflected in the rapid rise in the proportion of interest-bearing M1 in total M1 (see Chapter 5). Building societies extended their branch network in the 1970s and 1980s and introduced a wide range of accounts tailored to particular sections of the market. In a model that is already complex we cannot hope to capture these learning and marketing effects in a sophisticated manner and we have had to deal with them in a piecemeal fashion as described below.

In order to render the model tractable we have assumed weak separability between capital certain liquid assets and liabilities and capital uncertain assets. Weak tests of separability, namely adding additional 'price' variables other than those pertaining to the subset of weakly separable assets, indicated that our a priori choices concerning separability are broadly acceptable (e.g. Barr and Cuthbertson, 1989a, b).

In order that the reader is not overwhelmed by a plethora of coefficient estimates we have concentrated on presenting our preferred set of equations and we examine their economic properties in some detail. Our aim here is to demonstrate that the models broadly fit the data set, while satisfying certain theoretical restrictions, and yield plausible parameter estimates. In this chapter we are not primarily interested in classical hypothesis testing but such tests can be found in a wide range of companion papers on the FOF project (Barr and Cuthbertson, 1989a–f). In short our primary aim here is to demonstrate that the resulting equations could be used as part of a working financial model with sensible simulation properties. We now present the empirical results for liquid assets.

8.5 EMPIRICAL RESULTS: LIQUID ASSETS OF THE UK PERSONAL SECTOR

The asset categories modelled are notes and coin (NC), sight deposits (SD), time deposits (TD), building society deposits (BS) and National Savings investment account (NS). Data on the sight–time deposit split are only available post-1975 and the full estimation period (after lags) is therefore 1977 Q4 to 1986 Q4. Experiments with other categories of national savings proved problematic (Hood, 1987) as did the minor category local authority temporary debt (Weale, 1986), and these are excluded from the analysis. Interest rates used are the end of quarter rate on seven-day deposit accounts (for TD), the ordinary share rate (for BS) and the standard rate on the NS investment account. All interest rates are net of income tax at the standard rate.

The long-run share equations 8.11 in vector notation are reproduced here:

$$s^* = D + A \ln p^\tau + K\text{RW} + Jx \tag{8.18}$$

where x is the vector of additional variables (e.g. expenditure). As before an asterisk indicates the long-run or equilibrium value of a variable. The fitted values from OLS on 8.18 can be interpreted as target long-run shares because the co-integrating regression provides super-consistent estimates of the long-run parameters (Stock, 1987).

The retail price index (RPI) is used to deflate nominal wealth and interest rates. The additional explanatory variables in x are future real expenditure and a time trend starting in 1983 Q4. The former measures differential transactions demand and the latter the introduction of new interest-bearing checking accounts and the increasing pace of financial innovation (Barr and Cuthbertson, 1989a–f). In future work a stochastic trend or logistic relationship could be used to incorporate 'learning' (e.g. Baba *et al.*, 1988).

Inflation enters the model through its effect on real interest rates, which have a substitution effect on the shares (via the matrix A) and an income effect (via the matrix K). The latter arises because an increase in real rates represents an increase in real (future) wealth, and changes in wealth may alter the portfolio composition. For each asset the real rate is its own nominal rate minus expected inflation. In the case of the non-interest-bearing assets in this model (notes and coin, and sight deposits) the real rate is simply the negative of the inflation rate.

Homogeneity implies that the rows of A should sum to zero. In particular, since inflation appears in all the real rates, changes in inflation have no effect via matrix A. However, the income effect via K remains. All these restrictions are imposed in the long-run co-integrating equations reported.

The short-run EFEs are

$$s_t = C\Delta p_t + B\Delta\text{RW}_t + F\Delta x_t + L(s - s^*)_{t-1} \tag{8.19}$$

where C, B, F and L are conformable matrices (vectors) of parameters. L is the matrix of adjustment coefficients which determine the dynamic stability of the system. Levels of all the variables in 8.18 are found to be $I(1)$ (Table 8.1), and the Dickey–Fuller and augmented Dickey–Fuller (ADF) statistics (Dickey and Fuller, 1979) indicate a co-integrating set of variables (Table 8.2) when homogeneity and symmetry are imposed (in the TD, BS, and NS equations).

The long-run substitution coefficients in Table 8.2 have the signs that would be expected, i.e. negative on the diagonal and positive off it. The innovation trend variable leads mainly to a shift into sight deposits and out of time deposits. This almost certainly reflects the increasing number of sight deposits paying interest as agents learn of the existence of such accounts. Wealth and expenditure have opposite effects, as indicated by theory (see Equation 8.13) with the latter raising the share of the transactions assets (NC and SD) and lowering that of the savings assets (TD, BS

Table 8.1 Liquid assets: order of integration of variables[a]

	$I(0)$		$I(1)$	
	DF	*ADF*	*DF*	*ADF*
S_1(NC)	0.5	−0.8	−5.5	−2.8
S_2(SD)	−0.8	−1.2	−5.2	−1.5
S_3(TD)	+0.1	−0.4	−3.5	−1.9
S_4(BS)	−0.3	+0.2	−4.0	−1.9
S_5(NS)	−2.0	−0.4	−5.4	−4.0
g_z	−3.0	−2.2	−10.8	−4.7
$\ln p_3$	−2.0	−2.2	−7.2	−4.1
$\ln p_4$	−1.7	−1.7	−6.8	−4.6
$\ln p_5$	−1.4	−1.6	−9.5	−4.1
RW	+3.0	+1.3	−6.8	−2.0
y[b]	−1.6	+0.4	−7.6	−1.7

[a]The critical values for the DF and ADF statistics are about −2.8. A negative test statistic with absolute value greater than 2.8 indicates a stationary series.
[b]y is real aggregate consumption, the transactions variable.

Table 8.2 Liquid assets: long-run co-integration regressions[a,b]

	Price matrix A			
Share	NIB[c] NC + SD	TD	BS	NS
1 NC	−0.6	0.4	0.2	0.0
2 SD	−1.8	1.0	0.8	0.0
3 TD	1.4	−2.5	0.8	0.3
4 BS	1.0	0.8	−2.2	0.4
5 NS	0.0	0.3	0.4	−0.7

	Wealth	*Expenditure*	*Trend* (×100)	a[d]	*DF*[e]	*ADF*[e]
1 NC	−0.2	0.14	0.1	−0.4	−2.8	−0.4
2 SD	−0.4	0.29	0.7	−0.5	−3.3	−0.7
3 TD	0.2	−0.37	−0.6	−0.3	−2.2	−0.3
4 BS	0.3	−0.01	−0.1	−0.3	−2.5	−0.3
5 NS	0.1	−0.05	−0.1	−0.5	−3.4	−0.7

[a]The t statistics from this regression are invalid and are not reported.
[b]Adding-up, symmetry and homogeneity constraints are imposed in both the long- and short-run equations.
[c]NC and SD both have a real rate equal to minus the rate of inflation. Consequently, the separate effects of inflation on NC and SD cannot be identified. However, the sum of those effects can be estimated and is reported in the non-interest bearing, (NIB) column. The symmetry constraint is imposed on the lower 3 × 3 (a_{ij}) elements for TD, BS and NS, and on the appropriate row and column sums for NC and SD.
[d]a is the coefficient in the equation $\Delta e_t = ae_{t-1} + \Sigma_i(b_i \Delta e_{t-1i})$, where the e_t are the residuals from the long-run share equations.
[e]The critical values for the DF and ADF tests, at the 5% significance level, are about −4.

and NS). The Slutsky matrix (Equation 8.8a) has all eigenvalues negative and therefore satisfies the theoretical negativity condition.

The long-run elasticities and semi-elasticities are shown in Table 8.3. The semi-elasticities of NC and SD with respect to the (annual) inflation rate are around −2.0, reflecting a move out of transactions assets at high rates of inflation. This result is broadly consistent with results from aggregate M1 equations. The sum of the wealth and expenditure elasticities is positive for all assets and if, in the long run, wealth and expenditure increase at the same rate, all assets are 'normal goods' with respect to these two scale variables. TD, BS and NS are substitutes and the own rate semi-elasticities are larger than their respective cross-rates. The long-run elasticity results are therefore acceptable on a priori grounds.

The short-run parameters (Table 8.4) are all smaller than their long-run counterparts except for the response of NC to a change in the rate on BS deposits. Note that the share of NS does not respond immediately to changes in any interest rate. Equivalently the NS interest rate has no impact effect on the other shares. These restrictions are imposed on a priori grounds and in the interest of parsimony but are accepted by the data. (The Wald tests for short-run symmetry and homogeneity are SYM(3) = 1.3, HOM(4) = 6.9, with critical values of 7.8 and 9.5 respectively.)

The lag coefficients also have a reasonable structure with negative effects due to own shares in excess of target and positive effects due to excess holdings of other assets. The eigenvalues of the appropriate elements of the L matrix have modulus (0.6, 0.9, 0.8, 0.4) and indicate a dynamically stable system.

The restrictions on the co-integrating parameters (symmetry, homogeneity and zero restrictions) in the EFEs are acceptable on an adjusted quasi-likelihood ratio test QLF*(28) = 76 (with adjusted critical value of 95) but are not accepted without such adjustments (Pudney, 1981; Bewley, 1983).

Table 8.3 Long-run elasticities[a]: homogeneity and symmetry imposed[b]

	g_z^a	R_3	R_4	R_5	RW	y
1 NC	−1.9	1.4	0.75	0*	−1.5	1.7
2 SD	−2.6	−1.5	−1.3	0*	−1.3	1.7
3 TD	1.6	1.4	−1.0	−0.3	1.9	−1.7
4 BS	0.5	−0.5	1.4	−0.3	1.6	−1.0
5 NS	0*	−1.9	−2.5	4.5	3.5	−2.0

[a]The figures denote elasticities with respect to real wealth RW and expenditure y. If a_i is the stock of (real) assets the elasticities are $(da_i/a_i)/(dX_i/X_i)$ where X = (RW, y).
For interest rates R_3, R_4, R_5 and the annual inflation rate g_z^a, semi-elasticities (i.e. $100(da_i/a_i)/dX_i$) where $X_i = (r_3, R_4, R_5, g_z^a)$ are quoted. Asset shares at the sample mean are used in all the calculations.
[b]An asterisk indicates an imposed coefficient.

Table 8.4 Liquid assets: short-run error-feedback equation coefficients[a]

	'Price' matrix C			
	NIB NC + SD	*TD*	*BS*	*NS*[b]
NC	−0.5	0.0	0.5	0.0
	(1.3)		(1.5)	
SD	−0.5	0.5	0.0	0.0
	(1.8)	(1.8)		
TD	0.5	−0.7	0.2	0.0
	(1.2)	(1.2)	(0.4)	
BS	0.5	0.2	−0.7	0.0
	(1.5)	(0.4)	(1.5)	
NS[b]	0.0	0.0	0.0	0.0
	Wealth	*Expenditure*		*Trend* (×100)
NC	−0.1	0.1		−0.1
	(1.0)	(0.7)		(0.2)
SD	−0.2	0.2		0.5
	(2.0)	(2.2)		(3.6)
TD	0.0	−0.1		−0.5
	(0.002)	(1.0)		(2.7)
BS	0.2	−0.1		0.2
	(2.1)	(1.0)		(1.3)
NS	0.1	−0.1		−0.1
	(2.4)	(1.6)		(1.6)

Coefficients on lagged disequilibrium terms

	Adjustment matrix L				
	(1) NC	*(2) SD*	*(3) TD*	*(4) BS*	*(5) NS*
NC	—	0.1	0.1	0.2	0.3
		(0.5)	(1.1)	(1.7)	(0.6)
SD	—	−0.4	0.0	0.0	0.0
		(2.6)			
TD	—	0.3	−0.1	0.0	0.3
		(1.1)	(1.3)		(0.7)
BS	—	0.0	0.0	−0.2	0.0
				(1.7)	
NS	—	0.0	0.0	0.0	−0.6
			(0.8)		(3.7)

Goodness of fit: error-feedback equations[c]

Equation	R^2	BP(4)
1 NC	0.3	9.1
2 SD	0.6	5.5
3 TD	0.5	8.4
4 BS	0.4	9.4
5 NS	0.3	9.1

[a]Asymptotic *t* statistics are given in parentheses.
[b]Column and row coefficients constrained to zero.
[c]BP(4) is the Box–Pierce statistic for serial correlation of up to order 4. Under the null of no serial correlation the critical value at a 5% significance level is 9.5.

Overall these results are encouraging on economic and statistical grounds and the R^2 values (Table 8.4) are satisfactory for share equations.

8.5.1 Simulations: liquid asset equations

In the context of a large-scale financial model it is important that the dynamic simulation properties yield sensible interpretable results. This is as important a set of criteria as the conventional statistical properties of the equations. Here we present some illustrative simulations for the liquid assets submodel (for further details see Barr and Cuthbertson (1989b)).

The model was simulated by fixing all the exogenous variables at their 1986 Q4 values and allowing the system to run to convergence. The resulting profiles formed the base runs. The effects of changes in the building society deposit rate and in wealth were then simulated by raising the former by 0.5% (point) and the latter by £1 billion (about 0.5%) in 1988 Q1.

8.5.2 Building society rates +0.5%

The simulation results are seen most easily in Figs 8.1 and 8.2. BS (Fig. 8.1) adjust smoothly throughout from an increase on impact of £220 million to

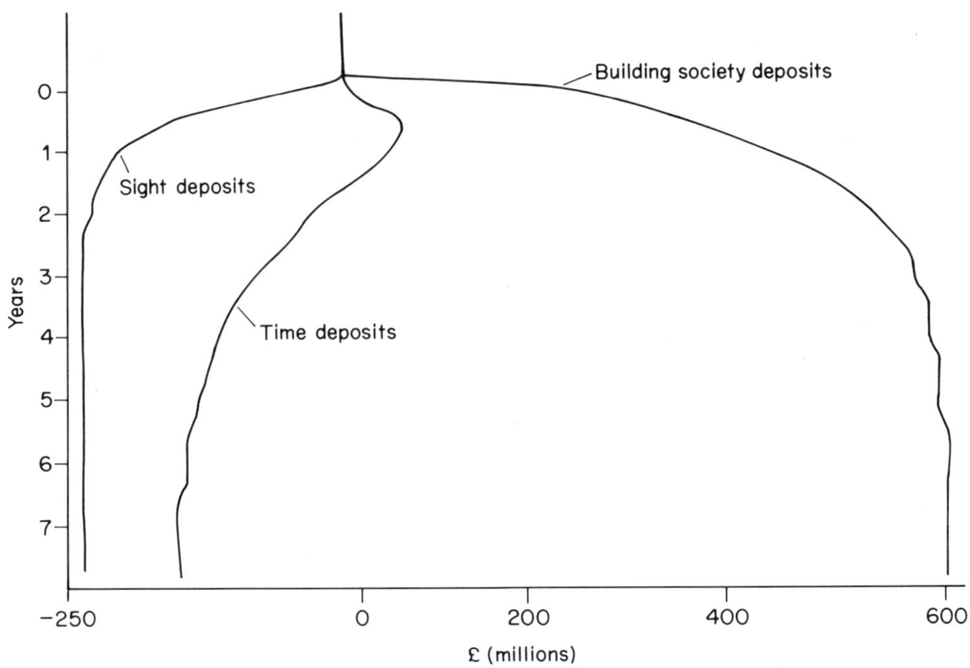

Fig. 8.1 Building society rate $+\frac{1}{2}\%$ (deviations from base).

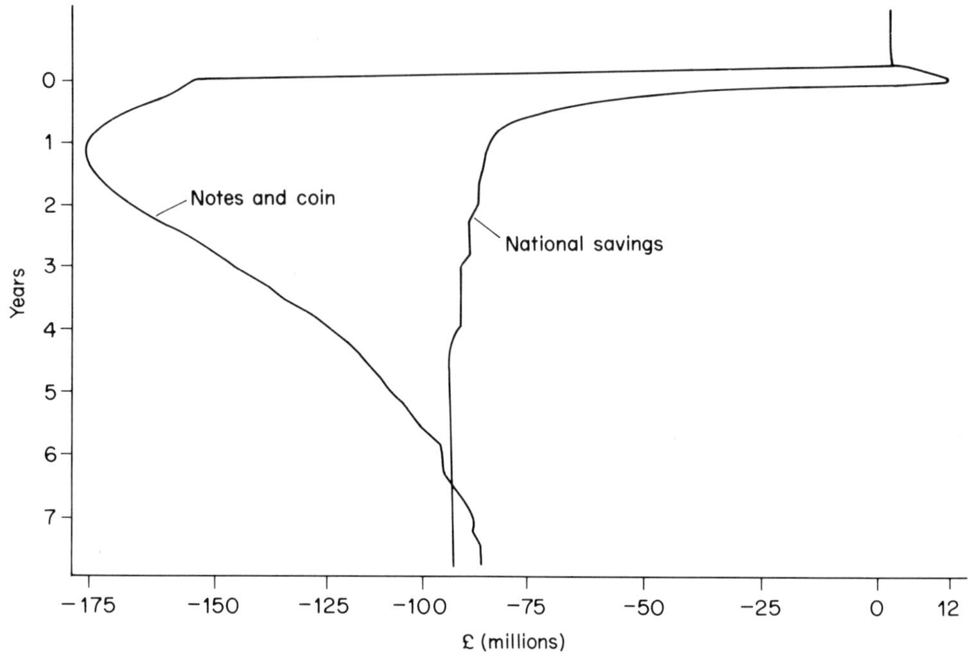

Fig. 8.2 Building society rate $+\frac{1}{2}\%$ (deviations from base).

a rise of £600 million in the long run. SD move quite slowly initially but reach their long-run decline of £250 million within 2 years. TD fall by around £50 million on impact and by £100 million in the long run. However, the adjustment embodies a small overshoot as time deposits increase temporarily after the initial fall. NC (Fig. 8.2) fall immediately by around £150 million and decline further over the subsequent year by £25 million. From that point they recover to show a net reduction of about £90 million. NS increase on impact because the only effect here is due to the increased level of wealth associated with a rise in the building society deposit rate. Subsequently this increase is quickly offset and within a year the new equilibrium effect is reached at around minus £90 million.

8.5.3 Total liquid assets +£1 billion

The behaviour of three of the assets—TD, BS and NS—is reasonably straightforward. BS absorb about £0.8 billion initially and this increases to £0.9 billion in the long run. TD receive about £0.1 billion initially, rising to £0.2 billion, and NS receive £0.16 billion on impact with no subsequent change. NC and SD, however, fall in both the short and long run: they are 'inferior goods'. If some assets (e.g. TD, BS, NS) are to be 'luxury goods', i.e. the wealth coefficient $\beta_i > 0$ (see Table 8.2), then adding up implies that other assets must be 'inferior goods'. The simulation reported here is a little artificial in that we would expect the level of transactions and real wealth to increase at about the same rate in the long run. The sum of the long-run wealth and transactions elasticities are positive for NC and SD and therefore an equal percentage increase in both 'scale variables' will yield an increase in holdings of these assets.

The simulation properties for the liquid assets equations therefore yield plausible responses both qualitatively and quantitatively.

8.6 CONCLUSIONS

We shall be brief and confine our remarks mainly to the methodology employed. The general to specific methodology advocated by Hendry (1979, 1983) has powerful arguments in its favour if one is to avoid specification errors due to mis-specified dynamics. However, in the context of a systems approach where the economic restrictions apply to the long-run parameters, testing down is difficult (because of the large number of simplification paths) and the final parsimonious equation may be undesirable on economic grounds (e.g. coefficients that are implausible with respect to size or sign) or on statistical grounds (e.g. the variables may not form a co-integrating vector; see Chapter 5 and Hall (1986)).

The Granger–Engle two-step approach allows a co-integrating vector with plausible long-run parameters to be established at stage one. The specification search over the short-run dynamic coefficients in stage two does not alter these long-run equilibrium parameters. Hence considerable simplification is achieved throughout the search procedure, which is of great importance in a system of equations with many parameters. The approach is flexible in that marginal adjustments can easily be made to the long-run or short-run parameters around the basic parsimonious model. We found the method to be useful in establishing plausible equations for personal sector liquid assets which conform to theoretical priors and which capture the main features of the data.

REFERENCES

Akerlof, G. A. and Milbourne, R. D. (1980) The short run demand for money. *Economic Journal*, **90**, 885–900.

Anderson, G. and Blundell, R. (1983) Consumer non-durables in the UK: a dynamic demand system. *Economic Journal, Conference Papers Supplement*, **94**, 35–44.

Baba, Y., Hendry, D. F. and Starr, R. M. (1988) US money demand 1960–1984, Nuffield College Discussion Paper No. 27.

Backus, D., Brainard, W. C., Smith, G. and Tobin, J. (1980) A model of UK financial and non-financial economic behaviour. *Journal of Money Credit and Banking*, **12**, 259–93.

Barr, D. G. and Cuthbertson, K. (1989a) Modelling the flow of funds, Bank of England Discussion Paper, Technical Series No. 21.

Barr, D. G. and Cuthbertson, K. (1989b) Econometric modelling of the financial decisions of the UK personal sector: preliminary results, Bank of England Discussion Paper, Technical Series No. 22.

Barr, D. G. and Cuthbertson, K. (1989c) An interdependent error feedback model of UK company sector asset demands, Bank of England Discussion Paper, Technical Series No. 25.

Barr, D. G. and Cuthbertson, K. (1989d) Neoclassical consumer demand theory and the demand for financial assets, Bank of England mimeo.

Barr, D. G. and Cuthbertson, K. (1989e) A data-based simulation model of the portfolio decisions of UK 'other' financial intermediaries, Bank of England mimeo.

Barr, D. G. and Cuthbertson, K. (1989f) The overseas sector's holding of short-term assets in the UK, Bank of England mimeo.

Barr, D. G., Cuthbertson, K. and Griffin, R. (1989) A consistent stock flow matrix for the UK financial sector, Bank of England mimeo.

Baumol, W. J. (1952) The transactions demand for cash: an inventory theoretic approach. *Quarterly Journal of Economics*, **66**, 545–56.

Berndt, E. R. and Savin, N. E. (1975) Estimation and hypothesis testing in singular equation systems with autoregressive disturbances. *Econometrica*, **43**, 937–57.

Berndt, E. R., McCurdy, T. H. and Rose, D. E. (1980) On testing theories of financial intermediary portfolio selection. *Review of Economic Studies*, **47**, 861–73.

Bewley, R. A. (1979) The direct estimation of the equilibrium response in a linear dynamic model. *Economics Letters*, **3**, 357–61.

Bewley, R. A. (1983) Tests of restrictions in large demand systems. *European Economic Review*, **20**, 257–69.

Brainard, W. C. and Tobin, J. (1968) Econometric models: their problems and usefulness: pitfalls in financial model building. *American Economic Review*, **2**(2), 99–122.

Christensen, L. R., Jorgenson and Lan, L. J. (1975) Transcendental Logarithmic Utility Functions. *American Economic Review*, **65**, 367–83.

Christofides, L. N. (1976) Quadratic costs and multi-asset partial adjustment equations. *Applied Economics*, **8**, 301–5.

Cohen, J. (1987) *The Flow of Funds in Theory and Practice: A Flow Constrained Approach to Monetary Theory and Policy*, Kluwer, Dordrecht.

Courakis, A. S. (1975) Testing theories of discount house portfolio selection. *Review of Economic Studies*, **42**, 643–8.

Courakis, A. S. (1980) In search of an explanation of commercial bank short-run portfolio behaviour. *Oxford Bulletin of Economics and Statistics*, **42**, 305–35.

Courakis, A. S. (1988) Modelling portfolio selection. *Economic Journal*, **98**, 619–42.

Cumby, R. E., Huizinga, J. and Obstfeld, M. (1983) Two-step two-stage least squares estimation in models with rational expectations. *Journal of Econometrics*, **21**, 333–55.

Deaton, A. and Muellbauer, J. (1980) *Economics and Consumer Behaviour*, Cambridge University Press, Cambridge.

Dickey, D. A. and Fuller, W. A. (1979) Distribution of the estimators for autoregressive time series with a unit root, *Journal of American Statistical Association*, **74** 427–31.

Feige, E. L. and Parkin, J. M. (1971) The optimal quantity of money, bonds, commodity inventories and capital. *American Economic Review*, **61**(3), 335–49.

Feige, E. L. and Pearce, D. (1976) Economically rational price expectations. *Journal of Political Economy*, **34**(3), 499–522.

Friedman, M. (1956) The quantity theory of money: a restatement, in *Studies in the Quantity Theory of Money* (ed. M. Friedman), University of Chicago Press, Chicago, IL.

Gallant, A. R. and Jorgenson, D. W. (1979) Statistical inference for a system of simultaneous non-linear implicit equations in the context of instrumental variable estimation. *Journal of Econometrics*, **11**, 275–302.

Granger, C. W. J. (1986) Developments in the study of co-integrated economic variables. *Oxford Bulletin of Economics and Statistics*, **48**(3), 213–28.

Green, C. (1984) Preliminary results from a five-sector flow of funds model of the United Kingdom 1972–77. *Economic Modelling*, **1**, 304–26.

Hall, S. G. (1986) An application of the Granger–Engle two-step estimation procedure to UK aggregate wage data. *Oxford Bulletin of Economics and Statistics*, **48**(3), 229–40.

Hansen, L. P. (1982) Large sample properties of generalised method of moments estimators. *Econometrica*, **50**, 1029–54.

Hendry, D. F. (1979) Predictive failure and econometric modelling in macroeconomics: the transactions demand for money, in *Economic Modelling* (ed. P. Ormerod), Heinemann, London.

Hendry, D. F. (1983) Econometric modelling: the consumption function in retrospect. *Scottish Journal of Political Economy*, **30**, 193–220.

Hendry, D. F. (1985) Monetary economic myth. *Oxford Review of Economic Policy*, Oxford University Press, Oxford.

Hendry, D. F. (1986) Econometric modelling with cointegrated variables: an overview *Oxford Bulletin of Economics and Statistics*, **48**(3), 201–12.

Hendry, D. F., Pagan, A. R. and Sargan, J. D. (1984) Dynamic specification, in *Handbook of Econometrics* (eds Z. Griliches and M. D. Intriligator), Vol. 2, North-Holland, Amsterdam.

Hood, W. (1987) The allocation of UK personal sector liquid assets, Government Economic Service Working Paper No. 94, HM Treasury, London.

Johansen, S. (1988) Statistical analysis of cointegration vectors. *Journal of Economic Dynamics and Control*, **12**, 231–54.

Keating, G. (1985) The financial sector of the London Business School model, in *Advances in Monetary Economics* (ed. D. Currie), Croom Helm, London.

Mayes, D. and Savage, D. (1980) The contrast between portfolio theory and econometric models of the UK monetary sector, in *Modern Portfolio Theory and Financial Institutions* (eds D. Corner and D. G. Mayes), Macmillan, London.

Merton, R. C. (1973) An intertemporal asset pricing model. *Econometrica*, **41**, 867–89.

Miller, M. and Orr, D. (1966) A model of the demand for money by firms. *Quarterly Journal of Economics*, **80**, 414–35.

Minford, P., Brech, M. and Matthews, K. (1980) A rational expectations model of the UK under floating exchange rates. *European Economic Review*, **14**, 189–220.

Modigliani, F. and Shiller, R. J. (1973) Inflation rational expectations and the term structure of interest rates. *Economica*, **40**, 41–53.

Modigliani, F. and Sutch, R. (1967) Debt management and the term structure of interest rates. *Journal of Political Economy*, **75**, 569–88.

Owen, D. (1986) *Money Wealth and Expenditure*, Cambridge University Press, Cambridge.

Parkin, M., Gray, M. R. and Barrett, R. J. (1970) The portfolio behaviour of commercial banks, in *The Econometric Study of the United Kingdom* (eds K. Hilton and D. Heathfield), Macmillan, London.

Patterson, K. D., Harnett, I. R., Robinson, G. N. and Ryding, J. (1987) The Bank of England quarterly model of the UK economy. *Economic Modelling*, **4**, 398–629.

Pesaran, H. (1987) *The Limits to Rational Expectations*, Blackwell, Oxford.

Pudney, S. E. (1981) An empirical method of approximating the separable structure of consumer preferences. *Review of Economic Studies*, **48**, 561–77.

Rose, A. K. (1985) An alternative approach to the American demand for money. *Journal of Money Credit and Banking*, **17**, 439–55.

Rossi, N. (1987) An intertemporally quasi-separable demand system. *Review of Economic Studies*, **74**, 449–57.

Smith, S. G. (1975) Pitfalls in financial model building: a clarification. *American Economic Review*, **65**, 510–16.

Spencer, P. D. and Mowl, C. (1978) A financial sector for the treasury model. Government Economic Service Working Paper No. 17, HM Treasury, London.

Sprenkle, C. M. (1969) The uselessness of transactions demand models. *Journal of Finance*, **4**, 835–47.

Stock, J. H. (1987) Asymptotic properties of least squares estimates of cointegrating vectors. *Econometrica*, **55**, 1035–56.

Swofford, J. L. and Whitney, G. A. (1986) Flexible functional forms and the utility approach to the demand for money: a non-parametric analysis. *Journal of Money Credit and Banking*, **18**, 383–9.

Tobin, J. (1956) The interest elasticity of the transactions demand for cash. *Review of Economics and Statistics*, **38**, 241–7.

Tobin, J. (1958) Liquidity preference as behaviour towards risk. *Review of Economic Studies*, **25**, 65–86.

Tobin, J. (1969) A general equilibrium approach to monetary theory. *Journal of Money Credit and Banking*, **1**, 15–29.

Tsiang, S. C. (1972) The rationale of the mean–standard deviation analysis, skewness preference and the demand for money. *American Economic Review*, **62**, 354–71.

Varian, H. R. (1983) Non-parametric tests of consumer behaviour. *Review of Economic Studies*, **50**, 99–110.

Wallis, K. (ed.) (1984) The assessment of monetary and fiscal policy. *Models of the UK Economy*, Oxford University Press, Oxford, Chapter 5.

Weale, M. (1986) The structure of personal sector short-term asset holdings. *Manchester School*, **54**, 141–61.

Weissenberger, E. (1986) An intertemporal system of dynamic consumer demand functions. *European Economic Review*, **30**, 859–91.

White, W. R. (1975) Some econometric models of deposit bank portfolio behaviour in the UK: 1964–70, in *Modelling the Economy* (ed. G. A. Renton), Heinemann, London.

Zellner, A. and Theil, H. (1962) Three stage least squares; simultaneous estimation of simultaneous equations. *Econometrica*, **30**, 54–78.

9

Optimal control of stochastic non-linear models

S. G. HALL AND M. J. STEPHENSON

9.1 INTRODUCTION

The use of large macroeconometric models has become central to the policy work of many national and international agencies. The models are not only complex in terms of their size but also invariably non-linear. Using such a model in policy formulation inevitably leads towards specifying a set of objectives and trying to meet these objectives as closely as possible. The natural formal framework in which to characterize this procedure is clearly that of optimal control (see, for example, Fair (1984) who summarizes a great deal of work in this area or Chow (1975)). However, econometric models are by their very nature stochastic and when they are also non-linear the solution to the deterministic control problem may differ substantially from the solution to the stochastic problem.

It is now over 10 years since the Report of the Committee on Policy Optimisation (House of Commons Select Committee, 1978) (the Ball Report) appeared. During that period the use of optimal control techniques has become more widespread and a considerable research effort has been made towards overcoming some of the difficulties identified in the Ball Report. In particular, three main objections were made to the use of control techniques: the uncertainty which exists as to the correct specification of the economic model, the problem of identifying a suitable objective function and the difficulty of formulating policy when the economy is made up of rational agents who alter their behaviour as the policy changes. The problem raised by rational agents has been the subject of an enormous body of literature over recent years—indeed, it has even given rise to whole new areas of discussion, such as the time inconsistency and credibility debates.

There has been less obvious progress as to the correct specification of appropriate objective functions, but this is perhaps more an area where experience is needed rather than new techniques and theoretical insights, and experience of conducting optimal control exercises has grown enormously. In our view the main remaining objection to the use of optimal control in practical policy formulation now lies in the uncertainty over the true structure of the economy. It seems unlikely that economists will reach a consensus as to the true model of the economy in the near future, and even if such a consensus were reached there would still be some uncertainty attached to the model in the form of stochastic parameters and error terms. There is therefore a need for a practical procedure which would allow optimal control techniques to be extended to stochastic non-linear models.

This problem has been addressed by Chow (1976) from a theoretical standpoint, and he outlines an algorithm which calculates optimal control rules for stochastic non-linear models. The Chow algorithm, in essence, works by iterating over a number of linearizations of the stochastic model using standard dynamic control theory to optimize the stochastic linearized model at each iteration. The key feature of the algorithm is that is the stochastic model which is linearized, not the deterministic model. To linearize a large stochastic model once would be enormously difficult and to include this as part of an iteration procedure would be an order of magnitude more complex. As far as we know the Chow (1976) algorithm has never been implemented in its full form. A few applications exist of stochastic optimal control of fairly small models (e.g. Bray, 1975), but this work has generally proceeded by linearizing the deterministic model rather than the full stochastic model. These applications then tend to produce solutions close to the deterministic solution (as we would expect)—indeed, if they are performed using fixed parameters and only error-term uncertainty, this algorithm converges on the deterministic solution.

There have been two other areas of development in applied work which contribute towards the development of optimal control techniques for stochastic non-linear models, although they both offer only a partial answer to the problem. Some studies have been undertaken which allow across-model optimization exercises to be carried out (e.g. Becker *et al.*, 1986; Hall and Henry, 1988). This approach recognizes that we are uncertain as to which of a range of models may truly represent the real world and so optimization is carried out subject to a range of models weighted together. This approach is useful when we are faced with a small range of discrete alternatives but it is not a practical way of dealing with general uncertainty; indeed it cannot even allow for the stochastic terms in a single non-linear model. The other approach is to derive simple, supposedly robust, feedback rules for use in policy formulation (e.g. Vines *et al.*, 1983; Currie and Levine, 1985; Taylor, 1985; Edison *et al.*, 1988). These simple rules are not generally optimal feedback rules, although their parameters may sometimes be chosen using an optimal control technique. This means that the use of a simple rule must inevitably lead to a loss in overall economic performance relative to the full optimal policy. The claim of robustness, which is often made, has no strong theoretical foundation. The full optimal feedback rule is not robust to changes in model structure, and there is no reason why a simple rule should be any more robust except that it may be so inefficient that a changing model structure has no real effect on it.

There is therefore a need for a practical algorithm for the direct calculation of optimal control solutions for a non-linear stochastic model. The purpose of this chapter is to propose a new technique which combines the approach of stochastic simulation with standard optimal control techniques to produce an algorithm which allows such calculations. In section 9.2 we outline the algorithm and contrast it with an existing approach. In section 9.3 we present an illustration of the approach using the large forecasting model of the Bank of England.

9.2 THE ALGORITHM

Suppose that we define the solution of a non-linear model to be

$$f_i(Y, X, \Omega, A, e) = 0 \qquad i = 1, N \tag{9.1}$$

where Y is a vector of N endogenous variables, X is a vector of M exogenous variables and Ω represents the variance–covariance matrix of the parameters A and the error terms e. If we define Y^* to be the solution to 9.1 subject to the stochastic parameters and error term, then we can define

$$E\{f_i(Y^*, X, \Omega, A, e)\} = 0 \qquad i = 1, N \tag{9.2}$$

and Y^* will be the mathematical expectation of Y.

The deterministic solution to the model can be defined as $\hat{Y}$ where

$$f_i\{\hat{Y}, X, 0, E(A), 0) = 0 \qquad i = 1, N \tag{9.3}$$

That is, the variance–covariance matrix of the parameters is set to zero and the error terms take their mean value, which is assumed to be zero without loss of generality. We know that, when the model is non-linear,

$$\hat{Y} \neq Y^*$$

We can extend this framework to include optimal control by splitting the X vector into two sections: a vector Z of exogenous variables and a vector u of control variables. We then only need to specify a suitable objective function which is to be minimized: for the purposes of exposition we shall use a conventional quadratic objective function. Therefore let

$$E(J) = E\left\{\sum_{i=1}^{N} A_i(Y_i - \bar{Y}_i)^2\right\} \tag{9.4}$$

where $\bar{Y}_i$ is the desired value for variable Y_i and 9.4 is to be minimized subject to the model

$$f(Y, Z, u, \Omega, A, e) = 0 \tag{9.5}$$

with respect to the control variables u. Again without loss of generality, we assume a one-period time horizon so as to simplify the notation; the multi-period extension is trivial.

We can now rewrite 9.4 in the following way:

$$E(J) = \sum_{i=1}^{N} A_i E(Y_i^2 + \bar{Y}_i^2 - 2Y_i\bar{Y}_i) \tag{9.6}$$

$$= \sum_{i=1}^{N} A_i\{E(Y_i^2) + \bar{Y}_i^2 - 2\bar{Y}E(Y_i)\} \tag{9.7}$$

and, given that $E(Y_i^2) = E(Y_i)E(Y_i) + \text{var}(Y_i)$, then

$$E(J) = \sum_{i=1}^{N} A_i\{E(Y_i)E(Y_i) + \text{var}(Y_i) + \bar{Y}_i^2 - 2\bar{Y}_i E(Y_i)\} \tag{9.8}$$

and we can define $E(Y_i) = \hat{Y}_i + E(d_i)$, i.e. the expected value of Y_i equals the deterministic model solution $\hat{Y}_i$ plus the expected deviation $E(d_i)$ of the deterministic value from the mean value. Substituting this into 9.8 gives

$$E(J) = \sum_{i=1}^{N} A_i\{\hat{Y}_i\hat{Y}_i + E(d_i)E(d_i) + 2\hat{Y}_i E(d_i) + \text{var}(Y_i)$$

$$+ \bar{Y}_i^2 - 2\bar{Y}_i\hat{Y}_i - 2\bar{Y}_i E(d_i)\} \tag{9.9}$$

The advantage of 9.9 over 9.4 is that the stochastic elements of the solution have been isolated in the terms $\text{var}(Y_i)$ and $E(d_i)$ and we are able to provide numerical estimates for both these terms through the use of stochastic simulation.

Stochastic simulation is a numerical technique which allow estimates to be made of the density function of the endogenous variables of large non-linear models. We shall not discuss the details of this technique here; a general discussion of the approach can be found in Hall (1986a) or Hall and Henry (1988). The main point of interest here is that stochastic simulation provides numerical estimates of both $\text{var}(Y_i)$ and $E(d_i)$. This suggests a solution algorithm which involves iterating between conventional optimal control exercises and stochastic simulation exercises to produce a solution to the full stochastic optimal control problem. This might be done by using the following step-by-step algorithm.

1. Calculate the optimal solution to the deterministic problem given by 9.4 and 9.3. Let the solution be u^*.
2. Perform a set of stochastic simulations around the base given by u^* to produce estimates of $\text{var}(Y_i)$ and d_i, $i = 1, N$.
3. Using these estimates of d_i and $\text{var}(Y_i)$ we can now minimize 9.9

subject to 9.3 to produce a new optimal solution u'. If u' is within a convergence criterion of $u^*(|u' - u^*| < \text{EPS})$, then stop. If the convergence criterion is not met, then set $u^* = u'$ and return to step 2.

This algorithm will still entail a small degree of approximation at convergence, although this will be much less than the usual method of producing a linear approximation to the non-linear model. The conventional procedure of linearizing the deterministic model, discussed by Kendrick (1981), would involve producing a linear approximation to the model and then appealing to the certainty equivalence theorem to solve the resulting quadratic–linear model deterministically. The problem with this approach is that when the objective function is quadratic and the parameters are known, this procedure simply reproduces the deterministic solution.

We can see the source of the above approximation by noting that in general $\text{var}(Y_i)$ and d_i are both functions of the control variables u. Without loss of generality we can simplify the notation by considering an example with only one control variable u and one state variable Y. Then, following the notation in 9.9, we can define

$$\hat{Y} = f(u) \tag{9.10}$$

$$\text{var}(Y) = g(u) \tag{9.11}$$

$$E(d) = h(u) \tag{9.12}$$

These terms can then be substituted into 9.9 to give

$$\begin{aligned} E(J) = {} & f(u)f(u) + h(u)h(u) + 2f(u)h(u) + g(u) \\ & + \bar{Y}^2 - 2\bar{Y}f(u) - 2\bar{Y}h(u) \end{aligned} \tag{9.13}$$

This is now an unconstrained function in u which will be minimized when the following FOC[1] is met:

$$2f(u)f' + 2h(u)h' + 2f(u)h' + 2h(u)f' + g' - 2\bar{Y}f' - 2\bar{Y}h' = 0 \tag{9.14}$$

In the algorithm given above, the partial derivatives g' and h' are set to zero during the calculation of the optimal solution, and so the solution which is calculated will be characterized by

$$2f(u)f' + 2h(u)f' - 2\bar{Y}f' = 0 \tag{9.15}$$

The standard technique of linearizing the model would also set $h(u) = 0$ and so this term would also be lost in the approximation. It must be appreciated at this point that $h(u)$, the deviation between the deterministic value of Y and its expected value, is of a quite different order of magnitude from g' and h', the derivatives of the deviation and the variance with respect to u. For most model applications g' and h' are likely to be so small that ignoring them is a reasonable approximation to make. However, if it is

[1]FOC First order condition

felt that a particular model is so non-linear that this is a damaging assumption, then it is possible to reduce this level of approximation by estimating a simple linear approximation for $g(u)$ and $h(u)$: two sets of stochastic simulations could be performed for different levels of u, and a simple linear function for $g(u)$ and $h(u)$ could be calculated. Under normal circumstances, however, the main effect of the stochastic parts of the model will be captured by the term $h(u)$.

Finally it is perhaps worth noting that the well-known certainty equivalence theorem can be demonstrated via equations 9.9 and 9.14. Certainty equivalence states that, if the objective function is quadratic and the model is linear, then the optimal control trajectory for the stochastic problem is identical with the solution to the deterministic problem when the error terms take their expected values. This can be seen as follows: when the model is linear $h(u) = g' = h' = 0$ and so 9.14 reduces to

$$2f(u)f' - 2\bar{Y}f' = 0 \tag{9.16}$$

which is identical with the FOC for the deterministic model.

9.3 FEEDBACK RULES AND MINIMIZING VARIANCES

For many forms of applied policy-making the possibility of stochastic optimal control is itself not a complete answer to the problem of uncertainty. The reason for this is that for many purposes we may not simply want to minimize the expected value of some objective function but we may also wish to add an effect related to the variance of the outcome relative to some baseline. As an example, suppose that we wish to target a particular level of gross domestic product (GDP) and have a choice of either fiscal policy (in the form of government expenditure) or monetary policy (in the form of interest rates) as control variables. This is a one-target two-instrument problem, and conventional deterministic control techniques will not be able to choose a single policy mix. However, if we also want to minimize the variance of GDP around its desired level then a unique choice of policy instruments can generally be made. Another example where the variance is an important consideration is in the calculation of optimal feedback rules. Again in this case we might well not only want to achieve, a given target for the state variables but we might also want to minimize the variance around the target level.

We can again use information from stochastic simulation to construct an objective function which will make allowance for this effect. In particular Hall (1986b) and Fair (1980) give an algorithm which evaluates the density function of a model's simulation properties. That is, if we change a variable u then the resulting change in Y will have a degree of uncertainty attached to it. As a simple approximation we can assume that $\Delta Y_i \sim \{\delta_{ij}\Delta u_j,$

$(\sigma_{ij}\Delta u_j)^2\}$ where δ_{ij} is the partial derivative of Y with respect to u and σ_{ij} is the standard error of this change.

We could then augment the standard objective function 9.4 by terms in the variance of Y associated with different control variables. This would have the following general form:

$$E(J) = E\left\{\sum_{i=1}^{N} A_i(Y_i - \bar{Y}_i)^2\right\} + B\sum_{i=1}^{N}\sum_{j=1}^{v}\{\sigma_{ij}(u_j - \bar{u}_j)\}^2 \qquad (9.17)$$

The first term is the standard one from Equation 9.4 and the second term represents the variance in the state variables caused by the active use of the control variables relative to some baseline value $\bar{u}$. B is a weighting parameter which evaluates the important of minimizing the variance relative to the target levels of the state variables.

If we were using this to calculate simple feedback rules then the control variables would be parameters of the feedback rule. In this case an obvious value for $\bar{u}$ would be zero, i.e. not operating a feedback mechanism.

The advantage of an objective function of this type is obvious: in standard control exercises we often have a selection of control variables which can be used which vary enormously in the degree of uncertainty over their effect. An obvious example here is direct government expenditure and interest rate policies. In most models the size and the sign of fiscal policies are fairly well defined; interest rates, however, work throught the foreign exchange sectors and have an enormous degree of uncertainty attached to them. A conventional deterministic control exercise may well exploit the interest rate effects of the model to a great extent, making no allowance for the degree of uncertainty attached to these effects. An objective function of the form of 9.17 would give much more weight to the more certain policy instruments and would not therefore tend to exploit the less well determined control variable.

9.4 AN APPLICATION

To illustrate the technique described above, we give a simple optimal control example using the Bank of England's quarterly forecasting model, which is a large non-linear econometric model involving aroung 600 variables. In this example the objective function was constructed so as to penalize deviations of the current account of the balance of payments from zero, using government current expenditure on goods and services as the control variable. This simplifies both the standard objective function 9.4 and the extended version 9.9 by setting $\bar{Y}_i$ to zero for all i. Thus the final three terms in 9.9 are set to zero.

The version of the Bank model employed is that deposited with the ESRC Macroeconomic Modelling Bureau in January 1988, and described by

Patterson *et al.* (1987), updated by Harnett and Patterson (1989). The time period used in the problem is 1988 Q1 to 1990 Q4, using the data base supplied to the Bureau with the model deposit. The stochastic simulations performed in stage two of the procedure are run over 500 replications, using the method of McCarthy (1972) to generate the random shocks to the residuals.

Figure 9.1 shows the outcome for the target variable. After some variation in the first two quarters, the original optimal control solution u^* settles down to track the target value of zero quite closely. However, the mean of the stochastic simulation $E(u^*)$ around this base deviates quite markedly from the target value in both the early and late quarters of the solution period.

The effect of including d_i and $\mathrm{var}(Y_i)$ in the objective function for the second-round optimal control solution u' is to produce an 'offset' for the deviation between u^* and $E(u^*)$, so that the solution path deviates from the target value in the early and late quarters in the opposite direction to $E(u^*)$.

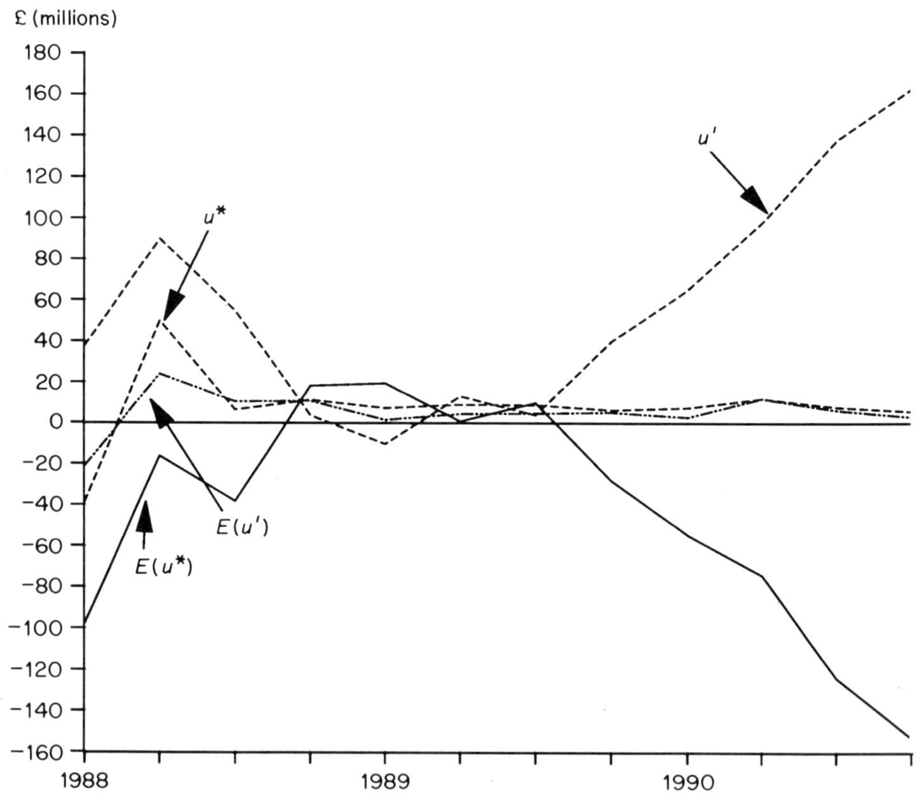

Fig. 9.1 Outcomes for current balance.

When a stochastic simulation is performed around u', the mean $E(u')$ tracks the target solution well throughout the solution period. No further rounds of the procedure were found to be necessary. Table 9.1 shows root mean squared errors for the four solution paths. Figure 9.2 shows that the time paths for the control variable (in deviations from base). As can be seen, the amendments to this path to generate u' as opposed to u^* are quite small in this case compared with the overall deviation from base.

This example illustrates two important points. The deviation caused by the non-linearities in the model is quite important in the sense that while the deterministic optimal trajectory follows the desired path quite closely its

Table 9.1

Solution	u^*	$E(u^*)$	u'	$E(u')$
RMSE	19.78	70.77	78.45	11.23

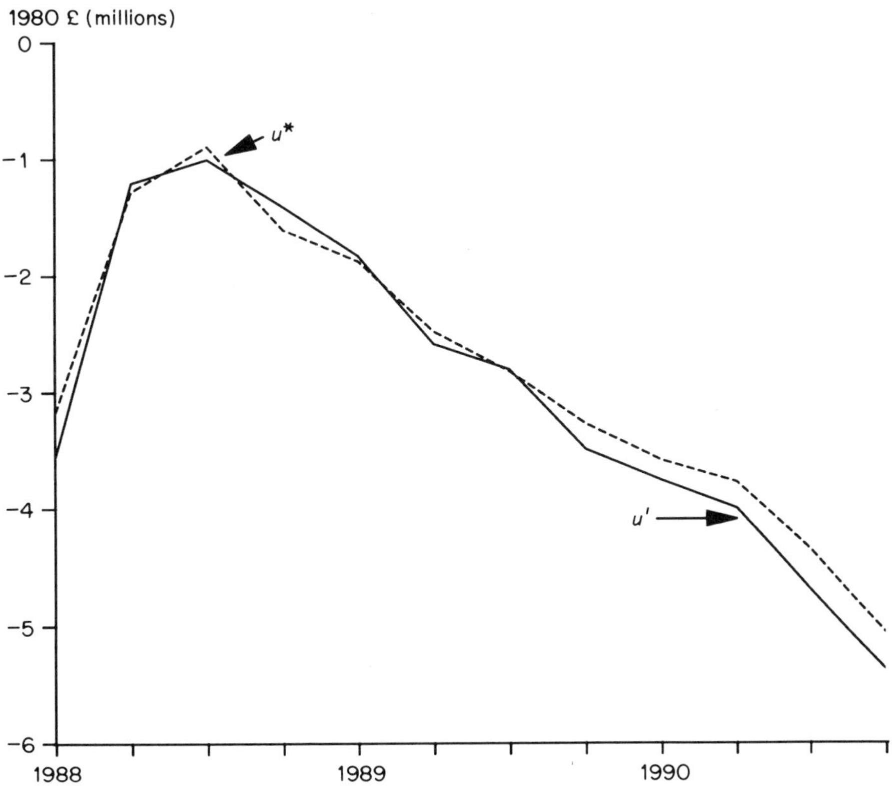

Fig. 9.2 Control variable outcomes (deviations from base).

expected value does not. Second it is clear that the order of approximation involved in the stochastic control algorithm itself is actually negligible relative to the convergence criteria of the optimal control algorithm.

REFERENCES

Becker, R. G., Dwolatzky, B., Karakitsos, E., and Rustem, B. (1986) The simultaneous use of rival models in policy optimisation. *Economic Journal*, **96**, 425–48.

Bray, J. (1975) Optimal control of a noisy economy with the UK as an example. *Journal of the Royal Statistical Society, Series A*, **138**, 339–73.

Chow, G. C. (1975) *Analysis and Control of Dynamic Economic Systems*, Wiley, New York.

Chow, G. C. (1976) The control of non-linear econometric systems with unknown parameters. *Econometrica*, **44**, 685–95.

Currie, D. A. and Levine, P. (1985) Simple macroeconomic policy rules in an open economy. *Economic Journal*, **85**, 60–70.

Edison, H., Miller, M. and Williamson, J. (1988) On evaluating and extending the target zone proposal. *Journal of Policy Modelling*, **3**, 37–70.

Fair, R. C. (1980) Estimating the uncertainty of policy effects in non-linear models. *Econometrica*, **48**, 1381–91.

Fair, R. C. (1984) *Specification, Estimation and Anaysis of Macroeconometric Models*, Harvard University Press, Cambridge, MA.

Hall, S. G. (1986a) The application of stochastic simulation techniques to the National Institute's model 7. *Manchester School*, **54**, 180–201.

Hall, S. G. (1986b) Estimating the uncertainty of the simulation properties of large non-linear econometric Models. *Applied Economics*, **18**, 985–93.

Hall, S. G. and Henry, S. G. B. (1988) *Macro-Econometric Models*, North-Holland, Amsterdam.

Harnett, I. R. and Patterson, K. D. (1989) An analysis of changes in the structural and simulation properties of the Bank of England quarterly model of the UK economy, *Economic Modelling*, **6**, 20–55.

House of Commons Select Committee (1978) *Report on Policy Optimisation*, Cmnd 7148, HMSO, London.

Kendrick, D. (1981) *Stochastic Control for Economic Models*, McGraw-Hill, New York.

McCarthy, M. D. (1972) Some notes on the generation of pseudo structural errors for use in stochastic simulation studies, in *Econometric Models of Cyclical Behaviour* (ed. B. Hickman), Columbia University Press, New York.

Patterson, K. D., Harnett, I. R., Robinson, G. N. and Ryding, J. (1987) The Bank of England quarterly model of the UK economy. *Economic Modelling*, **4**, 398–629.

Taylor, J. B. (1985) International co-ordination in the design of macroeconomic policy rules. *European Economic Review*, **28**, 53–82.

Vines, D., Maciejowski, J. M. and Meade, J. E. (1983) *Stagflation*, Vol. 2, *Demand Management*, George Allen and Unwin, London.

Index

Advanced Corporation Tax (ACT) 197, 199, 203, 213
Akerlof, G.A. 225
Allum, P. 78
Almost ideal demand system (AIDS) xvii, 225–9, 232, 233
Anderson, G. 187n, 233
Andrews, M. 2, 4
Arbitrage pricing theory (APT) 168
Artis, M.J. 127
Attfield, C. 75
Auerbach, A.J. 188, 189, 190

Baba, Y. 143, 175, 224, 237
Backus, D. 224
Bain, A. 187n
Balestra, P. 204
Ball Report (Report of the Committee on Policy Optimisation) 247
Banerjee, A. 128
Bank borrowing 50, 53–4, 59, 63, 212
Banks, role of 187–8
Bankruptcy xiv, 199–200, 201
see also Risk
Barclays Bank 115, 117, 118, 120–1
Bar-Ilan, A. 75
Barr, D.G. 225, 234, 235, 236, 237, 241
Baumol, W.J. 225
Bean, C. 75
Becker, R.G. 248
Bennett, A. 152
Bernanke, B. 75
Berndt, E.R. 224, 235
Bernheim, D. 75
Bewley, R.A. 234, 235, 241
Bhattacharya, S. 189
Blinder, A. 74, 75
Blundell, R. 233
Bollerslev, T. xvi, 57, 95, 120, 168, 171
Borooah, V.K. 91
Boskin, M. 73, 74, 76
Bover, O. 75
Bradford, D. 189
Brainard, W.C. 224, 233
Bray, J. 248
Breeden, D.T. xvi, 168, 180, 181
Brennan, M. 189
Breusch, T.S. 11, 22
Bruno, M. 21
Budd, 18

Capital asset pricing model (CAPM) xiv, xv, xvi, 111–13, 116–19, 167–70, 180–4
Capital costs 52
Carr, J. 127
Carruth, A.A. 6, 41
Castanias, R. 187n
Chang, H.S. 212
Chant, J. 107
Chen, A.H. 189
Chow, G.C. 247, 248
Chowdhury, G. 187n, 188, 198, 199n
Christofides, L.N. 233
Clegg Commission, the 18
Cohen, J. 224

Company debt xvi, 188, 190–1, 196, 198–9, 202–3, 208, 211–14, 216, 218–20
stocks of 194–5, 201, 214, 216
Company liquidity 49–52, 59, 61–3
Company taxation 191, 199, 202–3, 213, 215–16, 218, 219
Company sector, financial behaviour of xvi, 49–50, 51, 187–220
according to size 218–19
Competition 73, 99
Consumer prices 2, 5, 10, 31, 36–7, 40, 139
Consumers' expenditure 36, 73–101, 181
on durables 73, 75, 76–9, 86, 87–91, 99
interest elasticity of xiii, 73–4, 75, 88–9
on non-durables 74, 75, 86, 91–6, 99
Cost–push 40
Courakis, A.S. xvii, 224, 226
Crowder, M.J. 171
Cumby, R.E. 235
Currie, D.A. 248
Cuthbertson, K. 75, 78n, 127, 187n, 225, 234, 236, 237, 241

Darby, M. 127
Davidson, J. 75, 96, 99, 127
Davis, E. 75, 76, 94, 95
De Angelo, H. 190
Deaton, A. xvii, 74, 75, 225, 227, 230n
Debt, *see* Company debt
Demand for money 127–164
Deregulation policy 73, 79
Desai, M. 6, 7
Dhrymes, P. 187n, 199n
Dickens, R. 171
Dickey, D.A. 131, 237
Dicks, M. 79, 92, 97, 99
Dividend controls 206–8, 216–17, 219–20
Dividend decisions xvi, 195–7, 198, 199, 203, 211–14, 216, 219–20
Drayson, S. 79
Durlauf, S.N. 129

Earnings 2, 8, 9, 10
growth of 6–7, 20, 21, 34
in public sector 7, 18

Easton, W.W. 76, 96
Economic and Social Research Council (ESRC) ix
Edison, H. 248
Edwards, A. 76, 80, 95, 187n, 189, 215n
Employers' labour taxes 2, 3, 8, 11, 15, 21, 23, 30, 31, 40
Engle, R.F. xiii, 51, 56, 57–8, 120, 127, 128, 129, 168, 170, 171, 172, 243
Ericsson, N. 127
Exchange rate 39, 40, 41

Fair, R.C. 247, 252
Fama, E.F. 167, 187n, 199n
Feige, E.L. 225, 235
Feldstein, M. 189, 190
Ferber, R. 74
Financial firms 107–8
Financial innovation 134–6, 143–4, 156, 236, 237
Financial Services Act (1986) 107, 223
Financial Times Share Index xvi
Flemming, J. 96
Flow of funds project xvii, 223–43
Foster, N. 1
French, K.R. 176
Friedman, M. 225, 226
Fuller, W.A. 131, 237

Gallant, A.R. 235
GARCH formulation xiii, xvi, 56–7, 66–71, 118–20, 168, 171–3, 175–7, 181, 183
Godfrey, L. 11, 22
Goodhart, C. 107
Government expenditure 36
Granger, C.W.J. 57–8, 127, 128, 129, 224, 243
Gregory, M. 41
Green, J. 189, 190, 223
Grice, J. 152

Hall, S.G. 3, 5, 33, 41, 51, 65, 128, 129, 224, 243, 250, 252
Hansen, L.P. 235
Harnett, I. xvii, 75, 95, 97, 99, 252
Harvey, A.C. 11
Hausman, J.A. 205, 208, 212
Hendry, D.F. 75, 76, 77, 95, 100, 127, 129, 148, 224
Henry, S.G.B. 3, 5, 41, 51, 248, 250

Holly, S. 3, 8, 13
Holmans, A.E. 79
Hood, W. 236
Hours worked 8
Hubbard, R.G. 75, 96
Hylleberg, S. 95

Incomes policies 6–7, 11, 13, 16, 18, 40
Index of manufacturing production 55
  see also Sales
Inflation, 34, 152, 154, 225, 237
Inflationary expectations 2, 3, 5–6, 11, 13, 14, 16, 40, 41, 75
Institute of Fiscal Studies (IFS) 197
Interest rates 50, 63, 65, 73–5, 86, 90–1, 95–7, 131, 139, 143, 152, 154, 201–2, 213, 215, 218, 237, 239
Investment 36, 52, 212
Ireland, J. 50, 53, 127

Jackman, R. 96
Jenkinson, N. 96
Jensen, M. 167
Johansen, S. 128, 129, 133, 134, 135, 136, 147, 153, 156, 162, 164, 234
Johnston, R.B. 127, 143, 144
Jorgenson, D.W. 235
Judd, K.L. 96

Kaufman, G. 108
Keating, G. xvii, 224
Kelly, C. 50
Kendrick, D. 251
Kim, E.H. 189
King, M.A. 187n, 188, 189, 190, 199
Klemkosky, R. 168
Kurz, M. 187n, 199n

Labour costs 52
Labour market 1, 51
Labour productivity 2, 3, 11, 14, 15, 40
Layard, R. 5
Lee, C.F. 212
Levine, P. 248
Lewis, M.K. 127
Lintner, J. 111, 167, 168, 183
Liquid assets 50, 77, 78, 80, 86, 87, 90, 96
  demand for 224–44
Liquidity, *see* Company liquidity
Liverpoool model 96
Lloyds Bank 115, 117, 118, 120, 122
London Business School model 82, 85, 86, 87
Lubrano, M. 127

McCallum, B.T. 6
McCarthy, M.D. 254
Mackie, D.J. 7, 33
Mandlebrot, B. 114
Mankiw, G. 75
Manufacturing, earnings from xii, 1, 8, 10–13, 14, 24–5, 34–5, 38, 45
Marcus, A.J. 110
Market efficiency 123–5
Markowitz, H. 111, 167
Marquand, J. 107
Marshall, W. 187n, 199n
Martin, J. 168
Masulis, R.W. 190
Mayer, C.P. 190, 199
Mayes, D. 224
Mellis, C. 55
Merton, R. 120, 169, 226
Midland Bank 115, 117, 118, 120–1
Milbourne, R.D. 225
Miller, M.H. 187n, 188, 189, 198, 226
Minford, P. 224
Mizon, G.E. 127
Modigliani, F. 187n, 188, 198, 223
Monetary aggregates, determination of xv, 127, 129, 131–62
Mortgage lending 79, 82, 86, 87, 90
Mowl, C. 224
Muellbauer, J. xvii, 75, 225, 227, 230n

NIESR model 1, 82, 85, 86, 87
National Westminster Bank 115, 117, 118, 120, 122
Nerlove, M. 204
Newbold, P. 128, 129
Nickell, S.J. 2, 3, 4, 5, 51
Non-manufacturing sector, earnings from xii, 1, 8, 11, 13, 15–17, 26–7, 34–5, 38, 45
Non-trading sector, earnings from xii, 1, 11, 18–20, 28–9, 35, 39, 45

Optimal control techniques xvii–xviii, 247–57
Orr, D. 226
Oswald, A.J. 4, 6, 41
Output 54–5, 56, 59, 65–6, 67, 70, 71, 131, 156

Owen, D. 50, 224

Pagan, A. 56
Pakes, A. 208
Park, J.Y. 129
Parkin, M. 224, 225
Patterson, K.D. 74, 75, 76, 78, 91, 92, 96, 99, 127, 224, 254
Pearce, D. 235
Pennachi, G.G. 110
Pension plans 75–6
Personal liquidity 75, 76, 78, 86
Personal sector taxes 2, 3, 7–8, 21, 40
Pesaran, H. 235
Phillips, P.C.B. 129
Pissarides, C.A. 96
Portfolio risk 107–15, 123–5, 167–9, 177–84
Poterba, J. 187n
Prices 2, 9, 10, 11, 13, 14, 23, 34–6, 54, 139, 143, 156
Production costs 52–3
Productivity growth 21, 40–1
Pudney, S.E. 228, 235, 241

Rational expectations hypothesis (REH) 51, 57–8, 68, 111–12, 124
Real wages 5, 7
Retentions ratio 7, 11, 21, 22, 23, 43–5
Risk xiv, 56–7
  measurement of 107, 117, 167–8, 173, 180–2, 184, 201, 214, 219
  see also Bankruptcy
Roll, R. 167, 168
Ronn, E.I. 110
Rose, A.K. 224
Ross, S. 168, 189
Rossi, N. 227
Rowlatt, P.A. 4, 6, 8, 41

Sachs, J.D. 21
Sales, as determinant of stocks 52–3, 54–5
  see also Index of manufacturing production
Sargan, D. 75
Sargent, T.J. 51
Savage, D. 224
Savin, N.E. 235
Scholes, M.S. 188, 189
Schwartz, E. 189
Schweppe, F. 171
Schwert, G.W. 167
Securities and Investment Board, the (SIB) 110
Securities Association, the (TSA) 110
Selective employment tax 8, 16
Shaked, I. 110
Sharpe, D.R. 91, 111, 167, 168, 183
Shiller, R.J. 223
Short-term unemployment rate 3, 11, 17, 18, 21–3, 38
Shoven, J. 75
Smirlock, M. 187n, 199n
Smith, P. 3, 8, 13
Smith, S.G. 233
Spencer, P.D. 224
Spenkle, C.M. 225
Stiglitz, J.E. 96, 188
Stock, J.H. 129, 237
Stock appreciation 54
Stock prices 107, 110–11
Stockbuilding xii–xiii, 49–71, 199
Stockholding costs 59, 64, 65
Summers, L. 74, 187n
Sutch, R. 223
Sutton, J. 96
Swofford, J.L. 227

Taylor, J.B. 248
Taylor, M.P. 127, 152
Tax exhaustion 190–1, 197–9, 213, 215–16, 219
Taxation, *see* Company taxation
Theil, H. 235
Tobin, J. 224, 225, 226, 233
Townend, J. 96
Treasury model 82, 85, 86, 87, 96
Trundle, J. 127
Trustee Savings Bank 149
Tsiang, S.C. 226
Turnbull, P. 4

Ullah, A. 56
Unemployment 4, 36, 95, 97
  long-term 4–5
  short-term 2, 4, 5, 21, 36, 38, 40
Ungern-Sternberg, T. von 75, 76, 77, 96

Varian, H.R. 227
Verma, A.K. 110
Vines, D. 248

Wage bargaining xii, 2–4, 9, 13
Wage settlements 8, 18
Wallis, K.F. 1, 59, 224
Weale, M. 232, 236
Weiss, A. 96, 129
Weissenberger, E. 227
White, W.R. 224
Whitley, J.D. 6, 7
Whitney, G.A. 227
Wilcox, J. 100
Wren-Lewis, S. 7, 50, 51, 53

Zeldes, S. 96
Zellner, A. 234, 235